THE MIDDLE EASTERN STATES AND
THE LAW OF THE SEA

CONTEMPORARY ISSUES IN THE MIDDLE EAST

To my family

THE MIDDLE EASTERN STATES AND THE LAW OF THE SEA

by

ALI. A. EL-HAKIM

LIC-ÉN-DROIT (BEIRUT), DIP. SHIPPING LAW;
LL.M. (LONDON), PH.D. (CANTAB)

SYRACUSE UNIVERSITY PRESS
1979

Copyright © 1979 by A. A. El-Hakim

All rights reserved

First published in the United States of America 1979 by arrangement with Manchester University Press

Syracuse University Press
Syracuse, New York 13210

Library of Congress Cataloguing in Publication Data
Hakim, Ali A.
　The Middle Eastern States and the law of the sea.

　(Contemporary issues in the Middle East)
　A revision of the author's thesis, Cambridge.
　Bibliography: p. 275.
　Includes index.
　1. Maritime law – Near East. 2. Territorial waters – Near East. 3. Continental shelf – Near East. 4. Ocean bottom (Maritime law). 5. Aqaba, Gulf of – International status. 6. Tiran, Strait of – International status. I. Title. II. Series.
JX4422.N4H34　　　　1979　　　341.44'8'0956　　　79-17456
ISBN 0-8156-2217-1

Printed in Great Britain

CONTENTS

List of tables and maps	*page* ix
Foreword *by Professor R. Y. Jennings*	xi
Acknowledgements	xiii
Table of cases	xv
Abbreviations	xvii
Introduction	xix

PART ONE: GENERAL PRACTICE AND POLICIES	1
I Existing national claims to offshore jurisdiction	3
A Territorial sea	5
1 Breadth of the territorial sea	5
2 Measurement of the territorial sea	7
3 Delimitation of the territorial sea between States with adjacent or opposite coasts	10
4 Innocent passage through the territorial sea	10
5 Straits	11
6 Islands: legal status of Perim, Kamaran and Kuria Muria	17
B Functional zones beyond the territorial sea (excluding continental shelf)	20
1 Contiguous zones: supervision zones	20
2 Marine pollution control	21
3 Exclusive fishing zones: exclusive economic zones	26
C Continental shelf	29
1 Legal history of the continental shelf doctrine	29
2 Practice of the Middle Eastern States	31
D Conclusion	42
II Trends as reflected in the third United Nations conference on the law of the sea	43
A Recommendations of the Arab League	44
B Substantive issues before the conference	47
1 Jurisdictional limits	48

CONTENTS

    2 Establishment of an international regime and authority for exploration and exploitation of the seabed and ocean floor and subsoil thereof beyond the limits of national jurisdiction 67
    3 Control of marine pollution and regulation of scientific research and transfer of technology 73
  C Conclusion 78

PART TWO: SPECIFIC REGIONAL ISSUES 81

III Legal problems of offshore boundaries in the Arabian Gulf 83
  A Settled problems 86
    1 Bahrain–Saudi Arabia Boundary Agreement 86
    2 Agreement concerning the Sovereignty over the Islands of Al-'Arabiyah and Farsi and the Delimitation of the Boundary Line separating the Submarine Areas between the Kingdom of Saudi Arabia and Iran 91
    3 Agreement for Settlement of the Offshore Boundary and Ownership of Islands between Abu Dhabi and Qatar 95
    4 Offshore Boundary Agreement between the Amirates of Abu Dhabi and Dubai 99
    5 Agreement concerning the Boundary Line dividing the Continental Shelf between Iran and Qatar
        Agreement concerning Delimitation of the Continental Shelf between Bahrain and Iran
        Agreement concerning the Boundary Line dividing Parts of the Continental Shelf between Iran and the United Arab Emirates (Dubai)
        Agreement concerning Delimitation of the Continental Shelf between Iran and Oman 99
  B Outstanding problems 107
    1 Kuwait–Saudi Arabia: partitioned zone offshore lateral boundaries and the question of the islands of Qaru and Umm al-Maradim 107
    2 Iran–Kuwait–Saudi Arabia: offshore boundary between Iran and the Kuwait–Saudi Arabia partitioned zone 110

CONTENTS

    3 Iran–Iraq–Kuwait: offshore boundaries and Iraq–Kuwait dispute over the islands of Warbah and Bubiyan   111
    4 Qatar–Saudi Arabia: offshore boundary   121
    5 Bahrain–Qatar: offshore boundary and the question of the Hawar islands   121
    6 Iran–Sharjah–Umm al-Qaiwain: the question of Abu Musa island   122
    7 Iran–Ras al-Khaimah: the question of the Tumb islands   128
  C Conclusion   130

IV Legal status of the Gulf of Aqaba and the Straits of Tiran and the rules governing the right of passage therethrough   132

  A Geographical and historical position of the Gulf of Aqaba   133
  B Occupation of Umm Rashrash and the struggle for control of the Gulf of Aqaba, 1949–76   135
    1 Occupation of Umm Rashrash   135
    2 Egypt–Saudi Arabia accord concerning the islands of Tiran and Sanafir and the question of sovereignty thereover   136
    3 Egyptian regulations relating to navigation through the Straits of Tiran   137
    4 The 1956 Sinai campaign and the 1967 Arab–Israeli armed conflict   138
  C Main assertions and arguments regarding the controversy surrounding the Gulf of Aqaba and the Straits of Tiran   139
    1 The Egyptian position   139
    2 The Israeli position   141
  D Analysis of the problem   142
    1 Legal description of the Gulf of Aqaba   144
    2 Juridical status of the Gulf of Aqaba   144
    3 The rules governing the right of passage through the Gulf of Aqaba and the Straits of Tiran   151
    4 Israeli withdrawal from Sinai Peninsula in March 1957 and the right of passage through the Gulf of Aqaba and the Straits of Tiran   167
    5 The 'exceptional—possibly unique' case of the Gulf of Aqaba   172
  E Conclusion   176

CONTENTS

V Legal aspects of the Red Sea hot brines and other metalliferous mud deposits ... 178

   A Discovery and location ... 178
   B Nature and economic potential ... 179
   C Legal rights ... 180
      1 The Saudi Arabian law relating to the acquisition of the Red Sea resources ... 180
      2 Agreement between Sudan and Saudi Arabia relating to the Joint Exploitation of the Natural Resources of the Sea Bed and Subsoil of the Red Sea in the Common Zone ... 185
      3 Conference of States bordering the Red Sea ... 187

General conclusions ... 189

Appendices ... 193

I National legislation and international agreements ... 195

II Limits of national claims to offshore jurisdictions ... 200

III Letter from the Political Agent to Shaikh Saqr, Ruler of Sharjah ... 201

IV Declaration concerning the Exclusive Sovereign Rights of the State of Qatar in the Zones contiguous to the Territorial Sea, 2 June 1974 ... 202

V Declaration concerning the Limits of the Exclusive Fishing Zones of Saudi Arabia in the Red Sea and the Arabian Gulf, 1974 ... 204

VI A Decree No. 15 concerning the Territorial Waters of the Yemen Arab Republic, 30 April 1967 ... 205
   B Decree No. 16 concerning the Continental Shelf of the Yemen Arab Republic, 30 April 1967 ... 207

VII Documents on the Understanding concerning the Island of Abu Musa ... 208

Notes ... 212

Selected bibliography ... 275

Index ... 288

LIST OF TABLE AND MAPS

TABLE

National allocations of the continental shelf and sea bed in the oceans and seas adjacent to the Middle Eastern States under various proposals on delimitation of outer limits of national jurisdiction and coastline measurements of those States *page* 57

MAPS

1	The Middle East	xxii
2	The Straits of Bab el-Mandeb	13
3	The Strait of Hormuz	16
4	The Arabian Gulf	85
5	Bahrain–Saudi Arabia continental shelf boundary	87
6	Iran–Saudi Arabia continental shelf boundary	93
7	Abu Dhabi–Qatar continental shelf boundary	96
8	Iran–Qatar continental shelf boundary	101
9	Bahrain–Iran continental shelf boundary	102
10	Iran–United Arab Emirates (Dubai) continental shelf boundary	104
11	Iran–Oman continental shelf boundary	106
12	Kuwaiti territorial sea and continental shelf	114
13	Iraqi territorial sea and continental shelf	116
14	Khor Abdullah	119
15	The Gulf of Aqaba and the Straits of Tiran	134
16	Red Sea median line and location of brine deposits	181
17	Trackline of the *Oceanographer* through the Red Sea	182

FOREWORD

The law governing the use, conservation and delimitation of the sea and its resources is today a major preoccupation of all governments, whether maritime or landlocked, for the use of the resources of the sea has in a relatively short time become a focus of the principal groupings, rivalries, power struggles, ambitions and ideals of a greatly enlarged international society of States. The United Nations Third Conference on the Law of the Sea has accordingly been very much more than a conference on the law of the sea. Dr El-Hakim's careful, sensitive and objective study of the attitudes of an important group of States towards these questions is therefore of more than ordinary importance; in addition, the very well researched studies of particular problems and issues provide a valuable store of source material for students of maritime legal questions and particularly of maritime boundary questions in any part of the world. It is with pleasure and confidence that I commend this book.

R. Y. Jennings

ACKNOWLEDGEMENTS

I would like to thank the staff of the Squire Law Library in Cambridge for their help in finding references which I needed and Manchester University Press for their care and helpfulness. I would like also to acknowledge my indebtedness to Dr D. W. Bowett, President of Queens' College, Cambridge, and Professor I. Brownlie of the LSE, who read the manuscript and made invaluable criticism and useful suggestions. Most of all, I wish to express my sincere gratitude to Professor R. Y. Jennings, of Jesus College, Cambridge, for his constant guidance, encouragement and inspiring suggestions throughout my research under his supervision for the doctoral thesis on which the present work is based. The views maintained as well as the shortcomings are mine alone.

A. El-Hakim
Cambridge
February 1978

TABLE OF CASES

Anglo-Norwegian Fisheries (I.C.J., 1951), 214, 215
Buttes Gas & Oil Co. v. Armand Hammer and Occidental Petroleum Corp. and Occidental Petroleum Corp. v. Buttes Gas & Oil Co. and John Boreta (Q.B.D., 1974; C.A., 1974), 251, 252
Corfu Channel (I.C.J., 1949), 14, 45, 52, 143, 144, 145, 151, 152, 153, 155, 157, 158, 160, 163, 167, 227, 231, 261, 262, 264, 267, 268, 270
Fisheries Jurisdiction (United Kingdom v. Iceland), Merits (I.C.J., 1974), 54, 232
Genocide (I.C.J., 1951), 157, 266
Gulf of Fonseca (Central American Court of Justice, 1917), 140, 149, 150, 259, 262, 264
North Sea Continental Shelf (I.C.J., 1969), 31, 32, 56, 63, 89, 90, 91, 98, 107, 113, 114, 116, 117, 131, 159, 185, 187, 189, 221, 222, 223, 225, 233, 235, 242, 249, 250, 255, 267, 274
Occidental Petroleum Corp. v. Buttes Gas & Oil Co. (C.D. Cal., 1971), 252
Occidental Petroleum Corp. v. Buttes Gas & Oil Co. (F. 2nd, 1972), 252
Petroleum Development (Qatar) Ltd v. Ruler of Qatar (1950), 222
Petroleum Development (Trucial Coast) Ltd v. Sheikh of Abu Dhabi (1951), 222
Trucial States (Ajman, Sharjah, Umm Al Qaiwain) Mediation (1970), 201, 214, 251, 252

ABBREVIATIONS

A/AC.138/1 *et. seq.*, A/AC. 138/SR.1 *et seq.*;
A/AC.138/SC.I (II) or (III)/L.1 *et seq.*;
A/AC.138/SC.I (II) or (III)/SR.1 *et seq.*;

	Documents and Summary Records of the UN Plenary Committee on the Peaceful Uses of the Sea Bed and the Ocean Floor beyond the Limits of National Jurisdiction and its three Sub committees
AALCC	Asian-African Legal Consultative Committee
A.J.I.L.	*American Journal of International Law*
A.S.C.L.	*Annual Survey of Commonwealth Law*
BIICL	British Institute of International and Comparative Law
B.Y.I.L.	*British Yearbook of International Law*
C.L.J.	*Cambridge Law Journal*
Cmd, Cmnd	Command Papers (United Kingdom)
Dept. of State Bull.	United States, Department of State *Bulletin*
FAO	Food and Agriculture Organisation
GAOR	United Nations, General Assembly, Official Records
Hague *Recueil*	*Recueil des Cours,* Académie de Droit International de la Haye
Har.I.L.J.	*Harvard International Law Journal*
H.C. Deb.	United Kingdom: Parliamentary Debates (Hansard) House of Commons Official Reports
H.L. Deb.	House of Lords Official Reports
ICNT	Informal Composite Negotiating Text
I.C.J.	International Court of Justice
I.C.L.Q.	*International and Comparative Law Quarterly*
ILC	International Law Commission
I.L.M.	*International Legal Materials*
IMCO	Intergovernmental Maritime Consultative Organisation
Indian J.I.L.	*Indian Journal of International Law*
Int. Conc.	International Conciliation
J. Mar. L. and Comm.	*Journal of Maritime Law and Commerce*
L.N.T.S.	League of Nations Treaty Series
Louisiana L. Rev.	*Louisiana Law Review*
LSCOR (1st)	First United Nations Conference on the Law of the Sea, Official Records
LSCOR (2nd)	Second United Nations Conference on the Law of the Sea, Official Records
LSCOR (3rd)	Third United Nations Conference on the Law of the Sea, Official Records
M.E.E.D.	*Middle East Economic Digest* (London)

ABBREVIATIONS

M.E.E.S.	*Middle East Economic Survey* (Beirut)
M.L.R.	*Modern Law Review*
Netherlands I.L.Rev.	*Netherlands International Law Review*
Netherlands Y.I.L.	*Netherlands Yearbook of International Law*
N.R.L.	*Natural Resources Lawyer*
O.A.U.	Organisation of African Unity
Ocean Development	*Ocean Development and International Law Journal*
OPEC	Organisation of Petroleum Exporting Countries
R.E.D.I.	*Revenue Egyptienne de Droit International*
SCOR	United Nations, Security Council, Official Records
S.I.	Statutory Instrument (United Kingdom)
ST/LEG/Ser.B/1, B/2	United Nations Legislative Series, Laws and Regulations on the Regime of the High Seas, 1951, vols. I and II respectively
—B/6	United Nations Legislative Series, Laws and Regulations on the Regime of the Territorial Sea, 1957
—B/8	United Nations Legislative Series, Supplement to Regulations on the Regime of the High Seas (vols. I and II) and Laws Concerning the Nationality of Ships, 1959
—B/15	United Nations Legislative Series, National Legislation and Treaties relating to the Territorial Sea, the Contiguous Zone, the Continental Shelf, the High Seas and to Fishing and Conservation of the Living Resources of the Sea, 1970
—B/16	United Nations Legislative Series, National Legislation and Treatise Relating to the Law of the Sea, 1974
—B/18	United Nations Legislative Series, National Legislation and Treaties Relating to the Law of the Sea, 1976
—B/19	United Nations Legislative Series, National Legislation and Treaties Relating to the Law of the Sea (preliminary issue), 1978
U.K.T.S.	United Kingdom Treaty Series
UNCTAD	United Nations Conference on Trade and Development
UNEP	United Nations Environment Programme
UNESCO	United Nations Educational, Scientific and Cultural Organisation
UNITAR	United Nations Institute for Training and Research
U.N.T.S.	United Nations Treaty Series

INTRODUCTION

The sea covers 70·8 per cent of the earth's surface. Through the advances of science and technology the world community has become more aware of the urgency of establishing a generally agreed regime which would ensure that the sea and its vast resources are used and developed fairly, rationally and peacefully for the benefit of all mankind. The need for a radical reconsideration of the traditional law of the sea was emphasised by the decision of the Twenty-fifth Session of the General Assembly to convene in 1973, a comprehensive Third United Nations Conference on the Law of the Sea. So far, the conference has held seven sessions and has made substantial progress on most aspects, but it is clear that it will need further sessions to accomplish its task of adopting a convention dealing with all matters relating to the law of the sea.

The present work was motivated partly by these developments and partly by a feeling that the theme has not received sufficient attention. The Middle Eastern States covered in these pages include the State of Bahrain, the Arab Republic of Egypt, the United Arab Emirates, the Islamic Republic of Iran, the Republic of Iraq, the Hashemite Kingdom of Jordan, the State of Kuwait, the Republic of Lebanon, the Socialist People's Libyan Arab Jamahiriyah, the Sultanate of Oman, the State of Qatar, the Kingdom of Saudi Arabia, the Democratic Republic of the Sudan, the Syrian Arab Republic, the Yemen Arab Republic and the People's Democratic Republic of Yemen.[1]

The significance of the law of the sea to the Middle Eastern States hardly needs emphasis. Their coasts, enormous and diversified, embrace the heart of world communications. Continuous and uninterrupted, their shores start from the eastern Mediterranean and extend through the Suez Canal into the Red Sea. From the Red Sea they continue through the Straits of Bab el Mandeb, into the Gulf of Aden which opens into the Arabian Sea, and, touching the Indian Ocean, they run right through the Gulf of Oman, up to the Strait of Hormuz and the Arabian (Persian)

---

[1] For the purpose of brevity, short-form names will be used throughout. Thus the State of Bahrain will be referred to as Bahrain and the People's Democratic Republic of Yemen as Democratic Yemen. The term 'the Middle Eastern States' will be used henceforth to mean only the States named above.

INTRODUCTION

Gulf.[2] The continental shelf areas, together with the land territories, of the Middle Eastern States are reputed to contain between 50 and 75 per cent of the world's proved oil reserves. Thus for the oil-rich Middle Eastern States the sea is of vital importance to their economic and social progress. Besides, in coastal areas of many Middle Eastern States, especially those of the Arabian Gulf and the Red Sea, valuable fish resources and, in the case of the Red Sea, brine deposits, occur and need to be safeguarded and developed prudently. Again, their coasts are vulnerable to pollution, especially from oil, and need adequate protection against such dangers. Moreover, like most developing countries, the Middle Eastern States still lack the technology and the know-how necessary for the exploitation of sea resources and so require the co-operation and assistance of the appropriate United Nations Agencies and of the technologically advanced countries. Furthermore, while some States such as Saudi Arabia have considerable natural resources, others, such as Yemen, are more or less barren and, for that reason, have a paramount interest in the establishment of an international regime that would ensure that the natural resources of the sea bed beyond the limits of national jurisdiction are used and developed for the benefit of all mankind.

In brief, this work is an attempt to explore and analyse the practice and policies of the Middle Eastern States with regard to certain aspects of the international law of the sea. This is not, it must be stressed, a comprehensive treatment of all issues of the law of the sea. Some are treated briefly or completely omitted. The book falls into two main parts.

Part One deals with general practice and policies of the Middle Eastern States in the field of the international law of the sea. In Part Two special consideration is given to three specific regional issues, each of which is dealt with in a separate chapter.

Chapter I is devoted to an account and analysis of existing national claims to offshore jurisdiction, both as concerns the physical extent of the offshore area involved and the legal nature of the claim.

Chapter II is intended to provide some insight into the position which the Middle Eastern States are taking in the Third United Nations Conference on the Law of the Sea.

Chapter III is concerned with certain legal problems of offshore

---

[2] See Map 1. It is not intended to deal with the controversy regarding the use of 'Arabian' or 'Persian' Gulf. In a work largely concerned with Arab States, 'Arabian' seems more appropriate. However, the term 'Persian Gulf' as used in various quotations and documents relied upon in this book will remain unchanged.

boundaries in the Arabian Gulf. It surveys and analyses those settled, and some outstanding problems regarding continental shelf boundaries and islands of disputed sovereignty in the Arabian Gulf.

The controversy surrounding the legal status of the Gulf of Aqaba and the Straits of Tiran as well as the rules governing the right of passage through them has interesting legal implications and warrants special consideration. Chapter IV is accordingly devoted to a study of certain aspects of this problem.

Recent exploration activities in the Red Sea deeps have shown its potentialities as a source of mineral resources, the commercial exploitability of which has already drawn the attention of the littoral States to such issues as offshore boundary delimitation and joint exploitation projects. Legal aspects of this problem are discussed in Chapter V.

In a final section, some general conclusions are attempted.

I have endeavoured to state the law in accordance with the sources available to me on 1 January 1978, though in some instances subsequent developments were also taken note of.

The notes to each chapter are on pp. 212–274.

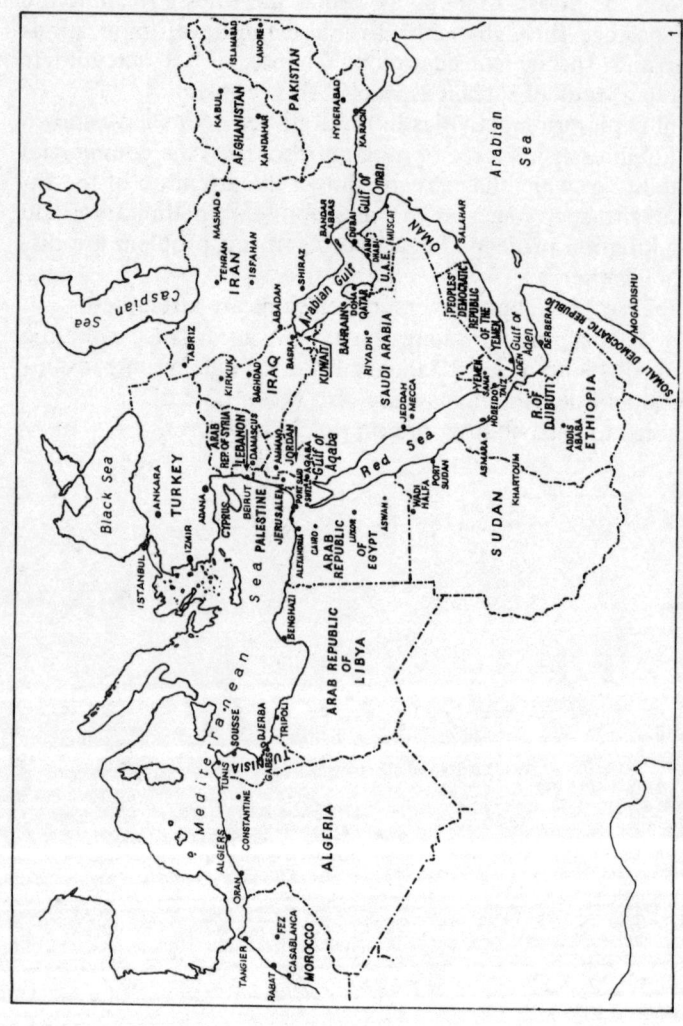

1 The Middle East. After *Middle East Annual Review*, 1975–76, pp. 6–7.

PART ONE

GENERAL PRACTICE AND POLICIES

CHAPTER I

EXISTING NATIONAL CLAIMS TO OFFSHORE JURISDICTION

Claims to offshore or maritime zones of jurisdiction vary from State to State, and current State practice exhibits such a variety of claims and such a lack of stability that identification of an effective list of types of jurisdiction is not practicable. However, five traditional jurisdictional zones may be distinguished:

In the first two zones, internal waters and the territorial sea, the predominant principle is that of sovereignty but, already in the territorial sea, the existence of a right of innocent passage reflects the landward reach of the principle of the freedom of the seas. In the next two zones, the various functional zones and the continental shelf, the position is reversed; the basic principle is that of the freedom of the seas but certain limitations on that freedom reflect the seaward extension of sovereign rights. Finally, in the zone beyond the continental shelf, in the high seas proper, the reach of territorial sovereignty is practically exhausted and jurisdictional claims are in the main limited to quasi-territorial jurisdiction over national vessels.[1]

In so far as the territorial sea and functional zones are concerned, it may be observed that, at the present time, while some States are asserting traditional territorial sea claims, supplemented by claims to various functional zones, others have dispensed with such refinements and are making comprehensive territorial sea claims of very considerable dimensions. Others again are experimenting *de lege ferenda* with new compromise formulae such as 'the patrimonial sea' or the 'exclusive economic zone', which are being discussed at the Third United Nations Conference on the Law of the Sea.[2]

In this chapter the present legislation of the Middle Eastern States, where it exists, in relation to the first four of the abovementioned five jurisdictional zones will be analysed. But since the basic question in relation to the zone of internal waters relates to the rules governing the outer limits of these waters, that is, the baseline from which the breadth of the territorial sea is measured, discussion of this question will be incorporated with that concerning the territorial sea zone.

3

As will be seen, most of the Middle Eastern States have adopted domestic territorial sea and continental shelf legislation; many of them have claimed contiguous or supervision zones beyond the territorial sea; few of them have made laws for the purpose of marine pollution control; and only Iran, Oman, Democratic Yemen, Qatar, and Saudi Arabia have made actual claims to exclusive fishing zones of considerable extent. Some of the Middle Eastern States are, presumably, awaiting the outcome of the Third Conference on the Law of the Sea before making legislation or formal claims, where none now exists, in regard to various aspects of the law of the sea.[3]

At the outset it is also worth noting that, with the exception that in March 1970 Sudan acceded to the 1958 Geneva Convention on the Continental Shelf, none of the Middle Eastern States has so far ratified or acceded to any of the four conventions adopted at the 1958 United Nations Conference on the Law of the Sea in Geneva[4]—though, as will be shown in more detail, on 28 May 1958 Iran signed the four conventions, but with reservations. On the same date also Lebanon signed three of the conventions; it did not sign the Convention on the Territorial Sea and the Contiguous Zone.[5] The reluctance of the Arab States to ratify or accede to those conventions is mainly due to their dissatisfaction with Article 16 (4) of the Territorial Sea Convention, which provides for the right of non-suspendable innocent passage through '... straits which are used for international navigation between one part of the high seas and ... the territorial sea of a foreign State', and which, according to one view, applies to the Straits of Tiran, the entrance to the Gulf of Aqaba.[6] With respect to the Convention on the Continental Shelf in particular, it has been observed that non-ratification by the Arab States and Iran may well have been dictated by a desire for prior settlement of existing disputes with neighbouring States and, in some cases, the conviction that the convention is better designed for States bordering the open seas than for those in areas such as the Arabian Gulf.[7] The latter conviction was expressed by Iran at the 1958 Conference on the Law of the Sea.[8]

A final introductory note: since the national laws of the Middle Eastern States reveal a great degree of similarity, a topical approach will be followed in their analysis, with differences and special or remarkable circumstances, where they arise, pointed out.[9]

EXISTING NATIONAL CLAIMS
A. TERRITORIAL SEA

With the exception of Bahrain, the United Arab Emirates (except the Emirate of Sharjah), Jordan, Lebanon and Qatar, all the Middle Eastern States are known to have made laws which dealt specifically with their respective territorial seas, though some of these laws have treated only very basic matters such as the breadth of the territorial sea.

1. Breadth of the territorial sea

Throughout the development of the law of the sea, the breadth of the territorial sea has been one of the most controversial questions, but at the present time it would seem that there is a consensus among the majority of States for a general agreement on a twelve-mile territorial sea.[10] This limit may be regarded as the general Middle Eastern standard at present, for it has been adopted by eleven of the sixteen Middle Eastern States, and as will be seen in Chapter II the others have already expressed support for it. It was adopted by Saudi Arabia and Egypt on 16 and 17 February 1958 respectively. Prior to these dates each of these two States had claimed a six-mile territorial sea.[11] According to one view, the timing of the Saudi and Egyptian extension of the territorial sea was primarily designed to assert general Arab claims with regard to the Gulf of Aqaba at the impending 1958 United Nations Conference on the Law of the Sea.[12] However, the immediate impact of the Saudi move was on relations with Bahrain and Qatar, whose territorial waters overlap those of Saudi Arabia.[13] Shortly after the issue of the Saudi decree extending the Saudi territorial waters, on 22 February 1958, Bahrain and Saudi Arabia signed an agreement defining their maritime boundaries.[14]

Up to 1958 the practice of Iraq in dealing with the regime and breadth of its territorial sea was the application of the general rules recognised by public international law.[15] But in November of that year Law No. 71 fixed the Iraqi territorial sea at twelve miles measured from the low-water mark of the Iraqi coast. Because the Iraqi coastline is concave and extends for about ten nautical miles only, the Iraqi territorial sea and continental shelf zones become narrower towards the high seas until each of them ends almost in a point. It may be observed also that the low-water mark of the Iraqi coast is moving slowly and gradually, but evenly, towards the sea because of a regular and slow accretion which is estimated to be about two miles per century; this is due to the Shatt al-Arab river's alluvial deposit (some 35 million cubic metres per year).[16] The Shatt al-Arab falls into the Arabian Gulf.

On 18 February 1959 Libya extended its territorial sea to twelve nautical miles.[17] During the 1958 Conference on the Law of the Sea the Libyan delegate supported his argument for a twelve-mile territorial sea by reference to the importance of fisheries as a source of food and of fish and sponges as 'valuable Libyan exports'. He also said that 'Libya was constantly faced with the problem of foreign fishermen who were wrongfully exploiting the resources of its territorial sea'.[18]

In March 1959 the Council of the League of Arab States recommended that all the Arab States should adopt the twelve-mile territorial sea.[19] On 2 August 1960 Sudan resolved that its territorial sea should have a breadth of twelve miles.[20] This resolution was confirmed by Article 5 of the Sudanese Territorial Waters and Continental Shelf Act of 28 November 1970.

In 1963 the territorial sea of the Syrian Arab Republic was extended to twelve nautical miles. The same limit was adopted by the Yemen Arab Republic on 30 April 1967, by Kuwait on 17 December 1967, by the People's Democratic Republic of Yemen on 9 February 1970 (this law was rescinded by a new law adopted in 1977 which also claimed the same limit) and by the Sultanate of Oman on 17 July 1972.[21] Before 1967 Kuwait never officially defined the extent of its territorial sea. But since it was a British protectorate (until 1961) and following the British practice in this respect, it was assumed that Kuwait's territorial sea was three miles. For the purpose of oil concessions, however, the territorial sea of Kuwait was defined in many agreements, concluded prior to and during 1961, to extend to six nautical miles.[22] This shows, even in an indirect way, that the authorities concerned were inclined to take the six nautical miles limit as a basis for Kuwait's territorial waters at that time, although there was no explicit reference to the fact.[23] It has also been suggested that Kuwait extended its territorial sea to twelve miles, hoping to reach an agreement with Iran on the delimitation of the continental shelf, for, whereas Iran has a twelve-mile limit, Kuwait was still an adherent to the 'six mile' rule and the question centred around the equitable basis for establishing the median line of the Arabian Gulf.[24] No such agreement, however, has been concluded yet.[25] Another justification for the extension of Kuwait's territorial sea is, according to the 'Explanatory Note' attached to the 1967 Kuwaiti decree on the territorial sea, the precedent set by other States in the area. In this Kuwait was preceded by Iran, Saudi Arabia and Iraq as well as a number of Arab States which followed the recommendation of the Arab League referred to above.

Jordan and Lebanon have not made any specific legislation regarding their respective territorial sea limits yet, but these limits have been defined for the purpose of fishing and other functional zones. Thus, in Jordan, Article 2 of the Fisheries Act No. 25 of 2 December 1943 provides that:

> In this Act, unless the context otherwise requires ... 'Transjordan' includes that part of the sea which is contiguous to the coast of Transjordan and lies within a distance of three nautical miles from the low-water line.[26]

In Lebanon, the Fisheries Order of 14 November 1921, issued by France for both Lebanon and Syria when they were under French mandate, limited the territorial sea of Lebanon to a distance of six miles from the coast or Lebanese islands.[27] For the purpose of the application of the Penal Law, the Lebanese Penal Code enacted by Legislative Decree No. 340-NT on 1 March 1943 extends the territorial sea of Lebanon to a distance of twenty kilometres measured from the line of the low tide.[28] And the Customs Code of 15 June 1935, which was also issued by France for both Lebanon and Syria, established for Lebanon a customs zone of twenty kilometres from the shore.[29]

Similarly, Bahrain, Qatar and the United Arab Emirates (with the exception of Sharjah Emirate) have so far not defined the limit of their respective territorial seas. But it is assumed that the three-mile limit sponsored by Britain is still in force in these States.[30] However, like Jordan and Lebanon, these States, as noted above, are in favour of the twelve-mile limit, and are expected to follow the lead of other Arab States and Iran and formally adopt this limit.[31]

In a decree dated 10 September 1969 the ruler of Sharjah declared that the extent of the territorial waters of Sharjah and its dependencies, and the territorial waters of its islands, is twelve nautical miles.[32] A supplementary decree issued on 5 April 1970 contained a similar provision.[33]

Finally, on 12 April 1959 Iran extended its territorial sea to twelve nautical miles.[34]

2. *Measurement of the territorial sea*

The principles governing the baseline from which the territorial sea is measured—or the outer limit of internal waters—are now fairly well established and, as formulated in Section III of the 1958 Geneva Convention on the Territorial Sea and the Contiguous

Zone, are 'probably generally accepted even by non-parties to the Convention',[35] and it is likely that they will be adopted by the Third Conference on the Law of the Sea.[36] According to these rules the normal baseline from which the width of the territorial sea is measured is the low-water line, but—and this is a restatement of the principle laid down by the International Court of Justice[37]—in localities where the coastline is deeply indented or cut into, or where there is a fringe of islands along the coast in its immediate vicinity, it is permissible to draw straight baselines by joining appropriate points on the coast, and to measure the territorial sea from these straight baselines.

In this regard the practice of the Middle Eastern States varies. The legislation of some States such as Kuwait,[38] Oman and Sharjah Emirate refers to or establishes baselines generally in accordance with the provisions of the 1958 convention; the legislation of other States, such as Saudi Arabia, Egypt, the Yemen Arab Republic, Syria, Sudan and Democratic Yemen, adopts detailed provisions which in some respects do not conform to the rules established in 1958. The legislation of others again, such as Iraq, refer merely to the low-water line. The Iranian law stipulates that the baseline will be determined by the government 'with due regard to the established rules of public international law'.

The provisions adopted in the laws of Saudi Arabia, Egypt, the Yemen Arab Republic, Syria, Sudan and Democratic Yemen are nearly identical. These provisions were first adopted by Saudi Arabia in the Royal Decree No. 6/4/5/3711 of 28 May 1949, which was revoked by the Royal Decree No. 33 of 16 February 1958.[39] It will first be noted that those laws contain provisions defining the internal waters and others for the determination of the baseline for the measurement of the territorial sea, although both provisions have practically the same effect. However, according to these provisions the baseline of the territorial sea is shifted out to the fringe of islands and shoals within twelve miles of the coast. It is also provided that, where there is an island group which may be connected by lines not more than twelve nautical miles long, lines may be drawn along the shore of all the islands of the group if the islands form a chain, or along the outermost islands of the group if the islands do not form a chain. Except in the Syrian legislation, which in its definition of an 'island' conforms with the 1958 Territorial Sea Convention, an island is defined to include any islet, reef, rock, or permanent artificial structure not submerged at lowest low tide. According to the 1958 convention an island is 'a naturally formed area of land, surrounded by water, which is above water at high tide'. Besides, whereas the latter convention speaks of a low-tide elevation which is 'surrounded and above water at low-tide submerged at high tide', the above-mentioned legislation speaks of shoals or elevations which are 'not submerged by' rather than those which are above lowest low water.[40] Moreover, each of the laws in question includes a provision to the effect that in cases where the measurement of the territorial sea according to the provisions of the legislation concerned leaves behind a region of high seas surrounded by the territorial sea from all sides and extending not more than twelve nautical miles in any direction, such a region will form part of the territorial sea. Furthermore, according to the legislation of Saudi Arabia, Egypt, the Yemen Arab Republic, Sudan and Democratic Yemen, a bay, whose waters may be included in the internal waters, includes any islet, lagoon or other arm of the sea. Thus a 'bay' does not have to meet the semicircularity requirement or the twenty-four nautical miles closing limit of Article 7 of the 1958 convention.[41] In the Syrian legislation a 'bay' is defined according to the semicircle requirement, but no maximum limits for the closure are indicated in the legislation. In the case of Egypt, it has been indicated that the following are considered to be bays within the meaning of the Egyptian law of 1951:[42]

Bay	Distance between headlands (miles)	Greatest distance from closing line to inner shore (miles)
1. Gulf of Salum	45·4	19·9
2. Abu Hashaifa Bay	31·6	7·9
3. Arab Gulf (El-Arab)	94·7	25·7
4. Bay of Pelusium	49·3	13·3
5. Bay of El-Arish	65·0	11·8

In a commentary by the government of Egypt in 1957 on the International Law Commission's draft articles concerning the law of the sea of 1956, Egypt considered that the provisions which dealt with 'bays' were 'unsatisfactory' and 'open to serious objection', and noted that:

The requirement that a *bay,* to be legally so considered, should be of an area large as that of a semicircle drawn on its mouth, would not respond to the practical situation presented in the case of countries like Egypt where a coast is marked by a succession of well-recognised bays of considerable breadth and relatively small depth.[43]

THE LIBYAN GULF OF SURT. In a declaration made on 9 October 1973 the Libyan Arab Republic claimed that the Gulf of Surt or Sirte '... constitutes an integral part of the territory of the Libyan Arab Republic and is under its complete sovereignty', and that '... it constitutes internal waters, beyond which the territorial waters of the Libyan Arab Republic start'.

The Gulf of Surt does not meet the semicircularity test or the twenty-four nautical miles closing limit required of a legal bay as described in Article 7 of the 1958 Territorial Sea Convention. However, Article 7 does not apply to so-called 'historic' bays, and it appears that Libya has based its claim with respect to the Gulf of Surt both on historic considerations and on the principle of vital bays. The Libyan declaration thus asserted that:

> Through history and without any dispute, the Libyan Arab Republic has exercised its sovereignty over the Gulf. Because of the Gulf's geographic location commanding a view of the southern part of the country, it is, therefore, crucial to the security of the Libyan Arab Republic. Consequently, complete surveillance over its area is necessary to ensure the security and safety of the State.

The declaration, furthermore, stated that private and public foreign ships are not allowed to enter the Gulf without prior permission from the authorities of the Libyan Arab Republic and in accordance with the regulations established by it in this regard.[44]

3. Delimitation of the territorial sea between States with adjacent or opposite coasts.

The 1958 Geneva Convention on the Territorial Sea and the Contiguous Zone lays down that where the territorial seas of two States would otherwise overlap, in the absence of an agreement between them to the contrary, neither may extend its territorial sea beyond the median line between the baselines of their respective territorial seas.[45] This rule has been referred to expressly in the territorial sea legislation of Kuwait, Sharjah, Oman and Iran. On the other hand the legislation of Iraq, Saudi Arabia, Egypt, Sudan, Syria, the Yemen Arab Republic and Democratic Yemen refer in this regard to agreement according to equitable or recognised rules of international law.

4. Innocent passage through the territorial sea

Whereas some Middle Eastern States, such as Egypt, Iraq, Saudi Arabia, and the Yemen Arab Republic, claim that their sovereignty over their respective territorial sea is subject to the provisions of international law as to the innocent passage of vessels of other nations through the territorial sea without making any distinction between merchant and military vessels, others, such as Syria, Democratic Yemen and Sudan, require the coastal State's prior permission for the innocent passage of warships. In this regard the 1958 convention is not absolutely clear, but the Informal Composite Negotiating Text prepared at the sixth session of the Third Law of the Sea Conference makes it clear that warships have the same rights of innocent passage through the territorial sea as merchant ships.[46]

The supplementary decree on the territorial sea issued by Sharjah Emirate in 1970 recognises the 'right of transit' and the 'right of over flight' by all vessels and aircraft of all nations with which Sharjah is at peace in that portion of Sharjah's territorial sea which is contiguous to the territorial sea of an opposite coast of another State in such a way that none of the waters between the land territories of Sharjah and the other State are high seas. This provision applies to Sharjah's dependencies on the coast of the Gulf of Oman, namely Husn Diba, Khor Fakkan and Kalba, for the territorial sea of these enclaves overlaps the territorial sea of the opposite State, Iran.

5. *Straits*

Article 16 (4) of the Geneva Convention on the Territorial Sea states that there shall be no suspension of the innocent passage of foreign ships through straits which are used for international navigation between one part of the high seas and another part of the high seas or the territorial sea of a foreign State. However, in accordance with the demands of the maritime powers, it is likely that the Third Law of the Sea Conference will adopt a rule which would provide for 'transit passage' through straits linking one area of the high seas or an exclusive economic zone and another area of the high seas or an exclusive economic area while leaving the right of non-suspendable innocent passage to apply to straits between one part of the high seas or an exclusive economic zone and the territorial sea of a foreign State.[47]

The Straits of Bab el-Mandeb and the Strait of Hormuz are two international straits where one or more of the Middle Eastern States are coastal States. The two straits, each in turn, and the practice of the Middle Eastern States concerned in relation to them, will therefore be examined here.[48]

THE STRAITS OF BAB EL-MANDEB. In a study of straits which constitute routes for international maritime traffic, Commander R. H.

Kennedy describes the Straits of Bab el-Mandeb in a statement which is necessary to quote at some length:

1. These Straits join the high seas of the Gulf of Aden to those of the Red Sea and form part of the international route from the Mediterranean to the Far East. The name is strictly applied to the waters lying between Ras Bab el Mandeb and Ras Si Ane about 14½ miles south-westward and comprising the Large Strait between that island and Arabia. Large Strait is about 9¼ miles wide and Small Strait about 1½ miles in breadth. For the purpose of this study, however, the water area in the vicinity less than 26 miles wide will be considered. This extends from Mokha in the north to a position about 20 miles eastward of Ras Bab el Mandeb, a distance of approximately 50 miles.

2. The following States border these Straits:
On the south-west, Ethiopia and French Somaliland [since 1968 known as Territoire Français des Afars et des Issas—French Territory of Afars and Issas; now the independent Republic of Djibouti]. On the north-east, Yemen [Arab Republic] and Aden Protectorate [now the independent People's Democratic Republic of Yemen].

3. *(a)* The length of the Straits may be considered as 50 miles.
(b) The general width of the Straits is 19½ miles but this width is restricted over a distance of about seven miles both by the peninsula of which Ras Bab el Mandeb forms the southern end on the northern side, and by Perim Island, which divides the main Strait into two—Large Strait and Small Strait.
(c) Small Strait between Perim Island and Ras Bab el Mandeb is about three miles long and varies in width from about three miles to one-and-a-half miles.
(d) Large Strait between Perim Island and the African coast is about 10 miles long with a general width of about 10½ miles. The narrowest part is 9¼ miles wide between the southern end of Perim Island and Jezirate Seba, a group of six islands extending about six miles from the African coast and south-south-westward of Perim Island.

4. The whole Strait, with the exception of Small Strait, throughout its length of about 50 miles, is deep water varying from about 100 fathoms or more in the middle to approximately three to six fathoms close off the coastal reefs. There are no navigational changes throughout its length. Small Strait has depths varying from 12 to 15½ fathoms and is free from changes in the fairway. Tidal streams are, however, strong and irregular, and, as many casualties have occurred there, the use of Large Strait is recommended.

5. In addition to Perim Island and Jezirat Seba, described above, the only island in the area is Dumerra, the outer edge of which lies about a mile from the African coast and about 14 miles west-north-westward of Perim Island.

There are no ports within the area.

6. Navigation is possible on both sides of median line drawn through the main Strait and through Large and Small Straits.[49]

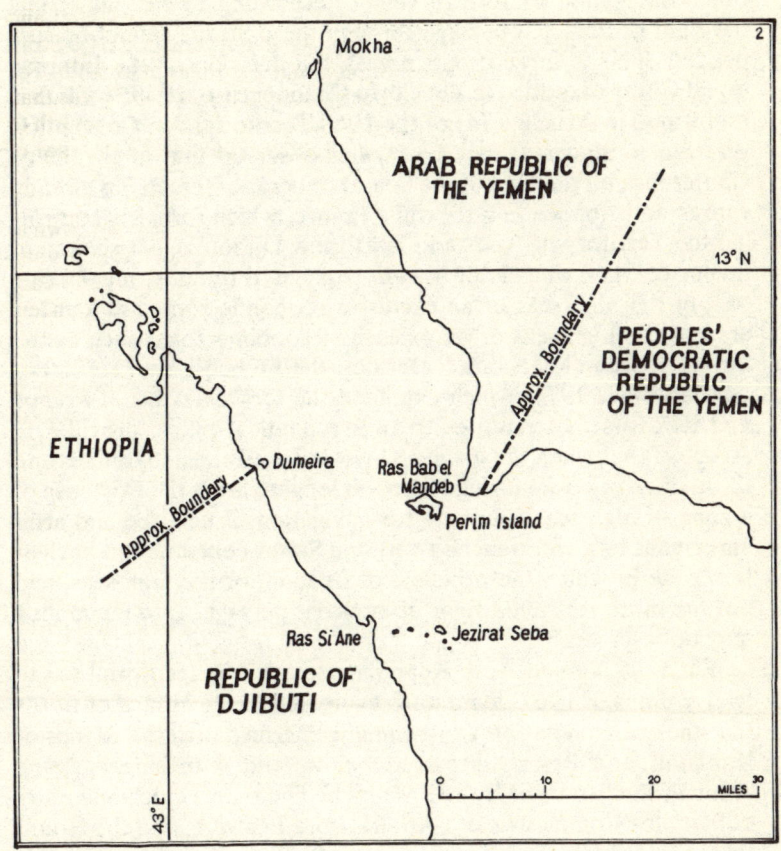

2 The Straits of Bab el-Mandeb. After R. H. Kennedy, 'A brief study of straits', *op. cit.*, p. 145.

The narrower part of the Straits of Bab el-Mandeb lies wholly within the territorial seas of Democratic Yemen and the Republic of Djibouti. Each claims a twelve-mile territorial sea.[50] However, since the Straits of Bab el-Mandeb join the high seas of the Gulf of Aden to those of the Red Sea and are actually used for international navigation by foreign vessels, according to customary law the right of innocent passage through these Straits cannot be suspended. This is in accordance with the decision of the International Court of Justice in the Corfu Channel case, 1949,[51] which is reaffirmed in Article 6 (4) of the 1958 Territorial Sea Convention referred to above. It may be further observed that at the Third Conference on the Law of the Sea, Democratic Yemen has already expressed its opposition to, while France, which formerly controlled the Territory of Afars and Issas (now Djibouti), has spoken in favour of, the principle of 'transit passage' through straits linking part of the high seas or an exclusive economic zone and another area of the high seas or an exclusive economic zone, such as the Straits of Bab el-Mandeb.[52] Besides, the French Law 71-1060 of 24 December 1971, which extended the territorial sea of France and its overseas territories to twelve nautical miles, provides in Article 3 that when the distance between the French baselines and those of an opposite foreign State no longer allows the existence of a zone of high seas adequate for navigation, if need be and after agreement has been reached with the States concerned, a navigation zone in which the principle of freedom of the high seas, and not the more restricted right of innocent passage, is to be applied may be reserved.[53]

When the Yemen Arab Republic extended its territorial sea to twelve miles in 1967, fears were expressed in the House of Lords that the government of Yemen might interfere with the islands of Kamaran and Perim, discussed below, and with ships passing through the Straits of Bab el-Mandeb. The then Under-Secretary of State for Commonwealth Affairs, Lord Beswick, told the House that '. . . Her Majesty's Government will take any action necessary to prevent interference by the Yemen authorities with the islands of Kamaran and Perim'. He also said:

> . . . the fact is that the extension of any territorial waters cannot affect the status of islands which belong to or are dependencies of another country and which are within the additional area of sea now claimed. So far as access to the Red Sea is concerned, this is guaranteed by international Convention, and we shall seek to ensure that that Convention is observed.[54]

Until 1971 there had been no interference with ships passing through the straits. The first incident, however, took place on 11 June of that year, when a Liberian-flag tanker, the *Coral Sea*, chartered by Israel, was fired on from an unmarked launch. Bazooka shells ripped three holes in the ship but failed to ignite the 30,000 tons of crude oil.

During the Arab–Israeli conflict of October 1973, reports were published that the government of Democratic Yemen had announced a blockade of the Straits of Bab el-Mandeb against ships sailing under the Israeli flag, operated by Israeli companies, or bound for Israel, and declared the straits a 'war' zone.[55] It has been reported also that during the Arab summit meeting at Rabat in October 1974 Egypt concluded an agreement with Democratic Yemen for the lease of the strategic island of Perim as a naval base to enable her to blockage the Israeli port of Eilat.[56] This, however, was denied by the government of Democratic Yemen, which in an announcement also stated that 'the so-called lease of the island [of Perim], was not a subject for debate by anyone at the Seventh Arab Summit Conference in Rabat'.[57]

THE STRAIT OF HORMUZ. The Strait of Hormuz joins the high seas of the Arabian Gulf to those of the Gulf of Oman, which opens to the Arabian Sea and the Indian Ocean. Since the end of World War II, with the development of the extensive petroleum resources which are found in the Arabian Gulf area, the importance of the strait as an international waterway has notably increased.[58] In 1973 it was shown that an average of one oil tanker every fourteen minutes passed through it, and that about 17 million barrels of oil—roughly a third of the non-communist world's consumption—left the Arabian Gulf through this narrow strait daily.[59] Geographically, the Strait of Hormuz:

lies between Iran on the north and north-west and Oman on the south. Its northern shores are formed by the eastern part of Quishm Island together with its off-lying islands of Jezirat Henjam. Its southern shores are formed by the western and northern sides of Musandam Peninsula, the most northerly part of the mainland of Oman, and its offlying islets.

From the Gulf of Oman the approach to the Strait is in a northerly direction and is about 30 miles wide. The Strait itself runs in a general south-westerly direction; it is constricted to a breadth of 20¾ miles at the northern end between Jezirat Larak and Great Quoin, an islet 8½ miles northward of Musandam Peninsula; thence between this peninsula and the eastern coast of Qishm Island the general width is about 28 miles.[60]

The twelve-mile territorial seas of Iran and Oman overlap in the narrower part of the Strait of Hormuz, leaving no high seas area

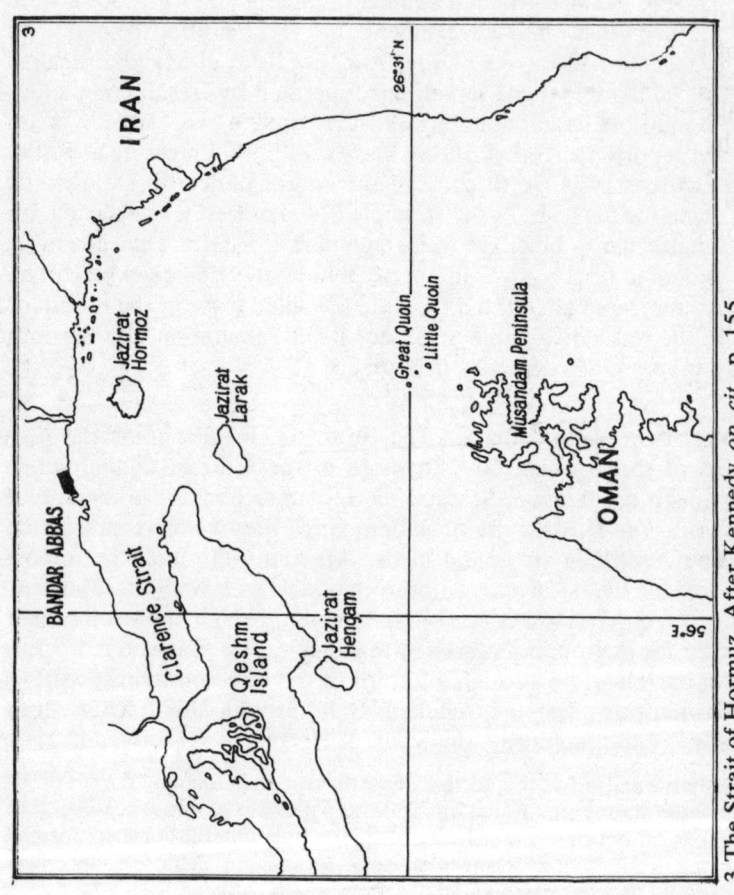

3 The Strait of Hormuz. After Kennedy, op. cit., p. 155.

within this part. However, since the strait is used for international navigation between the high seas of the Gulf of Oman and those of the Arabian Gulf, innocent passage of foreign ships through the strait cannot be suspended. This is by virtue of the customary rule laid down in the Corfu Channel case, 1949, and restated in the 1958 Territorial Sea Convention and referred to above. The Strait of Hormuz would also qualify for the application of the rule concerning 'transit passage' through straits, which, as mentioned above, is being considered at the Third Conference on the Law of the Sea. At that conference, however, Oman and Iran stressed that any proposed rules concerning passage through international straits should be based on the concept of innocent passage and not on the right of 'transit passage'.[61] It may be further observed that the 1972 Omani decree concerning the territorial sea also speaks of the principle of innocent passage of ships and planes of other States through international straits.

6. Islands: legal status of Perim, Kamaran and Kuria Muria

Perim and Kamaran are two strategically situated islands belonging to the People's Democratic Republic of Yemen. The former lies within the narrow Straits of Bab el-Mandeb, the southern entrance to the Red Sea, whereas the latter lies about four miles off the coast of the Yemen Arab Republic. For sometime there had been some controversy about the legal status of these two islands and the Kuria Muria islands, which lie in the Arabian Sea and belong to the Sultanate of Oman.[62]

It may be recalled that the People's Democratic Republic of Yemen (prior to 30 November 1970 the 'People's Republic of Southern Yemen') came into existence on 30 November 1967, the date on which the territory became independent after 129 years of British rule.[63] On the same day a 'Consensus' on Aden was adopted by the United Nations General Assembly which, *inter alia*, wished 'peace and prosperity to the Territory on its accession to independence', and affirmed the 'unity and territorial integrity of the whole Territory, including all the islands as prescribed in General Assembly Resolution 2183 (XXI) of 12 December 1966'.[64] The latter resolution indicated that the Territory of Aden includes 'in addition to Aden, the Eastern and Western Aden Protectorates and the Islands of Perim, Kuria Muria, Kamaran and other offshore islands'.[65]

However, on 30 November 1967 the United Kingdom informed the General Assembly that:

... in view of the negative reaction of the United Nations to the proposal for the internationalisation of Perim, the British had consulted the people, who had confirmed their wish to remain with South Arabia, accordingly, Perim would be part of the new Republic. The people of Kamaran had decided to unite with Aden and accordingly, it too would be part of the new State. However, the people of Kuria Muria had made it clear that they wished to be returned to Muscat and Oman, to which they had previously belonged. Therefore, sovereignty over these islands would be transferred to the Sultan of Muscat and Oman.[66]

THE KURIA MURIA ISLANDS. An agreement for the cession of the Kuria Muria islands (Halaaneea, Jibleea, Soda, Haski and Ghurzoud) to Muscat and Oman was concluded between the United Kingdom and the Sultan of Muscat and Oman and took effect on 30 November 1967.[67] The treaty noted that the five islands known as the Kuria Muria islands were ceded in 1854 to Queen Victoria by His Highness Saud bin Sultan, Sultan of Muscat, and that the inhabitants of the islands had expressed the wish that the islands should be reunited with the Sultanate of Muscat and Oman.[68] Although the Preamble to the treaty acknowledges that the act of cession was the result of the express wish of the inhabitants, Article 1 of the treaty asserts that Her Britannic Majesty ceded her 'sovereignty' over the Kuria Muria Islands. It is, therefore, arguable whether the act was a cession of *British legal sovereignty* or merely *British jurisdiction and control*.

During the adoption by the General Assembly of the 'Consensus' on Aden referred to above, many Arab States expressed their concern at the 'separation' of Kuria Muria from the new Republic of Southern Yemen.[69] And on 3 December 1967 the first President of Southern Yemen said that Britain had 'no right' to cede Kuria Muria to the 'so-called Sultan of Muscat and Oman', adding that the Republic of Southern Yemen had 'the legitimate right to recover our sovereignty over every inch of our territory, including the Kuria Murias, Perim and Kamaran'.[70] On 1 December 1967 the President of Yemen appointed a Governor for Perim, Kamaran and Kuria Muria Islands.[71] However, in February 1974 the Sultan of Oman affirmed that the Kuria Muria islands were under his 'Sultanate's sovereignty'.[72]

THE KAMARAN ISLANDS. Kamaran, which include the island of Kamaran and its adjacent islets, lies inside the Red Sea, about four miles off the coast of the Yemen Arab Republic and more than two hundred miles to the north of Perim island.[73] Turkey renounced all rights over Kamaran under Article 16 of the 1923

Treaty of Lausanne.[74] When under British rule, Kamaran was administered from Aden by a Commissioner as a protectorate under the Foreign Jurisdiction Act of 1890.[75] However, as noted above, on 30 November 1967 the Crown's power and jurisdiction in Kamaran were terminated and the territory became part of the Republic of Southern Yemen.[76]

In 1956 the government of Northern Yemen protested to the British government against the granting of oil exploratory concessions in Kamaran, on the ground that the island formed part of Northern Yemen. The Secretary of State for the Colonies replied that the government of Northern Yemen:

... have been informed that Her Majesty's Government are unable to accept that the King of Yemen has any claim to Kamaran Island, and that accordingly Her Majesty's Government see no reason why the concession should be cancelled.[77]

The Northern Yemen claim does not appear to have been raised again, though in 1967 it was observed that when British administration is withdrawn from Kamaran 'it appears that the Yemen will be confronted by the South Yemen Republic as an adverse claimant of the island'.[78]

PERIM ISLAND. Perim island is located at the narrowest point of the Straits of Bab el-Mandeb, the southern entrance to the Red Sea. Its area is about five square miles. It has a population of about 500, mostly fishermen, and has a small harbour and an airfield. As shown earlier, Perim divides the main Strait of Bab el-Mandeb into two—Large Strait and Small Strait. It is separated from the Arabian coast—Democratic Yemen and the Yemen Arab Republic—by the Small Strait, which is about three miles long and varies in width from three to one and a half miles. From the African coast—Ethiopia and the Republic of Djibouti—it is separated by the Large Strait, which is about ten miles long, with a general width of about ten and a half miles.

Perim island was first occupied by France in 1738: in 1799 it came into the possession of the British, who occupied it for the purpose of preventing the French in Egypt from establishing communications with the Indian Ocean via the Red Sea, but was later evacuated.[79] It was reoccupied by the British in January 1857 and used as a coaling station. The island was administered as part of the Indian Empire until 1937, when it became part of the British colony of Aden and was administered from Aden by a Commissioner under the British Settlement Acts of 1887 and 1945. In 1963 a separate administration was set up for Perim.[80]

During the debate on the Aden, Perim and Kuria Muria Islands Bill in the House of Commons in June 1967 proposals were made to exclude Perim from the Bill and place it under United Nations administration, because of its strategic location and because it was thought that the Yemen Arab Republic might claim sovereignty over this island.[81]

However, on 30 November 1967, the Foreign Secretary told the Commons that he had received confirmation from the United Nations that the proposal for the internationalisation of Perim 'would not be entertained because it was contrary to the letter and spirit of the United Nations Resolutions [on Aden]'.[82] He informed the House that after consultations with the inhabitants, the latter had opted in favour of remaining with South Arabia.[83] Eventually Britain relinquished sovereignty over the island under the Aden, Perim and Kuria Muria Act, 1967, and the island became part of the new Republic of Southern Yemen.[84]

B. FUNCTIONAL ZONES BEYOND THE TERRITORIAL SEA (EXCLUDING THE CONTINENTAL SHELF)

It has been shown that the functional zone claims beyond a twelve-mile territorial sea asserted by States in 1973, with few and insignificant exceptions, related to fishing, fishery conservation, pollution, and the exploitation of natural resources.[85] This is believed to be the position at the present time also.[86] However, few Middle Eastern States have actually asserted such claims, whereas more of them have claimed functional zones relating to security, navigation, fiscal, customs, sanitary and immigration matters, which have been referred to as 'contiguous' or 'supervision' zones.

1. Contiguous zones: supervision zones

The notion of the 'contiguous zone', as formulated in the 1958 Territorial Sea Convention, is to give the coastal State, in a zone of the high seas contiguous to its territorial sea, the control necessary to prevent infringement of its customs, fiscal, immigration or sanitary regulations within its territory or its territorial sea. This zone may not extend beyond twelve miles from the baseline from which the breadth of the territorial sea is measured. In accordance with the wish of Iran and of many Arab and other States, this idea has been retained in the Informal Composite Negotiating Text, July 1977, of the Third Law of the Sea Conference, but the breadth of the zone has been extended to twenty four miles measured from the baseline of the territorial sea.[87]

However, at present the Middle Eastern States of Egypt, Saudi Arabia, Democratic Yemen, the Yemen Arab Republic, Sudan and Syria each claim a contiguous (in the case of Syria 'supervision') zone extending for a distance of six nautical miles (in 1977 Democratic Yemen extended its contiguous zone to twelve nautical miles) from the outer limit of their respective twelve-mile territorial seas. But, whereas the contiguous zones claimed by Egypt, Saudi Arabia and the Yemen Arab Republic relate to security, navigation, fiscal and sanitary matters, those claimed by others relate to security, customs, sanitary, fiscal and (only in the case of Sudan) immigration matters. Iraq and Kuwait have not made any specific claims in this regard, but they have expressly reserved their right to claim contiguous zones beyond their respective territorial seas, in accordance with the rules of international law.

One interesting observation in relation to the contiguous zone claims of the Middle Eastern States is that they refer to security matters.[88] As indicated above, the 1958 Territorial Sea Convention does not recognise special security rights in the contiguous zone. In this regard, a commentary in the 1956 ILC's draft articles concerning the law of the sea indicated that:

> The Commission did not recognize special security rights in the contiguous zone. It considered that the extreme vagueness of the term 'security' would open the way for abuses and that the granting of such rights was not necessary. The enforcement of customs and sanitary regulations will be sufficient in most cases to safeguard the security of State. In so far as measures of self-defence against an imminent and direct threat to the security of the State are concerned, the Commission refers to the general principles of international law and the Charter of the United Nations.[89]

2. Marine pollution control

Since they border the Mediterranean Sea, the Red Sea, and the Arabian Gulf, which may be described as some of the busiest international trade routes and most vulnerable to oil pollution, the Middle Eastern States have a general as well as direct interest in the control of marine pollution. In the Arabian Gulf the transport of oil is by far the largest item of maritime traffic. It was estimated that in December 1972 a daily total of 19½ million barrels (2·9 million tons) of crude oil were produced from oilwells in the surrounding countries and in the sea bed of the Arabian Gulf, and that about 90 per cent of this enormous quantity (in the form of either crude oil or refined products) required the services of twenty-five to thirty large tankers daily, the average cargo of each exceeding 100,000 tons.[90] It has also been indicated that about one-tenth of the total production of crude oil in the Arabian Gulf comes from a large number of sea wells.[91] Hence the risk of oil pollution, whether from sea bed activities or shipping, is too great, particularly in view of the shallowness of the waters of the Arabian Gulf. In the event of a major accident in the narrow Strait of Hormuz or any part of the Arabian Gulf, all shipping could come to a halt for a considerable time and would cost the oil-exporting littoral States millions of dollars a day. Serious harm, also, could be done to the rich marine life of the waters of the Gulf.

In the Mediterranean Sea most sources of pollution are land-based. It has been estimated that as much as 1,000 million tons of industrial waste and untreated sewage are deposited every year.[92] This critical situation is attributed to increased industrialisation, the rise in population and the absence of adequate controls. In addition, about 300,000 tons of petroleum spilt from ships and 20,000 tons from refineries have to be taken into account.[93] Five coastal States have terminals for loading crude oil and refined products, including Syria, Lebanon and Libya, and there are reception terminals in all the other States round the seaboard. Some of the crude oil is loaded into large tankers for trans-ocean delivery, but part of it, and nearly all the black oil products, are destined for other Mediterranean ports. They are carried by smaller tankers, many of which are engaged on a shuttle service. In consequence these vessels seldom have the opportunity, while on the return journey to the loading terminals, effectively to operate retention-on-board routines.[94] It is also indicated that, in the Mediterranean, the turnover of the first 150 m depth of water requires a period of about eighty years, and this makes it particularly vulnerable to pollution.[95]

The Red Sea, linking Europe with Asia and Africa, is also exposed to oil pollution from oil tankers and other traffic which ply through it.

Despite this, few steps have so far been taken by the Middle Eastern States, at the national, regional or international level, to establish legal requirements for the control of marine pollution.

A. INTERNATIONAL LEVEL. Egypt, Jordan, Kuwait, Lebanon, Libya, Saudi Arabia, Syria and Democratic Yemen are parties to the International Convention for the Prevention of Pollution of the Sea by Oil, 12 May 1954, as amended 13 April 1962.[96] The other Middle Eastern States have so far not ratified this convention, and it appears that none has yet taken action on other multilateral anti-pollution measures, including the 1972 London Con-

EXISTING NATIONAL CLAIMS

vention on the Prevention of Marine Pollution by Dumping of Wastes and other Matter,[97] and the International Convention for the Prevention of Pollution from Ships, 1973.[98] The latter designates the Mediterranean Sea, the Red Sea and the 'Gulfs area'—that is, the Arabian Gulf and the Gulf of Oman—among the 'Special areas' that required additional precautions for the protection of the marine environment.[99]

B. REGIONAL LEVEL. First, as regard the Arabian Gulf, at a conference held in Kuwait on 15–24 April 1978[100] the States participating—Bahrain, Kuwait, Iran, Iraq, Oman, Qatar, Saudi Arabia and the United Arab Emirates—adopted and signed the Kuwait Regional Convention for Co-operation in the Protection of the Marine Environment from Pollution and a Protocol concerning Regional Co-operation in Combating Pollution by Oil and other Harmful Substances in Cases of Emergency.[101]

'Reference may also be made to the agreement concluded on 11 July 1972 to deal with oil spillages resulting from offshore operations in the Gulf.[102] Under this agreement, thirteen oil companies in the region have established the Gulf Area Oil Companies Mutual Aid Organisation for the purpose of providing a joint capability to clear up oil spills larger than could be dealt with by a single party. Membership of the organisation is open to all oil companies working in the Arabian Gulf area. Each participant is required to submit oil-spill contingency plans and to keep on hand specified quantities of equipment and supplies to be made available to other participants in emergencies.

During a conference held in January 1976 in Jedda, Saudi Arabia, at the invitation of the Arab League Educational, Cultural and Scientific Organisation (ALECSO), to study the issue of scientific research on, and the preservation of, the marine environment of the Red Sea basin and the Gulf of Aden, the participants—Egypt, Ethiopia, Jordan, the Republic of Somalia, Sudan, Saudi Arabia, Democratic Yemen and the Yemen Arab Republic—declared that the Red Sea and the Gulf of Aden were part of their national responsibility. Accordingly, the Jedda Declaration added, these States intended to shoulder their responsibility as regards the conservation of environmental conditions from the dangers of pollution and environmental degradation. It also declared that the States would co-operate in setting up a network for monitoring the meteorology of the environment of the Red Sea and the Gulf of Aden; in adopting a convention for the protection and preservation of the marine environment of these waters; and in establishing a regional programme for scientific research as well as a special fund to finance such a programme.

In the Mediterranean Sea, an important step towards control of marine pollution has been taken by the adoption, in Barcelona on 16 February 1976, of the Convention for the Protection of the Mediterranean Sea against Pollution. The convention is accompanied by two protocols for control of two specific sources of pollution, the Protocol Concerning Co-operation in Combating Pollution of the Mediterranean Sea by Oil and other Harmful Substances in Cases of Emergency, and the Protocol for the Prevention of Pollution of the Mediterranean Sea by Dumping from Ships and Aircraft.[103] The convention and the protocols were signed by the Mediterranean coastal States of Cyprus, Egypt, France, Greece, Italy, Lebanon, Malta, Monaco, Morocco, Spain and Turkey.[104]

Article 2(a) of the convention defines 'pollution' as:

the introduction by man, directly or indirectly, of substances or energy into the marine environment resulting in such deleterious effects as harm to living resources, hazards to human health, hindrance to marine activities including fishing, impairment of quality for use of sea water and reduction of amenities.

The protocol on the prevention of dumping from ships and aircraft binds the parties to take all possible steps to prevent the dumping of crude oil and hydrocarbons, mercury and cadmium, certain levels of radio-active wastes, persistent plastics and other persistent synthetic materials which may seriously interfere with fishing, navigation or other legitimate uses of the sea, and certain other dangerous products. The dumping of other products such as arsenic, lead, copper, zinc, nickel, cyanides and fluorides can be authorised, but only under a special permit from the competent national authorities.

The other protocol calls for co-operation among Mediterranean States whenever the presence of oil or other harmful substances polluting or threatening to pollute the sea presents a grave and imminent danger to the marine environment, coast or related interests (that is, fishing, tourism, public health or the preservation of living resources) of one or more contracting parties. This protocol also provides for the setting up of a regional oil-combating centre to develop and apply a communication system for receiving, channelling and despatching reports on discharges or spillages of oil or other harmful substances observed at sea, as well as on any incident causing or likely to cause pollution and presenting a grave and imminent danger to the marine environment, coast or related interests of one or more of the contracting parties.[105]

C. NATIONAL LEVEL. In Oman the 1974 'Marine Pollution Control Law'[106] establishes a 'Pollution-free zone' encompassing the twelve-mile territorial sea of the sultanate and those waters extending for thirty-eight nautical miles beyond the territorial sea. Where the coast of another State is opposite or adjacent to the coast of Oman, the limits of the 'Pollution-free zone' will not extend beyond such limits as may have been agreed to with such other States or, if there is no such agreement, the median line shall be the boundary line. As noted in Chapter III, Oman has already concluded an agreement with the opposite State, Iran, delimiting the boundary of the continental shelf areas between the two States.

Under the Omani law the term 'pollutant' is defined to include oil or oily mixture; any substance of a dangerous or noxious nature such as sewage, refuse, waste or garbage which, if added to any waters, would degrade those waters to an extent that is detrimental to their use by man or by any animal, fish or plant that is useful to man; any water which contains a substance such as the aforementioned; and any substance which may be designated by the Minister concerned to be a pollutant. The Omani law makes it illegal for any person to discharge a 'pollutant' into the 'Pollution-free zone' from a vessel, a place on land, or an oil transmission apparatus. It is also illegal for any vessel to discharge a 'pollutant' into the 'Pollution-free zone'; and for any vessel registered in the sultanate to discharge a 'pollutant' into any waters beyond the 'Pollution-free zone' of Oman.

Other provisions of the Omani law deal with such matters as relate to violations of the law, record-keeping, reporting and insurance requirements, enforcement, and civil liability for costs and damages.[107]

No other Middle Eastern State is known to have yet claimed a pollution control zone or passed any legislation concerning marine pollution control, but reference may be made to some legal instruments which made general reference to the problem of marine pollution. Thus Article 2 of the Iraqi Law No. 229 of 1970 concerning 'Preservation of Oil wealth and Natural Hydrocarbons'[108] provides that all oil operations in the region of the Iraqi Republic including its territorial sea and continental shelf must be carried out 'in accordance with scientific and efficient methods, and in conformity with the safe practice of oil industry'. Article 3 states that the operator must take necessary measures to prevent, *inter alia*, pollution of the air, and surface and sub-surface waters.

It is understood that a draft law for the control of marine pollution is still pending before the Iranian Parliament, but the Iranian Petroleum Act of 6 August 1974, which is applicable with respect to petroleum operations in inland and coastal waters and the continental shelf, specifically provides that:

> The National Iranian Oil company shall, during operations related to each agreement, be mindful and pay full attention to the conservation of the Natural Resources (especially Natural Gas) and also prevention of pollution of the environment (air, water and land). The Party to the Agreement shall also be bound to observe in its operations all regulations announced and/or communicated to it by the Government or National Iranian Oil Company, for the said purpose.[109]

In April 1971 Iran and Russia took the first step towards reducing pollution in the Caspian Sea by signing a protocol which may lead eventually to a treaty on the prevention of pollution of the Caspian Sea.[110] Iranian officials claimed that the Caspian Sea had been turned into a vast sewer by oil leakages and industrial waste. They believed that about 300,000 to 400,000 tons of oil seeped into the Caspian each year from offshore wells.[111]

In Kuwait, Article II(2) of Law No. 12 of 26 February 1964 'Regarding Prevention of Pollution of Navigable Waters by Oil', which implements the International Convention for the Prevention of Pollution of the Sea by Oil, 1954, to which Kuwait is a party, provides that the Minister of Finance and Industry may issue regulations to change the 'prohibited zones' described in Annex 1 of the law in accordance with any amendment of the provisions of the latter convention or any other convention ratified by the State of Kuwait.[112] It is also worth noting that in the offshore concession agreements with the government of Kuwait general reference was made to the problem of pollution.[113] The agreements refer to the company proceeding 'diligently with the drilling',[114] but the provisions which dealt with pollution are marked by their brevity: 'The Company shall conduct its operations in a workmanlike manner and by scientific methods and shall take all reasonable measures ... to prevent the pollution of the sea ...'.[115]

3. Exclusive fishing zones: exclusive economic zones

Both the 1958 and 1960 Conferences on the Law of the Sea failed to produce any agreement on the question of exclusive fisheries jurisdiction, but, as shown in the next chapter, the prospects in the

Third Law of the Sea Conference seem good for general agreement on a 200-mile exclusive economic zone in which the coastal State would have sovereign rights with regard to the living and non-living resources, and jurisdiction with regard to other activities, including scientific research and the preservation of the marine environment.

However, at December 1975, of the 129 coastal States, seventy-six have claimed exclusive fishing zones of twelve nautical miles' limit, whereas thirty-six have claimed exclusive fishing zones in excess of the twelve-mile limit.[116] As to the Middle Eastern States in particular, in their respective domestic continental shelf and territorial sea legislation many of them, including Egypt, Saudi Arabia, Kuwait, Bahrain, Qatar, the various members of the United Arab Emirates, and Iran, have expressly reserved their rights with respect to fishing in waters beyond the limits of the territorial sea. Up to the present, however, and with the exception of Oman, Iran, Saudi Arabia, Qatar and Democratic Yemen, the Middle Eastern States appear to have made no effort to police or control fishing in waters beyond the limits of their territorial seas.

In 1972 and 1973 respectively Oman and Iran, which border on both the Arabian Gulf and the Gulf of Oman, followed the precedent of other States which believed that fishing limits could be unilaterally decided upon, and each proclaimed an exclusive fishing zone of fifty nautical miles (in 1977 Oman extended its exclusive fishing zone to two hundred nautical miles) measured from the baselines of the territorial sea; but in the Arabian Gulf the limits of the Iranian exclusive fishing zone were said to be those of the waters superjacent to the Iranian continental shelf, which, it has been indicated, in general did not exceed fifty miles.[117] According to the Iranian proclamation, where Iran had continental shelf demarcation agreements with other countries in the Gulf, the demarcation line would constitute the limits of the Iranian exclusive fishing zone, and where such agreements had not yet been concluded, unless otherwise agreed, the median line between the Iranian and opposite or adjacent shores would be considered the limit of the exclusive fishing zone of Iran. Iran has indicated that in the Gulf of Oman, as in the case of the exclusive fishery zones proclaimed by Pakistan and Oman, the criterion of fifty nautical miles had been adopted because there the continental shelf ends abruptly a short distance from the coast.[118]

The Omani proclamation expressly provides that the sultanate exercises sovereign rights over its exclusive fishing zone for the purposes of exploring, developing and exploiting its living resources, 'including but not limited to fish'.[119]

The Iranian proclamation was made, according to its Preamble, in order to 'safeguard the fishing rights and interests of Iran in the seas adjacent to its coast and the coast of its islands'. The Preamble added that the coastal communities of Iran have throughout history been engaged in fishing activities in the seas adjacent to the Iranian coast and that the natural resources of these seas are of 'vital importance to the economic and social progress of Iran'.[120] Introducing the proclamation to the Iranian Parliament, the Foreign Minister of Iran told the Majlis that 'overfishing by foreign trawlers was depleting the fish stock in Iranian territorial waters'.[121]

In 1974 Saudi Arabia and Qatar issued declarations claiming exclusive sovereign rights in zones contiguous to their territorial seas.[122] The Qatar declaration reaffirms the rights of Qatar in its continental shelf as asserted in the proclamation of June 1949, and states that, in the zones contiguous to the territorial sea of its coast and the coasts of its islands, the State of Qatar alone has the exclusive sovereign rights with respect to fishing and all related activities and the exploitation and conservation of the marine wealth and natural resources and the rights with regard to the construction of installations and safety and control zones, and any type of research. The outer limits of those zones would be defined according to bilateral agreements already concluded with Qatar, but where no such agreements existed, and unless otherwise agreed, the limits would be defined by reference to the outer limits of the continental shelf of Qatar or to the median line between the baselines of the territorial seas of Qatar and the opposite or adjacent State concerned.

The Saudi declaration, which applies to the coasts of Saudi Arabia in the Arabian Gulf and the Red Sea, asserts 'exclusive fishing zones' in areas not specifically determined but stated to be 'contiguous to the coasts of the Kingdom and the coasts of its islands, from the coastal sea [i.e. territorial sea] of the Kingdom towards the high seas'. Thus there is some obscurity about the outer limits of the Saudi exclusive fishing zone, but it appears that they correspond to the median line between the baselines of the territorial seas of the coasts of Saudi Arabia and the coasts of the opposite or adjacent States, for the Saudi declaration stipulates that, if the exclusive fishing zone of Saudi Arabia should overlap with those of another coastal State, the boundary shall be the median line between the baselines of the territorial seas of the States concerned. Besides, the proclamation, referred to above, made by Iran and Oman had adopted similar criteria.

If the above-considered claims of Iran, Oman, Saudi Arabia and Qatar—and more particularly the claim of Qatar—are understood in conjunction with the respective continental shelf claims, discussed below, of these States, it would appear that these States are actually asserting claims which fall into line with the exclusive economic zone concept referred to above.[123]

It may be observed also that if, as Iran already suggested,[124] similar actions with regard to fishing were to be taken by the other coastal States of the Arabian Gulf, the living resources of the whole Gulf would be covered by the exclusive jurisdictions of the coastal States.[125] Suggestions have already been made for declaring the Gulf an 'inland sea' like the 'Bay of St Lawrence', in an agreement between the littoral States, to enable them to control pollution as well as fishing activities.[126] As mentioned in the next section, in the days when pearl fisheries were of prime importance to the inhabitants of the Gulf recommendations were also made for treating it as a *mare clausum* for the purposes of pearl diving. It is worth noting, however, that Kuwait has already stated that it favours the view that every coastal State should have 'special rights' in a zone contiguous to its territorial sea, but does not approve of the 'principle of closing the Gulf to the fishing vessels which belong to the States not bordering on it'. According to Kuwait, such action would be contrary to the principle of freedom to fish the high seas. Kuwait added the fear that other States might apply the same principle against the interests of Kuwaiti fishing vessels. However, Kuwait considers that it is possible for the States bordering on the Gulf to agree among themselves to regulate fishing activities in the Gulf for the purpose of the conservation of its fish resources, in accordance with the 1958 Geneva Convention on Fishing and Conservation of the Living Resources of the High Seas.[127]

Finally, in 1977 Democratic Yemem claimed an exclusive economic zone the breadth of which extends two hundred nautical miles from the baseline of its territorial sea.

C. THE CONTINENTAL SHELF

1. Legal history of the continental shelf doctrine

The law on the continental shelf began with the development of technically feasible and economically justifiable means for the exploitation of the mineral and non-living resources of the sea bed and subsoil of the submarine areas contiguous to the territorial sea. The need for new oil resources prompted the government of the United States to issue, on 28 September 1945, a proclamation, generally known as the 'Truman Proclamation'.[128] This proclamation 'soon came to be regarded as the starting point of the law on the subject' of the continental shelf and

> the chief doctrine it enunciated, namely that of the coastal State as having an original, natural, and exclusive (in short a vested) right to the continental shelf off its shores, came to prevail over all others, being now reflected in Article 2 of the 1958 Geneva Convention on the Continental Shelf.[129]

The Truman proclamation declared, *inter alia,* that:

> the Government of the United States regards the natural resources of the subsoil and sea bed of the continental shelf beneath the high seas but contiguous to the coasts of the United States, subject to its jurisdiction and control.

In justification of this claim, the Preamble to the proclamation stated that:

> the exercise of jurisdiction over the natural resources of the subsoil and sea bed of the continental shelf by the contiguous nation is reasonable and just, since the effectiveness of measures to utilize or conserve these resources would be contingent upon co-operation and protection from the shore, since the continental shelf may be regarded as an extension of the land-mass of the coastal nation and thus naturally appurtenant to it, since these resources frequently form a seaward extension of a pool or deposit lying within the territory, and since self-protection compels the coastal nation to keep close watch over activities off its shores which are of the nature necessary for utilisation of these resources.

The Truman proclamation itself made no specific reference to the outer limit of the continental shelf, but a related White House press release issued on the same day referred to 'an underwater area 750,000 square miles in extent' and stated that 'Generally, submerged land which is contiguous to the continent and which is covered by no more than 100 fathoms (600 feet) of water is considered as the continental shelf.' With regard to the delimitation of boundaries between the continental shelves of adjacent or opposite States, the proclamation stated that such boundaries 'shall be determined by the United States and the State concerned in accordance with equitable principles'.

However, the Truman proclamation was followed by a series of similar claims and by the support of legal writers,[130] culminating in the 1958 Geneva Convention on the Continental Shelf, whose first three articles, as observed by the International Court of Justice, were 'the ones which, it is clear, were then regarded as reflecting, or as crystallizing, received or at least emergent rules of customary international law relative to the continental shelf'.[131] Amongst them are those relating to the question of the seaward extent of the shelf; the juridicial character of the coastal State's entitlement; the nature of the rights exercisable; the kind of natural resources to which they relate; and the preservation intact of the legal status as high seas of the waters above the shelf, and the legal status of the superjacent air space. Article 1 defines the continental shelf as referring:

(a) to the sea bed and subsoil of the superjacent areas adjacent to the coast but outside the area of the territorial sea, to a depth of 200 metres or, beyond that limit, to where the depth of the superjacent waters admits of the exploitation of the natural resources of the said areas;
(b) to the seabed and subsoil of similar submarine areas adjacent to the coasts of island.[132]

2. *Practice of the Middle Eastern States*

The first Middle Eastern State to proclaim its 'jurisdiction and control' over the sea bed and subsoil, or at least over the resources of the sea bed and subsoil lying under the seas contiguous to its territorial sea, was Saudi Arabia, by a Royal Pronouncement dated 28 May 1949.[133] In June 1949, with the exception of Fujairah, the Trucial States of the Arabian Gulf (Bahrain, Kuwait, Qatar and various members of the new United Arab Emirates) made similar proclamations.[134] Similar action was taken by Iran and Libya in 1955, Iraq (1957), Egypt (1958), Syria (1963), Fujairah (1966),[135] the Yemen Arab Republic (1967), Democratic Yemen and Sudan (1970; in Democratic Yemen a revised law was enacted in 1977 and entered into force on 15 January 1978), and by Oman in 1972. Jordan and Lebanon have not made any express proclamation, but as the 1958 Geneva Convention on the Continental Shelf provided, no proclamation or any other act is necessary. This is because, as the International Court of Justice confirmed in the North Sea Continental Shelf cases:

the rights of the coastal state in respect of the area of continental shelf that constitutes a natural prolongation of its land territory into and under the sea exist *ipso facto* and *ab initio*, by virtue of its sovereignty over the land, and as an extension of it in an exercise of sovereign rights for the purpose of exploring the sea bed and exploiting its natural resources. In short, there is here an inherent right.[136]

The 1949 proclamations of the Trucial States and Saudi Arabia, and more particularly the pronouncement of the latter, are clearly influenced by the Truman proclamation. Thus each of these countries declared the sea bed and subsoil contiguous to or extending to a reasonable distance from its coast to appertain to its land and to be subject to its jurisdiction and control. In justification of the claim, emphasis was placed on the need for the greater utilisation of the world's natural resources, the reasonable and just nature of the claim, the adjacency of the area and the concern for the urgency of conserving and prudently utilising its natural resources. As in the Truman proclamation, too, the present proclamations left the boundaries of the continental shelf to be determined more precisely in accordance with 'equitable' or 'just' principles, after 'consultation' or, according to the Saudi pronouncement, 'agreement' with neighbouring States. These two concepts, of delimitation by mutual agreement and delimitation in accordance with equitable principles, as the International Court of Justice found in the North Sea cases, have underlain all the history of the development of the legal regime of the continental shelf, and have from the beginning reflected 'the *opinio juris* in the matter of delimitation'.[137] This finding of the Court constituted 'the essential reason' for its ruling that the equidistance method of delimitation, as formulated in Article 6 of the 1958 Convention on the Continental Shelf, is not a rule of customary law, for, the Court said, if the rule were to be compulsorily applied in all situations, this would not be consonant with the two basic concepts referred to above.[138] It may be recalled also that the decision of the Court dealt with the delimitation of lateral boundaries between adjacent States, and the Court ruled that delimitation must be effected by agreement in accordance with equitable principles, and listed certain geographical and geological factors which should be taken into account in the course of the negotiations.[139] However, many of the required continental shelf boundary lines in the Arabian Gulf have already been delimited by mutual agreements between the States concerned, and, despite the fact that none of the Gulf States is a party to the 1958 Convention on the Continental Shelf, in most cases the delimitation has been carried out largely according to Article 6 of that convention, which stipulates that the boundary of the continental shelf areas between opposite or adjacent States is, in the absence of agreement on a specific boundary, and unless another boundary line is justified by special circumstances, the median line or the line of equidistance between the baselines of the territorial seas of the States concerned.[140]

To return to the proclamations of the Trucial States and Saudi Arabia, like the Iranian Act of 1955, but unlike the Truman proclamation, which regarded only the natural resources of the continental shelf to be subject to the jurisdiction and control of the United States, these proclamations consider that the continental shelf as well as its resources 'belong' or 'appertain' to the coastal State. Similarly, the legislation of Egypt and Democratic Yemen claims rights of sovereignty over the sea bed and subsoil of the continental shelf and over its resources.[141] It has been stated, however, that from a practical point of view the difference between the two versions appears to be slight, 'since any control of the submarine resources will necessarily involve control of the subsea area as such'.[142] Moreover, it has been observed, the United States effectively exercises its jurisdiction over the continental shelf, not only over its resources. This fact is shown in the construction by the United States of what were called 'Texas towers' for military purposes.[143] Article 2 (1) of the 1958 Convention on the Continental Shelf provided that the coastal State exercises over the continental shelf sovereign rights for the purpose of exploring it and exploiting its natural resources. The convention did not provide the coastal State with 'sovereignty' over the continental shelf, mainly because this was considered to be inconsistent with the concept of the legal status of the superjacent waters as high seas and that of the air space above those waters, a concept which was specifically affirmed in Article 3 of the convention.[144] In so far as the continental shelf laws of the Middle Eastern States are concerned, they expressly provide for the latter concept.[145] It is worth noting also that many of the continental shelf agreements already concluded between States of the Arabian Gulf have specifically spoken of the desire of the States concerned to establish the boundary line between 'the respective areas of the continental shelf over which they have sovereign rights in accordance with international law'.[146]

The continental shelf legislation of Egypt, Syria, the Yemen Arab Republic, Sudan and Oman adopts the Geneva formula and determines the extent of the continental shelf on the basis of a depth of 200 metres and the exploitability test. But the Omani law departs from the Geneva formula in that sovereign rights are asserted over the continental shelf of 'the coast of the mainland or of an island, *rock, reef, or shoal* . . .'.[147] Like the Iranian legislation, the laws of Sudan and Egypt expressly provide for the right to construct and maintain or operate on the continental shelf installations and other devices necessary for its exploration and the exploitation of its natural resources, and the right to establish safety and protection zones around such installations and devices.

Such rights are specifically affirmed in Article 5 of the 1958 Convention on the Continental Shelf.[148]

Democratic Yemen has claimed a continental shelf which extends throughout the natural prolongation of the Republic's land territory to the outer limit of the continental margin, or to a distance of two hundred nautical miles from the baselines from which the breadth of the territorial sea is measured where the outer edge of the continental margin does not extend to that distance.

Libya has not made any legislation to deal exclusively with its continental shelf. Libya's assertion of rights over its continental shelf was laid down in Article 4 (1) of the Petroleum Law No. 25 of 1955 concerning the boundaries of the country's petroleum zones, which provides that

This law shall extend to the sea bed and subsoil which lie beneath the territorial waters and the high seas contiguous thereto under the control and jurisdiction of the United Kingdom of Libya. Any such sea bed and subsoil adjacent to any zone shall for the purposes of this law be deemed to be part of that zone.[149]

Thus no precise definition of the Libyan continental shelf was given. Besides, the continental shelf boundaries in the central Mediterranean between Libya, Tunisia, Italy and Malta have not been determined yet. This problem has become more urgent because oil companies exploring the central Mediterranean have already made successful strikes in Tunisian and Libyan areas, and it is feared that some oil may be found in areas claimed by two or more of these States.[150] Discussions between Libya and Malta over oil exploration rights began about four years ago, since Malta has granted oil exploration permits over some offshore areas to the south of the island, but some of these areas are claimed by Libya.[151] The discussions have not been successful and the two countries, therefore, agreed to refer their dispute to the International Court of Justice and to determine the boundary line between their respective continental shelves in accordance with the Court's decision.[152]

The laws of Iraq and Libya are equally vague on the definition of the continental shelf. The Iraqi law issued on 27 November 1957 declares that all natural resources existing on the sea bed and the subsoil of 'the maritime zone extending outwards to the sea and contiguous to the Iraqi territorial sea', are the property of Iraq and that Iraq has exclusive general jurisdiction over such resources and over their preservation and exploitation.

The timing of the Iraqi legislation was directly related to the increased Iranian interest in offshore zones, as manifested, mainly, in the agreement between the National Iranian Oil Company (NIOC) and Agip-Minerarie (SIRIP) signed on 24 August 1957, which defined the concession area as including 'a zone of the continental shelf located in the northern part of the Persian Gulf ...'.[153]

Actual study by Iran of bids presented to her in the spring of 1958 by various oil companies prompted the Iraqi government to issue, on 9 April 1958, a new proclamation which affirmed its 1957 proclamation and asserted that:

Such works and constructions as have been or will be undertaken in [the Iraqi territorial sea] zone or the zone encompassing the waters contiguous to it are subject to the sovereignty of the Iraqi State, and that the undertaking of such works and constructions is permissible to none other than the Iraqi authorities or to such quarters as may be duly authorised by Iraqi authorities.

Furthermore, the new proclamation declared Iraq's

non-recognition of any proclamation, declaration, legislation or planning pertaining to territorial waters or to contiguous waters issued by any neighbouring country in contradiction with the contents of this proclamation.

In addition the Iraqi government declared 'its adherence to international practice in this respect and to the principle of equidistance ...'.[154]

The 1955 Iranian Act on the continental shelf, which applies only in respect of the Arabian Gulf and the Gulf of Oman,[155] mainly refers to 'the continental shelf adjacent to the Iranian coast and to the coasts of Iranian islands' in defining the outer limit of the continental shelf. But in cases where the continental shelf of Iran overlaps that of another opposite or adjacent State, the Act provides that any eventual differences concerning the delimitation of boundary shall be settled according to 'the principles of equity and the Government shall take the necessary measures for the settlement of such eventual differences'. As shown above, the legislation of the Arab States of the Gulf adopts similar provision. The Iranian Act makes no further reference to the question of delimitation, but at the 1958 Conference on the Law of the Sea Iran made proposals concerning this question which are worthy of mention. Iran made the observation that the conference's draft articles referring to the exploration and exploitation of the sea bed were not in conflict with existing legislation in Iran. However, Iran added, some of the criteria referred to, though suitable for application to open seas, such as the Sea of Oman and Iranian waters west of the Straits of Hormuz, could not apply to shallow waters covering submerged lands, especially if they were of a deltaic type, as in the Arabian Gulf. Accordingly Iran said that it would submit amendments with a view to making the articles more applicable to such special conditions as it had described.[156] Later on, in the Fourth Committee of the conference, Iran indicated that the existence of extensive sedimentary mudflats near its coast, deposited by large bodies of water, makes identification of the low-water mark very difficult by visual observation or photography.[157] Iran considered this as a special case and, therefore, suggested that 'in such circumstances the boundary of the continental shelf should be measured from the high-water mark instead of the low-water mark'.[158] In a reply to a statement made by the Netherlands, Iran said that, although the high-water mark might not always be clearly defined, experts who had studied the question in the Arabian Gulf had found that visual or photographic identification was more practicable for the high-water mark than for the low-water mark.[159]

Iran also pointed out that it might be a complicated matter, where there were islands on a continuous continental shelf—a clear reference to the situation in the Arabian Gulf—to identify the low-water line for each island.[160] Iran said that it in no way disputed the fact that each island could have a continental shelf, but queried the way of tracing the median line in relation to islands and thought that if they were to be taken into account 'serious complications would arise and the benefit of having adopted the median line rule would be lost by difficulty of applying it'.[161] Accordingly Iran made the following proposal:

Where special circumstances ... so warrant, the median line may be measured from the high-water mark along the coastline of the States concerned.

Where an island or islands exist in a region which constitute a continuous continental shelf, the boundary shall be the median line and shall be measured from the low-water mark along the coasts of the States concerned, provided, however, that where special circumstances so warrant, the median line shall be measured from the high-water mark along the coastline of such State.[162]

The Iranian proposal, however, was rejected at the committee stage, and such ideas do not, therefore, appear in the 1958 Geneva Convention. After the rejection of the proposal, Iran stated that the acceptance of the principle of the median line could in no way infringe the sovereign rights of Iran over any Iranian island situated beyond any median line that might be established in the Arabian Gulf.[163] And on signing the 1958 convention Iran made a reservation with respect to Article 6, to the effect that the Iranian government accepted that one method of determining the boundary line in special circumstances would be that of measurement from the high-water mark.[164] It may be recalled that according to Article 6 of the convention the boundary of the continental shelf between adjacent or opposite States is, in the absence of agreement, and unless another boundary line is justified by 'special circumstances', the line of equidistance or the median line between the baselines of the territorial seas of the States concerned. It has been observed that the Iranian reservation was designed to claim a particular interpretation of the three-point formula of Article 6 and, therefore, there was no question of rejecting the formula.[165] In the light of the conference's rejection of the Iranian proposal, however, it would appear that the particular interpretation claimed by Iran, as stated by A. Dean, runs 'counter to the precepts of the Convention'.[166]

The Iranian proposals are of special significance in relation to delimitation of continental shelf boundaries in the Arabian Gulf. Because the depth of water in the Gulf 'increases more rapidly from the Iranian than from the Arabian shore',[167] the application of the high-water mark, it was indicated, would leave 'the way open for [Iran] to claim more of the sea bed and subsoil than the Convention would normally allow'. The Iranian reservation in this regard, it was added, 'may well be the source of future disputes'.[168] With regard to the Iranian proposal for ignoring all islands on a continuous continental shelf, such a proposal would be more advantageous to Iran because it faces States with many islands off their coasts. Similar reasons, it is stated, led, in the 1958 conference, countries such as Iran to insist on the inclusion of the phrase 'special circumstances' in Article 6 of the Convention on the Continental Shelf.[169]

However, as indicated in Chapter III, in the 1968 continental shelf agreement between Iran and Saudi Arabia portions of the boundary line were delimited by treating islands in a manner quite inconsistent with Iran's earlier proposals. Farsi and Al-'Arabiyah, two islands situated well towards the middle of the Gulf, were neglected as base points for the purpose of plotting the median line, but were given their own twelve-mile territorial seas measured from the line of lowest low water on each of the islands.[170]

Another island, Khark, close to the Iranian mainland but outside the belt of the territorial sea, was used as a base point in that it was given half-effect in delimiting portions of the boundary line. At the same time several Saudi islands which may be connected by lines not more than twelve nautical miles long, of which the island nearest to the mainland is not more than twelve nautical miles from the mainland, were completely ignored.

In connection with the continental shelf claims of the Middle Eastern States, or more specifically the continental shelf claims in the Arabian Gulf, it is proposed to deal briefly with two subsidiary matters. These are the contention according to which, in the Gulf, the continental shelf concept is not applicable, or at least, as a matter of fact, no continental shelf exists; and the question of pearl fisheries of the Arabian Gulf.

THE CONTINENTAL SHELF CONCEPT AND THE ARABIAN GULF. The Arabian Gulf, the shallow marginal sea of the Indian Ocean that lies between the Arabian peninsula and south-east Iran, has an area of 92,500 square miles (24,000 square kilometres) and is rarely deeper than 300 ft (50 fathoms or 100 metres), although depths exceeding 360 ft are found at its entrance and at isolated localities in its southern part. It is noticeably asymmetrical in profile, with the deepest water occurring along the Iranian coast, and a broad shallow area, which is usually less than 120 ft deep, along the Arabian coast.[171] The shallowness of the waters had led to the widespread belief that, although the whole of the Gulf is in the legal sense continental shelf, it does not constitute a continental shelf in the technical or geological meaning of the term.[172] Thus R. Young refers to the Arabian Gulf as a 'narrow sea where the continental shelf doctrine is not applicable'.[173] He further writes: 'as a factual matter, no continental shelf exists in the Persian Gulf, which is merely a basin much less than 100 fathoms on the Asian continental mass'.[174] Similarly the late Sir Henry Lauterpacht said; 'In the Persian Gulf there is nowhere a rapid drop or a depth of 600 feet. To these areas the geographical concept, even in its general connotation, of the continental shelf does not seem to be applicable at all.'[175] This circumstance, he added, 'explains why there is no reference to the continental shelf in the Proclamations issued by the Rulers of the Shaikhdoms in the Persian Gulf'.[176]

E. Lauterpacht seems to share the same view. He argues:

in so far as the continental shelf technically is regarded as the seaward projection of the continental land mass up to the point where it falls away steeply to the ocean depths, the North Sea and the Persian Gulf are not a shelf because they have no outer edge. The sea bed simply extends from one coast to the opposite coast without ever falling below a depth of 200 metres. However, though not technically a shelf, the areas involved do possess the qualities of adjacency to and continuity with the coastal State which appear to be the principal identifying elements of the shelf.[177]

In support of this interpretation, he finds that:

... by and large, the impression that one may receive from a review of the debates in the I.L.C. and at the Geneva Conference is that when there was any discussion of departure from the geological concept of the continental shelf it was for the purpose of covering not the deep seas beyond, but the shallow depressions like the Persian Gulf.[178]

First, if E. Lauterpacht implies, as at least one writer has suggested,[179] that the exploitability criterion was added to the definition of the continental shelf as formulated in Article 1 of the 1968 Convention on the Continental Shelf to cover such areas as the Arabian Gulf, this is not quite the case. For the background to the International Law Commission's final decision on the criteria to be applied in defining the continental shelf was the conclusions reached by the Inter-American Specialised Conference on 'Conservations of Natural Resources: Continental Shelf and Oceanic Waters', held at Ciudad Trujillo (Dominican Republic—now Santo Domingo) in March 1956. Thus the exploitability test for the definition of the continental shelf which was adopted by the International Law Commission in its first report on the continental shelf in 1951[180] was abandoned in 1953 in favour of that of a depth of 200 metres.[181] At the same time the Commission noted that the new criterion would cover shallow submarine areas which were contiguous to the coast and which did not attain the depth of 200 metres, such as the Arabian Gulf, despite the fact that they were not believed to comprise part of the continental shelf as that term is 'generally understood'.[182] Eventually, in 1956, the Commission decided to combine the two approaches, the exploitability test and the depth criterion, in the light of the conclusions reached by the Ciudad Trujillo conference.[183] The latter had decided that the right of the coastal State should be extended beyond the 200 metre depth 'to where the depth of the superjacent waters admits of the exploitation of the natural resources of the sea bed and subsoil'.[184] With relatively slight amendments, this formula was eventually incorporated in Article 1 of the 1958 Convention on the Continental Shelf.

As to the contention that shallow areas such as the Arabian Gulf are not continental shelf in the geographical or technical sense, mention first may be made of the following generally accepted definitions of the terms 'continental shelf', 'shelf edge' and 'continental borderland', which were adopted by the International Committee on the Nomenclature of Ocean Bottom Features in 1953:

Continental shelf, shelf edge and borderland. The zone around the continent, extending from the low-water line to the depth at which there is a marked increase of slope to greater depth. Where this increase occurs, the term shelf edge is appropriate. Conventionally, its edge is taken at 100 fathoms, or 200 metres, but instances are known where the increase of slope occurs at more than 200 or less than 65 fathoms. When the zone below the low-water line is highly irregular, and includes depths well in excess of those typical of continental shelves, the term continental borderland is appropriate.[185]

Thus minimum depth is not a prerequisite for regarding certain submarine areas as part of the continental shelf. The depth requirement is a conventional criterion for identifying the outer limit of the continental shelf. It is rightly stated that:

the variation in depth of the 'shelf' does not preclude its existence, it only confirms the fact that a rigid depth line cannot be adhered to, and that the 'shelf' is unequally distributed around the continents.[186]

Besides, a committee of experts stated that shallow seas such as the Arabian Gulf 'incontestably form parts of the continental shelf'. Referring to the Gulf of Paria, the Arabian Gulf and the North Sea, the committee of experts said these areas 'can be considered a flooded part of the continent ... those areas merge imperceptibly and without any change in character morphologically or geologically with the adjoining shelves facing the wide oceans. Hence no doubt can arise as to their belonging to the shelf.'[187] In other words:

All the submerged area is ... part of the broad continental shelf which extends in the case of the Persian Gulf beyond the Gulf for a distance of 60 nautical miles into the Gulf of Oman. Simply because the submerged area within certain geographical confines (to wit, the area constituting the Persian Gulf) never reaches the maximum limit of 200 metres does not mean there is no continental shelf there. Whatever the distinction geologically between inner shelves and the normal continental shelf, in the interest of avoiding confusion such distinction should not be carried over into the law. To apply a criterion based on the method of formation or origin would be unwarranted limitation on the continental shelf doctrine.[188]

PEARL FISHERIES OF THE ARABIAN GULF. The geological formation of the bottom of the Arabian Gulf and the temperature and shallowness of its waters appear to be favourable in a high degree to the growth of pearl oyster. The largest and most productive of all the pearl banks are on the Arabian side of the Gulf, the richest being those to the north and east of Bahrain.

No national legislation claiming exclusive control over any of the fisheries is known to exist, but the continental shelf legislation of the Arab States of the Gulf expressly stated that the traditional freedom of pearling by the peoples of the Gulf would in no way be affected. The historical right of the inhabitants to exploit the sea bed of the Gulf, however, has never been challenged. Pearling was the first type of exploitation.[189] The pearl fisheries, which under the present law would come within the continental shelf doctrine as the exploitation of a 'sedentary species', and which long antedate the growth of national States in the area:

> are governed by customs and usages of immemorial standing. Basic among these is the concept that pearl banks are open equally to all the peoples of the Gulf on the common understanding that traditional methods and standards will be observed.[190]

Pearl fishing was the premier industry in the Arabian Gulf in the eighteenth, nineteenth and early twentieth centuries, and on it thousands of persons depended for their subsistence. In view of this fact, as well as of the possibility that the industry might actually be destroyed, Lorimer wrote, the British government had never ceased to oppose, by such means as presented themselves, the intrusion of foreigners—including Europeans and British subjects—into the fishery.[191] Lorimer also records that at one time the British Resident at Baghdad recommended that the government of India should treat the Arabian Gulf as a *mare clausum* for the purpose of pearl diving against all persons coming from ports or coasts situated beyond its limits and should by proclamation refuse protection to such persons. But the recommendation was rejected because it was considered a serious step which might bring the British government into conflict with European or American powers.[192] Lorimer also refers to the opinion given by the Law Officers of the Crown on 11 February 1905 to the effect that, within the three-mile limit and in any other waters which might justly be considered territorial, the tribes of the Arabian coast were entitled to exclusive use of the pearl fisheries. It was also held that there appeared to be grounds for asserting the possession by the tribes of an exclusive right of fishing over pearl banks outside the territorial waters but not in deep waters. With regard to the latter, where the tribes themselves had not been accustomed to fish it did not appear to the Law officers that a claim by the tribes to exclude aliens from such waters could be advanced with any chance of success.[193]

In the third decade of this century the introduction to world markets of Japanese cultured pearls and the coincidence of a world-wide monetary crisis led to a marked decrease in demand for natural pearls and adversely affected the economy of the Gulf. The discovery of oil led to a new era of economic development.

D. CONCLUSION

Notwithstanding the recent claims by the States of Iran, Oman, Democratic Yemen, Qatar and Saudi Arabia to exclusive rights, essentially for control of fishing activities, over areas of the sea much larger than those previously contemplated, in this regard, by international law, it may be stated that, unlike other States, most Middle Eastern States have so far abstained from making jurisdictional claims of considerable dimensions. Thus none of them claims a territorial sea in excess of twelve miles. The majority adhere to this limit, which may be regarded as being permitted under existing customary international law, although at present over twenty-four States claim territorial seas in excess of twelve miles, among them about nine States claiming limits of up to 200 miles. In addition, as noted above, only very few Middle Eastern States have actually claimed fishing zones beyond the territorial sea, although at present over thirty-five claim exclusive fishing zones in excess of twelve miles, amongst them over thirteen States asserting fishing limits of up to 200 miles.

Despite the fact that with the exception of Sudan none of the Middle Eastern States is a party to the 1958 Convention on the Continental Shelf, the domestic continental shelf legislation of these States generally conforms with the convention's guidelines.

Except in the case of those States which have so far not extended their territorial seas to twelve miles, it seems unlikely that the majority of the Middle Eastern States will unilaterally extend their territorial seas in the near future. The same may be observed with regard to functional zone claims beyond the territorial sea, whether for fishing or other purposes, but this cannot be ruled out completely and will probably depend largely on the progress and outcome of the Third United Nations Conference on the Law of the Sea, which is at present in being, with the aim of reshaping the international law of the sea, and to which the next chapter will turn with a view to providing some insight into the position which the various Middle Eastern States are taking.

CHAPTER II

TRENDS AS REFLECTED IN THE THIRD UNITED NATIONS CONFERENCE ON THE LAW OF THE SEA

Though at the First United Nations Conference on the Law of the Sea in 1958 four conventions concerning the use of the seas were adopted, both that conference and the Second, held in 1960, failed to produce solutions to the critical questions of the breadth of the territorial sea and the precise nature of the rights of coastal States with respect to the living resources off their coasts. Even the law as codified in the 1958 convention has been termed 'ambiguous and subject to varying interpretations'.[1] In addition 'the political and economic realities, scientific development and rapid technological advances of the last decade have accentuated the need for early and progressive development of the law of the sea, in a framework of close international co-operation'.[2]

The question of convening a new conference on the law of the sea, therefore, had been considered both within and outside the United Nations. Eventually, on 17 December 1970, the General Assembly, under Resolution 27500 (XXV), adopted by a vote of 108 to 7, with eight abstentions, decided to convene in 1973 a third conference on the law of the sea. In accordance with operative paragraph 3 of Resolution 3067 (XXVIII) of 16 November 1973, the conference is expected 'to adopt a Convention dealing with all matters relating to the law of the sea'.[3] The conference has now been in session for a total of fifty-one weeks over the past six years, including twelve weeks during its seventh session in 1978; an eighth session is scheduled at Geneva for six weeks beginning 19 March 1979, and further meetings are expected to be held. At the first session, which was held in New York on 3–14 December 1973, about 140 governments were represented. The conference, which normally functions by consensus, has not voted on or approved a single article yet, but to assist future negotiations an Informal Single Negotiating Text of three parts, setting out possible provisions for almost the entire range of issues to be dealt with in the projected convention, was prepared at the end of the third session in May, 1975, by the chairmen of the conference's three main committees.[4] A fourth part on the subject of settlement of disputes was prepared by the president of the conference and released in July 1975.[5] All four parts of the Informal Single Negotiating Text were revised during the fourth session of the conference and a new Revised Single Negotiating Text, Parts I-IV, was released on 6 May 1976.[6] No new negotiating text was prepared during the fifth session, but many changes were made in the text after the sixth session. The Informal Composite Negotiating Text (ICNT), issued on 20 July 1977, has sixteen main parts and contains 303 articles and seven annexes.[7] However, a number of new concepts have already emerged, including the concept that the sea bed and ocean floor, and the subsoil thereof, beyond the limits of national jurisdiction, as well as the resources therein, are the 'common heritage of mankind'; the need for an international sea bed regime and authority, and the 'exclusive economic zone' or 'patrimonial sea'.

The main object of this chapter is to examine the views of the Middle Eastern States as reflected in the Third Conference, but first it may be enlightening to survey in brief the recommendations of the Arab League to its member States with regard to this conference, for all but one (Iran) of the States with which the present study is concerned are members of this intergovernmental organisation.

A. RECOMMENDATIONS OF THE ARAB LEAGUE

Like many other regional organisations, in anticipation of the Third Conference the League of Arab States has in recent years been considering aspects of the law of the sea in an attempt to co-ordinate the policies of its members. For this purpose, the Council of the Arab League under Resolution 2978 of 13 September 1972 invited the Committee of Arab Experts on the Law of the Sea[8] to examine all aspects of the law of the sea and recommend a common Arab policy on the problems of particular importance to the Arab States, including 'the problem of navigation through international straits'. In the same resolution the council reaffirmed paragraph A of its Resolution 1759 of 26 March 1959, which requested the Arab States to delay their adhesions to the 1958 Convention on the Territorial Sea and the Contiguous Zone. The Council also recommended to the Arab States:

B.   Acceptance of the principle of freedom of navigation in Straits and Gulfs—but no other waterways—which link two parts of the high seas and are used since the past as routes for international navigation.

C. To work in all international assemblies, in co-operation with the friendly states, in order to foil every attempt which would permit freedom of passage in straits which do not link between two parts of the high seas or through historic Gulfs which, since the past, have not been customarily used for international navigation.[9]

The delegates of the People's Democratic Republic of Yemen and the Sultanate of Oman have made formal reservations with respect to the former paragraph.

It is clear that the resolution's special reference to the question of 'Straits and Gulfs' and reaffirmation of Resolution 1759 are mainly due to the Gulf of Aqaba and its entrance the Straits of Tiran, for the Arab States have so far refused to adhere to the 1958 Territorial Sea Convention because it provides for non-suspendable innocent passage through straits used for international navigation between one part of the high seas and the territorial sea of a foreign State. It is widely asserted that the latter rule applies to the situation in the Gulf of Aqaba.[10] The approval by the Council of the Arab League of the principle of 'freedom of navigation' through straits used for international navigation between one part of the high seas and another part of the high seas reflects the view of Iraq, which in two memoranda submitted to the League expressed support for the principle of 'freedom of passage' through straits, but only when they connect two parts of the high seas and are used for international navigation.[11] Iraq, according to the memoranda, considered that such policy would on the one hand guarantee for Iraqi and other ships freedom of passage through the Strait of Hormuz, which has a maximum width of about twenty-three miles and in the event of an international agreement on a twelve-mile territorial sea would fall entirely within the territorial seas of both Oman and Iran;[12] it would also be consistent with the common policy of the Arab States according to which there should be no freedom of passage through straits connecting one part of the high seas and the territorial sea of a foreign State. At the same time, so the Iraqi argument ran, this policy is in harmony with the judgement of the International Court of Justice in the Corfu Channel case, 1949.[13]

The reservation entered by Democratic Yemen and Oman reflects their attitudes that only 'innocent passage' should be permitted through international straits.[14] During 1972 the States of Kuwait, Lebanon, Qatar and the United Arab Emirates transmitted to the Arab League separate memoranda expressing their support for the principle of 'freedom of passage' through international straits.[15] The difference in opinion between the Arab States on the question of straits is mainly due to their varied geographical situations. While States such as Iraq and Kuwait are located at the inner part of the Arabian Gulf and thus have no control over any part of its entrance, States such as Oman and Democratic Yemen border the Strait of Hormuz and the Straits of Bab el-Mandeb respectively. As will be seen, this difference in opinion has also been reflected at the Third Conference.

As to the Committee of Arab Experts, prior to the convening of the first substantive session, it held three sessions and adopted a number of similar sets of recommendations that had subsequently been approved by the Council of the Arab League.[16] The set of recommendations upon which attention will be focused here was adopted during the third session, which met from 2 to 10 March 1974. These recommendations, it has been indicated,[17] have been co-ordinated with the measures adopted in the Declaration of the Organisation of African Unity on the Issues of the Law of the Sea.[18] Unlike the latter, however, neither the present nor any other recommendations of the Arab League have been circulated in a document for the use of the Third Law of the Sea Conference. Thus, it is believed, they are not regarded as representing a common international policy of member States of the Arab League, they are mere guidelines for the use of those States. On the territorial sea, the Arab States are urged, if they have not already done so, to claim a territorial sea of twelve miles, and to seek an international agreement on the same, taking into account 'the special positions of some Arab States and other friendly States, but without prejudice to the Arab common interest'. It is not very clear how this recommendation can be put into effect, but it would seem to take into consideration particularly the claims of the Republic of Somalia and the Islamic Republic of Mauritania, the only two Arab States which claim territorial seas in excess of twelve miles.[19] According to the recommendations, 'warships should be required to obtain prior authorisation from, or give prior notification to the Coastal State concerned' before entering the territorial sea.

On straits, the Committee of Arab Experts recognised that its members have overwhelmingly supported the principle of 'freedom of navigation' through straits which are used for international navigation between parts of the high seas, but only in so far as merchant shipping and civil aviation were concerned. As to non-commercial navigation such as the passage of warships, submarines and military aircraft, the committee has not been able to arrive at any decision. The committee has also recognised the existence between the Arab States of a clear tendency for the principle of a 'contiguous zone' of six nautical miles beyond the territorial sea, for security, navigation, customs, sanitary, fiscal and immigration purposes.[20] It therefore invited those Arab States which had not yet claimed such zone to do so.

On other matters such as the exclusive economic zone and the establishment of an international regime and authority for the sea bed beyond the limits of national jurisdiction, the recommendations of the Arab League closely followed the OAU Declaration. They approved the concept of a 200-mile exclusive economic zone in which the coastal State would have exclusive rights over the living and non-living resources, but neighbouring landlocked and geographically disadvantaged States would be entitled to share in the exploitation of the living resources.[21] The international authority, it was recommended, should assume strong and comprehensive powers for the exploration and exploitation of, and regulation of activities in, the sea bed and ocean floor beyond national jurisdiction.[22]

The recommendations of the Arab League make no reference to a few issues of particular importance to certain Arab States. For instance, no reference is made to 'historic rights' and particularly to 'historic bays'. In view of the claims of Arab States that the Gulf of Aqaba and other bays in Egypt and Libya are historic bays,[23] it is not very clear just why the Committee of Arab Experts has not made any suggestion in this regard.[24]

Finally, as a regional organisation, the Arab League should have been able to assume a more active role and make a considerable contribution towards the current attempt to reshape and develop the law of the sea.

B. SUBSTANTIVE ISSUES BEFORE THE CONFERENCE

We now turn to the deliberations of the Third Conference on the Law of the Sea with a view to identifying and analysing the policies and reactions of the Middle Eastern States with regard to some of the main issues and trends. In defining their policies, the Middle Eastern States, like most States, are expected to be guided primarily by their national needs and interests. It must, however, be recognised that in defining policies regarding coastal jurisdiction States *(a)* act not only on the basis of their real interests but also (or perhaps primarily) on the basis of what they subjectively perceive as their interests; *(b)* are influenced by considerations that are not related to their interests in the utilisation of the sea.

With the exception that Jordan was not represented at the second session of the conference, all Middle Eastern States were invited to, and are actually participating in, the Third Law of the Sea Conference.[25]

The discussion of the main trends will develop under three main headings, corresponding to the division of work between the three main committees at the conference, namely: (1) jurisdictional limits, (2) establishment of an international regime and authority for the exploration and exploitation of the resources of the sea bed and ocean floor and subsoil thereof beyond the limits of national jurisdiction, and (3) control of marine pollution and regulation of scientific research and transfer of technology.

1. Jurisdictional limits

A. TERRITORIAL SEA (INCLUDING STRAITS USED FOR INTERNATIONAL NAVIGATION). The question relating to the breadth of the territorial sea has been one of the most controversial questions throughout the development of the law of the sea. Linked with this is the extent of the right of passage of foreign ships through the territorial sea and straits used for international navigation. The rules relating to the measurement of the territorial sea as formulated in the 1958 Territorial Sea Convention are widely accepted by States and, generally, have not been questioned at the Third Conference, except in relation to archipelagic States. Of the Middle Eastern States only Bahrain is an island State, consisting of six principal islands—most of them are close to the largest, Bahrain.[26]

(i) Breadth of the territorial sea. In December 1975, of the 129 independent coastal states, fifty-seven had claimed a territorial sea of twelve miles; forty-eight were still claiming less than twelve miles (thirty of them claimed three miles only); and twenty-three had claimed more than twelve miles (nine of them claiming 200 miles).[27] It is hardly surprising, therefore, that at the Third Conference the majority of States, including the Middle Eastern States, had already expressed their readiness for formal agreement on a maximum twelve-mile breadth for the territorial sea.[28] What is surprising, however, is that a number of maritime States, such as the U.S.A., have regarded the acceptance of an agreement on a twelve-mile territorial sea as a concession on their part and have therefore insisted that such agreement must 'be coupled with agreement on free transit of Straits used for international navigation'.[29] On the other hand, a number of Latin American and African States, led principally by Peru, Brazil and Ecuador, have

insisted that States should have the right to extend their territorial sea up to 200 miles.[30]

As shown in Chapter I, the majority of the Middle Eastern States have, in their national laws, adopted the modest limit of twelve miles. At the Third Conference, generally speaking, they have also expressed support for an international agreement on the same limit.[31] Kuwait favoured the twelve-mile limit because it considered it the best possible compromise.[32] The United Arab Emirates, which have not yet formally defined the extent of their territorial sea, maintained that every coastal State, taking into consideration its peculiarities, had the right to determine the breadth of its territorial sea.[33] They gave no indication, however, as to the breadth which they themselves favoured, but as noted elsewhere are likely to follow other Arabian Gulf States and adopt the twelve-mile limit. Egypt and Oman both stressed that they applied the twelve-mile limit, but at the same time they affirmed that they would accept whatever limit the conference might determine.[34] At the meeting of the Asian–African Legal Consultative Committee in 1971 Jordan said that the twelve-mile limit of territorial sea was 'desirable and appropriate', but pointed out that certain coastal States had adopted the limit of 200 miles, which 'could be justified for economic and security reasons'.[35]

Iran supported a general agreement on the twelve-mile limit and considered that its acceptance 'would merely amount to recognition of a rule applied by the majority of States'.[36] It did not, however, exclude the possibility of 'bilateral or multilateral agreements in cases where special circumstances existed'.[37]

(ii) Navigation through the territorial sea. The regime of innocent passage enshrined in the 1958 Territorial Sea Convention has been generally accepted at the Third Conference, but a number of States have called for a stricter definition of the meaning of 'innocent passage' and of the right of passage of warships through the territorial sea.[38] Oman and the Yemen Arab Republic jointly with other two straits States submitted draft articles on navigation through the territorial sea, including straits, which, *inter alia,* give the coastal State the right to require prior notification to or authorisation by its competent authorities of the passage of warships through its territorial sea.[39] The coastal State is also given the right to regulate the passage of ships with special characteristics, including nuclear-powered ships, oil tankers, chemical tankers and marine research ships.[40] The concern of Oman and the Yemen Arab Republic is clearly due to the fact that their territorial seas extend to the Strait of Hormuz and the Straits of Bab el-Mandeb

respectively. The traffic through these straits is heavy, and they are used by a considerable number of oil tankers. However, the Middle Eastern States have expressed more interest in and concern about the question of navigation through international straits.

(iii) Straits used for international navigation. A problem directly affected by the breadth of the territorial sea is navigation through straits which constitute routes for international traffic. An extension of the breadth of the territorial seas would change the status of many areas and consequently foreclose high-seas rights in these areas and the international straits that happened to fall within them.

It has been shown that an extension of the territorial sea from three to twelve miles would mean that some 116 straits would become territorial waters, including such important passages as the Dover Straits, the Bering Straits, the Straits of Gibraltar, the Malacca Straits, the Strait of Hormuz and the Straits of Bab el-Mandeb.[41] Accordingly the major maritime powers, concerned first of all with their strategic mobility and secondly with their commercial interests, argued that, in the event of an international agreement on a twelve-mile territorial sea, the regime of non-suspendable innocent passage through international straits contained in the 1958 Territorial Sea Convention would no longer be adequate: in particular that the test of innocence was open to subjective interpretation by coastal States.[42] The major powers, therefore, introduced and insisted on the new concept of 'free transit' or 'transit passage' for all shipping and aircraft through and over straits used for international navigation. This demand would '... *extend* rather than merely resist encroachment upon the right of [innocent passage] that has been made in the law of the sea for a very long time',[43] to secure the same rights of navigation and overflight in territorial straits as were now enjoyed as part of the freedom of the high seas in the area beyond territorial waters.

A number of countries bordering on straits, and archipelagic States, concerned about their right to security in view of the risk involved in the passage of warships and military aircraft through areas close to their coasts and air space, and the protection of their coasts against pollution and other hazards, have strongly opposed the 'free transit' proposals and considered that the basic regime of innocent passage already provided for in the 1958 Territorial Sea Convention would suffice for international straits. Other States have recognised the need for more precision in the regime of innocent passage. A large number of developing countries, however, showed readiness to recognise the principle of 'free transit' with regard to merchant ships.[44]

The attitudes of the Middle Eastern States towards this question have varied. As a State with borders on the strategic Strait of Hormuz, Iran stressed that, while certain exceptions to the sovereignty of the coastal State might be envisaged in the interests of international trade and communication, any proposed rules regarding passage through international straits should be based on the concept of innocent passage and should take into account the need to protect the security and other interests of the coastal State, including the protection of the marine environment and the regulation of the passage of vessels through sea corridors.[45] In support of its standpoint Iran noted that 'at least in times of peace, coastal States had seldom imposed restrictions on transit through Straits used for international navigation'.[46] More recently, however, Iran had implicitly expressed its readiness to recognise the principle of 'free' or 'transit' passage with regard to merchant ships when it said that:

the passage of foreign ships, *particularly warships,* through territorial waters, including those of Straits, should be subject to the principle of innocent passage and conducive to the development of international commerce and communications [emphasis added].[47]

The views of the Arab States largely reflected those they expressed inside the Arab League. Speaking on behalf of five other Arab States and for itself, Kuwait recalled, in an implicit but clear reference to the issue of passage through the Strait of Tiran, that these Arab States had not acceded to the 1958 Territorial Sea Convention because they opposed Article 16(4) of that convention, which treated all straits alike; it also stressed that the term 'Straits used for international navigation' should be strictly confined to straits that connected two parts of the high seas.[48] For itself, Kuwait also suggested that 'freedom of transit' should be guaranteed for all merchant vessels, while the concept of 'prior notification' could serve as a compromise formula to be applied to warships and military aircraft 'in view of the risk involved in their passage'.[49] Iraq has reiterated its view in favour of the freedom of navigation through straits used for international navigation between parts of the high seas, and therefore expressed disagreement with the draft on the territorial sea submitted by Spain[50] because it referred to straits as part of the ordinary territorial sea.[51]

Egypt believed that the proven regime of innocent passage should be the starting point for the development of the regime of passage through international straits.[52] Elsewhere Egypt strongly critised the 'free transit' proposals:

GENERAL PRACTICE AND POLICIES

... such a freedom which allows submerged submarines, nuclear or otherwise to pass unseen cannot be called anything other than licensing for the spread of terror.[53]

Oman and the Yemen Arab Republic, as noted earlier, submitted with other States some draft articles on the territorial sea, including 'straits used for international navigation'.[54] The draft, which applied 'to any Strait which is used for international navigation and forms parts of the territorial sea of one or more states', referred to the regime of navigation through straits as a 'right of innocent passage'. As explained by the delegate of Oman, who introduced the draft to the conference, the draft applied to straits as defined by the International Court of Justice in the Corfu Channel case,[55] and therefore did not apply to straits which historically had not been used for international navigation.[56] This express interpretation may have been motivated by the issue of passage through the Straits of Tiran. The draft articles also required prior notification to or authorisation by the coastal State of the passage of foreign warships through its territorial sea and the straits falling within it, but it was expressly stipulated that the passage of foreign merchant ships through straits should be presumed to be innocent.[57]

Similarly, Democratic Yemen, whose territorial sea extends to the narrower part of the Straits of Bab el-Mandeb, said that foreign commercial vessels should have the right of innocent passage while non-commercial vessels, including warships and submarines, should obtain prior authorisation for passage through international straits.[58]

Lebanon and the United Arab Emirates, without any elaboration, declared that there should be freedom of navigation through international straits.[59] Saudi Arabia supported the principle of 'free passage in international Straits, connecting different parts of the high seas', and said that it 'had no objection to the claims of archipelagic States if the channels of international navigation were respected'.[60] Finally, in the Sea Bed Committee the Libyan delegate expressly stated that 'in view of the fact that the great powers often made use of the Mediterranean for their military activities' his country was 'in favour of the idea of innocent passage' through international straits.[61]

B. THE CONTIGUOUS ZONE. The concept of the contiguous zone as an area of the high seas adjacent to the territorial sea where the coastal State may exercise preventive or protective control for certain purposes has been resorted to by States since the seventeenth century, especially in order to enforce their customs and fiscal regulations. As understood at present the contiguous zone concept serves similar purposes, but was accepted at the 1958 Law of the Sea Conference as a means of limiting the extent of the territorial sea while at the same time providing protection for the legitimate interests of coastal States which considered that a narrow territorial sea would not provide the necessary protection.

At the Third Conference this concept received little attention, because many States considered that on the establishment, by general acceptance, of a twelve-mile territorial sea and an exclusive economic zone of 200 miles the concept of a contiguous zone would become superfluous. This was the view taken, for example, by Lebanon.[62] Others, including most of the other Arab States and Iran, called for the retention of the contiguous zone concept to extend to an agreed area beyond the twelve-mile territorial sea, believing that the establishment of a contiguous zone was not inconsistent with the concept of an exclusive economic zone, since the latter related only to jurisdiction over resources.[63] For this purpose many Arab States, together with Iran and other States, submitted a draft article which envisaged the establishment of a 'contiguous zone' beyond the territorial sea, but no certain limit was indicated and, unlike the laws of some Arab States in this regard, no reference was made to 'security' matters. Reference was made, as in the 1958 Territorial Sea Convention, only to matters relating to customs, fiscal, immigration and sanitary regulations. The ICNT includes an article which envisages the creation of a contiguous zone for the latter purposes, and expressly states that the contiguous zone of a State may not extend beyond twenty-four nautical miles from the baseline from which the breadth of the territorial sea is measured.[64]

C. THE EXCLUSIVE ECONOMIC ZONE.

(i) The general concept. Whilst existing conventional international law recognises the coastal State's sovereign rights over its continental shelf for the purpose of 'exploring it and exploiting its natural resources',[65] it accords no special control or jurisdiction over the living resources of the superjacent waters, or of any waters beyond the territorial sea. Since the 1958 and 1960 Law of the Sea conferences, however, there have been two important developments—the technological revolution in fishing which hit the world in the mid-1960s, and the emergence of the poor and hungry Third World as a self-conscious and self-assertive force. These developments led developing coastal States to demand addi-

tional rights in respect of fisheries in adjacent waters. As a consequence extensive jurisdictional claims were made over relatively broad areas of adjacent maritime spaces.[66] In its judgement in the Fisheries Jurisdiction case, 1974, the International Court of Justice noted that:

> Two concepts have crystallised as customary law in recent years arising out of the general consensus revealed at the 1960 Conference. The first is the concept of the fishing zone .... The second is the concept of preferential right of fishing in adjacent waters in favour of the coastal state in a situation of special dependence on its coastal fisheries ...[67]

The Court described the exclusive fishing zone as an 'area in which a state may claim exclusive fishing jurisdiction independently of its territorial sea', and as being 'a *tertium genus* between the territorial sea and the high seas', adding, 'the extension of that fishery up to a twelve-mile limit from the baselines appears now to be generally accepted'.[68]

In the contemporary debate on the law of the sea, however, many of the developing countries have tended to link the question of the rights of coastal States over living resources in the waters adjacent to their territorial seas with the question of jurisdiction over the resources of contiguous submarine areas. These countries have persuasively developed the argument that the coastal State should be entitled to have sovereign or exclusive rights for the purpose of exploration and exploitation of the living and non-living resources of an economic zone extending to 200 miles from the baseline from which the breadth of the territorial sea is measured. In that zone the coastal State would also have the necessary control over pollution and the regulation of scientific research, but there would be freedom of navigation and overflight and freedom to lay submarine cables and pipelines, on the understanding that these freedoms would not unjustifiably interfere with the coastal State's rights over its resources. This concept, variously described as the patrimonial sea or exclusive economic zone, first emerged from the developing countries of Latin America and Africa, and has been quickly embraced by other developing countries and a significant number of developed ones.[69] Even the distant-water fishing nations such as the United States, the Soviet Union and the United Kingdom have now indicated their readiness to accept this concept, if their demands with regard to other basic questions are accepted.[70] Thus, at the end of the Caracas session of the Third Conference, the chairman of the second committee was able to say that:

The idea of a territorial sea of twelve miles and exclusive economic zone beyond the territorial sea up to a total maximum distance of 200 miles was the keystone of the compromise solution favoured by the majority of States participating in the Conference, although acceptance of the idea was of course dependent on the satisfactory resolution of other issues, such as passage through straits used for international navigation, the outermost limit of the Continental Shelf and the aspirations of the landlocked and other geographically disadvantaged countries, and there were still differences of opinion over the nature and characteristics of the concept of exclusive economic zone.[71]

The ICNT envisages the establishment of a 200-mile exclusive economic zone, which is defined as 'an area beyond and adjacent to the territorial sea, subject to the specific legal regime established in this Part, under which the rights and jurisdictions of the coastal State and the rights and freedoms of other States are governed by the relevant provisions of the present Convention'.[72]

In the exclusive economic zone the coastal State would have *(a)* sovereign rights for the purpose of exploring and exploiting, conserving and managing the natural resources, whether living or non-living, of the sea bed and subsoil and the superjacent waters, and with regard to other activities for the economic exploitation and exploration of the zone, such as the production of energy from the water, currents and winds; *(b)* jurisdiction with regard to the establishment and use of artificial islands, installations and structures; marine scientific research and the preservation of the marine environment; *(c)* other rights and duties provided for in the new proposed convention.[73] The text also provides that where the coastal State does not have the capacity to harvest the entire allowable catch of the living resources of its economic zone, it shall, through agreements or other arrangements and pursuant to the prescribed terms, conditions and regulations, give other States access to the surplus of the allowable catch.[74] The text also provides that landlocked States shall have the right to participate in the exploitation of the living resources of the exclusive economic zones of adjoining coastal States on an equitable basis, through bilateral, sub-regional or regional agreements with the States concerned.[75]

Before surveying the views of the Middle Eastern States with regard to the exclusive economic zone concept, a brief assessment will be made of the influence on them of geographic and other factors.

(ii) Factors influencing Middle Eastern States. With the exception of Democratic Yemen and Oman, which partly border on the open

ocean, all Middle Eastern States border on or are located within relatively narrow seas. Most important of these are the Mediterranean, the Red Sea and the Arabian Gulf. It has been shown that beyond a depth of 200-metres there would be 77 per cent of sea bed in the Mediterranean, 55 per cent in the Red Sea and none in the Arabian Gulf, and that by the shift seaward of the limits of national jurisdiction from the 200-metre depth to forty miles from the shore, 65 per cent of the water area of the Mediterranean, 85 per cent of that of the Red Sea, and 85 per cent of that of the Arabian Gulf would be closed off. If the seaward extent of national limits is fixed at 200 miles from the shore, then 100 per cent of the water area of each of these seas would be closed off.[76] These figures show that a 200-mile zone for sea bed resources exploitation would give most of the Middle Eastern States nothing, or little more than they enjoy at present under the continental shelf doctrine, whether based on the criteria of the 1958 Convention on the Continental Shelf or on the theory of 'natural prolongation' propounded in the North Sea Continental Shelf cases, 1969.[77] In other words, owing to geographic considerations, most of the Middle Eastern States could not fully benefit from the proposed 200-mile exclusive economic zone. Such would be the case also even if it is agreed, as some States have proposed, that the coastal State's jurisdiction over adjacent submarine areas should extend to the outer edge of the continental margin where this extends beyond the 200-mile limit.[78] Among the Middle Eastern States the principal beneficiaries in terms of shelf area from a 200-mile zone for sea bed resources are Democratic Yemen and Oman—both border on the Indian Ocean—whilst Iraq, with only ten miles of coastline, and Jordan, with only about fifteen miles, would come off worst: each would be allocated only 200 square miles of sea bed area. (Table 1)

It should not be forgotten, however, that the main interest behind the idea of an exclusive zone is in the living resources of the zone. Although, as with sea bed resources, many of the Middle Eastern States would not be able to claim a full 200-mile exclusive fishing zone, the establishment of a 200-mile zone for living resources would doubtless be an attractive proposition for them. A broad fishery zone would give these countries greater control and jurisdiction over fisheries in areas adjacent to their territorial waters than they enjoy at present. As noted in Chapter I, only Iran, Oman, Qatar and Saudi Arabia have actually claimed exclusive fishing zones beyond the territorial sea. Such protection would also seem necessary for the others, especially in view of the fact that

Table I

National allocations of the continental shelf and sea bed in the oceans and seas adjacent to the Middle Eastern States under various proposals on delimitation of outer limits of national jurisdiction, and coastline measurements of these States (all figures nautical square miles, except the first column—nautical miles)

	Length of coastline	40 n.m.	200 n.m.	200 m depth	End of continental margin
Bahrain	68	1,400	1,500	1,500	1,500
Egypt	1,307	36,700	50,600	10,900	28,900
United Arab Emirates	420	17,300	17,300	17,300	17,000
Iran	990	33,200	45,400	31,200	45,400
Iraq	10	200	200	200	200
Jordan	15	200	200	200	200
Kuwait	115	3,000	3,500	3,500	3,500
Lebanon	105	4,100	6,600	1,300	4,600
Libya	910	38,100	98,600	24,400	60,100
Oman	1,005	36,700	163,800	17,800	44,500
Qatar	204	6,600	7,000	7,700	7,000
Saudi Arabia	1,316	43,800	54,300	22,100	54,000
Sudan	387	18,300	26,700	6,500	26,500
Syria	82	2,900	3,300	1,100	3,000
Yemen Arab Republic	244	9,000	9,900	7,200	9,900
Democratic Yemen	654	10,800	160,500	15,100	90,100

Source. The first column is based on U.S. Department of State, *Sovereignty of the Sea* (Geographic Bulletin No. 3, revised October 1969), table II. (Note. The coastline of the Kuwait–Saudi Arabia neutral zone, which was partitioned in 1965, measures forty nautical miles and it is assumed that half this distance now belongs exclusively to Kuwait and the other half to Saudi Arabia.) The other columns are based on U.S. Department of State, the Geographer, *Theoretical Area Allocations of Sea Bed to Coastal States, based on Certain U.N. Sea Bed Committee Proposals,* Limits in the Seas, No. 46, (12 August 1972). According to the latter source as well, the principal beneficiaries in terms of shelf area, whether the seaward extent of the national limit is fixed at the 200 m depth, 40 or 200 miles from the shore, or at the end of the continental margin, include the United States, Australia, Canada, Indonesia and the Soviet Union.

many Middle Eastern States, particularly those situated along the Arabian Gulf and the Red Sea, have in recent years been developing fishing industries, primarily to meet the requirement of their inhabitants and with view to develop their economies.

Finally, it may be recalled that none of the Middle Eastern States is landlocked, and that with the exception of Afghanistan, which borders Iran on the east, there are no landlocked States in their region.

(iii) Trends among Middle Eastern States. Generally speaking, the majority of the Middle Eastern States have expressed or indicated their willingness to accept an international agreement on a 200-mile exclusive economic zone. But whereas some of them, such as Egypt, Libya, Oman and Democratic Yemen, came out with strong support for the idea, others, such as Iraq, Iran and Bahrain, have accepted it in the name of solidarity with the aspirations of other developing countries. Others again, such as Lebanon, have accepted the new concept with great reluctance. Kuwait does not on the whole favour it.

Egypt, Democratic Yemen, Saudi Arabia, Sudan, Oman, the Yemen Arab Republic and the Libyan Arab Republic have extended a warm welcome to the idea of a 200-mile zone. The first four might have been partly motivated by the existence of mineral-rich brines in the Red Sea deeps.[79] Thus, since 1971, Sudan has expressed the view that it:

... would certainly not view with favour any suggestion that it should renounce its title to that area of the Red Sea in which it had already been carrying out exploratory and prospecting activities for a number of years, since it possessed these rights under existing law ... and the Red Sea fisheries were an important source of food.[80]

Egypt described the exclusive economic zone as a '... natural outcome of the developing countries' philosophy and was designed to overcome the numerous shortcomings of the regime of the continental shelf as prescribed in the 1958 Geneva Convention'.[81] Libya noted that the aim of those who sought to reduce to a minimum the sovereignty of the coastal State over its economic zone 'was to enable their fishing fleets to invade the coastal waters of the developing countries, monopolise fishery resources, transform them into finished products and sell them at high prices', and regarded this approach as 'contrary to the equitable principles that should prevail in the elaboration of a new law of the sea'. Libya for this reason 'favoured the establishment of exclusive economic zone in which the coastal state would have complete sovereignty over living and non-living resources'.[82] The United Arab Emirates have adopted a similar attitude.[83]

Bahrain and Iraq have 'recognised the aspirations of the coastal states to extend their marine jurisdiction' to an economic zone of 200 miles, but stressed that this idea should not be applied to semi-enclosed seas such as the Arabian Gulf, where 'A proper solution would be the establishment of regional arrangements for conservation, exploration, management, protection from pollution and development of the living resources of the sea'.[84] Elsewhere Iraq emphasised that the doctrine of the economic zone, if eventually adopted, should take into account not only the interests of the landlocked countries but also the interests of the countries with a very limited coastline.[85] Because of its limited coastline, Iraq considered itself a geographically disadvantaged State and therefore shared the view of many landlocked and other geographically disadvantaged States that they should be entitled to participate in the exploitation of the living and non-living resources of the economic zones of neighbouring coastal States.[86] Iraq, however, pointed out that geographically disadvantaged States such as those which were unable to extend their economic zones to the limit to be agreed upon in the proposed convention should not be compelled to make contributions to the international sea bed authority out of the revenues derived from the exploitation of the living resources of their economic zones.[87] This restrictive interpretation was clearly designed to apply to States such as Iraq.

Prior to its claim of a fifty-mile exclusive fishing zone,[88] Iran found the idea of the economic zone attractive because it was in line with a growing tendency to link the extent of the fishing zones in many cases with the extent of the continental shelf, and justifiable on the ground that many of the world's more productive fishing areas are situated in relatively shallow waters.[89] More recently, however, Iran noted that because of its geographical position it could not benefit fully from the proposed 200-mile exclusive economic zone, but that it would support the aspirations of those coastal States which were able to exercise jurisdiction up to 200 miles.[90] Nevertheless, Iran maintained that the coastal State held exclusive and inalienable rights over its continental shelf and, therefore, could not agree with any proposal that would involve the sharing of revenues derived from the exploitation of the continental shelf.[91] This standpoint reflects Iran's concern about its huge offshore oil resources, for, as indicated earlier, it has borders with the landlocked State of Afghanistan, which insisted that landlocked and other geographically disadvantaged States should be entitled to some rights in the renewable and non-renewable resources of the economic zones of neighbouring countries.[92] Iran, however, agreed that coastal States should, under regional or bilaterial agreements, accord to the nationals of the landlocked States of their region or sub-region 'preferential rights to fish in certain areas of their exclusive economic zone'.[93] It has already been noted that the ICNT refers to participation by landlocked and geographically disadvantaged States only in the living resources of the exclusive economic zones of neighbouring coastal States.

Lebanon 'had accepted the principle of a 200-mile economic zone with great reluctance, for such a zone in the Mediterranean would be meaningless'; nevertheless, it had not wanted to oppose the will of the great majority of States, which 'did not trust an international community controlled by the great maritime powers'.[94] Lebanon feared that the establishment of an exclusive economic zone would mean the end of the concept of the territorial sea, and as a compromise suggested the idea of a 'contiguous fishing zone' under which the coastal State in a 'high sea area' adjacent to its territorial sea would exercise 'sovereign rights' for the purposes of exploration and exploitation of all types of natural resources, and perhaps also with regard to scientific research and preservation of the marine environment. Such a formula, the Lebanese representative continued, would settle the question of sovereignty in a reassuring manner, resolve a difficult problem of terminology, and omit the concept of residual rights.[95]

Without reference to the concept of the exclusive economic zone or other proposals concerning fisheries beyond the territorial sea, Kuwait stated that:

All States should be allowed to satisfy their animal protein requirement from the resources available in the sea and they had an equal interest in conserving those resources; thus, it was desirable to maintain the total yield from a stock at a high level.[96]

It is clear that Kuwait does not on the whole favour the exclusive zone concept. Kuwait instead seems to accept the view, favoured by many distant-water fishing nations, according to which coastal States should have only preferential rights with regard to the fisheries adjacent to their coasts and that foreign vessels should have access to the surplus of the allowable catch of such fisheries. This is because Kuwait, which has one of the largest fishing fleets in the Arabian Gulf area, has developed a distant-water fishing fleet which fishes off the coasts of Africa and in the Indian Ocean, thousands of miles away from home.[97] For this reason also Kuwait has disapproved of the principle of closing the Arabian Gulf to foreign fishing vessels.[98]

D. THE CONTINENTAL SHELF.
(i) Relationship to the exclusive economic zone. In the debate at the Third Conference concerning the outer limits of national jurisdic-

tion over adjacent sea bed resources two main approaches have evolved. First, there were States which not only sought the retention of the continental shelf doctrine but also made it clear that coastal States' jurisdiction should extend to the outer edge of the continental margin where this extends beyond 200 miles, the limit proposed for the exclusive economic zone.[99] Secondly, there were States which advocated that the concept of the continental shelf should be subsumed under the concept of the exclusive economic zone, and that the area beyond should be part of the international area to which the 'common heritage of mankind' concept should apply and where no activities could be carried on without the approval of the international authority on such conditions as it might determine.

The ICNT incorporates the first approach, but with the proviso that coastal States should make payments or contributions in kind to the international authority in respect of the exploitation of the resources of the continental shelf beyond 200 nautical miles.[100]

Although a few of the Middle Eastern States, as will be seen below, have for one reason or another called for the retention of the continental shelf doctrine as such, none has supported the first of the two approaches referred to above. This attitude is understandable, for in terms of sea bed area allocation most of the Middle Eastern States would be better off under the 200-miles proposition than under that which advocates the extension of the coastal State's jurisdiction to the limit of the continental margin where this extends beyond 200-miles, or at least they would be in the same position.[101] This is because, as indicated earlier, none of the Middle Eastern States can claim a full 200-miles exclusive economic zone, and because most of these States are either shelf-locked, such as those located around the Arabian Gulf, i.e. their continental shelf abuts on that of their neighbours so that no portion of it descends below the 200-metre depth (the formula designated in the 1958 Continental Shelf Convention) on to the continental slope; or have very limited outer continental margins, such as those bordering on the Red Sea, in the sense that their adjacent sea bed areas descend very sharply into the deep sea, that is, the area beyond the limits of the margin, so that the sea bed area which could be allocated to each of them under a 200-mile limit would be larger than that they could acquire by virtue of the end of the continental margin proposition.[102] In addition, the stand favoured by the Middle Eastern States, if eventually adopted, would give them the opportunity of gaining a share of the revenue from future exploitation of resources on other countries' sea bed areas that extend beyond 200 miles but which are considered part of their continental margins, in accordance with the proposition reflected in the ICNT referred to above.

Most of the Middle Eastern States that called for the retention of the continental shelf doctrine as such agreed that the seaward limit of the shelf should be delimited by reference to a fixed distance measured from the shore instead of the criteria of depth and exploitability which were endorsed in the 1958 Continental Shelf Convention.

Kuwait, which, as noted earlier, does not appear to favour the exclusive economic zone, considered that:

> if the concept of the common heritage of mankind was to become a reality, a definition of the outer limit of the continental shelf was urgently needed. The depth criterion recognising the exclusive sovereign rights of the coastal state to the sea bed and subsoil thereof to a depth of 200 metres outside the limits of the territorial sea should be retained, while the exploitability criterion should be discarded. For those coastal states disadvantaged by the application of the depth criterion above, a supplementary distance criterion could be applied.[103]

Kuwait, however, has not suggested a definite limit. The Kuwaiti position might have been motivated by suggestions that no considerable quantities of petroleum or natural gas are likely to be found in areas beyond the outer limit of the continental margin. For since Kuwait is a shelf-locked State and a major oil-producing country, it might be advantageous to her if the quantities of oil that might be found in areas beyond the 200-metre isobath but within the continental margin were left to the control of the international sea bed authority. Iraq and Iran have advocated similar positions and, perhaps, have been motivated by similar reasons.[104]

Bahrain has supported the retention of the continental shelf doctrine, 'as defined in bilateral agreements or in accordance with the principles laid down in the 1958 Convention', but in areas which had narrow shelves or were shelf-locked it favoured the replacement of the continental shelf concept by that of the economic zone.[105]

Among the Middle Eastern States which considered that the concept of the continental shelf should be subsumed under the concept of a 200-mile economic zone, if it were adopted, is Lebanon, whose delegation of the Third Conference explained that:

> The criterion of the 200-metre isobath might eventually be kept. If, however, it were to be extended to 4,000 metre isobath, as certain favoured states seemed to wish, there would remain nothing for the International Sea Bed Authority except abyssal depths. There would then be little point

in establishing an Authority. The sea bed prizes would go to technologically or geographically favoured nations.

If the ideas of exploitability and depth were eliminated, there remained only the criterion of distance, which led back to the idea of the economic zone. The concept of the continental shelf should be replaced by that of the economic zone. To retain the shelf concept would be unfair and undemocratic. It might well be argued that those were acquired rights, but such rights had impeded the progressive development of international law. If a mistake had been made in 1958, there was no need to perpetuate it.[106]

(ii) Delimitation. Most of the Middle Eastern States have stressed the importance of the question of the delimitation of submarine or continental shelf boundaries between adjacent and opposite States. This is natural, since, as noted earlier, the waters of the Mediterranean, the Red Sea and the Arabian Gulf would be completely closed off by the extension of the outer limits of national jurisdiction to 200 miles. Although many of the boundary lines in the Arabian Gulf have been delimited, a few are still to be finally determined, notably the Iraq–Kuwait and Iraq–Iran boundaries.[107] The question of offshore boundary delimitation has also gained importance in the Red Sea following the discovery in its deeps of metalliferous hot brines,[108] and has been highlighted in the central Mediterranean, in areas between Libya and its neighbours Tunisia and Malta, where some successful strikes for oil have already been made.[109]

At the Third Conference many of the Middle Eastern States have emphasised the importance of the principle of equidistance for offshore boundary delimitation between opposite or adjacent States, and frequently reference was made to the finding of the International Court of Justice in the North Sea Continental Shelf cases.[110] Reference was also made to the principle of 'special circumstances', which it was thought needed further elaboration, and to the situation with regard to islands and their effects on the boundaries of the continental shelf, which was considered to be equally ambiguous and required clarification also. The Middle Eastern States, however, made no specific proposals concerning such matters.[111]

The ICNT provides that delimitation of continental shelf boundaries between adjacent and opposite sides should be effected 'by agreement in accordance with equitable principles, employing, where appropriate, the median or equidistant line, and taking account of all the relevant circumstances'.[112] The text does not include any special provisions on the treatment to be accorded to islands in delimiting boundaries of the continental shelf, for, while some States have insisted that islands should receive the same treatment as continental areas, others argued to exclude or limit the jurisdiction around islands. However, the text envisages that islands might generate their own territorial seas, contiguous zones, exclusive economic zones, and continental shelves. This does not apply, though, to rocks which cannot sustain human inhabitation or economic life.[113]

Finally, in relation to the continental shelf reference may be made to the draft article which was submitted to the Third Conference by thirty-seven States, including Iran and the Libyan Arab Republic. The draft article provides that:

> No State shall be entitled to construct, maintain, deploy or operate on or over the continental shelf of another state any military installations or devices or any other installations for whatever purposes without the consent of the coastal State.[114]

This provision has not been reflected in the ICNT, which, however, provides that 'The delineation of the course' for the laying of submarine cables and pipelines on the continental shelf shall be subject to the consent of the coastal State.[115] On signing the future convention, Iran and Libya might decide to place reservations to that effect. On signing the 1958 conventions on the continental shelf and on the high seas, Iran made a similar reservation,[116] which led to objections from the United States and other countries.[117]

E. ENCLOSED AND SEMI-ENCLOSED SEAS. The question of the so-called 'enclosed and semi-enclosed seas' has been raised at the Third Conference, mainly in connection with the exclusive economic zone concept, by a number of States including Middle Eastern ones which believed that the latter concept should not be applied to such seas. These States, bordering enclosed or semi-enclosed seas, maintained that the problems raised by this category of seas with regard to the management of their resources, international navigation and the preservation of the marine environment 'justified granting them a particular status constituting an exception to the general rule' which would take into account 'the needs and interests of all the coastal states in the region'.[118]

The Middle Eastern States referred particularly to the Mediterranean Sea, the Red Sea and the Arabian Gulf.[119] Under proposals submitted by Iran the term 'enclosed sea' refers to 'a small body of inland waters surrounded by two or more states which is connected to the open seas by a narrow outlet'; whereas the expression 'semi-enclosed sea' is used to mean 'a basin located along the margins of the main ocean basins and enclosed by the land territories of two or more States'.[120] Examples of the former category, according to Iran, are the 'Persian Gulf' and the Baltic Sea; the latter category refers to such seas as the Caribbean and the Andaman.[121] The Iranian proposals emphasise the need for a special legal regime for enclosed and semi-enclosed seas, by providing for additional power and jurisdiction for the coastal States to adopt preventive and restrictive measures under regional arrangements regarding the uses of those seas, including the management and exploitation of the renewable resources, scientific research which would be conducted only with the consent of the coastal State concerned, and the prevention of marine pollution. No reference, however, is made to the question of international navigation through such seas, but in a statement made by the delegate of Iran it was stated that the coastal States of enclosed or semi-enclosed seas would have the right of 'freedom of passage' through straits connecting these seas to the oceans; while 'a different regime would apply to the navigation of other states whose ships could pass through straits connecting oceans with the semi-enclosed seas only for the purpose of calling at one of the ports of the semi-enclosed sea', because 'semi-enclosed seas such as the Persian Gulf were seas of destination rather than transit'.[122]

In contrast, the draft articles on enclosed and semi-enclosed seas submitted by Iraq place the emphasis on the freedom of navigation through semi-enclosed seas and the straits which connect them with the open oceans.[123] The Iraqi draft provides, *inter alia,* for freedom of navigation both in 'Semi-enclosed seas which constitute part of the high seas', and in straits 'which are customarily used for international navigation' and 'connecting two parts of the high seas, whether they are open seas or semi-enclosed seas'. According to the badly drafted Article 5:

The term 'Semi-enclosed seas which constitute part of the high seas' means an inland sea which is surrounded by two or more States, which may provide a corridor of the high seas between opposite and adjacent States and which is connected with other parts of the high seas by a narrow outlet.

Clearly the Iraqi proposal is designed so as to apply particularly to the Arabian Gulf and its entrance, the Strait of Hormuz. As noted elsewhere, the latter falls entirely within the territorial waters claimed by both Iran and Oman and can be controlled from the nearby Iranian-held islands of Abu Musa and Greater and Lesser Tumbs.[124] Thus the delegate of Iraq said that the item of 'enclosed and semi-enclosed seas' was of great importance to his country because Iraq:

> lay on a narrow semi-enclosed gulf that was its only access, through the Hormuz Strait, to the high seas. It was vital to his country to have free transit through that Strait and freedom of navigation in the area as a whole. Furthermore the existence of islands in the area should not hamper the freedom of navigation.[125]

However, the Iraqi draft also provides that the riparian States of semi-enclosed seas, through regional arrangements and with due consideration to the activities of the competent international organisation, should co-operate for the management and exploitation of the living resources and control of marine pollution of their sea.

Democratic Yemen, which borders the Straits of Bab el-Mandeb at the entrance of the Red Sea, asserted that 'the Red Sea was a semi-enclosed sea only in respect of matters relating to pollution', and said that it could not accept the concept of free passage in a vital region that was subject to heavy straits traffic; '... the question of navigation in straits must be decided on the basis of the principle of innocent passage', Democratic Yemen added.[126]

The Yemen Arab Republic, another Red Sea State, noted that the intensive and diverse activities that were carried on in 'closed and semi-closed' seas tended to centre on the exploitation of the natural resources of these waters. It therefore believed that 'If a comparison of interest was adopted as a basis for the control that a State might exercise over its adjacent waters, the coastal States [of closed and semi-closed seas] must be given full control and jurisdiction over such areas'.[127]

The Libyan Arab Republic considered that the Mediterranean Sea conformed to the definition of the 'semi-internal or semi-enclosed sea', and accordingly maintained that it should be 'a sea of peace, free from any foreign fleets that might threaten the security and health of the coastal peoples'.[128] The Soviet Union, on the other hand, claimed that the Mediterranean was neither enclosed nor semi-enclosed, but 'an immense body of water used as a high sea by all countries for all international shipping'.[129] Undoubtedly the Libyan call for the exclusion of foreign fleets from the Mediterranean is motivated by the deployment in that sea of naval fleets by the two super-powers. This was also the reason behind the proposal of Yugoslavia in 1968 to the other littoral States that a conference be convened to agree upon the exclusion of naval vessels of non-littoral countries.[130]

According to the provisions on 'enclosed and semi-enclosed seas' which are contained in the ICNT, the Mediterranean, the Red Sea and the Arabian Gulf would be considered as enclosed or semi-enclosed seas. The text makes no distinction between 'enclosed' and 'semi-enclosed' seas; both are collectively defied as:

> a gulf, basin, or sea surrounded by two or more States and connected to the open seas by a narrow outlet or consisting entirely or primarily of the territorial seas and exclusive economic zones of two or more coastal States.[131]

The text, however, sets up no special regime for enclosed and semi-enclosed seas, it provides only that States bordering such waters shall, in a manner consistent with other provisions of the convention, co-operate with each other directly or through an appropriate regional organisation in the exercise of their rights and duties under the convention. To this end, they shall co-ordinate the management, conservation, exploration and exploitation of the living resources of the sea; and co-ordinate the implementation of their rights and duties with respect to the preservation of the marine environment, and their scientific research policies.[132] These provisions reflect more the position of States which saw no need to make enclosed and semi-enclosed seas subject to a special regime or rules.[133]

2. Establishment of an international regime and authority for exploration and exploitation of the sea bed and ocean floor and subsoil thereof beyond the limits of national jurisdiction

It may be recalled that in an explanatory memorandum dated 17 August 1967[134] Ambassador Arvid Pardo of Malta submitted for consideration before the General Assembly of the United Nations an item which was allocated to the First Committee and inscribed on the agenda 'Examination of the question of the reservation exclusively for peaceful purposes of the sea bed and the ocean floor, and the subsoil thereof, underlying the high seas beyond the limits of national jurisdiction, and the use of their resources in the interests of mankind'.

On the recommendations of the First Committee, the General Assembly on 18 December 1967 decided to establish an *ad hoc* committee 'to study the peaceful uses of the sea bed and the ocean floor beyond the limits of national jurisdiction',[135] and on 15

December 1969 adopted Resolution 2574D (XXIV) which declared that, pending the establishment of an international sea bed regime:

(a) States and persons, physical or juridical, are bound to refrain from all activities of exploitation of the resources of the area of the sea bed and ocean floor, and the subsoil thereof, beyond the limits of national jurisdiction:

(b) No claim to any part of that area or its resources shall be recognised.[136]

Eventually on 17 December 1970, the General Assembly adopted Resolution 2449 (XXV), which contained the Declaration of Principles Governing the Sea Bed and the Ocean Floor, and the subsoil thereof, beyond the Limits of National Jurisdiction, by a vote of 108 in favour, none against, and 14 abstentions. The declaration set forth some fifteen principles which were to govern the sea bed and ocean floor beyond the limits of national jurisdiction. It begins with the principles that the international sea bed area and its resources 'are the common heritage of mankind', and 'shall not be subject to appropriation by any means by States or persons, natural or juridical, and no State shall claim sovereignty or sovereign rights over any part thereof'. The declaration further declares, *inter alia,* that:

3. No State or person, natural or juridical shall claim, exercise or acquire rights with respect to the area or its resources incompatible with the international regime to be established and the principles of this Declaration.

9. On the basis of the Principles of this Declaration, an international regime applying to the area and its resources and including appropriate international machinery to give effect to its provisions shall be established by an international treaty of a universal character generally agreed upon. The regime shall, *inter alia,* provide for the orderly and safe development and rational management of the area and its resources and for expanding opportunities in the use thereof, and ensure the equitable sharing by states in the benefits derived therefrom, taking into particular consideration the interests and needs of the developing countries, whether landlocked or coastal.[137]

Since its adoption the Declaration of Principles resolution has become the cornerstone of the negotiations for the establishment of an international regime and authority for the exploration and exploitation of the sea bed and the ocean floor beyond the limits of national jurisdiction. At the Third Conference these negotiations have centred on three major issues: the extent or limits of the international sea bed area, the nature of the international sea bed regime and authority, and the economic effects of deep sea bed exploitation. These issues will now be considered in more detail, each in turn.

A. LIMITS OF THE INTERNATIONAL SEA BED AREA. The question of the limits of the international sea bed area has in fact already been discussed above when the concept of the exclusive economic zone was considered. For it is generally agreed that the international area must begin where national jurisdiction ends. Thus the ICNT provides that the 'Area' means 'the sea bed and ocean floor and subsoil thereof beyond the limits of national jurisdiction'.[138] As noted above, the prevailing trends are those which provide that the outer limits of national jurisdiction should end, at least as far as sea bed resources are concerned, either at 200 miles or at the outer edge of the continental margin where this extends beyond 200 miles.

B. NATURE OF THE INTERNATIONAL SEA BED REGIME AND AUTHORITY. It is generally accepted that any system for the exploration and exploitation of the resources of international sea bed area (hereinafter called the 'area') should be based on principles which would give full effect to the concept of the 'common heritage of mankind' which was embodied in the Declaration of Principles. The terms of the latter would seem to indicate that the basic ideas of the 'common heritage of mankind' concept are that the area and its resources are the common heritage of mankind; the area shall not be subject to appropriation by any means by States or persons, natural or juridical; the area shall be open to use exclusively for peaceful purposes by all States; and that the exploration of the area and the exploitation of its resources shall be carried for the benefit of mankind as a whole.[139]

The views of States, however, have sharply differed on the ways and means of implementing these basic ideas. First, there have been differences on the question of who may explore and exploit the area. Two main approaches have been put forward. The developed or industrial countries would prefer all exploration and exploitation to be carried out by a contracting party or group of contracting parties or natural or juridical persons under its or their authority or sponsorship, subject to the terms and conditions set down in the proposed convention and to regulations by the international authority.[140] The role of the latter would thus be limited to a licensing role. This approach, according to its advocates, would have the advantage of avoiding the practical and financial

GENERAL PRACTICE AND POLICIES

difficulties of exploitation by the international authority itself. It has been opposed by the developing countries, who believe that, in accordance with the concept that the resources of the area are the 'common heritage of mankind', the international authority should have powers to control and undertake direct all activities relating to exploration and exploitation in the area, to ensure that the benefits derived therefrom will go to the benefit of all mankind. Accordingly, the developing countries of the 'Group of Seventy-seven'[141] proposed a system giving the international authority the right to engage direct in the exploration of the area and the exploitation of its resources and all other related activities, including those of scientific research, but which would allow the international authority, if it considered it appropriate, to confer certain tasks upon juridical or natural persons through service contracts or other means.[142]

Secondly, whereas the proposals submitted by a number of industrial countries contain some detailed rules and regulations as well as technical details regarding the terms and conditions of exploration and exploitation of the area, the 'Group of Seventy-seven' holds the view that the proposed treaty should contain only the basic essential principles to guide the international authority in establishing detailed rules and regulations. The developing countries prefer a flexible approach because they fear that the inclusion of rigid rules and regulations in the treaty might weaken the power of the international authority, and could have a paralysing effect on its role in future decades.

As to the Middle Eastern States, many of them have emphasised the importance of the Declaration of Principles and especially the concept of the 'common heritage of mankind' because they contain the basic guidelines fundamental to the establishment of an international regime and authority for the deep-sea-bed area.[143]

As oil-producing countries Kuwait and Iraq have expressed strong opposition to the idea that the international authority should be merely a licensing authority. Thus Iraq expressed that it:

> had greatly suffered from the activities of oil companies and did not want the Authority to fall into the hands of monopolies. It should not be merely a licensing agency, but should undertake exploration and exploitation directly or through contracts with States. In any case, all activities should be under its strict control and supervision.[144]

Kuwait believed that the international authority should have comprehensive powers and functions, including 'the organisation, administration, control and co-ordination of all operations relating to the development of Sea Bed resources'.[145]

Similarly, Iran considered that:

> The powers of the International Authority should be as wide as possible. It should not only have the right to undertake directly the exploration and exploitation of the resources of the international zone but also be empowered to resolve all problems arising from such operations. It should make use of market studies to prevent any harmful consequences from the mining of minerals.[146]

Libya stressed that the main function of the international authority should be to control all economic and related activities in the area and to carry out direct exploration and exploitation of the sea bed and its resources. It emphasised:

> A licensing system would not be in keeping with the interests of the developing countries, which were well aware that joint management was the most important and revolutionary aspect of the concept that the international area was the common heritage of mankind.[147]

Egypt has accepted the proposal of the 'Group of Seventy-seven' because it 'had been formulated in a spirit of compromise' and 'it contained an element of flexibility in the form of provisions enabling the Authority to enter into contractual arrangements with third parties'.[148]

Finally, it is worth noting that Annex II of the ICNT contains draft provisions relating to the basic conditions of exploration and exploitation of the area in which, according to Article 151 of the text, the activities shall be 'carried out on the Authority's behalf' either by the enterprise (the organ through which the authority would directly carry out activities in the area) or, in association with the authority, by States parties to the convention, their entities or firms. Article 151 adds that national and private entities engaged in such activities must undertake, 'through contractual or other arrangements, ... to contribute the technological capability, financial and other resources necessary to enable the Authority to fulfil its functions'.[149]

C. ECONOMIC EFFECTS OF DEEP-SEA-BED EXPLOITATION. In the Preamble to the Declaration of Principles resolution the General Assembly stressed, *inter alia,* that the development of the area and its resources should be undertaken in such a manner as to 'minimise any adverse economic effects caused by the fluctuation of prices of raw materials from such activities'. In the related Resolution 2750A (XXV), 17 December 1970, therefore, the Assembly requested the Secretary General to identify in collaboration with the United Nations Conference on Trade and Development

(UNCTAD) and other competent organisations of the UN, the problems arising from the extraction of certain minerals from the area and examine the impact they would have on the economic well-being of the developing countries, in particular on prices of mineral exports on the world market.

In 1971 the United Nations secretariat prepared a preliminary assessment which, in brief, showed that it was apparent that technological developments would eventually make deep-sea petroleum and manganese nodule exploitation not only technically possible but also commercially feasible. But it was found unlikely that in the near future petroleum markets would be affected in any significant way by production from areas beyond the 200-metre isobath because of the higher cost of deep-water production and the wide availability of petroleum in shallow parts of the shelves. It was felt, however, that manganese nodules which contain copper, cobalt, manganese and nickel in great quantities, might be simultaneously produced from deep waters but that the impact of such production on world markets was expected to be fairly minor by 1980, and probably still not very serious by the end of the century. Since the weight ratio of the metal recoverable from the nodules is very different from that of the world metal demand, the impact of nodule exploitation on the markets will vary considerably from one metal to another.[150]

More recent and comprehensive studies of the economic implications of sea bed mining were considered at the Third Conference.[151] During the discussion it was indicated that all the proved reserves to date of hydrocarbon resources fall within the limit of the proposed 200-miles exclusive economic zone, and that the total ultimate hydrocarbon resources of the areas seaward of 200 nautical miles were estimated to be equivalent to approximately 284 billion barrels of oil or 13 per cent of total offshore resources. But in view of the great depth of these areas the economic possibilities were considered to be remote. It was also shown that any adverse economic impact as a result of commercial mining of sea bed manganese nodules, when or if commercial production was undertaken, would fall most heavily upon the developing countries of Morocco and Zambia as the main exporters of cobalt. The production of nickel, copper and manganese, it was indicated, would not have a serious effect on land-based production as a whole, but cobalt production from the deep sea bed could account for about half the volume of world output and might cause a substantial reduction in the price of cobalt by 1985. But it was stressed that 'There appears to be a consensus, even among experts, that, in the nature of things, no available figures are in fact entirely reliable in reflecting current realities, let alone future ones'.[152] However, it was suggested that the international authority might have to establish a permanent technical subsidiary organ for the purpose of ensuring that no adverse effects flow from future exploitation, and which would also have the power to exercise control over the rate of exploitation. A few industrialised countries, including the United States, the United Kingdom and Japan, argued that demand for manganese nodules would increase in the future and that any resources acquired from the deep sea bed would simply represent a small marginal supplement to supplies from land-based resources and would not cause a reduction in prices.[153] These countries, therefore, have opposed the idea of the international authority exercising control over the rate of future sea bed exploitation of manganese nodules.

However, the ICNT envisages the setting up of an Economic Planning Commission which, *inter alia*:

... in consultation with the competent organs of the United Nations, its specialised agencies and any other intergovernmental organisation with responsibilities relating to minerals which are also derived from the Area, shall review the trends of, and factors affecting, supply, demand and prices of raw materials which may be obtained from the Area, bearing in mind the interests of both consuming and producing countries, and in particular the developing countries among them.[154]

In view of the above considerations, and the fact that none of the Middle Eastern States is a producer of manganese nodules, it seems that the production of such minerals from the sea bed would not have any adverse impact on their economy. However, the oil-producing countries, especially Iran, Iraq and Kuwait, presumably fear that there might be some adverse effects on the price of oil from future sea bed exploitation. These States, therefore, have stressed that:

Only an International Authority with comprehensive powers ... would ensure rational exploitation and would prevent waste and mismanagement. It should establish an order of priority for exploitation based on the requirements of world development, taking into account the special situation of developing countries that produce non-renewable minerals.[155]

3. *Control of marine pollution and regulation of scientific research and transfer of technology*

A. CONTROL OF MARINE POLLUTION. At the Third Conference the question of marine pollution control has been discussed with

GENERAL PRACTICE AND POLICIES

reference to both the area within the limits of national jurisdiction, that is the exclusive economic zone, and the area beyond these limits, the international sea bed area. Three main sources of marine pollution have been considered: vessel-source pollution, pollution from sea bed exploitation, and pollution from land-based sources. As regards the latter, which is considered the major source of marine pollution, the developing countries insisted that any international standards should take into account their economic capacity and their need for economic development. If this concern were taken into consideration, the developed countries felt, it would permit double standards. It has, therefore, been generally accepted that it would suffice to include in the proposed treaty some general obligation to encourage States to take national and regional measures to prevent and control land-based pollution.[156]

With respect to pollution from sea bed exploitation, the main question has been that of pollution arising from activities carried on in areas within the limits of national jurisdiction. The developing coastal States emphasised that they should exercise the necessary jurisdiction for pollution control in areas corresponding to their respective exclusive economic zones. The maritime powers, however, argued that regulations made by States in these cases might lead to restrictions on the freedom of navigation and create problems for international shipping. They have therefore demanded that States should apply only international standards in such areas.[157] As to pollution arising from activities carried out in the international sea bed area, it is generally agreed that the international authority would take the appropriate measures for the adoption and implementation of international rules and standards for the prevention of marine pollution.[158]

With regard to pollution from shipping, there has been widespread support for the regional and general multilateral agreements that have dealt with this source of pollution, including the International Convention for the Prevention of Pollution from Ships, 1973,[159] and the 1972 London Convention on the Prevention of Marine Pollution by Dumping of Wastes and other Matter.[160] Differences arose, however, on the question of the extent of the rights of coastal States to deal with this type of pollution within the exclusive economic zone. The developing countries took the position that the coastal States should have complete jurisdiction to establish and enforce national regulations in addition to the international standards contained in existing international conventions. The maritime States, supported by landlocked States, argued that coastal States should have no jurisdiction over foreign vessels in areas beyond the territorial sea.[161]

Since they border on some of the busiest international sea routes and are most vulnerable to oil pollution, the Middle Eastern States have a general as well as direct interest in the preservation of the marine environment and control of marine pollution. At the Third Conference, therefore, many of them expressed support for international and regional regulations to preserve the marine environment from further deterioration and control marine pollution. They stressed the importance of the 1973 International Convention for the Prevention of Pollution from Ships, which designates the Mediterranean Sea, the Red Sea, and the 'Gulfs area', that is, the Arabian Gulf and the Gulf of Oman, among the 'special areas' that required additional precautions for the protection of the marine environment. They also urged further regional cooperation for the control of marine pollution in such areas and emphasised the important role that could be played by the Intergovernmental Maritime Consultative Organisation (IMCO) and other organisations. Kuwait commended the work of IMCO and hoped that the Third Conference would be able to integrate its contribution in the articles on pollution.[162]

Egypt took the view that within the 200-mile exclusive economic zone the coastal States must observe and enforce international standards, especially with regard to shipping and sea bed mining. She recognised, however, the need for special arrangements between coastal States whose area of national jurisdiction could not extend for 200 miles without overlapping, 'as in the case of certain closed and semi-closed seas'.[163] This is probably a reference particularly to the Red Sea and the Mediterranean, on which Egypt borders. Egypt also emphasised the need for a revision of existing international rules on liability in view of the 'rapid development in ship design, sea transport techniques and navigation aids', believing also that a future convention 'must contain clear obligations for flag States and port States without unduly hampering shipping schedules'.[164]

With a coastline 2,000 kilometres long, Libya stated that it took marine pollution problems seriously, especially 'because it was planning the use of the water for drinking and agriculture to compensate for its shortage of fresh water'. It considered that 'national laws were needed which gave States the right to intervene in order to prevent pollution', and called for the establishment of checking points 'in order to verify that ships were complying with international regulations concerning pollution'.[165]

Both Iraq and Iran considered that in semi-enclosed seas such as the Arabian Gulf regional and sub-regional measures to prevent and control marine pollution would be most effective.[166] In addition, Iran subscribed to the zonal approach for the preservation of the marine environment, and in co-operation with Canada and other States submitted to the Third Conference some draft articles which, *inter alia,* provide that coastal States should take all necessary measures to prevent pollution of the marine environment from any source and to ensure that activities under their jurisdiction or control do not cause damage to areas beyond their national jurisdiction. The articles also express that the coastal State, as a consequence of its jurisdiction over its exclusive economic zone, had the obligation to preserve the marine environment and to take adequate steps for the purposes of preventing and controlling pollution.[167]

B. REGULATION OF SCIENTIFIC RESEARCH AND TRANSFER OF TECHNOLOGY. The discussion of the question of marine scientific research has centred mainly on research in the area within national jurisdiction, for the developing countries wanted all research in the economic zone to be subject to the consent of the coastal State. The developed countries, on the other hand, at the beginning urged the need for full freedom of scientific research in the zone, but later proposed to distinguish between so-called 'pure research', where notification should suffice, and research related to the resources of the economic zone, in respect of which the consent of coastal State should be required. This proposal has been criticised by the 'Group of Seventy-seven' and other countries on the grounds that it is impossible to distinguish between pure and resource-orientated research. On this point, the ICNT provides, *inter alia,* that:

Marine scientific research activities in the exclusive zone and on the continental shelf shall be conducted with the consent of the coastal State.[168]

Within the international sea bed area, the ICNT provides that marine scientific research shall be carried out exclusively for peaceful purposes and for the benefit of mankind as a whole.[169]

As to development and transfer of technology, the ICNT states, *inter alia,* that:

States shall promote the development of the marine scientific and technological capacity of the States which may need and request technical assistance in this field, particularly developing States, including landlocked and geographically disadvantaged States, with regard to the exploration, exploitation, conservation and management of marine resources, the preservation of marine environment, scientific research and other uses of the marine environment compatible with this Convention, with a view to accelerating the social and economic development of the developing States.[170]

Many of the Middle Eastern States took the view that scientific research within the area of national jurisdiction should be carried on only with the consent of the coastal State. They also emphasised the need to facilitate the transfer of technology. Thus Sudan subscribed to the view that marine scientific research in the area within the national jurisdiction of coastal States should be subject to the prior consent of the coastal State concerned, whereas in the area beyond national jurisdiction, scientific research should be conducted in compliance with 'the spirit and intentions of the concept that the resources of that area were the common heritage of mankind'.[171] With regard to transfer of technology, Sudan said that the envisaged international authority should co-ordinate all technical assistance programmes and transfer of technology, and that States in a region where scientific research was being conducted should participate in that research.[172]

Iran shared the view that in the exclusive economic zone the conduct of scientific research should be subject to the prior consent of the coastal State; it also considered that such research should be compatible with the research programmes of the coastal State, that personnel from that State should participate in the research activities and that the results should be placed at the disposal of the coastal State. In the international zone, according to Iran, the proposed international sea bed authority should be responsible for safeguarding the interests of the international community as a whole, and scientific research in that area would be subject to the consent of the authority, which could also engage in scientific research on its own.[173] On the question of transfer of technology, Iran stressed that:

> technology should cease to be the monopoly of certain states and that all countries should participate on an equal footing in the exploitation of what was termed 'the common heritage of mankind'. The transfer of technology could be carried out through the Authority, in collaboration with the International Hydrographic Bureau and the Intergovernmental Oceanographic Commission, on the lines of the work already carried out in that field by the fisheries commissions.[174]

Iraq believed that in areas where there were special circumstances, such as semi-enclosed seas, scientific research beyond the limits of the territorial sea should be conducted by all the coastal States through regional arrangements and with assistance from the specialised agencies and the technologically advanced countries.[175]

Libya proposed the setting up, under the supervision of the proposed international authority, of technical and scientific training programmes for personnel from developing countries.[176]

C. CONCLUSION

The Middle Eastern States are having less influence on the current reshaping of the international law of the sea than other developing States, such as those of Latin America. Indeed, their policies with regard to many of the issues discussed at the Third Conference are the result of their response or reaction to trends evolved through the practice of, and to proposals made by, other States. However, like many of the present members of the United Nations, many of the Middle Eastern States did not take part in previous United Nations conferences on the law of the sea; and the fact that all of them are actively participating in the work of the Third Conference is in itself a considerable contribution to the attempt at developing a law of the sea more satisfactory to the developing as well as the developed countries.

It is widely recognised that the aim of the Third Conference is to adopt a package deal, covering almost every aspect of the law of the sea and, at the same time, achieving an overall balance between all the interests involved. The Middle Eastern States, like most developing countries, have no great strategic interests; their interests are basically economic in nature. It is difficult to predict what the final outcome of the conference will be, but if it is successful at least parts of the package are likely to be satisfactory to the Middle Eastern States. No State can expect all its requirements to be fully met.

In conclusion, it may be worth summarising briefly the attitudes of the Middle Eastern States towards some of the main issues before the Third Conference. On the question of the breadth of the territorial sea, all the States seem ready to accept a general agreement on a twelve-mile limit. As far as straits are concerned, some Middle Eastern States, especially those bordering on straits, advocate the principle of non-suspendable innocent passage for foreign ships, particularly warships, whereas others, especially Iraq, support the newly introduced principle of 'free' or 'transit' passage; the majority of them, however, insist that the regime of straits should be strictly confined to straits which connect two parts of the high seas. As regards the 200-mile exclusive economic zone, the concept is generally acceptable to all Middle Eastern States except Kuwait. Finally, as far as the exploration and exploitation of the sea bed and ocean floor and subsoil thereof beyond the limits of national jurisdiction are concerned, like most developing countries, the Middle Eastern States believe that the proposed international authority should be essentially an operating rather than a licensing authority.

PART TWO
SPECIFIC REGIONAL ISSUES

CHAPTER III

LEGAL PROBLEMS OF OFFSHORE BOUNDARIES IN THE ARABIAN GULF

The Arabian Gulf is:

a body of water that extends southeastward for about 500 miles (805 km) from the mouth of the Shatt al-Arab Channel in Iraq to the Musandum Peninsula and varies in width from 50 miles (80 km) at the head to 200 miles (322 km) at it widest part. 'The Gulf', however, is a term frequently used to refer not only to the Persian Gulf proper but also to its outlets, the 50-miles (80 km) wide Strait of Hormuz and the Gulf of Oman, which open into the Arabian Sea. In the Persian Gulf the depth of water rarely exceeds 50 fathoms and increases more rapidly from the Iranian than from the Arabian shore. Off the Arabian coast there are large areas of water less than 20 fathoms deep where valuable pearl banks occur.

There are eight political units with shorelines on the Gulf. Iran occupies the entire north-eastern shore and the head east of Shat al-Arab. Iraq has a 40 miles (64 km) wide frontage west of that river. The Arabian side is divided among Kuwait, Saudi Arabia, Bahrain, Qatar, the United Arab Emirates and Oman.

The coasts of the Persian Gulf have a total length of nearly 2,000 miles (3,219 km).[1]

This chapter is concerned with legal problems of the delimitation of the boundaries of the continental shelf and the related issue of islands of disputed sovereignty in the Arabian Gulf.

It may be recalled that because the depth of the waters of the Gulf rarely exceeds 50 fathoms (100 metres), it is accepted internationally that the whole sea bed of the Gulf is in the legal sense continental shelf.[2] This being so, the continental shelf claims of the littoral States which are either opposite or adjacent to each other converge and overlap. Recognising this situation, as shown in Chapter I, in their relevant national laws, therefore, the Gulf States did not attempt to specify the seaward limits of their respective continental shelf areas. They expressly stipulated instead that sea bed boundaries shall be determined, as the opportunity calls, in accordance with 'equitable' or 'just' principles by 'agreement' or after 'consultation' with neighbouring States. The 1958 Iraqi proclamation, however, referred to 'international practice... and to the principle of equidistance'. Reference to this principle is also made in the Omani law, which in addition defines the continental shelf on the basis of the criteria adopted in Article 1 of the 1958 Convention on the Continental Shelf, that is, the 200-metre depth and the exploitability test.[3]

The problem of offshore boundaries in the Arabian Gulf has assumed significance in the eyes of the local governments primarily as a result of the discovery of oil there. It became quite evident then that possession of a few miles of submarine area could make the difference between owning or not owning a profitable oilfield.[4] As will be shown, conflicting claims over submarine boundaries, especially in the higher Gulf, have in many cases first arisen as a result of the overlapping of offshore oil concession areas. In some instances oil concessionaires refused to proceed with drilling operations in zones of overlap until some agreement or understanding on the delimitation of boundaries was reached, presumably because they feared to invest substantial amounts of money in exploration in areas which might subsequently be contested.

The Gulf exhibits features that in connection with the issue of boundaries raise many important and frequently complex problems. At the northern end of the Gulf a particular problem is caused by the special configuration and short extent of the Iraqi coastline. The presence of a large number of proven and probable petroleum deposits brings up the question of the relevance of the location of such deposits to the issue of delimitation.[5] The chief difficulty, however, is created by the presence of islands and other similar features, which are not only numerous and scattered throughout the Gulf but commonly the subject of disputed sovereignty.[6]

International law provides some principles and guidelines for the delimitation of national boundaries on the continental shelf, but by no means for all the questions involved. In the light of such and other relevant principles of international law, it is now proposed to consider in more detail the legal problems relating to the delimitation of continental shelf boundaries and islands of disputed sovereignty in the Arabian Gulf. Although in many cases such problems have been settled, a few important questions are still outstanding. The settled problems will be examined in the following section, and those outstanding in the following one, bearing always in mind that none of the Arabian Gulf States is a party to the Convention on the Continental Shelf or any of the other 1958 conventions on the law of the sea.

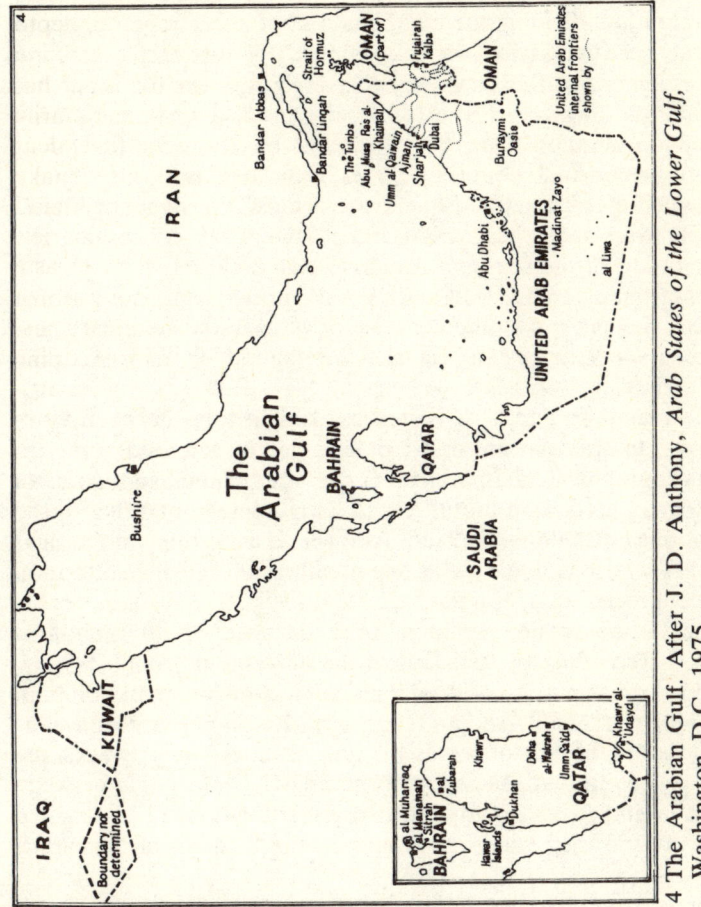

4 The Arabian Gulf. After J. D. Anthony, *Arab States of the Lower Gulf*, Washington, D.C., 1975.

SPECIFIC REGIONAL ISSUES
A. SETTLED PROBLEMS

1. Bahrain–Saudi Arabia boundary agreement[7]
The Bahrain–Saudi Arabia agreement on the delimitation of the boundary line dividing the continental shelf areas appertaining to each of these two States, whose coasts are opposite each other, and the settlement of the question of sovereignty over the islands of Lubainah al-Saghirah (little Lubainah) and Lubainah al-Kabirab (Greater Lubinah), is of special interest as it was the first of its kind to be concluded between States of the Arabian Gulf.

Having referred to the respective proclamations of Saudi Arabia and Bahrain of 29 May 1949 and 5 June 1949 concerning the exploitation of the sea bed, which, as noted earlier, refer for the delimitation of sea bed boundaries to the principle of equity and of justice, the present agreement provides that the boundary line between Saudi Arabia and Bahrain is delimited 'on the basis of the median line'.[8]

The boundary line is delimited by straight lines between fourteen points whose locations are determined by reference either to fixed geographical landmarks on both Bahraini and Saudi Arabian territory or to certain latitudes and longitudes. Everything to the left of this line belongs to Saudi Arabia and everything to the right of it belongs to Bahrain, with one qualification to which attention will be directed in a moment.[9]

The boundary line extends for a distance of 98½ nautical miles.[10] According to Article 1 of the agreement, points 1–7, 10 and 11 represent *mid-points* of lines connecting landmarks on both Bahraini and Saudi Arabian territory. It has, however, been indicated that in the case of points 1–4 and 7 small islands between the coasts were not utilised in determining the mid-point between Bahraini and Saudi Arabian territory.[11] If these small islands had been utilised they would have altered the location of the points involved.

Points 8 and 9 are located on the islands of Lubainah al-Sagirah and Lubainah al-Kabirah respectively, in such a way that the former island is left to Bahrain and the latter to Saudi Arabia. No territorial sea is attributed to any of these two islands, presumably because the surrounding area is constricted.[12]

Points 12–14 of the boundary line are determined by reference solely to geographical co-ordinates. As a result, the Fasht Bu Saafa hexagon, an area of proven petroleum resources and approximately double the size of Bahrain, is to the left of the boundary line and hence under the jurisdiction of Saudi Arabia. However,

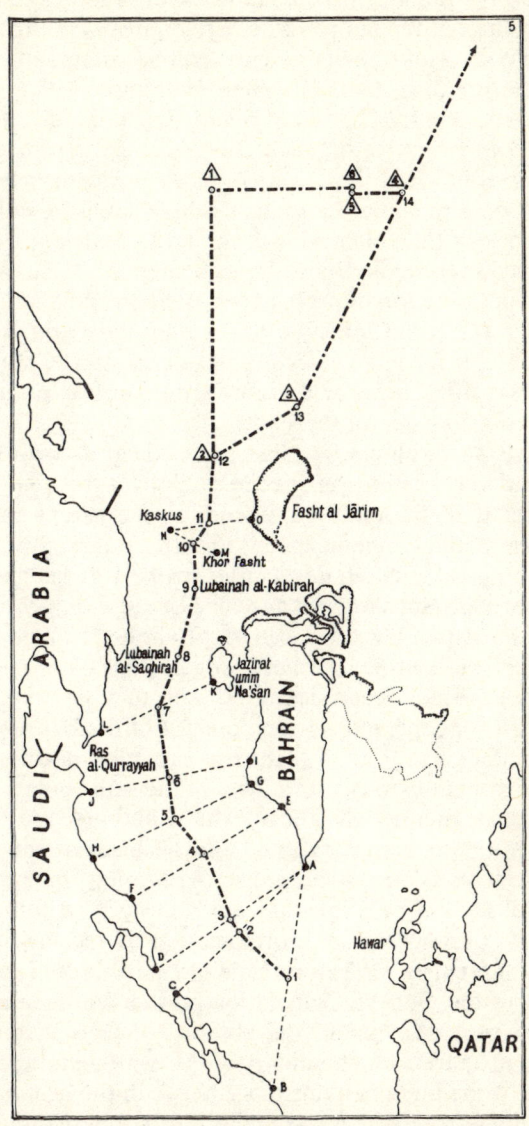

5 Bahrain–Saudi Arabia continental shelf boundary. After *Limits in the Seas*, Series A, No. 12, Office of the Geographer, Bureau of Intelligence and Research, U.S. Department of State, Washington, D.C., 10 March 1970.

Article 2 of the agreement provides that this area shall be developed in the manner which Saudi Arabia chooses, on condition that one half of the net revenue derived from the exploitation of the petroleum resources of this area shall be granted to Bahrain, on the understanding that this shall not impair 'the right of sovereignty and administration' of Saudi Arabia in the said area.

The locations of points 8, 9 and 12–14, and the solution concerning the resources of the Fasht Bu Saafa hexagon, were motivated by a desire to settle the long-standing claims of Bahrain to the two islands of Lubainah al-Sagirah and Lubainah al-Kabirah, and the Fasht Bu Saafa hexagon. It has been pointed out also that at one stage of the negotiations between Bahrain and Saudi Arabia the latter agreed to the principle of dividing the Fasht Bu Saafa hexagon, but later the present solution was accepted by both countries, because differences of opinion arose on the principle of drawing the dividing line of the Fasht.[13]

From point 14 the boundary line proceeds in a north-easterly direction, but no terminus is specified in the agreement, which instead states that the line then extends to the extent consistent with both the Saudi pronouncement and the Bahraini proclamation concerning the exploitation of the sea bed. It has been said that a northern terminus was not specified because of jurisdictional disputes then existing between Iran and Bahrain.[14] The boundary lines between the continental shelves of Bahrain–Iran and Saudi Arabia–Iran have now been delimited, and they meet at a point which lies 12¼ nautical miles from point 14 of the Bahrain–Saudi Arabia boundary line.[15] If the latter is extended north-easterly, therefore, it would obviously terminate in the same point.

Although, as mentioned above, the Bahrain–Saudi Arabia agreement refers to boundary lines 'on the basis of the median line' and also to 'mid-points', according to one view this agreement does not utilise 'the principle of equidistance'.[16] Another view suggests that it embodies an approximation to the median line, modified by agreement.[17] The principle of equidistance is reflected in Article 6 of the Geneva Convention on the Continental Shelf, 1958, which provides that in the absence of 'agreement' or of 'special circumstances', the boundary of the continental shelf is the median line or the line of equidistance between the nearest points of the baselines from which the breadth of the territorial sea of each State is measured. According to Article 1 of the same convention, which is regarded as reflecting a rule of customary international law,[18] islands as well as mainland coasts generate continental shelves.

Before commenting on these views, it may be useful to recall a few relevant considerations. First of all, like all the other States of the Arabian Gulf, Bahrain and Saudi Arabia are not parties to the Convention on the Continental Shelf, and their present agreement was signed and ratified before the signature of that convention; however, they must assuredly have been aware of the discussions on the contents of Article 6 and other provisions of the convention that had taken place in the International Law Commission.

Secondly, in its judgement in the North Sea Continental Shelf cases, 1969,[19] which dealt with the delimitation of lateral boundaries between adjacent States, the International Court of Justice, rejecting the view that the equidistance method of delimitation was a mandatory rule of customary law, and observing that there is no single method of delimitation the use of which is in all circumstances obligatory, has found that 'delimitation is to be affected by agreement in accordance with equitable principles'.[20] The Court also specified some of the 'factors' which States should take into account in the course of the negotiations for a delimitation. These include the configuration and length of the coasts of the States concerned and, so far as known or readily ascertainable, the physical and geological structure, and natural resources, of the continental shelf areas involved.[21]

Throughout its judgement the Court emphasised that, under certain conditions of coastal configuration which are frequently met with, a lateral equidistance line, despite its known advantages, leads unquestionably to inequity in the sense that it leaves to one of the States concerned areas that are a natural prolongation of the territory of the other.[22] On the other hand, the Court indicated that an equidistance line in the form of a median line is the only means for the delimitation of the continental shelf areas off, and dividing, opposite States and that, ignoring the presence of islets, rocks and minor coastal projections—the disproportionally distorting effect of which can be eliminated by other means—such a line leads to equitable results because it leaves to each of the States concerned all those parts of the continental shelf that can be claimed to constitute a natural prolongation of its land territory into and under the sea.[23]

This indication, taken together with other observations made by the Court in the course of its judgement,[24] may be understood to imply that in the opinion of the Court the equidistance line in its median line form may be regarded as a general principle of law.[25] This implication, however, is weakened by other evidence in the judgement, including the following view of the Court:

It emerges from the history of the development of the legal regime of the Continental Shelf ... that the essential reason why the equidistance method is not to be regarded as a rule of law is that, if it were to be compulsorily applied in all situations, this would not be consonant with certain legal notions which ... have from the beginning reflected the *opinio juris* in the matter of delimitation; those principles being that delimitation must be the object of agreement between the States concerned, and that such agreement must be arrived at in accordance with equitable principles.[26]

In the light of the foregoing considerations, it would appear that the main question with regard to the Bahrain–Saudi Arabia agreement is not whether it has utilised the principle of equidistance or not, but whether the delimitation has been affected in accordance with equitable principles. But since, as indicated by the International Court of Justice, the median line method of delimitation normally achieves an equitable limit between opposite States, and the first article of the present agreement, together with the revealed part of the negotiations, suggests that the median line has provided the starting point for the delimitation of the boundary line between Bahrain and Saudi Arabia, the question that may be asked is whether the deviation from the strict application of the median line is justified by 'special circumstances' or made in order to achieve a more equitable delimitation. Here attention will be focused on the two main instances where points of the boundary line between Bahrain and Saudi Arabia were not determined according to the equidistance principle. The first instance concerns points 1–4 and 7, where small islands between the coasts of the two countries were ignored.[27] This case, however, may be justified because, although, as noted earlier, the general principle is that islands should be taken into account in drawing the median line boundary, most authorities agree that the presence of minor islands or islets may constitute 'special circumstances' justifying the deviation of the boundary from the median line.[28] This understanding about small islands, as indicated above, was also recognised by the International Court of Justice in the North Sea Shelf cases, 1969, when it said that, ignoring the presence of islets, rocks and minor coastal projections, the disproportionately distorting effect of which can be eliminated by other means, a median line must effect an equal division of the particular area involved.[29]

The other instance involves points 12–14 of the Bahraini–Saudi Arabian boundary line, whose location is based on geographical co-ordinates and irrespective of the equidistance principle, presumably in order to preserve the unity of the Fasht Bu Saafa oil deposit. Although, in the North Sea Continental Shelf cases, 1969, the International Court mentioned natural resources 'so far as known or readily ascertainable' as a factor to be taken into account in the course of the negotiations for a delimitation,[30] this should not mean that just because a boundary line would otherwise divide a single deposit between two countries it should for that reason be diverted to give one or the other exclusive jurisdiction over it. For the Court did not consider that unity of deposit constitutes anything more than 'a factual element which it is reasonable to take into consideration in the course of the negotiations'.[31] As Judge Ammoun rightly maintained:

> If the preservation of the unity of deposit is a matter of concern to the Parties, they must provide for this by a voluntary agreement (by transfer or joint exploitation), and this does not fall within the category of a factor or rule of delimitation.[32]

Indeed, the existence of a common deposit 'would scarcely seem to constitute a "special circumstance", however, entitling a coastal State to demand a deviation' from the median line or equidistance line.[33] There seems to be no reason, therefore, why points 12–14 of the boundary line between Saudi Arabia and Bahrain have not been located on the basis of the median line. At the same time the parties could have agreed on joint exploitation or profit-sharing in the Fasht Bu Saafa oil deposit.[34] It should be said, however, that at the time Bahrain and Saudi Arabia concluded their agreement some authorities expressed support for the view that a boundary line should not cross a common deposit.[35]

2. Agreement concerning the Sovereignty over the Islands of Al-'Arabiyah and Farsi and the Delimitation of the Boundary Line separating the Submarine Areas between the Kingdom of Saudi Arabia and Iran[36]

The need to define the offshore boundaries between Iran and Saudi Arabia, which lie opposite each other, did not become pressing until the 1960s, when offshore explorations indicated the probable presence of large oil reserves towards the centre of the Arabian Gulf.[37] Thus in a statement issued on 15 June 1963[38] the Saudi government claimed that both the concession granted by Iran to the Iran Pan-American Oil Company (IPAC) in April 1958[39] and Area 2, District I, of the Iranian pre-announcement of 1 April 1958[40] constituted an infringement of the concession area granted by Saudi Arabia to the Arabian American Oil Company (ARAMCO) in 1948.[41] Talks between Saudi Arabia and Iran about this matter were held in August 1963, and it was agreed in principle that joint exploitation of the disputed area would be in the interest of the two sides.[42] On 13 December 1965 the two countries initialled an agreement based on the median line principle delimiting their submarine boundaries.[43] The agreement, however, was never ratified, because of the reluctance of the Iranians, who, after new oil resources were discovered in the northern zone of the 1965 proposed boundary line, felt that the agreement did not provide an equitable division of the area involved.[44]

The present agreement between Saudi Arabia and Iran, which, according to its Preamble, 'with due respect to the principles of the law and particular circumstances', determines 'in a just and accurate manner the boundary line separating the respective submarine areas over which each Party is entitled by international law to exercise sovereign rights', is a modification of the 1965 median line agreement. It revises the line between points 8 and 14 of the 1965 boundary line, giving only a slight net gain in sea bed area to Iran, but presumably a substantial increase in Iran's share of estimated oil reserves.[45] The agreement also resolves the long-standing difference between the two parties regarding sovereignty over the islands of Al-'Arabiyah and Farsi.

As regards the islands of Al-'Arabiyah and Farsi, these normally uninhabited islands have housed military garrisons in the past and are situated well towards the middle of the Gulf, but somewhat closer to the Saudi Arabian coast, with Farsi being the nearer to Iran. The maximum elevation on both islands is about 10 ft.[46] The problem of these two islands was settled by mutual recognition of the sovereignty of Saudi Arabia over the island of Al-'Arabiyah and of Iran over the island of Farsi.[47]

The boundary line between Saudi Arabia and Iran settles the longest single continental shelf boundary in the Arabian Gulf (some 138¾ nautical miles).[48] Except in the vicinity of Al-'Arabiyah and Farsi, the offshore boundary is determined by straight lines between some fourteen points whose latitudes and longitudes were specified in the agreement. The southern segment of the boundary line between points 1 and A is essentially a median line between the two opposite mainlands.[49] Point 1 is the site where the continental shelf boundaries between Iran–Saudi Arabia, Iran–Bahrain and Bahrain–Saudi Arabia, if extended north-easterly, would intersect.[50]

In the vicinity of Al-'Arabiyah and Farsi the boundary line reflects the agreement's settlement of the question of sovereignty over the two islands in question. The continental shelf boundary

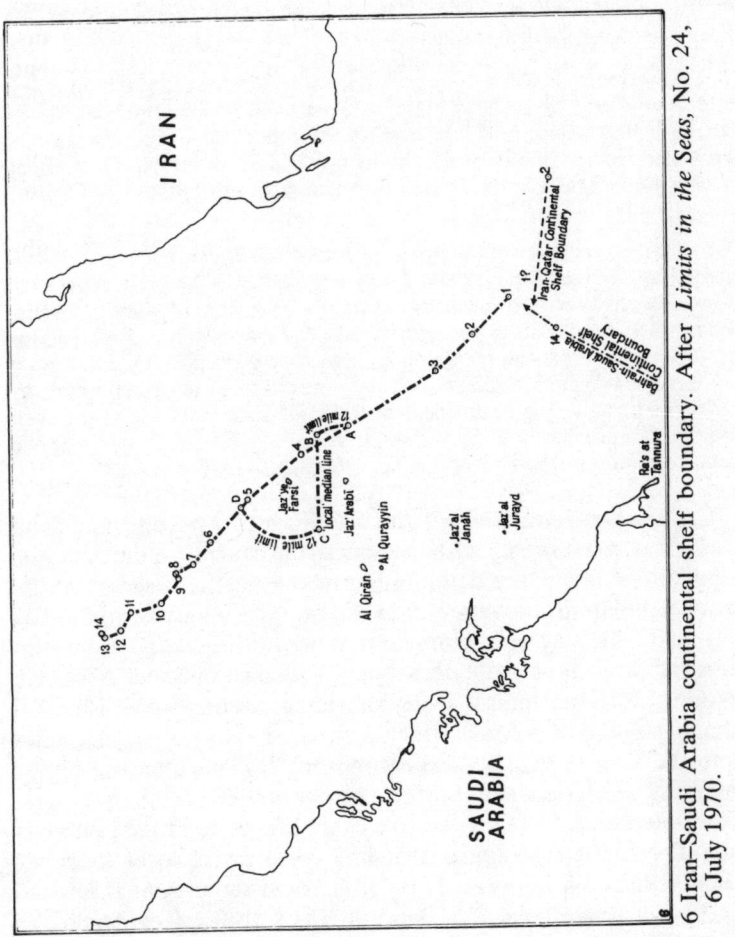

6 Iran–Saudi Arabia continental shelf boundary. After *Limits in the Seas*, No. 24, 6 July 1970.

around these islands was delimited by giving effect to the twelve-mile territorial seas of the respective islands to the extent of actually deviating the boundary from the median line. However, these two islands were not possessed of any continental shelf rights beyond their own territorial seas.[51] The effect given to these islands is described as follows:

> ... Furthermore, it was recognised that each island was entitled to a belt of territorial sea. Since both States claim a twelve-mile limit, this meant that each belt would not only overlap the other but would also extend across the median line between the two mainlands in the direction of the other State—slightly in the case of Al-'Arabiyah, substantially in the case of Al-Farisiyah.
>
> The solution reached would appear to conform fully with applicable legal principles. Between the two islands a median line was adopted, separating their respective territorial seas equidistantly on a basis identical with that described in Article 12 of the Territorial Sea Convention. With regard to the 'overspill' across the median line, it was recognised that the existence of a territorial belt belonging to one party would rule out by definition any rights occurring to the other party in the same area by virtue of the shelf doctrine. Hence the boundary should deviate to the extent necessary to respect the areas of territorial sea appertaining to each islet ...[52]

The median line between the baselines of opposite mainland coasts has presumably also provided the starting point for the negotiations about the delimitation of the northern sector of the Saudi Arabian–Iran continental shelf boundary between points D and 14.[53] The agreed boundary, however, deviates from this median line. It is actually drawn near the coast of Saudi Arabia in favour of Iran's claim, by giving half-effect to the Iranian island of Kharg (about 3 × 4 n.m.), which is situated about seventeen miles from the Iranian coast,[54] and recognising Iran's claim to a bigger share in the oil deposits (Marjan–Fereydoon reservoir), which, as indicated above, were known to exist in that zone of the boundary line. The half-effect line is that line constructed so as to divide equally the area between (1) a line equidistant from the Saudi Arabian mainland and the island of Kharg (full effect), and (2) a line equidistant from both the mainland of Iran and Saudi Arabia: Kharg (no effect), that is, when Kharg is given full effect it is considered to be part of the mainland, and when Kharg is given no effect it is ignored in determining the equidistant line.[55]

Article 4 of the Iran–Saudi Arabia agreement prohibits any oil-drilling operations within a zone extending 500 metres in width on either side of the demarcation line. This provision has been interpreted as prohibiting drilling operations within the 500-metre zone from installations located outside as well as inside the zone, with the exceptions of wells for conservation or observation purposes jointly agreed upon.[56] This clause is applicable to the Marjan–Fereydoon oil reservoir, which, as noted above, lies across the agreed boundary line.

The significance of the Saudi–Iranian agreement is in the methods employed in delimiting the continental shelf boundary in the presence of offshore islands located many miles from the mainland (in the case of Al-'Arabiyah and Farsi), and, further, the method employed in assigning an effect to an important island proximal to the mainland (in the case of Kharg). It should be stated, however, that it is not very clear whether the northerly segment of the Saudi Arabia–Iran boundary deviates from the median line between the mainlands of the two States merely because of the presence of the Marjan–Fereydoon deposits or owing to the presence of the island of Kharg. For, as stated elsewhere, the existence of a common deposit would scarcely justify a deviation from the median line.[57] It has thus been rightly observed that:

> Kharg most probably received this special allocation because the general outlines of the mid-Gulf oil fields were known and concessions had been granted ... The question arises, would the agreement have been made in the same manner if the resources were suspected but their exact location not known? or would the agreement have been the same if the oil deposits were farther to the west so that a half-effect line would have placed them entirely in Saudi Arabia?
>
> While the question essentially is academic, the answer probably would be negative ...[58]

Finally it may be observed that it is not clear either why the Saudi islands of Janah, al-Jurayd, al-Qurayyin, Qiran and Hurqus have had no effect whatever in delimiting the Saudi Arabia–Iran continental shelf boundary.[59] These islands are so located that they are within twelve-miles of the Saudi coast and each other, and therefore may be considered as being within the Saudi Arabian baseline, in accordance with the Saudi decree on the territorial sea.[60]

3. Agreement for Settlement of the Offshore Boundary and Ownership of Islands between Abu Dhabi and Qatar[61]

On 20 March 1969 Abu Dhabi and Qatar, two adjacent States, signed and ratified an agreement for the demarcation of the boundary line between their respective continental shelves and settle-

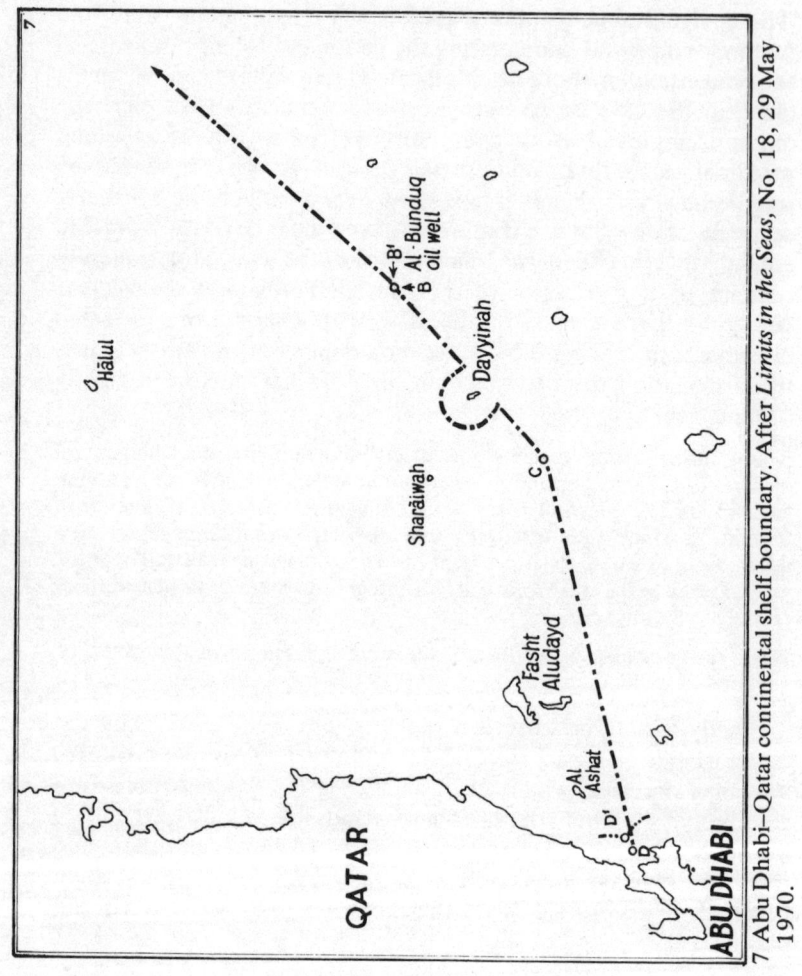

7 Abu Dhabi–Qatar continental shelf boundary. After *Limits in the Seas*, No. 18, 29 May 1970.

ment of the dispute about sovereignty over islands pertaining to their offshore areas.

The question of the disputed islands goes back many years. Halul is the largest of the islands and lies about sixty-one miles east-north-east of Dohah in Qatar.[62] In 1908 Lorimer stated that 'The political position of Halul appears to be indeterminate'.[63] According to Sir R. Hay, however, Halul 'in the past has usually been regarded as belonging to Abu Dhabi but is also claimed by Qatar'.[64] The dispute over Halul was intensified following offshore oil exploration in its vicinity. Eventually, in 1962, two British 'experts' found that Halul should belong to Qatar and several small islands to Abu Dhabi, but the question of two other islands, over which the claims of Abu Dhabi and Qatar were judged to be equal, was left undecided.[65] Following the experts' decision, the ruler of Qatar issued a decree declaring his concurrence with the decision regarding the establishment of Qatari right of ownership over the island of Halul and noting that the British government 'has approved the extension of Qatar's sovereignty to this island'.[66]

However, under the present agreement Abu Dhabi and Qatar have concluded that the island of Dayyinah (Daiyina or Daiyinah), considered further below, is part of the territory of Abu Dhabi, and that both the islands of Al-Ashat (Lashat) and Shara'iwah (Shura'awa) are part of the territory of Qatar.[67] Furthermore, the agreement provides that neither country now has any territorial claim upon the other with respect to the islands or offshore areas falling outside its agreed offshore boundary. Hence Halul, being an island situated on the Qatari side of the agreed boundary, has been mutually regarded as part of the territory of Qatar.

The agreed continental shelf boundary extends for a distance of 115 nautical miles.[68] The boundary line consists of straight line segments joining four terminal points (A, B, C, D), except for a fifteen-nautical-mile arc round the island of Dayyinah which places the island in Abu Dhabi territory and marks its three-mile territorial sea.[69] The island of Dayyinah did not have any further effect on the continental shelf boundary.[70]

Points A and D, it is pointed out, are equidistant from the coasts of both States, while point C is simply the intersection of the lines from points B and D and not a point equidistant from the coasts of the respective countries.[71] Point D, the landward terminus of the shelf boundary, is, according to Article 4(iii) of the agreement, the point where the three-mile territorial sea claims of Qatar and Abu Dhabi intersect.[72] Point A, the seaward extent of the boundary line, coincides with point 6, which marks the southern terminus of the continental shelf boundary between Iran and Qatar and is equidistant from the mainland of Abu Dhabi, Iran and Qatar.[73]

Point B of the boundary line, according to Article 4(i) of the agreement was designated to coincide with the location of an oilfield (al-Bunduq well No. 1).[74] It was selected independent of any consideration of the equidistance principle.[75] According to the provisions of the agreement, however, the al-Bunduq field is to be shared equally by the parties, and they agreed that in so far as the exploitation of the field is concerned they would from time to time consult each other on all matters pertaining to this field in order to exercise all the rights on an equal basis. Furthermore, the agreement provides that the al-Bunduq field shall be developed by Abu Dhabi Marine Areas Ltd (ADMA) in accordance with the terms of its concession with the ruler of Abu Dhabi, and all royalties, profits and other government fees due in respect of the aforementioned field under the said concession shall be equally divided between the governments of Qatar and Abu Dhabi.

The importance of the Abu Dhabi–Qatar agreement lies mainly in the method employed to accommodate the parties' common interest in the al-Bunduq oilfield. To avoid any dispute over ownership, the boundary line was drawn to coincide with the location of the field. Consequently the parties have agreed that the al-Bunduq field is to be shared equally. For economic reasons they have stipulated that the development of the field is to be carried out by one concessionaire, ADMA, according to the terms of its concession with the rule of Abu Dhabi. However, provisions were made for mutual consultation over the exploitation of the field and for equal sharing of all royalties, profits and other government fees due in respect of the field. This solution seems to be remarkably in harmony with the principles declared by the International Court of Justice in the North Sea Continental Shelf cases, 1969,[76] to be applicable to such situations. Thus the Court pointed out that there will be areas in which, in accordance with the rules and principles of continental shelf delimitation, two States may have equally justifiable claims, or, in other words, areas in which those claims will overlap. In such situations, the Court added, the solution may be found in an agreed division of the overlapping areas or in an agreement for joint exploitation, 'the latter solution appearing particularly appropriate when it is a question of preserving the unity of a deposit'.[77]

The solution adopted with regard to the al-Bunduq oilfield may also be compared with that employed in the Saudi Arabia–Bahrain agreement of 1958 with respect to the Fasht Bu Saafa oil deposit.

In that agreement the boundary line was drawn near the Bahraini coast in order to place the Fasht Bu Saafa deposit under Saudi jurisdiction.[78] In both cases, however, the parties concerned have provided for equal sharing of the profit derived from the development operations and, further, followed the principle that 'two concessionaires should not tap the same pool, or in a descriptive parable: never two straws in one glass'.[79]

4. Offshore Boundary Agreement between the Amirates of Abu Dhabi and Dubai[80]

On 18 February 1968 Abu Dhabi and Dubai, whose coasts are adjacent to each other, signed an agreement on the redefinition of their lateral offshore boundary. Although the boundary between these two emirates is no longer an international boundary properly speaking because both of them are members of the new union of United Arab Emirates, it nevertheless may be useful to examine the agreement, because it definitely settles the dispute between the two emirates over the Fateh oilfield, which is located about 100 kilometres offshore, that it, towards the middle of the Arabian Gulf and because, as will be seen later, the seaward extent of the agreed boundary line coincides with point 1 of the boundary line agreed upon in 1974 and which divides parts of the continental shelf between Iran and the United Arab Emirates.[81]

According to the present agreement, the old offshore boundary between Abu Dhabi and Dubai:

Starts at Ras Hasian [Ra's Hasan] on the coast and extends seawards in a straight line in a northwesterly direction passing to the west of the Fateh wells belonging to the Amirate of Dubai.

This boundary was delimited in 1965 in an agreement reached through British mediation between the ruler of Abu Dhabi, Sheikh Shakhbut, and the ruler of Dubai. But in 1966, following the discovery by Continental Oil of Dubai of oil in the area of the Fateh wells, Shaikh Shakhbut questioned the validity of the 1965 agreement and laid claim to the area.[82]

However, the new agreement confirms Dubai's sovereignty over the Fateh wells and, further, annexes to Dubai an area of the sea forming a parallelogram and lying to the west of the Fateh wells, by adjusting the coastal point of departure of the old boundary line ten kilometres to the west—to Dubai's advantage.

5. Agreement concerning the Boundary Line dividing the Continental Shelf between Iran and Qatar; Agreement concerning

Delimitation of the Continental Shelf between Bahrain and Iran; Agreement concerning the Boundary Line dividing Parts of the Continental Shelf between Iran and the United Arab Emirates (Dubai); Agreement concerning Delimitation of the Continental Shelf between Iran and Oman[83]

The boundary lines dividing the continental shelf between Iran and its opposite neighbours, Qatar, Bahrain, the United Arab Emirates (Dubai), and Oman, were delimited in a series of agreements ratified respectively on 10 May 1970, 14 May 1972, 15 March 1975 and 28 May 1975.[84]

As noted at the outset, none of these States is a party to the Convention on the Continental Shelf or any of the other 1958 Geneva conventions on the law of the sea. In the Preamble to each of the present agreements, however, the parties concerned, in identical terms, express the desire

of establishing in a just, equitable and precise manner the boundary line between the respective areas of the continental shelf over which they have sovereign rights in accordance with international law.

Each of the agreed boundaries was delimited by reference to geodetic lines between points whose geographical co-ordinates were specified in the relevant agreement. The line between Iran and Qatar has a length of 131 nautical miles.[85] Point 2 of this line coincides with point 1 of the Bahrain–Iran continental shelf boundary,[86] while point 6, as noted elsewhere, is coextensive with point A, which marks the seaward extent of the Qatar–Abu Dhabi offshore boundary line.[87] The Iran–Qatar shelf boundary, it has been seen, is based on the equidistance principle with the exception that the presence of all islands between the two mainland coasts was ignored.[88]

The Bahrain–Iran continental shelf boundary extends for a distance of 28·8 nautical miles.[89] Two of its four terminal points were determined by existing continental shelf boundary agreements. For, as pointed out above, point 1 of this boundary line coincides with point 2 of the Iran–Qatar offshore boundary, while point 4 coincides with point 1 of the Iran–Saudi Arabia continental shelf boundary.[90]

According to the Geographer of the U.S. Department of State, points 1 and 4 of the Bahrain–Iran boundary line are nearer to Iranian territory (island of Nakhilu) than they are to Bahraini territory (islet north of Jazirat al Muharrag); while points 2 and 3 of the said line are nearly the same distance from Bahrain (islet north of Jazirat al Muharrag), and Iran (island of Nakhilu), so the

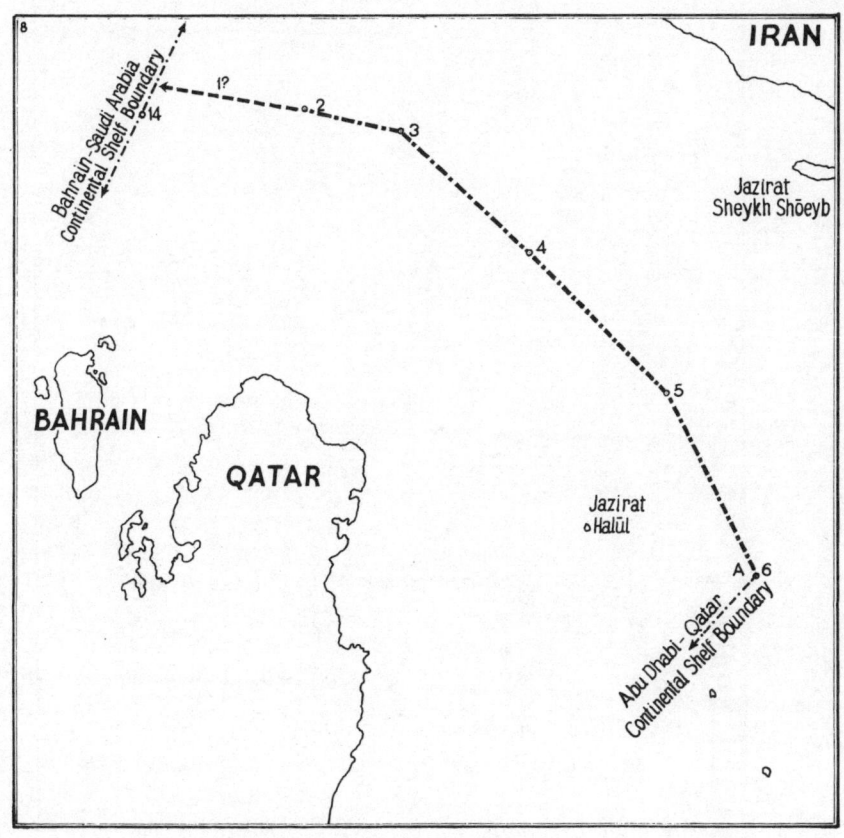

8 Iran–Quatar continental shelf boundary. After *Limits in the Seas*, No. 25, 9 July 1970.

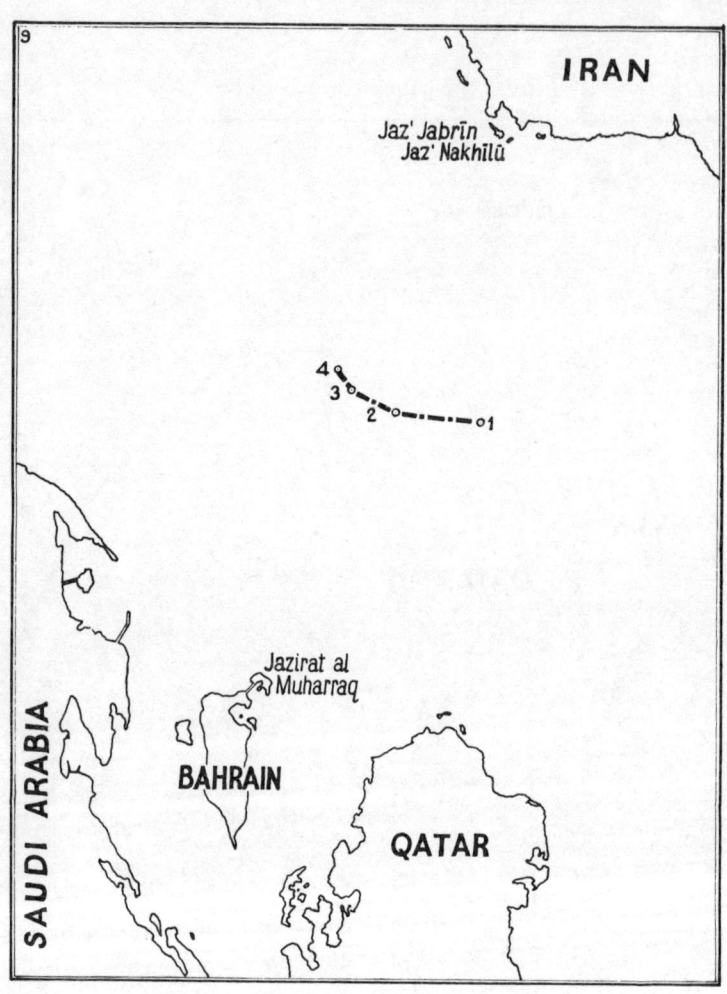

9 Bahrain–Iran continental shelf boundary. After *Limits in the Seas*, No. 58, 13 September 1974.

assumption, it is added, can be made that the latter two points are in fact equidistant points.[91] It has been observed, however, that according to the Bahrain–Iran agreement al-Muharraq, the second biggest Bahraini island, which is connected to the mainland by a causeway, has been ignored in drawing the median line; at the same time full effect has been given to the Iranian islands of Nakhilu and Jabrin, that is, they were considered as being within the Iranian baseline.[92]

As to the boundary line between Iran and the United Arab Emirates, which extends for a distance of 39.25 nautical miles,[93] it should first be made clear that the agreed boundary line delimits only some parts of the continental shelf between these two States, namely the area between Iran and the offshore lateral limits or boundaries of the emirate of Dubai. Point 1 of the agreed boundary appears to coincide with the lateral offshore boundary line between Dubai and Abu Dhabi as agreed upon in 1968,[94] while point 5, which marks the other end of the agreed boundary, seems to coincide with what Dubai in 1964 claimed to constitute its lateral offshore boundary line with Sharjah.[95] In view of the fact that the boundaries between the various members of the union of United Arab Emirates are no longer international boundaries properly speaking, it is not very clear why the present agreement between Iran and the United Arab Emirates defines only the shelf boundary between Iran and Dubai. One reason may be that the parties concerned have wished to avoid for the time being the issue concerning the islands of Abu Musa and the two Tumbs near the Strait of Hormuz, on which Iran landed troops on 30 November 1971,[96] and, another may be the dispute between Iran and Abu Dhabi over the island of Sir Bani Yas which is about 145 miles to the west of Abu Dhabi.[97]

The Iran–United Arab Emirates agreement does not state whether the principle of equidistance was utilised in determining the boundary line. It would appear, however, that the median line between the baselines of the mainland coasts of Iran and Dubai has basically been followed, with the exception that in the vicinity of the Iranian island of Sirri this median line has been displaced so as to coincide with the southern twelve-mile limit of the territorial waters of Sirri.[98] Sirri, however, has been disregarded for the purpose of determining the median line, in other words the island has not been recognised as being within the Iranian baseline. The treatment accorded to Sirri island is similar to that employed in the Iran–Saudi Arabia and Qatar–Abu Dhabi continental shelf agreements.[99]

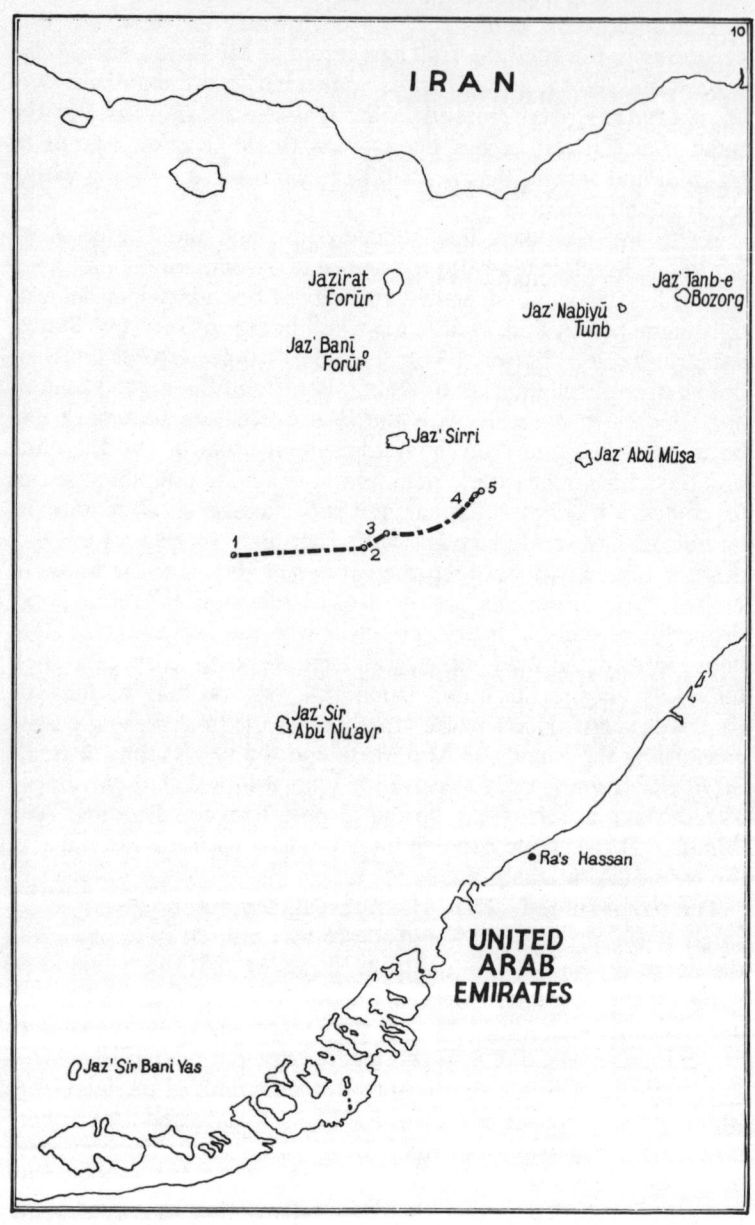

10 Iran–United Arab Emirates (Dubai) continental shelf boundary. After *Limits in the Seas,* No. 63, 30 September 1975.

The continental shelf boundary between Iran and Oman extends from the eastern section of the Arabian Gulf through the Strait of Hormuz to the Gulf of Oman and has a length of 124·85 nautical miles.[100] Although it is not stated in the agreement, it is presumed that the Iranian islands of Qeshm, Hengam, Hormoz and Larak, and the close inshore Omani islands of al-Ghanam, Great Quoin, Gap, Musandam, al-Fayyarin and Lima (Limah), were used as base-point for the purpose of plotting some points of the agreed boundary line.[101] Nor does the agreement state whether the equidistance principle was utilised in determining the shelf boundary, but it has been shown that, from the twenty-two terminal or turning points of the boundary line, turning points 3, 4, 9, 10, 14, 15 and 16 are equidistant from one point on each coast, while the other turning points are clearly close to one of the States, with point 21 being 4·40 nautical miles closer to Oman than to Iran territory.[102] In addition, the segment of the shelf boundary between points 9 and 10 was drawn to coincide with the twelve-mile limit of the territorial sea of the Iranian island of Larak.[103] However, two terminal points have not been precisely delimited. Point 1 of the boundary line is described in the agreement as being:

the most western point which is the intersection of the geodetic line drawn between point (O) having the coordinates of 55° 42′ 15″ E, 26° 14′ 45″ N, and point (2) having the coordinates of 55° 47′ 45″ E, 26° 16′ 35″ N with the lateral offshore boundary line between Oman and Ras Al Khaimah.

The other terminal point (point 22) is described in the agreement as being:

On an azimuth of 190° from point 21 to the intersection of the Oman–Sharjah lateral offshore boundary.

It should be noted that the Oman–Ras Alkhaimah and Oman–Sharjah lateral offshore boundaries have not been defined.

In almost identical terms, each of the four agreements under consideration provides safeguards against the existence across the agreed boundary line of any single geological structure or field of petroleum or any other mineral deposit. In such a case, and if the part of the structure or field which is located on one side of the demarcation line is exploitable wholly or in part by directional drillings from the other side of the boundary line, then no well shall be drilled on either side of the agreed boundary line so that any producing section thereof is less than 125 metres from the said boundary line except by mutual agreement between the two contracting parties as to the manner in which the operations on both sides of the boundary line could be co-ordinated or unitised.

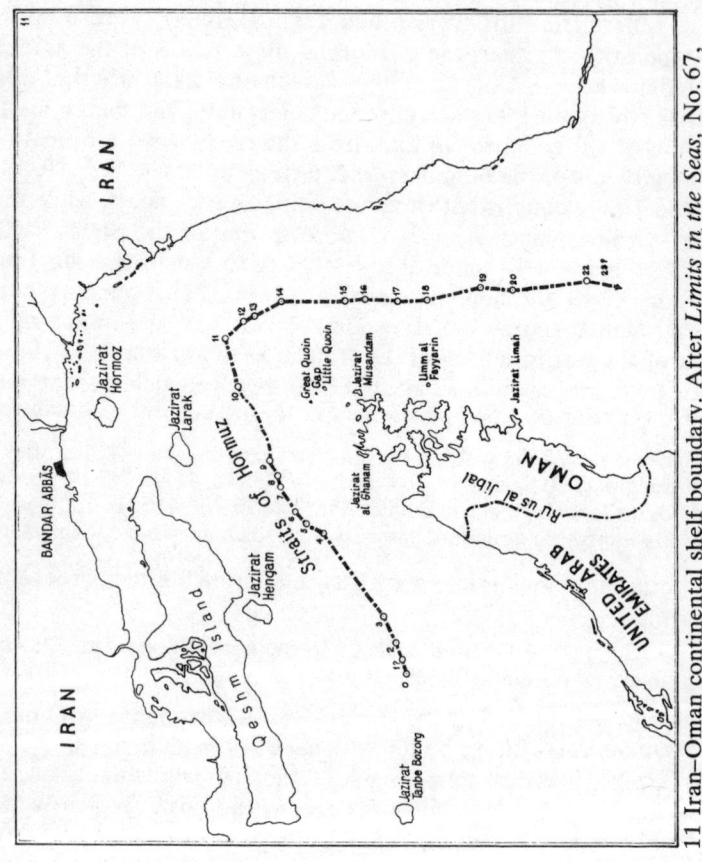

11 Iran–Oman continental shelf boundary. After *Limits in the Seas*, No. 67, 1 January 1976.

In this respect the parties concerned have followed the earlier practice of States in the North Sea, which was referred to with appreciation by the International Court of Justice in its judgement in the North Sea Continental Shelf cases, 1969, when it said:

> Yet it frequently occurs that the same deposit lies on both sides of the line dividing a continental shelf between two States, and since it is possible to exploit such a deposit from either side, a problem immediately arises on account of the risk of prejudicial or wasteful exploitation by one or other of the States concerned. To look no farther than the North Sea, the practice of States shows how this problem has been dealt with, and all that is needed is to refer to the undertakings entered into by the coastal States of that sea with a view to ensuring the most efficient exploitation or the apportionment of the products extracted.[104]

The International Court then referred in particular to the agreement on 10 March 1965 between the United Kingdom and Norway, Article 4; the agreement of 6 October 1965 between the Netherlands and the United Kingdom relating to 'the exploitation of single geological structures extending across the dividing line on the Continental Shelf under the North Sea'; and the agreement of 14 May 1962 between the Federal Republic and the Netherlands concerning a joint plan for exploiting the natural resources underlying the area of the Ems estuary where the frontier between the two States has not been finally delimited.[105] For instance, Article 4 of the United Kingdom–Norway agreement provides that:

> If any single geological petroleum structure or petroleum field, or any single geological structure or field of any other mineral deposit, including sand or gravel, extends across the dividing line and the part of such structure or field which is situated on one side of the dividing line is exploitable, wholly or in part, from the other side of the dividing line, the Contracting Parties shall, in consultations with the licenses, if any, seek to reach agreement as to the manner in which the structure or field shall be most effectively exploited and the manner in which the proceeds deriving therefrom shall be apportioned.

B. OUTSTANDING PROBLEMS

1. Kuwait–Saudi Arabia: partitioned zone offshore lateral boundaries and the question of the islands of Qaru and Umm al-Maradim

The Neutral Zone is an area of about 2,200 square miles between Saudi Arabia and Kuwait; off its coast lie the islands of Qaru and Umm al-Maradim. Since the Al Uquair convention of 2 December 1922, which delineated the land boundaries between Kuwait and Saudi Arabia, the Neutral Zone was run as a condominium, with both countries sharing equal responsibility for the administration of the entire territory. In 1965, however, the two countries agreed that in the future the southern half of the mainland would be administered directly by Saudi Arabia and the northern part by Kuwait.[106] According to Article 1 of the Partition Agreement, the boundary line between the two sections of the zone is to be the line which divides them into two equal parts. The agreement further provides that, for the purpose of exploiting the natural resources in the partitioned zone, not more than six marine miles of the sea bed and subsoil adjoining the partitioned zone shall be annexed to the mainland of that partitioned zone and that the two contracting parties shall agree to determine the boundary line which divides the territorial waters which adjoin the partitioned zone. As to the submerged area beyond the aforementioned six-mile limit, the agreement stipulates that the two contracting parties shall exercise their equal rights by means of joint exploitation, unless the two parties agree otherwise.

As stipulated in Article 1 of the Partition Agreement, the final boundary line between the two sectors of the partitioned area was precisely established by a supplementary agreement concluded on 18 December 1969.[107] The boundary line, however, ends at the coast and has not been prolonged offshore. It has been indicated that the southern offshore boundary of the partitioned zone with Saudi Arabia was delimited in notes exchanged between Saudi Arabia and Kuwait in May 1963.[108] More recently, however, it has been stated that the boundary has not yet been formally determined throughout its length, but the segment nearer the shore, which runs through the Safaniya and Khafji offshore oilfields, has been established *de facto* for a number of years.[109] It may be stressed also that the boundary line which divides the territorial waters that adjoin the partitioned zone has not been determined yet and it is not likely to be agreed upon until the dispute between Kuwait and Saudi Arabia, discussed below, over the islands of Qaru and Umm al-Maradim is resolved. Any future settlement of this question might affect the boundary line if it were to be based on the equidistance principle.

However, the questions regarding the demarcation of the northern offshore boundary of the partitioned zone with Kuwait and the rival claims of Saudi Arabia and Kuwait over the islands of Qaru and Umm al-Maradim are still unresolved.[110] Following the signature of the 1965 Partition Agreement, the Saudi Oil Minister described these two questions as 'purely legal', and announced that it had been agreed that both sides, Kuwait and Saudi Arabia, should submit their respective legal cases on these matters to a conciliation commission of impartial legal experts which would be asked to recommend a suitable solution to the two governments.[111] In addition, Article VIII of the Partition Agreement stipulated that, in determining the northern boundary of the submerged area adjoining the partitioned zone, it should be delineated as if the zone had not been partitioned. However, as noted above, no solution has been reached yet for either of the two problems. The rival claims of Saudi Arabia and Kuwait over Qaru and Umm al-Maradim will now be examined in more detail.

THE QUESTION OF QARU AND UMM AL-MARADIM. Lorimer reckons the maritime possessions of Kuwait to include the islets of Qaru and Umm al-Maradim.[112] In addition, it is indicated that the British government, which was responsible for the conduct of Kuwait's international relations until 1961, and the government of Kuwait itself have always taken the view that the islets, though situated off, do not pertain to, the Neutral Zone, because they were not the subject of the dispute for the settlement of which the Neutral Zone was created under the above-mentioned 1922 Uquair Convention.[113] On the other hand, though M. T. El-Ghoneimy believes that the Anglo-Turkish agreement of 1913 was the first international agreement to specify the islands by name, including them in the zone in which the Shaikh of Kuwait exercises autonomy, he expresses the opinion that the agreement had no effect as to identifying the legal status of the islands. Furthermore, he considers that a fair interpretation of the Uqair convention does not support Kuwait's pretension. El-Ghoneimy concludes that the conduct of Kuwait and Saudi Arabia since 1922 does not prove that Kuwait acquired sovereignty over the two islands, and that, in the absence of effective occupation and control by another State, the islands of Qaru and Umm al-Maradim automatically appertain to the Neutral Zone by virtue of their contiguity to its coast.[114]

However, on the assumption that Qaru and Umm al-Maradim are Kuwaiti islands, these islands together with the island of Kubar (Kubbar) off the coast of Kuwait proper were the subject of a sixty years' oil concession granted to the American Independent Oil Company (Aminoil), by the ruler of Kuwait on 22 September 1949.[115] Saudi Arabia is said to have protested against this action in due time, and as a consequence Aminoil stopped the drilling operations.[116] It is indicated, however, that in 1962 Aminoil conducted a seismic survey of the three islands and their surrounding waters.[117] In addition, it may be observed that the Kuwaiti Decree No. 6 of 1962 concerning the administrative division of Kuwait includes the islands of Qaru and Umm al-Maradim in the Ahmadi province.[118] More recently, the government of Kuwait reaffirmed that the islands of Kuwait are known and include, among others, the islands of Qaru and Umm al-Maradim which are off the partitioned zone and the sovereignty over which has not been, at any time, relinquished by Kuwait.[119] But it is worth noting that in late 1963 and again in early 1964, it was reported that Kuwait had offered to share equally with Saudi Arabia any income from future oil production from Qaru and Umm al-Maradim, on the understanding that Kuwait would retain 100 per cent ownership of the islands.[120]

The Saudi government, it is stated, has never officially declared its position on the matter, but all the indications are that it does not accept Kuwait's claim to exclusive sovereignty over the islands.[121] It is also indicated that Saudi Arabia argues that Qaru and Umm al-Maradim have the same legal status as the Neutral Zone before its partition, that is to say, joint rights equally shared with Kuwait.[122] The 1957 concession agreement between Saudi Arabia and the Arabian Oil Company (AOC) of Japan concerning the Saudi areas off the Neutral Zone makes no specific reference to the islands of Qaru and Umm al-Maradim,[123] but E. H. Brown reveals the existence of a confidential letter of agreement between AOC and the Saudi government concerning them.[124] According to E. H. Brown, the confidential agreement specifically refers to the two islands as being located in the concession area, but that, since the governments of Saudi Arabia and Kuwait were contemplating discussions as to their territorial rights over the islands, they were not mentioned in the original concession agreement. However, if at a future time it was determined that the islands belonged either to the Kingdom of Saudi Arabia or to the Neutral Zone, they would become subject to the terms and conditions of AOC concession agreement.[125]

2. Iran–Kuwait–Saudi Arabia: offshore boundary between Iran and the Kuwait–Saudi Arabia partitioned zone
Though the mainland of the Neutral Zone between Saudi Arabia and Kuwait was partitioned equally between the two States in 1965, as noted above, the submerged area adjoining the partitioned zone has not been partitioned and the two countries have agreed to exercise their equal rights in this area by means of joint exploitation.[126] A related and outstanding problem is the boundary

line between the submerged area adjoining the partitioned zone and the opposite State, Iran. In 1966 negotiations on this problem were held between Iran on one side and Kuwait and Saudi Arabia on the other, but ended inconclusively owing to the difficulty of finding an equitable basis for constructing the median line.[127] Because of the existence of some islands on both sides of the proposed boundary line, there has arisen between the parties concerned the question of whether these offshore islands should be taken into account or be ignored for the purpose of fixing the baselines from which the boundary line should be measured. Noticeable among these islands is the Iranian island of Kharg, which is situated about seventeen miles from the Iranian coast and was given half-effect in determining the offshore boundary between Saudi Arabia and Iran,[128] and the islands of Qaru and Umm al-Maradim off the coast of the partitioned zone whose sovereignty is disputed between Kuwait and Saudi Arabia.[129]

3. Iran–Iraq–Kuwait: offshore boundaries and Iraq–Kuwait dispute over the islands of Warbah and Bubiyan

A. OFFSHORE BOUNDARIES. Situated as it is at the northern end (or the top) of the Arabian Gulf, Iraq, with its limited and sharply curved coastline, is adjacent to both Kuwait and Iran; while the coasts of Iran and Kuwait are opposite each other. The disputes between these States over the delimitation of the boundary lines between their respective continental shelf areas first arose as a result of the overlapping of oil concessions. Thus both Kuwait and Iraq have protested against the pre-announcement of the National Iranian Oil Company (NIOC) of 1 April 1963 concerning offshore explorations.[130] Iraq claimed that most of the areas declared open for bidding under the Iranian pre-announcement were exclusively Iraqi territorial waters, and in a protest dated 1 May 1963 the Iraqi government declared that 'it will not recognise, nor permit, any concession granted to any party whatsoever for oil exploration in these areas', and that 'all the parties concerned must ascertain the ownership of these areas before seeking to grant or acquire any oil exploration concessions in them . . .'.[131] Similarly, in a statement issued on 4 June 1963, Kuwait considered that NIOC's action amounted to an infringement of its territorial sovereignty and continental shelf.[132] A further objection by Kuwait was against IPAC (Iran Pan-American Oil Company) concession, Area 1, which, according to Kuwait, interfered with its offshore concession area granted on 15 January 1961 to the Kuwait Shell Group.[133] Iran, on the other hand, claimed that the concession area held by Kuwait Shell has very greatly interfered with both IPAC and SIRIP (Iran-Italian Petroleum Company) concessions, granted in 1958 and 1957 respectively.[134] It was because of the latter claim that in 1963 Kuwait Shell decided to suspend its operations. The company informed the Kuwaiti government that 'its best drilling prospect now lies in the south-eastern part of the concession area which is nearer to IPAC Cyrus field, but that drilling in this area will not be possible until some agreement on the delimitation of offshore boundaries between Kuwait and Iran is reached'.[135]

However, despite lengthy negotiations between Iraq, Iran and Kuwait, and particularly between the latter two, on the delimitation of their respective offshore boundaries, no boundaries have yet been finally determined.[136] As to the boundary line between Iran and Kuwait, one main difficulty had been the treatment that should be given to the Iranian island of Kharg, which is more than twelve miles from the Iranian coast, and the Kuwaiti island of Failaka (Faylakah), which is about ten miles from the mainland, in drawing the boundary line.[137] This difficulty, it is understood, has now been overcome and the two parties have in principle agreed that both Kharg and Failaka should be given full effect, that is to say, they should be considered as being within the baselines of Iran and Kuwait respectively. Other reasons delaying a final agreement on the Iran–Kuwait boundary line include the outstanding problem concerning the offshore boundary line between Iran and the Kuwait–Saudi Arabia partitioned zone, and the fact that the principles adopted in any bilateral settlement between Kuwait and Iran as regards the baselines (shoals, islands, etc.) for demarcating the median line would also inevitably affect the other unresolved offshore boundary disputes in the area involving Saudi Arabia (in the northern boundary of the Kuwait–Saudi Arabia partitioned zone with Kuwait) and Iraq. Thus, following the official announcement in January 1968 that Iran and Kuwait had arrived at a solution in respect of their offshore boundary line,[138] Iraq reacted with a strong protest stressing its refusal to recognise

any communiqué, declaration, legislation, or plan of any neighbouring State which infringes upon Iraq's territorial waters and continental shelf in contravention with Iraq's sovereign rights.[139]

Again, on 11 July 1970, following a joint Kuwait–Iranian communiqué in July 1970 which referred to an agreement to accelerate the work of the joint technical committee concerned with the demarcation of the offshore boundary between the two countries,[140] the Iraqi Foreign Ministry reiterated its reservation. The Iraqi statement, *inter alia*, said that:

> Because of the rights which Iraq has in the area, and the overlap between its territorial waters and continental shelf and those of neighbouring countries, the Government of the Republic of Iraq affirms once again its insistence on complete rights of sovereignty over Iraq's territorial waters and continental shelf . . . and that works and installations which have been, or will be, erected and are in any way connected with this area, are subject to the Iraqi Republic's sovereignty.[141]

The Iraqi–Kuwait offshore boundary is still unresolved, and progress in settling it may be delayed mainly because of the current dispute, discussed below, between the two States over the islands of Warbah and Bubiyan.

As regards the offshore boundary between Iraq and Iran, the difficulty centres over the area near the mouth of the Shutt al-Arab (Shatt al-Arab) which was described as '[providing] a number of mixed legal problems with respect to the continental shelf'.[142] The problem was further complicated by the conflict between the two countries over their river boundary in the fifty-mile long Shutt el-Arab estuary and the abrogation by Iran's unilateral action of the 1937 'Boundary Treaty between Iraq and Iran' concerning the Shutt al-Arab waterway.[143] This conflict, however, has been resolved in a new treaty between Iran and Iraq, signed on 13 June 1975, which defines their maritime borders along the Shutt al-Arab river in accordance with the *thalweg* line.[144] No provisions were made for the delimitation of Iran–Iraq offshore boundaries in the Arabian Gulf because, according to one report, Iran has requested a postponement of the question pending the conclusion of a tripartite agreement in this regard between Iraq, Iran and Kuwait.[145]

Having explained that the offshore boundaries between Iran, Kuwait and Iraq have not yet been formally determined in international agreement, it may nevertheless be observed that Kuwait and Iraq have each made some indications of their offshore boundaries.[146] Thus Article 1 of the offshore concession agreement dated 15 January 1961 between Kuwait and Kuwait Shell Petroleum Development Co. Ltd provides specific co-ordinates indicating 'the approximate boundaries of the sea bed to which Kuwait is entitled'.[147] With reference to this article, a 'note' in the annex to the reply of the Federal Republic of Germany in the North Sea Continental Shelf cases, 1969, states that '[t]he dividing line follows the general direction of the land frontier and does not reflect

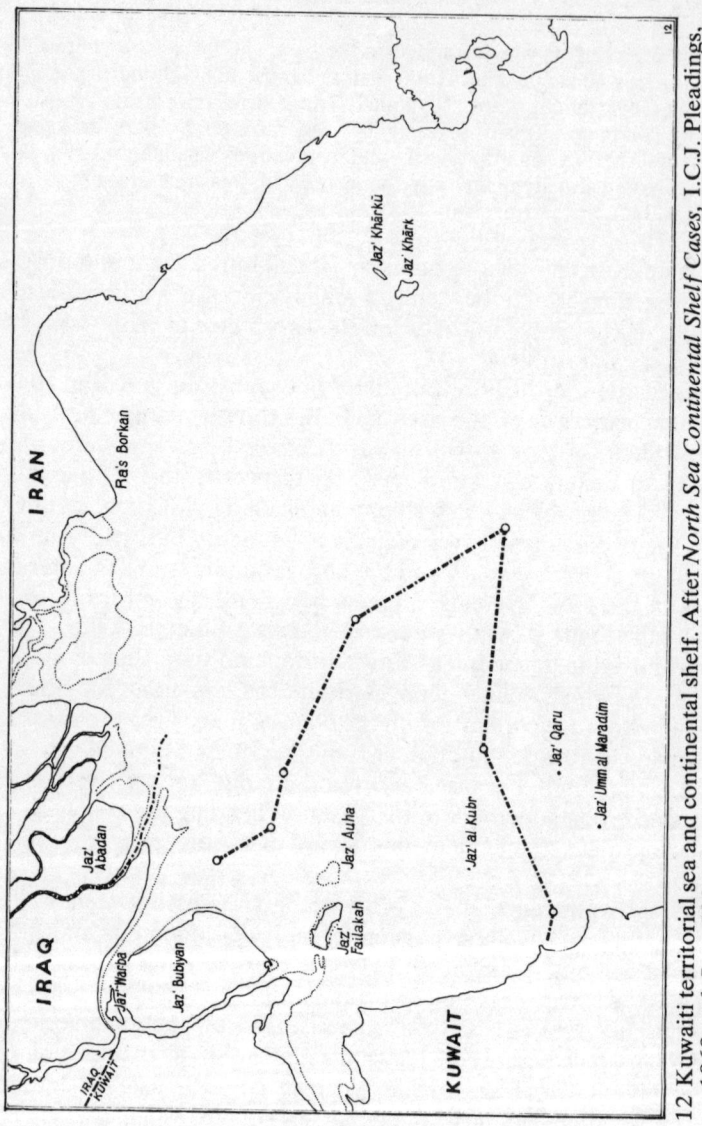

12 Kuwaiti territorial sea and continental shelf. After *North Sea Continental Shelf Cases*, I.C.J. Pleadings, 1968, vol. I, p. 580.

the principle of equidistance', and that 'this is not an international agreement in the strict sense of the word'.[148]

Commenting on the latter interpretation of the Federal Republic's, the Danish and Netherlands governments in their common rejoinder argued that:[149]

> This interpretation is not justified. Indeed, the very fact that the concession agreement speaks of the *approximate boundaries* of the sea bed to which Kuwait is entitled' and makes no reference to the geographical position of her land frontier is a strong warning against such an interpretation... The 'dividing line' in question... is a delimitation which concerns not only the adjacent State Iraq, but also the opposite State Iran, and the adjacent territory of the Neutral Zone. The Federal Republic's 'Note' in its Annex mentions only the general direction of the land frontier without specifying which. But the Danish and Netherlands Governments assume that the Federal Republic means to refer to a continuation of the general direction of the land frontier between Kuwait and Iraq. One thing is very clear: Iraq, Kuwait's adjacent neighbour, does not consider the continental shelf boundary to be a continuation of the general direction of their land frontier... (1) Iraq has based the delimitation of her territorial sea and continental shelf in the Persian Gulf, *vis-à-vis both States adjacent to her*, on the strict application of the equidistance principle.[150] (2) The northern boundary of the Kuwait–Kuwait Shell concession does not follow the general direction of the land frontier but is practically identical with the equidistance line claimed by Iraq as her territorial sea and continental shelf boundaries.[151] It is equally clear that the other boundaries of the Kuwait–Kuwait Shell concession are not continuation of the general direction of the land frontier. Study of detailed charts of this part of the Persian Gulf shows that the delimitation of the actual international boundaries between Kuwait and Iran and the Neutral Zone involves consideration of the use of various islands and low-tide elevations as base-points for the application of the equidistance principle; and it may be surmised that the other concession lines are 'working' boundaries pending the completion of negotiations between the States concerned.

In addition, reference may be made to a Kuwaiti note dated 15 July 1971, in which Kuwait declared that:

> Kuwait is not a party to the Convention on the Continental Shelf which was signed at Geneva on 29 April 1958. However, Kuwait is aware of the provisions of that Convention, and in exercise of its sovereign rights has adopted the 'median line' in delimiting the boundary of the continental shelf with its neighbours.[152]

So far as Iraq is concerned, it was stated in the above-mentioned rejoinder that a chart, prepared by a Norwegian expert at the request of the Iraqi government, showing the areas of territorial sea and continental shelf of Iraq demonstrates that Iraq 'has based the delimitation of her territorial sea and continental shelf in the

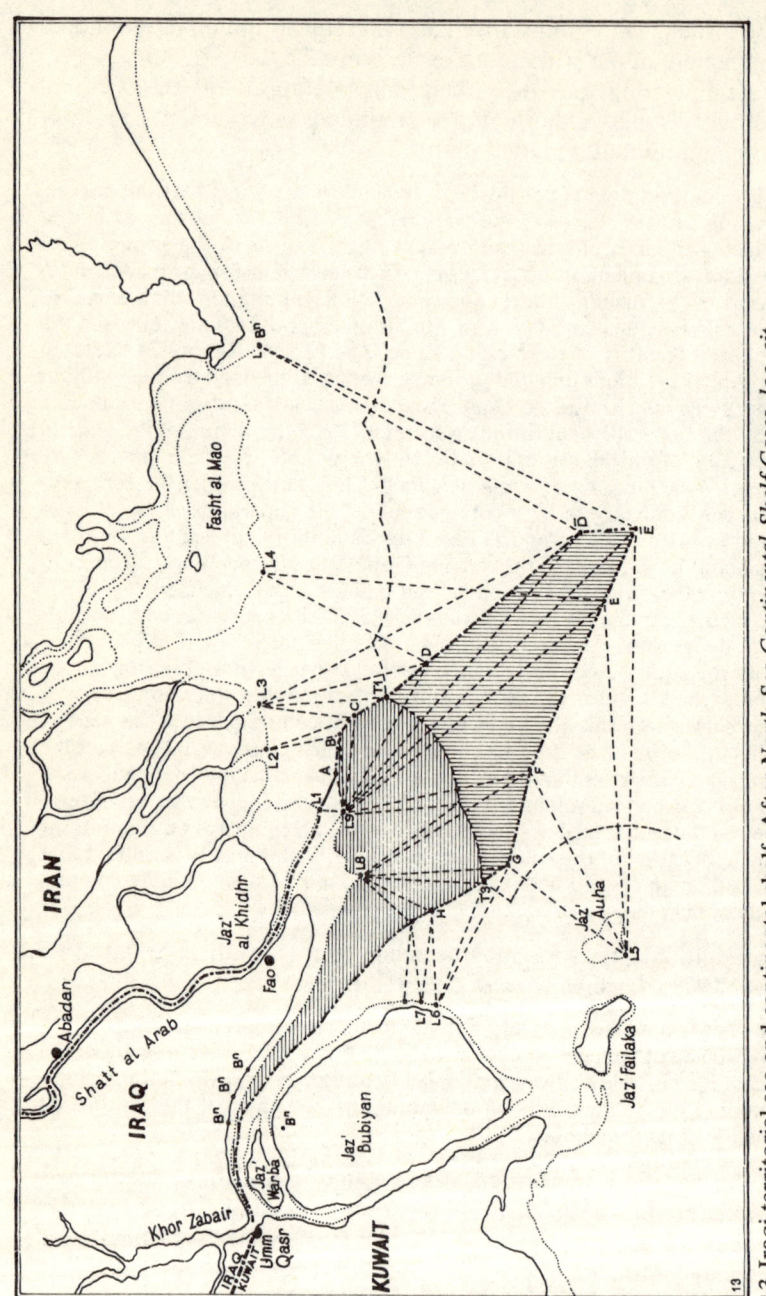

13 Iraqi territorial sea and continental shelf. After *North Sea Continental Shelf Cases, loc. cit.*

Persian Gulf, *vis-à-vis both States adjacent to her* [Iran and Kuwait], on the strict application of the equidistance principle', with the exception that 'a base point on the Iranian coast (named L4 on the chart) has been disregarded presumably because there were some doubts whether the base point—a low tide elevation—could be used as a true base point. Instead a more easterly base point (L4^1) was chosen for the delimitation of the Shelf.'[153]

It was also pointed out in the rejoinder that:

Like Belgium and the Federal Republic, Iraq is a country whose coast abuts upon a 'single natural continental shelf' and whose rights thereover, in the words of the Belgian Expose des motifs 'are necessarily limited in a concrete manner by the rights of other coastal States'. Again like Belgium and the Federal Republic, Iraq finds that the area of the continental shelf appertaining to her under the equidistance principle is not considerable. In other words, Iraq's situation has obvious parallels with that of Belgium and the Federal Republic, and more especially that of the Federal Republic. *Like Belgium, but unlike* the Federal Republic, Iraq has automatically considered that the equidistance principle expressed in Article 6 of the Continental Shelf Convention [1958] would govern the delimitation of her continental shelf in the absence of an agreement or of special circumstances justifying another boundary line.[154]

However, in the light of the judgement of the International Court of Justice in the North Sea Continental Shelf cases,[155] and because of the similarity between the geographical configuration of the coastlines of Iraq and the Federal Republic, in future negotiations Iraq may refuse to accept the application of the equidistance principle for the delimitation of the continental shelf with the neighbouring States Kuwait and Iran. Iraq might well argue that because of the great irregularity in her concave coastline, and since there is no outer boundary to the continental shelf in the Arabian Gulf, the application of the equidistance principle would not provide an equitable solution. For in the North Sea Continental Shelf cases the Court observed that in certain geographical circumstances, such as the presence of irregular coastlines and areas where there is no outer boundary to the continental shelf, the equidistance method, despite its known advantages, leads unquestionably to inequity in that it leaves to one of the States concerned areas that are a natural prolongation of the territory of the other.[156] Eventually the Court found that the use of the equidistance method of delimitation was not obligatory as between the parties and that delimitation is to be effected by agreement in accordance with equitable principles. The Court also indicated that the general configuration and length of the coastlines of the parties are 'factors' to be taken into account in the course of the negotiations for a delimitation.[157]

B. IRAQ–KUWAIT DISPUTE OVER WARBAH AND BUBIYAN[158] Warbah (or Warba) and Bubiyan are two barren and virtually uninhabited islands in the north-west corner of the Arabian Gulf. The two islands are very close to each other and to the mainland of Kuwait, and are within less than a mile from Iraq's ten-nautical-mile stretch of coastline along the Arabian Gulf.[159] They dominate the channel between Iraq's main port on the Gulf, Umm Qasr, and the Gulf itself, and thus command the narrow maritime lane through which Basrah-bound shipping has to pass. In 1905 Lorimer stated that:

> Excluding the island of Bubiyan, which is claimed by the Shaikh of Kuwait but is at present [1905] occupied by the Turks, and the island of Warbah, the ownership of which naturally follows that of Bubiyan, we may reckon the maritime possessions of Kuwait to consist of Failakah which, with its northern and southern outliers of Mashjan and Auhah, is situated at the mouth of Kuwait Bay, and the islets of Kubbar, Qaru and Umm-al-Maradim.[160]

In an agreement signed between Kuwait and Iraq on 4 October 1963 Iraq agreed to recognise the independence of the State of Kuwait and its complete sovereignty within the boundaries indicated in the letter of the Prime Minister of Iraq dated 21 July 1932 and which was accepted by the ruler of Kuwait in a letter dated 10 August 1932. The letter of the Iraqi Prime Minister indicates the land frontier between Kuwait and Iraq, and further recognises that the islands of 'Warbah, Bubiyan, Maskan (or Mashjan), Failakah, Auha, Kubar, Qaru, and Umm al-Maradim belong to Kuwait'.[161]

Moreover, the islands of Warbah and Bubiyan and their territorial waters were included in the concession area granted by Kuwait to Kuwait Oil Co. Ltd under an agreement dated 30 December 1951.[162] The two islands were also part of the concession area held by Kuwait Spanish Petroleum Company under an agreement between the latter and Kuwait ratified on 6 May 1968.[163]

However, the present disagreement between Kuwait and Iraq over Warbah and Bubiyan erupted on 20 March 1973 when Iraqi troops were reported to have occupied Kuwait's Samitah police post in the frontier area, just south of the Iraqi port of Umm Qasr.[164] According to Kuwait, the real cause of that incident was an 'Iraqi demand for Kuwait to relinquish its sovereignty over the two islands of Warbah and Bubiyan'.[165] Kuwait later explained

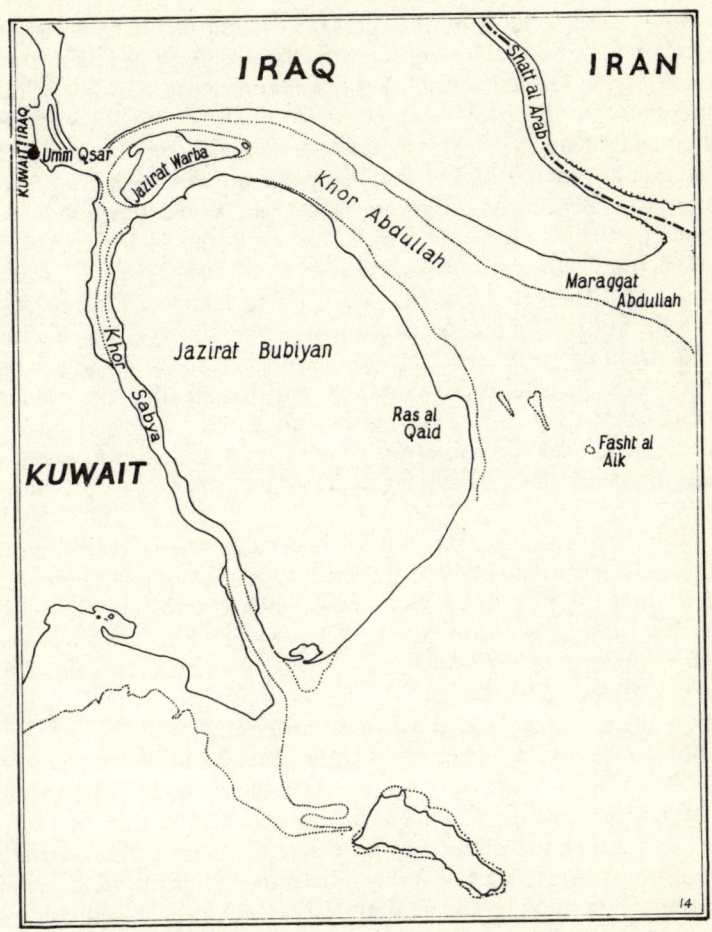

14 Khor Abdullah. After Kennedy, *op. cit.*, p. 233.

that, following the start of work on the development of the Iraqi North Romaila oilfield, Iraq approached Kuwait regarding its need for a suitable site for its proposed new deep-water oil terminal at the head of the Gulf. Kuwait responded by pointing out that all the waters surrounding the Kuwaiti islands were shallow, whereas deep waters are to be found off Kuwait proper, and that Kuwait was prepared to facilitate the passage of Iraq pipelines across its territory for eventual linking up with the proposed terminal. Iraq, it was further added, responded by submitting to Kuwait a draft agreement on this project which was found unacceptable and was rejected by Kuwait.[166] At the same time Kuwait issued two official statements which affirmed that Kuwait's borders with Iraq were internationally recognised frontiers and had been defined under an agreement concluded between the two countries in 1963.[167]

The Iraqi attitude was expressed by the Iraqi Foreign Minister, who stated that 'it is not that we want to take the islands from Kuwait, but rather that we are relinquishing our claim to Kuwait on account of them', and that 'the two islands are of the utmost importance to us and our condition for demarcating the boundaries is that they should be Iraqi'. The Foreign Minister added, 'There is an exchange of letters or agreement between us and the Kuwaitis, but there is no legal document defining the boundaries...'[168]

With a view to discussing the entire boundary issue between the two countries, official talks between Kuwait and Iraq were held in April and August 1973 but ended inconclusively, reportedly because Iraq insisted on having the two islands of Bubiyan and Warbah leased to her, while Kuwait was adamant in its refusal to even consider such a request. At the same time Kuwait insisted on discussing only the 1932 and 1963 border pacts.[169]

More recently, however, the Deputy Prime Minister of Kuwait said that Kuwait is willing to lease to Iraq the island of Warbah and a stretch of coastline to enable her to expand the port of Umm Qasr, in return for a piece of Iraqi territory. He added, Kuwait could not consider leasing Bubiyan because it lies in 'the heart of Kuwait'.[170] In addition, on 12 July 1975, the National Assembly of Kuwait adopted a resolution which, while expressing support for 'the positive steps which the Government has taken at all levels, designed to reach full mutual understanding' with Iraq, stressed 'Kuwait's sovereignty over all its territory within the borders which have been approved in accordance with international and bilateral agreements between Kuwait and its neighbours'.[171]

4. Qatar–Saudi Arabia: offshore boundary

The offshore boundary line between Qatar and Saudi Arabia in the Bay of al-Salwa (or Dohat al-Salwa) still remains formally undetermined. For it is uncertain whether the 1965 agreement between Qatar and Saudi Arabia is in force. This unpublished agreement, it is stated, defines both the land and sea boundaries between the two countries.[172]

5. Bahrain–Qatar: offshore boundary and the question of Hawar islands

When Bahrain and Qatar were still under British protection the British Foreign Office presented to Bahrain a tentative plan for the demarcation of her boundaries with Qatar, but Bahrain rejected it and presented a counter-plan claiming more areas of the sea bed than those indicated in the British plan.[173] So far, the offshore boundary between the two countries has not been determined, mainly because of their disagreement over the Hawar (or Hawwar) islands and the Bahraini claim to Zubarah. Zubarah is a piece of territory on the north-western coast of Qatar and at present forms an integral part of Qatar.[174] The Hawar islands lie about 900 metres off the north-western shore of Qatar Peninsula and at low tide can be reached on foot. Fishermen from Qatar go there to fish. The main island is approximately five kilometres in length and one kilometre in breadth. It has a small number of inhabitants, two Bahraini police stations, and one representative in the National Assembly of Bahrain. According to Sir R. Hay, the dispute with Qatar over the Hawar islands was settled by the British government in favour of Bahrain in 1938.[175] Qatar, however, considers that Hawar islands should be regarded as part of its territory because they lie close to its north-western shore.[176]

According to recent reports, however, an understanding to resolve the boundary dispute between Qatar and Bahrain was reached during a meeting between the rulers of the two States in London in August 1974. While one report suggested that Qatar had agreed to drop its claim to the Hawar islands,[177] according to another Qatar claimed sovereignty over Hawar, but in return offered to reclaim a part of the sea off Bahrain equal in area to that of Hawar because Bahrain argued that Hawar was needed for its increasing population.[178] Qatar, it is further reported, has made a few other offers, including the acceptance of a boundary line as a result of which Qatar would be ceding part of its continental shelf to Bahrain in return for Hawar. It also offered to share any revenue from oil that may be discovered in Hawar in future, to grant Bahrain $10 million and to build a bridge connecting Qatar via Hawar to Ras el-Bar, south of Bahrain.[179]

6. Iran–Sharjah-Umm al-Qaiwain: the question of Abu Musa

Abu Musa is an island situated towards the Arabian side of the Gulf, near the exit of the Strait of Hormuz.[180] It lies about thirty-five miles off the coast of the United Arab Emirates (Sharjah), and approximately forty-three miles off the Iranian coast opposite. It has a surface area of approximately thirty square miles, with a population of some 800 persons. Abu Musa is characterised by deep waters providing good anchorage, and by extensive deposits of red iron oxide which are extracted and exported.[181] The island has been the subject of a long-standing dispute between Iran and Sharjah, but in 1971 a 'Memorandum of understanding' was announced. Before examining this memorandum, it might be enlightening to describe briefly the conflicting claims of Iran and Sharjah, and the dispute which arose in 1970 between Sharjah and neighbouring Umm al-Qaiwain and their respective oil concessionaires over a drilling location situated within nine miles of Abu Musa.

A. IRAN–SHARJAH: CONFLICTING CLAIMS. In the summer of 1964 Abu Musa was reportedly occupied by Iran, 'when a Persian ship put a buoy near the island'.[182] While the report was subsequently denied by Iran, it is nevertheless a clear indication that this island has been the subject of a long-standing dispute between Iran and Sharjah.[183]

The Iranian claim to sovereignty over the island is understood to be based on three points: (1) that Abu Musa formerly belonged to Iran and was handed over to Sharjah after the British entry into the Arabian Gulf; (2) that the British government formerly acknowledged Iran's ownership; and (3) that the security of the Gulf and the protection of sea routes justify the Iranian government's assertion of sovereignty over the island.[184]

The Iranian claim became more insistent when the British government announced its intention of withdrawing from the Gulf, and after the eruption of the dispute, discussed below, between Sharjah and Umm al-Qaiwain over an oil promising area about nine miles out to sea from Abu Musa. Thus on or about 19 May 1970 Iran informed Her Majesty's government that in her view the island of Abu Musa and its territorial waters to a distance of twelve miles were under the sovereignty of Iran.[185] This assertion was reaffirmed in two letters dated 27 May and 23 June 1970 respectively, communicated from the National Iranian Oil Company to Sharjah's oil concessionaire, Buttes Gas & Oil Company.[186] In the letter of June 1970 NIOC informed Buttes, *inter alia,* that

> His Imperial Majesty's Government reserves the right to take any action whatsoever to maintain its sovereignty over the island of Abu Musa and its Territorial waters.

For its part, Sharjah asserted that the tribes on the island were branches of Arab tribes inhabiting Sharjah, and that Abu Musa:

> has since ancient times been recognised as an Arab island, and has never before been settled by any foreign power, having always been administered by its Arab rulers along the Omani coast.... The British Government affirmed this historical right of the Arabs and of Sharjah specifically on every occasion, and stated its official view through Sir William Luce, the Representative of the British Foreign Secretary in the Gulf area, with the words: 'The British Government did not seize Abu Musa from the Iranians and hand it over to Sharjah at the time of its entry into the Gulf. The British Government has since its entry into the Gulf considered Abu Musa to be Arab, and according to old documents in possession of the British Government the island was Arab...'.[187]

In addition Sharjah considered that:

(a) The security interests of a country cannot under any circumstances justify the occupation of another's territory, nor can the protection of sea routes be used as an excuse for claiming sovereignty over an island belonging to another state.
(b) Abu Musa has no military importance in the strategic sense, since it is well known that Iran possesses the most modern aircraft and most powerful naval units and can therefore cover any area of the Arabian Gulf with its modern weapons without making use of Abu Musa. Moreover, Iran has seized the island of Sirri, only some twenty miles distant from Abu Musa, and—assuming its object is security and protection of sea routes—is capable of doing so from this island or other Iranian islands at the entrance of the Gulf, which forms a bottleneck known as the Straits of Hormuz.[188]

B. SHARJAH—UMM AL-QAIWAIN: DISAGREEMENT. During November and December 1969 two offshore oil concessions were awarded to two American oil companies in the adjoining Gulf States of Umm al-Qaiwain and Sharjah. These were the concession agreement of 18 November 1969 between Umm al-Qaiwain and Occidental Petroleum Corporation, and that of 29 December 1969 between Sharjah and Buttes Gas & Oil Company.[189] Under the former agreement Occidental has the concession for 'the territorial and offshore waters of Umm al-Qaiwain'. In the latter agreement the concession area was defined to include:

All the territorial waters of the mainland of Sharjah within the jurisdiction of the Ruler, all islands within the jurisdiction of the Ruler and the territorial waters of the said islands and all the area of the sea bed and subsoil lying beneath the waters of the Arabian Gulf contiguous to the said territorial waters over which the Ruler exercises jurisdiction and control.

These concessions were approved by the Foreign and Commonwealth Office in conformity with the special treaty relations under which the British government at that time managed the international relations of the Trucial States. The maps issued by the Foreign Office at the time of the granting of the concessions showed a three-mile limit for Sharjah's territorial waters around the island of Abu Musa; they also showed that the concession of Occidental included the sea bed to the east of the island of Abu Musa beyond the said three miles. According to H.M. Government the areas of the two concessions were delimited on the basis of a sea boundary agreement concluded between Sharjah and Umm al-Qaiwain in 1964.[190]

However, as indicated earlier, in 1970 a dispute between Sharjah and Umm al-Qaiwain and their respective oil concessionaires erupted over an oil drilling location situated within nine miles off the island of Abu Musa and about thirty-two miles off the coast of Umm al-Qaiwain. The dispute arose following the discovery by an operating company in early 1970 in that location of favourable indications of an extensive oil and gas-bearing structure.[191] Matters came to a head in 1970, when British naval units prevented Occidental from taking a drilling rig to the promising area.[192] As a result of their action Occidental attempted to sue the British government for damages.[193] Eventually the dispute was stopped by direct British intervention and a three-month drilling stand-off in the disputed area was called, pending an investigation of the whole matter by a third party. Sir Gawain Bell was later appointed as mediator between the various factions.[194]

Umm al-Qaiwain claimed that the drilling location in question fell within the offshore concession area granted to its concessionaire, Occidental Petroleum, because it fell beyond the three-mile limit originally claimed around Abu Musa. This view was based on an assertion by Umm al-Qaiwain that, according to the above-mentioned 1964 sea boundary agreement, Sharjah agreed that Umm al-Qaiwain should have sovereign rights up to three miles off Abu Musa (thus leaving Abu Musa with three miles of territorial sea). This was contested by Sharjah, which argued that the 1964 agreement was about 'sea boundaries' and not 'sea bed boundaries', as the English translation from the Arabic puts it; that the agreement related to the points of departure and the compass courses of the lines of certain lateral boundaries; and that there was no evidence of any agreement touching frontal boundaries, nor of any agreement touching the breadth of which the territorial sea might be established.[195] In addition Sharjah, which considered the location to be within the concession area it had granted to Buttes Gas & Oil, asserted that the area never had been or could be within the jurisdiction and control of Umm al-Qaiwain because it fell within the twelve-mile territorial sea of Abu Musa as established by the first decree concerning the territorial sea of Sharjah and its dependencies which was made on 10 September 1969, antedating the concession held by Occidental. (Occidental alleged that this decree was fraudulently backdated.) Moreover, Sharjah said that '(ii) even apart from the effect of that Decree the area is within the "contiguous zone" of jurisdiction and has been at all material times', and that '(iii) even supposing neither the September Decree nor the contiguous zone were to have effect of excluding a claim by Umm al-Qaiwain, the area is still within Sharjah's sovereign rights on the continental shelf recognised by general international law'.[196]

Sir Gawain Bell was unsuccessful in his mediation, but following intensive negotiations with Sir William Luce, Britain's special envoy in the Arabian Gulf, Sharjah and Iran agreed on a 'Memorandum of Understanding', examined below, concerning future arrangements in respect of the island of Abu Musa and its twelve-mile territorial sea. Umm al-Qaiwain demanded the cancellation of the memorandum on the ground that the Sharjah authorities were not competent to sign such an agreement.[197] Following the discovery of oil in the disputed location by Buttes Gas & Oil in 1972, the government of Umm al-Qaiwain announced its intention of taking legal action against the company,[198] though no such action is known to have been entered upon.

The controversy between Sharjah and Umm al-Qaiwain was followed by litigation between their respective oil concessionaires before both United States and British courts. In the United States a private anti-trust suit brought by Occidental against Buttes Gas & Oil alleged that the latter had conspired with Sharjah, Umm al-Qaiwain, Great Britain and Iran to deprive Occidental of the oil-rich portion of its concession area from Umm al-Qaiwain. On 17 April 1971 the district court in California dismissed the suit on the ground that the doctrine of 'acts of state' as applied in the United States precluded any enquiry into acts of foreign sovereigns even if allegedly induced and procured by the defendants.[199] The dismissal was affirmed by the United States Court of Appeals on 23 June 1972,[200] and on 24 October 1972 the Supreme Court denied a petition for a writ of *certiorari*.[201] A further action by Occidental was brought towards the end of 1974 in the Western Louisiana district court, in which the company claimed title to the crude oil produced by Buttes Gas & Oil from the disputed location. The court, however, entered judgement in favour of Buttes, stating that no rights of Occidental had been confiscated by any of the countries involved; that in law Occidental would be unable to prove that it had any concessionary rights at the time Buttes produced the oil; and that a decision on possible confiscation of rights would involve determining a boundary dispute between Iran, Sharjah and Umm al-Qaiwain.[202]

Meanwhile in England on 15 October 1970 Buttes issued a writ of slander against Occidental and its chairman, who in a press conference had accused Buttes of wrong-dealing. On 7 April 1972 Occidental put in a defence and counter-claim. It affirmed that the accusation was true in substance and in fact, pleading fair comment on a matter of public interest. In addition, it counter-claimed against Buttes for conspiracy and made a claim for damages for libel in respect of a circular sent to Buttes shareholders. On 31 July 1974 Mr Justice May struck out the conspiracy counter-claim on the grounds that allegations of conspiracy would involve investigation of matters which were 'acts of state' of the governments of Sharjah, Umm al-Qaiwain, Iran and the United Kingdom, and were not justiciable in the courts of England. But the Judge allowed the action to continue in regard to the slander and the counter-claim in respect of the libel.[203] In the Court of Appeal, which considered the matter on 5 December 1974, Lord Denning, M.R., allowed an interlocutory appeal by Occidental but dismissed a cross-appeal by Buttes. Lord Denning held that there was no ground for striking out the counter-claim of conspiracy and no ground for saying that the counter-claim of libel should not proceed. He said that the courts of England had never extended the doctrine of 'acts of state' so as to prevent the defendants in such a case from pleading justification and proving the facts relied on, even though incidentally it would mean enquiring into acts done by a foreign power. But, Lord Denning added, it was well settled that the English courts would not enquire into the validity or invalidity of the legislation or decrees of a foreign government which had been recognised by the government of the United Kingdom; he further noted that none of the claims in the action or counter-action sought to challenge the validity of any foreign legislation or decrees. All that was sought was compensation for the consequences of them.[204] However, the case before the Court of Appeal was only interlocutory and the trial of the action is in theory still pending.

C. IRAN–SHARJAH: MEMORANDUM OF UNDERSTANDING. As has been indicated, through intensive efforts by the British government, Iran and Sharjah agreed on a 'Memorandum of Understanding' concerning future arrangements in respect of the island of Abu Musa and its territorial waters. The understanding was first announced on 29 November 1971 by the then ruler of Sharjah.[205] Just twenty-four hours after the ruler's announcement Iran's Prime Minister told the Iranian parliament that Iranian troops had landed on the Greater and Lesser Tumbs the day before and, taking up strategic positions on Abu Musa, had hoisted the Iranian flag there.[206]

The understanding does not determine the question of sovereignty over the island. For, under its terms, 'Neither Iran nor Sharjah will give up its claim to Abu Musa nor recognise the other's claim.' Thus the settlement appears to be of a temporary nature. Against this background the parties have agreed upon certain arrangements concerning jurisdiction and other related matters. It has been agreed that Iranian troops will be stationed in areas the extent of which is shown on a map attached to the memorandum. Within the agreed areas occupied by Iranian troops 'Iran will have full jurisdiction and the Iranian flag will fly'. Sharjah's rights of jurisdiction are described with some ambiguity: 'Sharjah will retain full jurisdiction over the remainder of the island. The Sharjah flag will fly over the Sharjah police post on the same basis as the Iranian flag will fly over the Iranian military quarters'. Apparently Sharjah's garrison police post will be purely symbolic, while the presence of Iranian troops will ensure for Iran control of the Strait of Hormuz.[207]

According to the memorandum both Iran and Sharjah recognised a twelve-mile limit of territorial waters around Abu Musa, and agreed that the exploitation of the petroleum resources of the island and the sea bed and subsoil beneath its territorial sea would be carried out by Buttes Gas & Oil Company under the terms of its concession with the ruler of Sharjah.[208] Revenues accruing from oil exploitation would be shared equally between Iran and Sharjah. It was also agreed that a 'financial assistance agreement will be signed between Iran and Sharjah'. In implementation of this provision an aid agreement was signed by the two countries, which provides for an annual payment by Iran of £1,500,000 for a period of nine years to the government of Sharjah to be used for public purposes. This payment will, however, cease when Sharjah's revenues from oil discovered in the area of Abu Musa reach a rate of £3,000,000 a year.[209] Finally, under the memorandum, Iranian and Sharjah nationals would have equal fishing rights in the territorial sea of Abu Musa.[210]

Although the validity of the arrangements regarding the island of Abu Musa has been challenged by some Arab States on the grounds that the then ruler of Sharjah concluded it under duress and that in any event he had had no authority to sign such an agreement,[211] the new ruler stated on 2 February 1972 that Sharjah intends to stand by its agreement with Iran. He added, however, that he would seek a new 'understanding with the Shah of Iran'.[212] As regards the United Arab Emirates, of which Sharjah is a member, it has been observed that the U.A.R. 'does not appear [to have] announced its position towards the Abu Musa Agreement, and it remains doubtful, therefore, whether the U.A.E. has legally succeeded to the obligations under the said Agreement'.[213]

7. *Iran–Ras al-Khaimah: the question of the Tumb islands*

As mentioned above, on 30 November 1971 Iran landed troops on the three small, but strategically placed, islands of Abu Musa, Greater Tumb and Lesser Tumb, which lie in the exit from the Strait of Hormuz, the important seaway at the entrance of the Arabian Gulf.[214] Greater Tumb (Tumb Kubra or Tanb-e-Bozorg), the easternmost, lies about fifteen miles from the approximately sixty-mile long Iranian island of Qeshm, which is separated from the Iranian mainland by the narrow and intricate Clarence (or Khuran) Strait, and about forty miles from the Arabian mainland. Lesser Tumb (Tumb Sughra or Nabiy Tumb), approximately eight miles west of its sister island, lies about twenty miles from Qeshm and forty-five miles from the Arabian side. The former island has about 150 Arab inhabitants, and the latter is virtually uninhabited.

During the whole period of British control the Tumb islands were considered part of the territory of Ras al-Khaimah, and the United Kingdom held the view that the islands belonged to Ras al-Khaimah.[215] Nevertheless, since the two islands have long been claimed by Iran,[216] Britain seems to believe that some arrangement about the future of the Tumbs should have been worked out between Iran and Ras al-Khaimah by the time of the British withdrawal from the Gulf at the end of 1971.[217] The British government, it is stated, made great efforts to this end, but it was not possible to achieve an agreed solution because the ruler of Ras al-Khaimah felt he could not reach an agreement with Iran.[218]

Iran claims the islands as Iranian territory:

> For more than a century, beginning in 1770, British maps marked the Tumb islands as being Persian ... these islands form part of a group of islands virtually constituting an archipelago, all of which has always been part of Iran.[219]

However, it is clear that Iran had felt it necessary, because the islands were of vital strategic importance, to control them after the British withdrawal.[220]

Though in the case of Abu Musa the landing of Iranian troops, as shown above, was in pursuance of the 'Memorandum of Understanding' between Sharjah and Iran, no such agreement existed in the case of the Tumbs. The occupation of these islands took place just one day before the United Kingdom ended its special treaty relations with Ras al-Khaimah and the territory became completely independent. Iran's action was strongly condemned by several Arab States, and on 9 December 1971 the Security Council of the United Nations began a consideration of a complaint by Algeria, Iraq, Libya and the People's Democratic Republic of Yemen about 'the dangerous situation in the Arabian Gulf area arising from the occupation by armed forces of Iran' of three islands in the Gulf on 30 November 1971.[221] The representative of the United Arab Emirates felt that Iran's action was 'untenable both historically and judicially' and that it was contrary to the Charter of the United Nations.[222] He also said that:

> The British Government itself has on numerous occasions stated its belief that these islands were Arab and that the Iranian claim to them was not based on any legitimate historical or legal basis.[223]

The British government was criticised by several Arab States on the grounds that at the time of the occupation Britain was still technically responsible for the islands' defence and in theory should have come to Ras al-Khaimah's rescue. Thus the representative of Iraq, with regard to the two Tumbs, stated that:

> the Government of the United Kingdom always acknowledged and reaffirmed on various occasions that they were an integral part of Ras al-Khaimah, and that they were Arab islands. Accordingly, the United Kingdom has failed to honour its obligations towards Ras al-Khaimah in

not defending those two islands, where protection was a British responsibility.[224]

The delegate of Kuwait said that his government had told Iran that:

it could refer the case to the International Court of Justice or accept arbitration. But all our bids for a peaceful solution were turned down. Iran [he continued] cannot adjust itself, apparently, to the undisputed fact that these islands have always been Arab islands and that the continuation of free passage through the Strait of Hormuz is not only essential to Iran's economic life but also equally essential and vital to Kuwait, Iraq and the other littoral States of the Gulf. The Gulf is our sole economic lifeline.[225]

Notwithstanding the complaint of the Arab States, the Iranian seizure of the Tumb islands continued.[226] From a legal point of view Iran's action was indefensible: it is certainly a manifest breach of the international law prohibitions enshrined in Article 2(4) of the Charter of the United Nations.[227] From ancient times the islands have always been recognised as Arab and as part of the territory of Ras al-Khaimah.

It is interesting to observe that before the Iranian landing on Abu Musa and the two Tumb islands the Shah of Iran argued that Iran should have the islands

for strategic reasons. It is true that they could be flattened by Iran's Phantoms if they were ever to fall into the wrong hands; but his aim is clearly to prevent such a confrontation, with all its explosive potential, from occurring in the first place. Iran, he argues, should be awarded sovereignty. At least (as Britain has informally suggested by way of compromise) Iran must get garrisoning rights.[228]

Clearly this argument is political and not legal.[229]

C. CONCLUSION

Despite the difficulties, indicated at the outset, involved in the problem of continental shelf delimitation in the Arabian Gulf, the offshore boundary agreements so far reached in that area seem to have achieved their aim of 'just' and 'equitable' solutions. In addition, and notwithstanding the fact that none of the Arabian Gulf States is a party to the 1958 Geneva Convention on the Continental Shelf, the principles followed in the agreements parallel the convention's guidelines with respect to jurisdiction and delimitation of boundary. It might even be suggested that a regional customary rule has come into existence on the three-point rule expressed in Article 6 of the Geneva convention.[230] Moreover it may be observed that on the whole the boundary agreements are in harmony with the rules and principles of international law laid down by the International Court of Justice in the North Sea Continental Shelf cases, 1969.[231] The Court ruled that 'delimitation is to be affected by agreement in accordance with equitable principles',[232] and that, if the application of these principles leads to an overlapping of the areas appertaining to the States concerned, such a situation must be dealt with 'either by an agreed, or failing that by an equal, division of the overlapping areas, or by agreements for joint exploitation, the latter solution appearing particularly appropriate where it is a question of preserving the unity of a deposit'.[233]

The treatment accorded to islands and especially to those lying on or near an agreed boundary line, such as the islands of Al-'Arabiyah and Farsi in the Saudi Arabia–Iran agreement and Dayyinah in the agreement between Abu Dhabi and Qatar, is particularly interesting. Such islands have usually been given continental shelf rights coinciding with their respective territorial waters, but were not used as basepoints for the purpose of plotting median or equidistance lines to fix continental shelf boundaries between opposite or adjacent States.

With respect to the remaining unresolved problems and especially the offshore boundaries between Iran and Iraq, Kuwait, the Kuwait–Saudi Arabia partitioned zone, and the United Arab Emirates (with regard to the remaining undefined sector), it is believed that progress on these will be accelerated as a result of the Iraqi–Iranian treaty concerning Shatt al-Arab and the more recent Iranian proposal to withdraw from the islands of Abu Musa and the Tumbs. However, the dispute between Kuwait and Iraq over the islands of Warbah and Bubiyan may hold up final settlement of the Kuwait–Iraq–Iran boundaries.

CHAPTER IV

LEGAL STATUS OF THE GULF OF AQABA AND THE STRAITS OF TIRAN AND THE RULES GOVERNING THE RIGHT OF PASSAGE THERETHROUGH

The problem of the Gulf of Aqaba first arose in modern times 'after the occupation of the fishing port situated on the Gulf of Akaba, Umm Rashrash, which was to become the Port of Eilat, by the Israeli forces on the 10 March 1949',[1] that is, shortly after the 'Palestine war' of 1948 had ceased. The latter Israeli action was viewed by the Arab States surrounding the Gulf of Aqaba as a violation of the truce imposed by the Security Council, and as a threat against their rights there, so they complained to the United Nations and later attempted to resist physically the Israeli occupation, but failed. Egypt, therefore, acting in full accord with Saudi Arabia, effectively occupied the islands of Tiran and Sanafir at the entrance to the Gulf of Aqaba, the Straits of Tiran. This action was immediately followed by Egyptian regulations aimed at prohibiting the passage of Israeli vessels, and of other vessels carrying strategic cargoes to Israel, through the Straits of Tiran and the Gulf. Soon the problem appeared, essentially, as one concerning the extent of Israel's right of navigation, if any, through those waters. Since then the problem has been one of the chief bones of contention in three rounds of armed conflict between Israel and neighbouring Arab States, in 1956, 1967 and 1973. It has also been the subject of vehement and intensive discussions both within and without the United Nations, has occupied the attention of numerous academic studies, and has continually attracted the press. The problem, however, remains unresolved.

The difficulty about the question of the Gulf is not only that it is linked with the political issue of Palestine, which awaits a final settlement, and that there is no international agreement regulating navigation in the waters concerned, but also that it involves a series of controversial issues of international law, including matters relating to acquisition of territory, 'war' and 'peace', breadth of the territorial sea, passage through territorial waters, straits, multinational and historic waters.

The first part of this chapter provides the background to the geographical and historical position of the Gulf of Aqaba, the occupation of Umm Rashrash by Israeli forces in 1949, and the struggle for control of the Gulf since then. In the second part it identifies some of the specific issues involved in the problem and analyses them in the light of the general principles of international law and other relevant conventional rules.

A. GEOGRAPHICAL AND HISTORICAL POSITION OF THE GULF OF AQABA

The Gulf of Aqaba, the Sinus Aelanticus of antiquity, is a long, narrow gulf on the eastern side of the Sinai Peninsula forming the north-eastern fringe of the Red Sea.[2] The gulf extends approximately ninety-six miles, from the southernmost tip of Sinai up to the Jordanian port of Aqaba. It is generally quite deep, measuring over 800 fathoms in the middle.[3] It varies in breadth:

> at the entrance between Nabq and Ras Fartak [it] is 5¾ miles. About seventeen miles above Ras Fartak the breadth is 14½ miles, which is the widest part of the Gulf: thence abreast El Kura it is 12½ miles wide, abreast El Mamleh, the width is 9 miles, thence this general width is maintained, varying from between 12 miles and 11 miles, to within 15 miles of the head. The head then narrows to a width of about four miles abreast Ras el Masri, whence a general width of about three miles is maintained for 4 miles to the head.[4]

The passage at the entrance of the gulf is hampered by the existence of two main islands, Tiran and Sanafir, and several smaller coral islets and rocks.[5] Tiran, about seven miles long and five miles wide, lies about four and a half miles south of Ras Fartak on the Saudi coast and is separated from the Egyptian coast by the Straits of Tiran, about three miles wide. Sanafir lies about two miles east of Tiran, with a reef in between.[6] The Straits of Tiran, the western and principal entrance to the gulf, is divided by a line of coral reefs into two channels; Enterprise Passage and Grafton Passage. Both of these passages are deep. The latter lies close to Tiran island, with a minimum breadth of 950 yards, the former, 1,300 yards wide, lies close to the Egyptian Sinai Peninsula at Ras Nasrani. The Enterprise Passage is the principal shipping channel, navigable by vessels of substantial size, thus placing the main entrance to the Gulf of Aqaba exclusively within Egypt's territorial sea. The eastern entrance to the gulf, the passages between the Saudi coast and the two islands of Tiran and Sanafir and between the two islands are not navigable, owing to the existence of several coral islets and rocks.[7] Apparently, because the Enterprise Passage

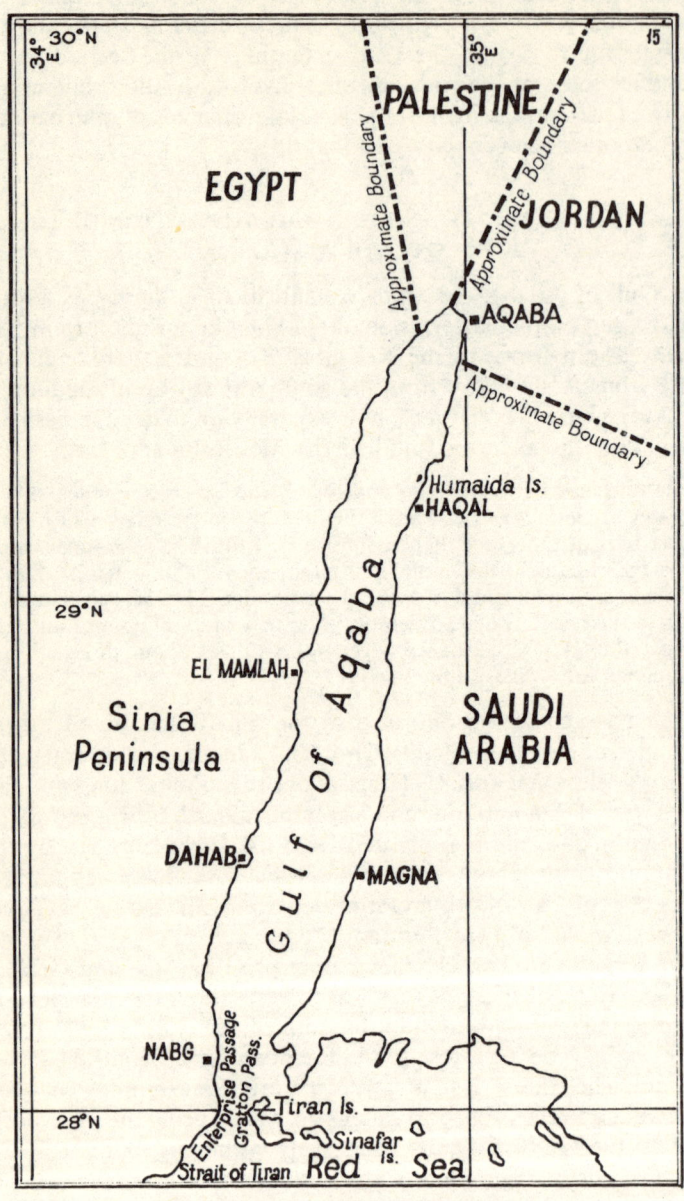

15 The Gulf of Aqaba and the Straits of Tiran. After M. P. Strohl, *The International Law of Bays,* The Hague, 1963, p. 390.

is the only navigable channel within the 'Straits' of Tiran, the term 'Strait' of Tiran is also used.

Historically,

> For over a thousand years the Gulf has been surrounded by Arab territories. By approximately 700 A.D. the Arab conquest of a large part of the area known today as the Middle East had been completed, and from that time until approximately 1517, when the Arab territories surrounding the Gulf were brought under the political control of the Ottoman Empire, the Gulf apparently was an exclusively Arab water area. From 1517 until the end of World War I the Gulf was controlled by the Ottoman Empire. During that long period the question of the Gulf's status does not appear to have arisen. When, however, during the Middle Ages a Crusader fleet made an incursion into the Gulf and the Red Sea from its base at the northern end of the Gulf, the whole Muslim world was shocked at the invasion of water areas which constituted a gateway of the Pilgrims to the Islamic holy cities of Mecca and Medine.[8]

At present, of approximately 230 miles coastline of the gulf, about 125 miles are in Egypt, ninety-six miles in Saudi Arabia, fifteen miles in Jordan,[9] and about four miles in Israeli territory.[10] There are four main ports on the gulf. Two lie at its head: on the eastern side, the port of Aqaba—Jordan's only outlet to the sea—and, on the western side, the Israeli port of Eilat (formerly Umm Rashrash). The other two ports are Magna in Saudi Arabia and Mersa Dahab in Egypt.

The extent of the territorial seas claimed by the countries surrounding the Gulf of Aqaba are: Egypt—twelve miles (1958); Israel—six miles (1956); Jordan—three miles (1943); Saudi Arabia—twelve miles (1958).[11]

B. OCCUPATION OF UMM RASHRASH AND THE STRUGGLE FOR CONTROL OF THE GULF OF AQABA, 1949–76

1. Occupation of Umm Rashrash

After the Israeli occupation, on 10 March 1949, of Umm Rashrash, the latter was declared, on 25 June 1952, to be the Israeli port of Eilat.[12] This occupation was established after the conclusion of the Egyptian–Israeli Rhodes General Armistice Agreement, 24 February 1949,[13] but before the signing of the Israeli–Jordan Rhodes General Armistice Agreement, 3 April 1949.[14]

The Israeli occupation occurred while the Israeli–Jordan armistice negotiations were still in progress.[15] This action, together with other military operations by Israeli forces in the southern part of the Negev in March 1949, was the subject of acute anxiety on the part of the United Nations acting mediator on Palestine, who following the Transjordanian complaint at Rhodes confirmed the Israeli occupation of 'Umm Reshresh, with the borders of Palestine on the Gulf of Aqaba in the afternoon of March 10'.[16] He therefore

> formally requested the Israeli and Transjordan delegations now at Rhodes to inform their Governments that military activity of this kind, regardless of whether actual fighting eventuates, must be regarded as contrary to the conditions of the truce imposed by the Security Council.[17]

The Israeli–Jordanian armistice agreement of 1949, leaving Umm Rashrash under Israeli control as 'dictated exclusively by military considerations', in no way prejudices 'the rights, claims and positions of either party hereto in the ultimate peaceful settlement of the Palestine Question'.[18]

In view of the above, Charles B. Selak affirms:

> For a final and complete determination of the status of the Gulf it may be necessary to await a final settlement of the Palestine question, for it is unclear at present what is the status of Israel's coastline on the Gulf.[19]

2. Egypt–Saudi Arabia accord concerning the islands of Tiran and Sanafir and the question of sovereignty thereover

Following the Israeli occupation of Umm Rashrash in March 1949, Egypt—with the concurrence of Saudi Arabia, which claims sovereignty over the islands of Tiran and Sanafir at the entrance of the Straits of Tiran—occupied these two islands and established its vigilance to exclude Israeli vessels and other vessels carrying strategic cargo to Israel from passing through the Egyptian territorial waters in the Straits of Tiran. The Egypt–Saudi Arabia accord was communicated specifically to the United Kingdom and the United States respectively on 30 January and 28 February 1950: the Egyptian *aide-mémoire* emphasised:

> 1. Taking into consideration certain velleities which have manifested themselves recently on the part of Israel authorities on behalf of the Islands of Tiran and Sanafir in the Red Sea at the entrance of the Gulf of Aqaba, the Government of Egypt acting in full accord with the Government of Saudi Arabia has given orders to occupy effectively these two islands. This occupation is now an accomplished fact.
>
> 2. In doing this Egypt wanted simply to confirm its right (as well as every possible right of the Kingdom of Saudi Arabia) in regard to the mentioned islands which by their geographical position are at least 3 marine miles off the Egyptian side of Sinai and 4 miles approximately off the opposite side of Saudi Arabia, all this in order to forestall any attempt on or possible violation of its rights.

3. This occupation is not conceived in a spirit to hinder in whatever way it may be the innocent passage across the maritime space separating these two islands from the Egyptian coast of Sinai. It goes without saying that this passage, the only practicable, will remain free as in the past being in confirmation with the international practice and the recognised principles of international law.[20]

Sovereignty over the islands of Tiran and Sanafir seems to be disputed between Egypt and Saudi Arabia. On 15 February 1954 Egypt informed the Security Council that the two islands had constituted Egyptian territory since 1906, at the time of the delimitation of the frontier between Egypt and the Ottoman Empire, and that the records of the Second World War contain official evidence that Egyptian units had been using these two islands as part of the Egyptian defensive system during the war.[21] On 31 March 1957, however, Saudi Arabia addressed a circular note to the missions of 'friendly Governments' in Jidda, in which it asserted that the two islands of Tiran and Sanafir 'are Saudi Arabian property'.[22] A further assertion was made in a memorandum to the United Nations stating that the two islands and the straits separating them 'are under the sovereignty and jurisdiction of the Kingdom of Saudi Arabia'.[23] More recently, nevertheless, it has been indicated that, although up to 1949 the legal status of Tiran and Sanafir was not determined, in that year Saudi Arabia and Egypt agreed that the latter would occupy the two islands to control the entrance to the gulf, but without prejudice to any Saudi claim.[24]

3. Egyptian regulations relating to navigation through the Straits of Tiran

Early in 1951 Egypt promulgated regulations requiring vessels transiting the Straits of Tiran to notify the Egyptian authorities and to submit to inspection. Egypt, it was contended, did not intend to prohibit the innocent passage of warships or commercial vessels of 'friendly countries', and this action was without prejudice to Egypt's 'legitimate right of control as a riparian power nor to the exercise of its exceptional rights of visit and seizure of contraband'. Egypt thus declared that 'enemy' warships were forbidden access to and passage through Egyptian territorial waters, including the Straits of Tiran, while 'enemy' commercial vessels could have access only at the risk of seizure and detention.[25]

In July 1951 the United Kingdom agreed that the Egyptian customs authorities at Suez or Adabia might visit and search British vessels, other than naval or military craft, sailing direct from Suez or Adabia to Aqaba.[26] These measures were agreed upon by the British 'to prevent the recurrence of incidents such as . . . the case of S.S. *Empire Roche* in the entrance to the Gulf of Aqaba'.[27] The *Empire Roche,* a British steamship bound for the Jordanian port of Aqaba with a cargo of arms, was fired on in the Straits of Tiran on 1 July 1951.[28]

Further Egyptian regulations relating to navigation through the Straits of Tiran were issued in 1954. A naval signal station was established and vessels approaching the area were ordered to keep 'a sharp lookout for signals made by this station'.[29] Presumably these instructions were complied with by U.S. merchant vessels passing through the straits, which were instructed by the U.S. Navy Hydrographic Office to hoist their signal letters on arriving within signalling distance of the signal station.[30]

On 10 July 1955 Mr David Ben-Gurion, then Prime Minister of Israel, declared that the port of Eilat was being completed so that passage into the Indian Ocean could be assured 'if necessary with the help of the Israeli Navy, Air Force, and Army'. A few weeks later, on 25 September 1955, Mr Ben-Gurion repeated his threat to use force to ensure Israeli use of the gulf, and he even set a time limit for these actions—'in a year or less'—but added that he would endeavour to open talks with the Egyptian President as soon as Eilat's port facilities were nearly complete.[31] Egypt's 'answer to the threat was to tighten her rules for entry into the Gulf'.[32] Thus on 5 September 1955 Egypt reaffirmed the prohibition against Israeli shipping and issued regulations requiring three days' advance notice from vessels heading towards the Gulf of Aqaba, and the 'Regional Boycotting Office for Israel' in Alexandria was appointed the sole authority for issuing permission to vessels to pass through the Egyptian territorial waters in the Gulf of Aqaba and the Straits of Tiran.[33]

4. The 1956 Sinai campaign and the 1967 Arab–Israeli armed conflict

Since the various Egyptian regulations regarding passage through the Straits of Tiran were announced, a series of incidents have occurred in these waters involving vessels of different flags.[34] During the 1956 Sinai campaign,[35] however, Israel occupied the islands of Tiran and Sanafir and took over the Egyptian positions in the Sharm el-Sheikh and Gaza areas. According to the Ministry for Foreign Affairs of Israel, 'on 3 November of that year . . . and for the first time in seven years, navigation through the Straits of Tiran, and in the Gulf of Aqaba was free to the ships and cargoes of all nations, as in every other international waterway'.[36]

In compliance with General Assembly Resolution 1124 (XI) of

THE GULF OF AQABA AND THE STRAITS OF TIRAN

2 February 1957,[37] the Israeli forces withdrew from the areas they occupied during the 1956 invasion and units of the United Nations Emergency Force (UNEF) were placed on the Egyptian–Israeli Armistice Demarcation Line of 24 February 1949.[38] The United Nations remained in control until May 1967, when the President of the United Arab Republic requested the Secretary General to withdraw UNEF 'from the territory of the United Arab Republic and Gaza Strip'.[39] The latter move was soon followed by the announcement of the President of Egypt on 22 May 1967 that 'the United Arab Republic has decided to prevent Israeli ships, and other ships carrying strategic cargoes to Israel, from passing through the mouth of the Gulf of Aqaba . . . "The Israeli flag shall not go through the Gulf," the President declared.'[40] As a result of the Arab–Israeli conflict which followed in 1967, Israel is now in control of Arab territories which include the western shore of the Gulf of Aqaba, the islands of Tiran and Sanafir, and Sharm el-Sheikh.[41]

C. THE MAIN ASSERTIONS AND ARGUMENTS REGARDING THE CONTROVERSY SURROUNDING THE GULF OF AQABA AND THE STRAITS OF TIRAN

Before any fruitful analysis of legal issues relating to the controversy surrounding the legal status of, and the right of passage through, the Gulf of Aqaba and the Straits of Tiran can be attempted, it is essential that the major assertions and arguments of the parties concerned be clarified. Perhaps the most useful approach to an accurate *exposé* of these matters is to describe them as expounded by Egyptian and Israeli spokesmen, noting that the controversy was discussed in the United Nations on several occasions and that it was also raised during the eighth session of the International Law Commission in 1956 and at the 1958 Geneva Conference on the Law of the Sea.[42]

1. *The Egyptian position*
Egypt asserts that Israel's claim to the right to navigate through the Straits of Tiran and across the Gulf of Aqaba is 'without foundation'.[43] The Egyptian argument in support of this assertion, as explained by spokesmen on several occasions,[44] rests essentially on the following propositions:

1. That 'Historically the Gulf [of Aqaba] has been under continued and uninterrupted Arab domination for over one thousand years. It always has been a national inland waterway subject to

absolute Arab sovereignty. Its geographical location is conclusive proof of its national character. By its configuration it has a nature of *mare clausum* which does not belong to the class of international waterways.'[45] In support of this proposition reference is made[46] to the Gulf of Fonseca case of 1917,[47] where the International Court of Central American Republics held that the gulf, bounded by Nicaragua, El Salvador and Honduras, was 'an historic bay possessed of the characteristics of a closed sea'.[48]

2. That Israel can assert no 'legal rights' on the basis of its possession of the port of Eilat, because this port is nothing but the Arab village of Umm Rashrash, which Israel occupied by the use of force in violation of the Egyptian–Israeli General Armistice Agreement of 24 February 1949, and decisions of the Security Council, including Resolution 54 (1948), 15 July 1948, ordering the parties 'pursuant to Article 40 of the Charter, to desist from further military action', and Resolution 56 (1948), adopted by the Security Council on 19 August 1948, in which it was stated that 'no party is entitled to gain military or political advantage through violation of the truce'.[49]

3. That, even if it is admitted that Eilat has been legally established on the Gulf of Aqaba, since Egypt is not a party to the 1958 Geneva Convention on the Territorial Sea and the Contiguous Zone, it is not bound by Article 16(4) in so far as it provides for free and innocent passage through straits which are used for international navigation between one part of the high seas and the territorial sea of a foreign State. Nor, so runs the argument, is this provision declaratory of customary international law. Furthermore, it is stated that, in any event, Article 16(4) 'is not applicable to the Straits of Tiran, for the latter do not connect the Red Sea with allegedly Israeli territorial waters. Indeed, a ship proceeding towards Elath must travel over 95 miles of Arab internal waters, after passing through the Straits, before reaching its destination.'[50] In addition, Egypt asserts that, under the 1958 convention, it can hinder or even deny passage to Israeli ships through its territorial waters in the Straits of Tiran and the Gulf of Aqaba on the ground that such passage is not innocent but 'prejudicial to the peace, good order or security of the coastal State'.

4. That the Egyptian–Israeli General Armistice Agreement of 24 February 1949 does not vitiate Egypt's right to impose restrictions on navigation in the Gulf of Aqaba because 'it is a general, incontestable rule of international law that the conclusion of a partial or general armistice agreement does not end the state of war. It only terminates the hostilities.'[51] Moreover, Egypt has

exercised such rights since 1950, and vessels flying American, British as well as various other flags accepted the Egyptian regulations until 1956, and the opening of the Gulf of Aqaba to Israel from autumn 1956 to spring 1967 was an accomplished fact imposed by the use of force.[52]

5. With reference to an Israeli assertion that the Egyptian *aide-mémoire* of 1950,[53] in which assurances were given that 'innocent passage' through the Straits of Tiran would remain free 'in conformity with international practice and recognised principles of the law of nations', should guarantee her free passage through the Straits of Tiran, Egypt replies that its declaration 'could never be construed to guarantee "free and innocent passage" to any enemy during a state of war'.[54]

Finally, it may be observed that although, on several occasions, Egypt announced its intention to 'prevent Israeli ships, and other ships carrying strategic cargoes to Israel, from passing through the mouth of the Gulf of Aqaba',[55] she nevertheless made it clear that she 'would permit innocent passage of the Straits of Tiran'.[56]

2. The Israeli position

Israel declares that 'the description of the Gulf of Aqaba as "closed Arab waters under exclusive Arab jurisdiction" was based neither on law nor on fact'.[57] She asserts that 'as a littoral State' on the Gulf of Aqaba, she should be able to 'exercise full rights of free passage in the Gulf of Aqaba and through the Straits of Tiran'.[58] For Israel believes that 'the Gulf of Aqaba comprehends international waters and that no nation has the right to prevent free and innocent passage in the Gulf and through the Straits giving access thereto, in accordance with the generally accepted definition of those terms in the law of the Sea'.[59]

The government of Israel considers that 'the Gulf of Aqaba is an international waterway in the sense that the territorial waters of at least four countries overlap within the Gulf, so that, if any one country were to assert the application of its sovereign rights in the territorial waters, we would ... achieve a maritime jungle ...'.[60]

In addition, with the Gulf of Aqaba in mind, the Israeli government, commenting on the provisional articles concerning the regime of the high seas and the territorial sea adopted by the International Law Commission at its seventh session in 1955,[61] has maintained that:

... where access to a given port—whether existing one or which at some future date a State may wish to establish—is only possible by traversing a strait (in the geographical sense), then it is quite immaterial whether that Strait is or is not within the waters classed as the territorial sea of one or more of the littoral States, or what is the legal nature (gulf, bay, high seas) of the waters on which the harbour is situated. In such circumstances the right of passage for the ships of all nations, and quite regardless of their cargo, is and must remain absolutely unqualified, and the littoral State or States have no right whatsoever so long as the matter is not regulated by Convention to hinder, hamper, impede or suspend the free passage of those ships. The same rule is also true as regards warships . . .

The interests of the international community must have absolute predominance over those of the littoral States whose territorial waters have to be traversed in making for a given harbour. In this respect the passage through Straits of this character is assimilated to the high seas themselves.

. . . regardless of their position as a territorial sea, straits in the geographical sense which constitute the only access to a harbour belonging to another State can under no circumstances fall within the regime of territorial sea.[62]

In support of its stand, Israel places heavy reliance on the rule in Article 16(4) of the 1958 Geneva Convention on the Territorial Sea and the Contiguous Zone, namely: 'There shall be no suspension of the innocent passage of foreign ships through straits which are used for international navigation between one part of the high seas and . . . the territorial sea of a foreign State'. Thus Israel declares that 'there could not be a more unequivocal affirmation of Israel's right of navigation through the Straits of Tiran than (Article 16(4)) of the Convention'.[63] Israel also maintains that:

For ten years and more, since the Sinai Campaign, the Straits of Tiran had been free and open to Israel's and to all shipping as a provision of the general settlement which led to the withdrawal of the Israel Defence Forces from the Peninsula.[64]

As indicated earlier, in a supplementary argument Israel asserts that the blocking of the Straits of Tiran against Israeli shipping is contrary to the Egyptian undertaking that the passage 'will remain free . . .' which is contained in the Egyptian *aide-mémoire* of 1950.[65]

D. ANALYSIS OF THE PROBLEM

Having thus outlined the principal assertions and arguments made by Israel and Egypt, we now turn to a closer examination of the legal issues involved. But in view of the diversity of these issues and the fact that the whole problem has been examined by several eminent writers, the analysis will concentrate on some of the less explored aspects. The question of whether or not Israel has lawfully acquired the territory bordering upon the Gulf of Aqaba, and Egypt's claim that a continuing state of 'war' and 'belligerency' exists between the two countries, will not be subjects for full analysis or conclusions here.[66]

As rightly observed by Professor R. R. Baxter, 'the problem of free navigation through the Gulf of Aqaba has been found inextricably linked with the question of passage through the Straits [of Tiran] which connect the Gulf with the Red Sea'.[67] The questions of passage through the actual straits and the status of the waters above the straits are indeed inseparable. It is submitted that the nature of the legal status of the Straits of Tiran is dependent on that of the gulf proper and, of course, on that of the waters below, i.e. the Red Sea. This is simply because, geographically, a strait is normally defined by reference to the two sections of waters it connects, for at present no precise measurements are required of a strait.[68] Thus in the Corfu Channel case, 1949, a geographical strait was defined as a passage 'between two parts of the high seas'.[69] Similarly, Professor Baxter, an authority on the question of international waterways, states: 'In geographic terms, a strait is normally a narrow passage connecting two sections of the high seas, but a precise delimitation cannot be made of width and length required of such a passage'.[70]

Article 16(4) of the 1958 Convention on the Territorial Sea and the Contiguous Zone also refers simply to straits 'between one part of the high seas and another part of the high seas or the territorial sea of a foreign State'. Likewise the recent ICNT, Part III, which was prepared after the sixth session of the Third Conference on the Law of the Sea speaks of straits between one area of the high seas or an exclusive economic zone and another area of the high seas or an exclusive economic zone or the territorial sea of a foreign State.[71]

In view of the above, it is essential that the legal description and status of the Gulf of Aqaba proper be examined before that of the straits which connect it with the Red Sea. As to the Red Sea, there seems to be no dispute regarding its legal status: at present it is generally recognised that it constitutes part of the high seas; the territorial seas of the littoral States are, of course, excepted.[72] If the exclusive economic zone concept which is at present being discussed at the Third Conference of the Law of the Sea is eventually adopted, the Red Sea would be considered as an exclusive economic zone, but this will not affect the freedom of navigation there.[73]

SPECIFIC REGIONAL ISSUES

1. Legal description of the Gulf of Aqaba

In geography the term 'bay', which is used interchangeably with the term 'gulf' because there is no single geographical conception of a 'bay' or 'gulf',[74] refers to a wide indentation of the sea into the land.[75]

A definition of the legal concept of a 'bay' which 'may be taken as expressive of customary law'[76] is to be found in Article 7 of the 1958 Convention on the Territorial Sea and the Contiguous Zone:

> For the purposes of these articles, a bay is a well-marked indentation whose penetration is in such proportion to the width of its mouth as to contain landlocked waters and constitute more than a mere curvature of the coast. An indentation shall not, however, be regarded as a bay unless its area is as large as, or larger than, that of the semicircle whose diameter is a line drawn across the mouth of that indentation.

In the light of these considerations, and having regard to the extent and restricted configuration of the Gulf of Aqaba,[77] it would appear that the latter is a 'bay' in the geographical and legal sense. The gulf may be described as a 'strait gulf'[78] or as an 'arm' of the sea,[79] but it is a body of water to which 'the rules of bays are applicable'.[80] It is a 'bay of the Red Sea'.[81]

Having ascertained this much, an attempt will be made now to arrive at a conclusion as to the juridical status of this gulf and, consequently, to the right of passage through it. The following analysis, therefore will be divided into two main headings: the juridical status of the Gulf of Aqaba, and the rules governing the right of passage through the gulf and the Straits of Tiran. Under the former heading will be discussed the question of the legal regime of the gulf from the point of view of territorial sovereignty. The discussion under the second heading will be devoted to issues relating to the extent of the right of passage through the gulf, taking account of the assertion that the Straits of Tiran fall into the category of international straits under the doctrine of the Corfu Channel case, 1949,[82] or that they would be an international waterway under Article 16(4) of the Convention on the Territorial Sea and the Contiguous Zone, 1958.

2. Juridical status of the Gulf of Aqaba

Various and conflicting propositions have been advanced with regard to the juridical status of the Gulf of Aqaba. It is not intended, however, to consider the claim of the Arab States that the gulf is an Arab 'historic' bay, an Arab *mare clausum*, because this claim, based on historic grounds, is directly connected with the question relating to the legality of Israel's possession of the territory bordering on the gulf, a question which, as stated earlier, is not for examination here. In addition, this particular issue has received detailed analysis from several eminent writers,[83] and no formal declaration or agreement seems to exist between the Arab littoral States of the gulf concerning this claim. As will be shown, however, there seems to be little or perhaps no doubt at all that, regardless of any historic considerations, the Gulf of Aqaba can be transformed into a 'closed' bay by agreement among all the littoral States.

A. EFFECT OF THE TERRITORIAL SEA CLAIMS. The assertion that the Gulf of Aqaba 'comprehends international waters', was advanced in 1957, particularly by the maritime nations, including the United States and the United Kingdom, in connection with the Israeli withdrawal from Gaza and Sharm el-Sheikh following the Sinai campaign of 1956. The advocates of this proposition are mainly those States which in 1957 were still refusing to recognise the extension of the territorial sea beyond the three-mile limit and, therefore, insisted that the three-mile limit rather than the six- or twelve-mile limit should apply to the Gulf of Aqaba. Accordingly they considered that 'there is a stretch of water in the middle of the Gulf of Aqaba outside the territorial waters of the Arab littoral States which constitutes international waters'.[84]

Since at present there seems to exist a sufficient international consensus of opinion for the twelve-mile territorial sea limit, as adopted by Egypt and Saudi Arabia and a great number of other States, to be regarded as a customary rule of international law, it can no longer be said that the Gulf of Aqaba 'comprehends international waters'. For owing to the narrowness of the gulf, the territorial seas of the littoral States overlap in all its parts, leaving no room for any high seas.[85] This situation seems to have been recognised now even by the maritime powers which in 1957 insisted that the gulf 'comprehends international waters', for, as will be seen later, more recently these States have based their claim for free and innocent passage through the gulf not on the doctrine of the Corfu Channel case[86] but rather on Article 16(4) of 1958 Convention on the Territorial Sea and the Contiguous Zone, with its reference to straits between one part of the high seas and the territorial sea of a foreign State.

B. LEGAL STATUS OF MULTI-STATE BAYS. A number of States and some writers have expressed the view that because the Gulf of

SPECIFIC REGIONAL ISSUES

Aqaba is bordered by more than one State it should be considered as part of the high seas.[87] This view is supported by reference to authorities such as Oppenheim[88] and Gidel.[89] The latter, with regard to the construction of the baseline of the territorial sea within bays bordered by more than one state, *inter alia*, writes:

> If the baseline of the territorial sea is drawn following the low-water mark, as general opinion in our view rightly maintains, the bay will not include internal waters other than the narrow belt immediately adjoining the shore together with ports and harbours. It will follow from this that navigation will be completely assured within the bay with a right of innocent passage for ships bound for the various coastal states. This situation could no doubt be modified by treaty provisions, but it is this situation which must be considered in our view to be produced by the application of the customary rule.
>
> Quite different is the status of the waters of the bay if the baseline of the territorial sea takes the form of straight line. In fact the maritime areas on the landward of this line must be considered internal waters. The solution which we have adopted as correct for the construction of the baseline of the territorial sea—the low-water mark—in bays with a number of coastal states provides the answer to the question of the juridical status of these waters, they are either high seas or territorial sea.[90]

Oppenheim proposes that:

> ... as a rule, all Gulfs and bays enclosed by the land of more than one littoral state, however narrow their entrance may be, are non-territorial. They are part of the open sea, the marginal belt inside the Gulfs and bays are excepted. They can never be appropriated; they are in time of peace and war open to vessels of all nations, including men-of-war, and foreign vessels cannot, therefore, be compelled to comply with municipal regulations of the littoral state concerning the mode of fishing.[91]

First, it will be noted that both Gidel and Oppenheim make it clear that the States of a multinational bay have the right to claim a territorial sea. Gidel's main concern appears to be that navigation should be completely assured in such a bay for ships bound for the various coastal States. He therefore takes the view that the baseline for the measurement of the territorial sea within the bay should be the low-water mark. This is to ensure that there remain within the bay some water areas which would be either territorial sea or, if the territorial waters of the various littoral States do not overlap, high seas and thus would be subject to the right of free or innocent passage as the case may be. This approach, according to Gidel, is part of customary law and could, no doubt, be modified by treaty provisions.

As to Oppenheim's proposition, some who have sought to rely

on this proposition have apparently failed to observe certain relevant qualifications. As already indicated, Oppenheim does not deny the States of a multi-State bay the right to a territorial sea, for he excluded the waters of the 'marginal belt inside the Gulfs and bays' from the application of his proposition. It therefore appears that when he says '... as a rule, all gulfs and bays ...', Oppenheim has in mind only the case of a bay too big to be wholly territorial waters. Besides, it may be observed that Oppenheim has assumed that the breadth of the territorial sea or 'marginal belt' is three miles.[92]

In the light of the foregoing observations and having regard to the fact that the territorial waters of the littoral States of the Gulf of Aqaba overlap in all parts of the Gulf, it may be safely suggested that in accordance with the propositions advanced by both Gidel and Oppenheim the Gulf of Aqaba is not part of the high seas but wholly territorial waters. According to Gidel's view, it appears that the gulf can even be transformed into internal waters by agreement between the riparian States.

The assertion that gulfs and bays surrounded by the land of more than one State can be claimed as internal waters is accepted by several legal authorities. Thus the American authority Charles Cheney Hyde says:

When the geographical relationship of a bay to the adjacent or enveloping land is such that the sovereign of the latter, if a single state, might not unlawfully claim the water as a part of its territory, it is not apparent why a like privilege should be denied to two or more States to which such land belongs, at least if they are so agreed, and accept as between themselves a division of the waters concerned. No requirement of international law as such deprives them of that privilege, notwithstanding the disposition of some who would have little room for its application.[93]

Accordingly, Hyde suggests that:

... the Bay of Fundy, by reason of its geographical relationship to the land into which it is projected, might be fairly dealt with by the United States and Canada, should they so agree, as a closed bay.[94]

In Article 6 of the 1929 Harvard Draft Convention on Territorial Waters George G. Wilson, Reporter, comments, *inter alia*:

This article deals with the delimitation of the waters within the seaward limit of bays when such waters are bordered by the territory of two or more States ... The situation does not frequently arise, and when it arises it will generally be dealt with by a Convention between the States concerned ...

Where the waters within the seaward limit are bordered by two or more

SPECIFIC REGIONAL ISSUES

States, it would seem that the bordering States should be permitted by international law to divide such waters between them as inland waters. If the same waters were bordered by one State only, that State would clearly be entitled, under Article 5, to treat the waters as inland waters. The power of two or more States should not be smaller than the power of one State in this respect if the States can reach an agreement.[95]

Judge P. Jessup states that a bay bordered by more than one State:

is clearly not a part of the high seas, and is properly considered by the bordering states as their common property. There is no reason why such states should be compelled to accept that the line of territorial waters follows the sinuosities of the coast.[96]

Introducing his discussion on 'the Bay within the Littoral of two or more States', Commander M. Strohl refers, *inter alia*, to Oppenheim's proposition that such a bay, however narrow its entrance may be, is non-territorial, but expresses doubt whether any general rule on such bays exists at the present time. He says:

In fact, both Professor Hyde and the Harvard Research suggest that there is no requirement of international law which prevents the riparian States from jointly claiming the bay and agreeing upon a division of its waters as inland waters.[97]

Strohl concludes:

... bays lying within the littoral of two or more States represent a special case ... Each bay of this type is in itself a special situation wherein the practices of the States concerned have usually evolved through the mutual recognition of their combined needs.[98]

Similarly, Professor J. Verzijl denies:

... the validity of any general theory according to which a wide bay with a narrow entrance should be considered as comprising a central pocket of open sea on the sole ground that it is surrounded by more than one State ... there is indeed no convincing authority for such a general theory. The riparian States are completely free to agree upon a solution of this sort but there is no mandatory rule to this effect in force. It is up to them to regulate the question as they think fit.[99]

In 1956 the International Law Commission was unable to propose rules applicable to multinational bays because it did not have 'sufficient data at its disposal concerning the number of cases involved or the regulations at present applicable to them'.[100] Accordingly, Article 7, concerning bays, of the 1958 Convention on the Territorial Sea and the Contiguous zone related 'only to bays the coasts of which belong to a single state'.[101]

It may be observed also that neither the Preparatory Committee of the current Third United Nations Conference on the Law of the Sea nor the conference itself has attempted to deal with the question of bays whose coastline is shared by more than one State.[102] This lends support to the view that each bay of this type 'is in itself a special situation'[103] which does not lend itself to the formulation of a general rule.

C. CONCLUSION. Taking into account the above views and considerations, the final conclusion with regard to the juridical status of the Gulf of Aqaba might be summed up as follows:

1. In principle and, regardless of any consideration which might be given to the claim that the gulf is an Arab 'historic' bay, the Gulf of Aqaba, in the words of Professor Hyde, ... 'might be fairly dealt with by [the littoral States], should they so agree, as a closed bay'.[104] This conclusion derives support from various writers,[105] as well as from the practice of certain States.[106] So far, however, there exists no agreement to that effect, nor has there been any formal agreement declaring the Gulf of Aqaba as an Arab 'historic' bay, in accordance with the claim of the Arab littoral States.

2. Under the present circumstances, therefore, it is suggested that the waters of the Gulf of Aqaba should be considered as *territorial waters*, with all the consequences which this term entails according to the generally accepted rules of the law of the sea.[107]

Before considering the question relating to the extent of the right of passage through the gulf, it is convenient to deal briefly with the Gulf of Fonseca case, 1917,[108] because it has been taken up in most discussions of the legal status of the Gulf of Aqaba.

D. THE GULF OF FONSECA CASE AND THE GULF OF AQABA. The Gulf of Fonseca, approximately fifty miles in length and thirty in breadth, is situated on the west coast of Central America and surrounded at its entrance by the territories of Nicaragua and El Salvador, and by the territory of Honduras as its head.[109]

The question of the status of the gulf was brought before the Central American Court of Justice in an action commenced and maintained by the government of the republic of El Salvador against the government of the republic of Nicaragua, arising out of the conclusion of a treaty by the latter with the government of the United States of America, known as the Bryan–Chamorro treaty, 4 August 1914, which relates, among other matters, to the leasing of a naval base in the Gulf of Fonseca.[110] The three riparian States were in accord in regarding the gulf as 'closed' sea, and the only question was whether the waters of the bay outside the territorial sea were held by the riparians jointly or severally.[111]

The Fonseca case has been referred to by the Arab States, mainly, in support of the claim that the Gulf of Aqaba is an Arab 'historic' bay, an Arab *mare clausum*.[112] But since that claim is not an issue for analysis here, the Gulf of Fonseca case will not be examined as authority for that proposition. Of interest, however, for the purposes of the present analysis is the position taken by the government of Nicaragua, which asserted that the true reason underlying the closed or territorial bay characteristic of the Gulf of Fonseca is the fact that it is 'small in extent, and, therefore belongs to the nations that own its coasts', and not the fact that the three States adjacent to the gulf belonged to a single international political entity, that is to say, not because of any 'historic' title.[113] The restricted geographical configuration of the Gulf of Fonseca was also stressed by the government of El Salvador: '. . ., apart from its character as a historic bay, the Gulf of Fonseca presents the particular condition that its entrance . . . is not of an extent greater than the ten miles fixed generally by the publicists as essential to considering a bay as "territorial" or "closed" . . .'.[114] It was also a factor which the Central American Court took into account when it decided that, taking into consideration 'geographical and historic considerations' as well as its 'situation, extent and configuration', the Gulf of Fonseca must be regarded as 'an historic bay possessed of the characteristics of a closed sea'.[115]

The above would seem to add weight to the argument advanced earlier to the effect that, regardless of any historic considerations, the Gulf of Aqaba, by common agreement between the littoral States, can be transformed into a 'closed' bay, especially that the Fonseca case was about a bay which could not be wholly territorial waters, while the entire waters of the Gulf of Aqaba are claimed to be territorial waters.

Reference may also be made here to the Gulf of Trieste, which lies at the north-east corner of the Adriatic Sea, between Yugoslavia and Italy. The penetration of that gulf is about thirteen miles, and the width of its entrance between Salvore Point in Yugoslavia and Porto Grado in Italy is about twelve miles. There does not exist a fixed boundary in the Gulf of Trieste, but because the territorial sea claims of both Italy and Yugoslavia leave no high-seas area within the gulf[116] it has been stated that 'the whole area of the Gulf of Trieste is under the sovereignty of Italy and Yugoslavia'.[117]

3. The rules governing the right of passage through the Gulf of Aqaba and the Straits of Tiran

Having established that the Gulf of Aqaba is a 'bay' and that, under the circumstances prevailing at present, the juridical status of its waters is that they are territorial, it should follow that the rules governing the right of passage should be those of the traditional concept of 'innocent passage'. This question, however, has been complicated by propositions according to which there should be 'free and innocent passage', that is non-suspendable or unrestricted innocent passage, through the Gulf of Aqaba for merchant vessels and warships of all nations, regardless of their cargo. It has even been argued that there should be 'free passage', i.e. as that exercised on the high seas, through the gulf. It is necessary, therefore, that such propositions be clarified and examined before any further consideration of the question of 'innocent passage' through the Gulf of Aqaba.

A. THE DOCTRINE OF THE CORFU CHANNEL CASE AND THE GULF OF AQABA. Prior to the 1958 Law of the Sea Conference and the adoption of Article 16(4) of the Convention on the Territorial Sea and the Contiguous Zone, which, *inter alia*, prohibits the suspension of the innocent passage of foreign ships 'through Straits which are used for international navigation between one part of the high seas and ... the territorial sea of a foreign State', the claim for a right of unrestricted innocent passage through the Gulf of Aqaba was based essentially on the doctrine of the Corfu Channel case, 1949.[118] In that case, on the facts before it, the International Court of Justice held that:

> It is, in the opinion of the court, generally recognised and in accordance with international custom that States in time of peace have a right to send their warships through Straits used for international navigation between two parts of the high seas without the previous authorisation of a coastal State, provided that the passage is *innocent*. Unless otherwise prescribed in an international convention, there is no right for a coastal State to prohibit such passage through Straits in time of peace.[119]

The argument has been that the Gulf of Aqaba 'comprehends international waters and that no nation has the right to prevent free and innocent passage in the Gulf of Aqaba and through the Straits giving access thereto'.[120] As demonstrated earlier, however, it can no longer be said that there are high seas within the Gulf of Aqaba, since the territorial seas of the littoral States overlap in all its parts. Consequently, unrestricted innocent passage cannot be claimed on the proposition that the 'Straits of Tiran' are a 'strait' connecting two parts of the high seas. This being so, it is scarcely necessary to consider whether the Straits of Tiran are 'used for international navigation'. Nevertheless, this question is examined later in the discussion.

The above situation was recognised by the International Law Commission during its seventh session in 1956. For, as will be shown later in more detail, when the question of passage through the Gulf of Aqaba was raised before the Commission by the Israeli government, M. François, the Commission's Special Rapporteur, pointed out that the doctrine of the Corfu Channel case 'related to Straits between parts of the high seas, and so did not apply to the Gulf of Aqaba which, though open to the high seas at one end, merely gave access to a port at the other'.[121] He also noted that '... the width of the gulf [of Aqaba] is never more than twice that of the territorial sea'.[122]

B. THE QUESTION OF NAVIGATION THROUGH TERRITORIAL WATERS WHICH CONSTITUTE THE ONLY ACCESS TO A PORT OF ANOTHER STATE—THE CASE OF THE GULF OF AQABA

(i) The International Law Commission consideration. The result of the above-explained position is that ships bound from the high seas of the Red Sea to the Israeli port of Eilat or the Jordanian port of Aqaba would have the right only of 'innocent passage' when traversing through the territorial waters of Egypt and/or Saudi Arabia within the Gulf of Aqaba. Recognising this situation, the government of Israel sought to guarantee for its vessels when traversing these waters a right of free passage or, if the latter was not accepted, a right of non-suspendable innocent passage. For this purpose Israel suggested that, in waters constituting the only access to a harbour belonging to a third State, coastal States could not claim any territorial sea, or that, if they were able to claim one, such territorial sea could under no circumstances fall within the regime of territorial sea. This proposition was put forward by the government of Israel to the ILC in 1956 in connection with its codification of the law of the sea.[123] In the ILC the proposition was recognised as referring to the Gulf of Aqaba, but was refused endorsement. M. François, the Special Rapporteur, noted that:

[Israel] appeared to have in mind the Gulf of Aqaba, at the head of which Israel had a port to which access was through the territorial seas of other coastal States, the width of the Gulf being never more than twice that of the territorial sea. The case was exceptional—possibly unique.[124]

As noted, M. François also pointed out that the doctrine of the Corfu Channel case 'related to Straits between two parts of the high seas, and so did not apply to the Gulf of Aqaba which, though open to the high seas at one end, merely gave access to a port at the other'.[125]

Mr Pal, a member of the ILC, said that:

the Israel Government appeared to consider that coastal states could not claim any territorial sea in straits constituting the only access to a harbour belonging to a third State. Such a claim called for serious consideration. He was not, however, prepared to accept it at that stage.[126]

Another member, Mr Spiropoulos,

wondered whether the problem could not be assimilated to that of bays. The right of access to a port such as that mentioned could be based on international agreements or on long usage. Strictly speaking, however, such a consideration was irrelevant, since the Commission was concerned with establishing general rules.[127]

Sir Gerald Fitzmaurice said that:

vessels would in any case enjoy the right of innocent passage through a gulf consisting entirely of the territorial waters of coastal states to a port belonging to a third state.[128]

Sir Gerald also agreed with Mr Sandstrom that 'the case under consideration was governed by Article 16 so far as the right of innocent passage was concerned.'[129]

Article 16 of the Commission's draft articles related to the meaning of the right of innocent passage. It stated, *inter alia,* that: '2. Passage means navigation through the territorial sea for the purpose either of traversing that sea without entering internal waters, or of proceeding to internal waters or of making for the high seas from internal waters.'[130]

The Soviet member, Mr Krylov, said that 'the question sounded far more like a case for the International Court of Justice than a matter on which the Commission could enunciate a general rule'.[131]

After further discussion of the Israeli proposal, the Commission came to the very significant—for the present discussion—decision that 'the question raised by the Israel Government related to an exceptional case which did not lend itself to the formulation of a general rule'.[132]

Moreover, in its final draft articles on the law of the sea, the ILC retained the above-quoted provision of Article 16, and in the article which dealt with straits it referred only to freedom of passage

SPECIFIC REGIONAL ISSUES

through straits 'used for international navigation between two parts of the high seas', commenting that:

> The question was asked what would be the legal position of Straits forming part of the territorial sea of one or more States and constituting the sole means of access to a port of another State. The Commission considers that this case could be assimilated to that of a bay whose inner part and entrance from the high seas belong to different States. As the Commission felt bound to confine itself to proposing rules applicable to bays, wholly belonging to a single coastal State, it also reserved consideration of the above mentioned case.[133]

In short, the International Law Commission refused to endorse the Israeli proposition; and its general reaction would appear to indicate the following:

1. The only access to the Israeli port of Eilat was through the territorial seas of other States, the width of the Gulf of Aqaba being never more than twice that of the territorial sea, which *a fortiori* meant that coastal States could claim territorial seas even in waters constituting the only access to a harbour belonging to another State.

2. The Gulf of Aqaba, though open to the high seas at one end, merely gave on to a port at the other, and therefore did not lend itself to the exceptional treatment provided for straits or channels of communication between two parts of the high seas.

3. The Straits of Tiran, the entrance to the Gulf of Aqaba, should be assimilated to the gulf itself, so that the rules regarding bays whose inner part and entrance from the high seas belong to different States apply to such straits and gulf. The Commission, however, refrained from proposing rules for such bays.

4. The right of access to ports such as the Israeli port of Eilat or the Jordanian port of Aqaba could be based on the traditional right of 'innocent passage' through territorial waters.

(ii) The First Conference on the Law of the Sea decision—Article 16(4) of the Convention on the Territorial Sea and the Contiguous Zone. The question of securing free navigation through territorial waters which constitute the only access to a port of another State was again discussed at the 1958 Law of the Sea Conference, on the initiative of the representative of Israel, who made direct reference to the Gulf of Aqaba.[134] Several proposals were introduced,[135] but the conference did not adopt any specific rule regarding that question. It decided, however, to change the ILC's provision on the non-suspendable innocent passage through straits used for international navigation between two parts of the high seas, which, as seen earlier, is a restatement of the customary rule enunciated by

the International Court of Justice in the Corfu Channel case, 1949, to include in the one legal category 'straits which are used for international navigation between one part of the high seas and another part of the high seas or the territorial sea of a foreign State'. This amended provision was embodied in the Convention on the Territorial Sea and the Contiguous Zone as Article 16(4).[136] It has been called the 'Aqaba article',[137] because ever since its adoption it has been asserted that the concept embodied in its last part, referring to '... or the territorial sea of a foreign State', is applicable to situations such as that of the Gulf of Aqaba.[138] It has also been heavily relied on by Israel[139] and other States, including the United Kingdom[140] and the United States,[141] as a guarantee for all nations and vessels of the right of non-suspendable innocent passage to the Gulf of Aqaba through the Straits of Tiran. The argument has thus been that the Straits of Tiran constitute an international strait because, so the argument runs, they connect the high seas of the Red Sea and the territorial seas of the States situated at the inner part of the Gulf of Aqaba and are used for international navigation by foreign ships. But this is an untenable argument, not only because Egypt and Saudi Arabia are not parties to the 1958 Territorial Sea Convention; because, as it is hoped to demonstrate below, the rule in question is not one of customary international law and the Gulf of Aqaba and the Straits of Tiran are actually not 'used for international navigation'; but also because the Straits of Tiran do not connect one part of the high seas and the territorial sea of a foreign State. Indeed, a ship bound from the high seas of the Red Sea to the Israeli port of Eilat or the Jordanian port of Aqaba has to traverse not merely the actual straits but also the approximately ninety-five-mile-long territorial sea portions of Egypt and/or Saudi Arabia within the gulf proper before reaching its destination.

A better view, therefore, would appear to be that situations like that in the Straits of Tiran are covered by the customary rules relating to the traditional right of innocent passage as formulated in Section III of the 1958 Territorial Sea Convention, which under Article 14(2) provides that 'Passage means navigation through the territorial sea for the purpose either of traversing the sea without entering internal waters, or of proceeding to internal waters, or of making for the high seas from internal waters'.[142]

A consideration of the circumstances surrounding the adoption of Article 16(4) referred to above and of the contention that the latter represented a rule of customary international law can only serve to suggest the foregoing view.

1. The adoption of Article 16(4), with particular reference to the position of Arab States

In committee meetings of the 1958 Law of the Sea Conference, Article 16(4) was adopted by thirty-one votes to thirty, with ten abstentions.[143] The Strait of Tiran, though not officially stated, 'was in everybody's mind',[144] and, therefore, all the Arab States voted against the adoption of Article 16(4),[145] with the Saudi representative expressing the opinion that 'the amended text no longer dealt with general principles of international law, but had been carefully tailored to promote the claims of one State'.[146]

In plenary meetings of the conference an attempt by the delegations of the Arab States, led by the Egyptian representative, to have a separate vote on Article 16(4) was defeated by the close vote of thirty-four to thirty-two, with six abstentions,[147] and the whole article containing that paragraph was adopted by sixty-two votes to one, with nine abstentions.[148] After the adoption of Article 16, the Saudi delegate explained that he had abstained from voting because:

he considered that Paragraph 4 was a mutilation of international law and had nothing to do with the principle of navigation, which had been used as a pretext to introduce ideas foreign to the principles of international law. The rules of law which the Conference was in process of adopting should deal only with general principles, whereas he believed that Paragraph 4 had been drafted with one particular case in view. Saudi Arabia would take the necessary steps to protect its national interest against the interpretation and application of Paragraph 4.[149]

The adoption of Article 16(4) was 'sufficient to explain the refusal of the Arab States to sign the Convention'.[150] But it might be asked why the Arab States, instead of keeping out of the convention altogether, have not signed it with a reservation against considering themselves bound by Article 16(4), as some of the delegations present at the conference expected.[151] On signing, Tunisia made such a reservation[152] but, like all the other Arab States, has never ratified the convention.[153]

The question of whether reservations were to be allowed or not was debated during the adoption of the Convention on the Territorial Sea and the Contiguous Zone. The strongest opponents of the final words of Article 16(4), the delegations of Egypt and Saudi Arabia, along with delegations of other governments were of the opinion that reservations should be allowed; other delegations, such as that of the United States, proposed that a clause should be included in the convention stating that no reservations would be admissible.[154] The final decision, originally proposed by

India, was that the convention should not contain any clause dealing with reservations.[155] This decision, however, was interpreted in 'diametrically opposite ways'.[156] Some delegations, for instance Saudi Arabia, considered that in the absence of a clause relating to reservations States were entitled to make whatever reservations they wished; whereas in the opinion of other delegations—such as that of the United Kingdom, which invoked the advisory opinion of the International Court of Justice in the matter of Reservations to the Genocide Convention, 1951[157]—in the absence of such a clause any reservation made by a particular State would be valid only *vis-à-vis* States which accepted it.[158] Despite this uncertainty at the time of signature, many States have made reservations to the Convention on the Territorial Sea and the Contiguous Zone, 1958. Those made by the governments of the Byelorussian SSR, Czechoslovakia, Hungary, Romania, the Ukranian SSR, the USSR and Venezuela were confirmed in their instruments of ratification.[159]

Nevertheless the Arab States have chosen not adhere to the Territorial Sea Convention at all. The decision may have been dictated by a desire to avoid any conflict that might arise in view of the 'deliberately created' uncertainty as to the 'intention of the legislator' on the admissibility or non-admissibility of reservations.[160] Thus Article 16(4) 'is considered by many States to be a serious obstacle to the ratification of the Convention, and thus defeats the intention of the Conference to bring about a worldwide harmonisation of State practice concerning the territorial sea'.[161]

2. Nature and binding effect of Article 16(4), with particular reference to the Straits of Tiran

Referring to Article 16(4), the chairman of the American delegation to the 1958 Geneva conference, Mr A. Dean, stated:

This highly controversial provision is grounded primarily in the decision of the International Court of Justice in the *Corfu Channel* case. But it goes further than did the decision in that case. It specifically determines the heated controversy between Israel and the Arab States as to the right of Israeli shipping to pass through the Straits of Tiran to the Gulf of Aqaba.[162]

After a brief statement of the Corfu Channel decision and the refusal of the International Law Commission to recognise Israel's claim to use the Straits of Tiran for her commercial shipping, Mr Dean continued:

... the Conference, by providing that the right obtained not only in straits linking 'one part of the high seas and another part of the high seas' but also between 'one part of the high seas ... and the territorial sea of a foreign state', adopted a rule which clearly applied to the Israeli–Arab controversy ...

The Geneva Conference thus, in a politically charged area, achieved agreement sufficient to write a new and beneficial rule of international law.[163]

With reference to the latter remark, Mr Dean, in a letter of 'clarification' to Professor Leo Gross, has said:

In making this statement I was thinking mainly in terms of the fact that the question of innocent passage through straits between one part of the high seas and the territorial sea of a foreign state had not been covered by the decision of the International Court in the Corfu Channel case or in the draft articles prepared by the International Law Commission. I did not intend to pass upon the question of whether or not this rule represented a codification of customary international law.[164]

Whether Mr Dean did or did not intend to pass upon the question of whether or not the rule regarding innocent passage through 'straits' between one part of the high seas and the territorial sea of a foreign State represented a codification of customary international law, it is submitted here that his observation clearly brings up what may be considered as strong evidence in support of the argument that that rule is a new conventional rule. For Mr Dean recognises that according to the Corfu Channel case[165] the right of unrestricted innocent passage could be exercised only in straits linking two areas of high seas, and emphasises that the International Law Commission refused to apply the Corfu decision to channels linking territorial sea with high seas, particularly to the Straits of Tiran.

Professor Leo Gross, however, submits that the rule in question represents 'a codification of customary international law although it could also be argued that it contains an element of progressive development of the law'.[166] The latter phrase seems to weaken his first proposition—that the rule represents 'a codification of customary international law'. Nevertheless, in support of his submission he refers to 'The very substantial vote in favour of the rule at the Conference', which, he believes, must be considered 'as an expression of the Conference in favour of free and innocent passage through international waterways'.[167] The fact that the rule received a 'very substantial vote in favour' of its adoption does not necessarily mean that the conference considered it an established rule of customary international law or that it has become a general rule of international law. Thus in the North Sea Continental Shelf cases, 1969,[168] while recognising that multinational conventions might generate rules which could gradually come to be accepted as forming part of customary law, the International Court of Justice set out a number of conditions which in its opinion would need to be fulfilled before this could happen. Clarifying these conditions, the Court, *inter alia*, noted that:

> With respect to the other elements usually regarded as necessary before a conventional rule could be considered to have become a general rule of international law, it might be that, even without the passage of any considerable period of time, a very widespread and representative participation in the Convention might suffice of itself, provided it *included that of States whose interests were specially affected.*[169]

It has already been shown that Egypt and the other Arab States which were present at the 1958 conference did not consent to the adoption of Article 16(4); they actively rejected it. It may be recalled also that the ILC refused to recognise the rule in question, and that up to 1973 the Territorial Sea Convention, which entered into force on 10 September 1964, received the limited number of forty-three ratifications and accessions only.[170] Besides, as is rightly emphasised by Professor J. Verzijl, who in his capacity as chairman of the Netherlands delegation to the 1958 conference played an active role in the adoption of Article 16(4), the rule was successfully achieved

as a result of the incidental fact that the disputed paragraph 4 obtained in an Article which in its first, second and third paragraphs gave the coastal States extensive rights of control in their territorial sea which even the strongest opponents of the final words did not wish to risk by voting against the entire Article. As a result this ultimately obtained an overwhelming majority. Had the subject of paragraph 4 formed a separate Article, it would certainly not have been adopted, as it would have failed to secure the necessary two-thirds majority.[171]

Dr Y. Blum shares the submission advanced by Professor Gross. He argues that Article 16(4) 'is not an innovation of the Conference, but merely the restatement of a rule which had already been in force prior to the adoption of the Convention'.[172] Dr Blum's data, however, are less convincing than those advanced by Professor Gross. He attempts to find support for his argument in the statement in Oppenheim that 'the rule that foreign merchantmen cannot be excluded from passage through territorial straits applies only when they connect two parts of the open sea'.[173] But this

SPECIFIC REGIONAL ISSUES

statement has no relevance to the rule under consideration. It is obvious that by including in the one legal category straits connecting two parts of the open sea and 'straits' linking territorial waters with high seas, Article 16(4) goes beyond the rule discussed in Oppenheim.[174] Moreover it may be argued that, according to the statement in Oppenheim, foreign vessels can be excluded from all 'straits' other than those connecting two parts of the open sea, for the latter statement is qualified by the use of the word 'only'.

Perhaps it is the thought of Dr Blum that the first part of Article 16(4)—namely 'There shall be no suspension of the innocent passage of foreign ships through straits which are used for international navigation between one part of the high seas and another part of the high seas . . .'—applies to the Straits of Tiran. If so, it must be recalled that the Strait of Tiran does not connect two parts of the high seas, because, as shown earlier, the territorial seas of the littoral States leave no room for any high seas within the Gulf of Aqaba. They overlap in all parts of the gulf, and not only, as Dr Blum assumes, 'in certain parts of the Gulf'.[175]

In the opinion of the present writer, the evidence rather suggests that the right of non-suspendable innocent passage through straits connecting two parts of the high seas is an established rule of customary international law, but that through 'straits' linking high seas to territorial waters it is merely a conventional rule.[176] Therefore Egypt, not being a party to the 1958 Territorial Sea Convention, is not bound by the latter rule. Accordingly, the Straits of Tiran are simply part of Egypt's ordinary territorial waters and not an 'international waterway'. In addition to the above-mentioned facts and observations, the latter opinion derives support from the following evidence.

The rationale usually appended to the unrestricted right of passage through straits is the special significance of such waterways to international navigation. Thus Hyde states that:

There are straits and straits.

When . . . a strait is an essential channel of international intercourse, as, for example, when it connects two open seas, the international society exhibits deep interest in the free use of that channel.[177]

Similarly Professor R. R. Baxter states that only those straits 'which are used to a substantial extent by commercial shipping or warships belonging to States other than the riparian nation or nations', are international waterways.[178]

It may be suggested, as the United Kingdom maintained in its argument in the Corfu Channel case, that 'for a strait to constitute a route for international maritime traffic, it is enough to show that it is a route serving a particular region';[179] however, under no circumstances could it be suggested that a passage which is used for navigation between one part of the high seas and the territorial sea of a foreign State may constitute 'a route for international maritime traffic'. For, as the United Kingdom in the latter case emphasised:

> It is simply the geographical fact that the strait connects two parts of the open sea where ships may lawfully wish to pass which distinguishes it as a strait subject to a special regime in international law.[180]

This geographical fact was considered by the International Court of Justice as a 'decisive criterion' in finding whether a strait belonged to the class of international highways through which a right of passage exists. The Court said:

> ... the decisive criterion is rather its geographical situation as connecting two parts of the high seas and the fact of its being used for international navigation.[181]

Had the Court thought that 'straits' other than those connecting two parts of the high seas could constitute what might be considered 'useful route(s) for international maritime traffic'[182] it would probably have been satisfied with the second of its tests, namely the fact that the strait is being used for international navigation.[183] The geographical test has been stressed also by Sir Henry Lauterpacht:

> It must, however, be stated that the rule that foreign merchantmen cannot be excluded from passage through territorial straits applies *only* when they connect two parts of the open sea [emphasis added].[184]

Thus the evidence shows that under general rules of international law the geographical fact that a strait connects two parts of the open sea is a prerequisite for finding whether it belongs to the class of international highways through which a right of passage exists. This is so, perhaps, because passages or channels which are used for navigation between one part of the high seas and the territorial sea of a foreign State, in the words of A. H. Charteris, 'are not usually channels of communication on the highway of the ocean which every maritime nation is concerned to keep open, but merely means of access to ports lying within them'.[185]

3. Third Conference on the Law of the Sea— the right of 'transit passage' through straits

It is worth noting that at the Third Conference on the Law of the

Sea the Arab States have stressed that the regime of straits should be strictly confined to straits linking two parts of the high seas,[186] whereas Israel has specifically expressed the view that all straits without exception must be open to free navigation, i.e. transit passage.[187] Israel accordingly has favoured, in this regard, the proposals of the United States[188] to those of the United Kingdom[189] and the socialist States,[190] because the proposals of the latter distinguish between straits linking two parts of the high seas and those connecting one part of the high seas and the territorial sea of a foreign State, and apply to the latter category the right of non-suspendable innocent passage, and not 'transit passage', which applies to the former category.[191] The ICNT, Part III, prepared after the sixth session of the Third Conference adopts the approach of the United Kingdom and the socialist States and thus provides for the right of 'transit passage' through straits which are used for international navigation between one area of the high seas or an exclusive economic zone and another area of the high seas or an exclusive economic zone. In straits used for international navigation between one area of the high seas or an exclusive economic zone and the territorial sea of a foreign State, the right of non-suspendable innocent passage would apply.[192]

In addition, Israel has suggested that the classification of a State as geographically disadvantaged should depend, among other matters, on its access to the high seas.[193] Israel, therefore, has considered that 'A country whose territorial sea was separated from the high seas by straits must have absolute freedom of navigation'.[194] Israel appears to have in mind the Gulf of Aqaba and its port of Eilat, but whatever geographical disadvantages she may suffer from in the Gulf of Aqaba, Israel has a relatively large Mediterranean coast as well, and, as shown in the next section, it is there that her most important ports are situated. Clearly, therefore, Israel cannot be regarded as a geographically disadvantaged State.

C. SHIPPING PRACTICE IN THE GULF OF AQABA AND THE RIGHT OF PASSAGE THERETHROUGH

Apart from the reasons discussed above, Article 16(4) of the Territorial Sea Convention could not apply to the Straits of Tiran because, as indicated earlier, the latter are not 'used for international navigation'. This conclusion, as will be shown below, is based on an examination of the practice of shipping through the Straits of Tiran and the Gulf of Aqaba. But first it may be useful to shed some light on the meaning of the expression 'used for international navigation'. There exists no strict or clear-cut definition, but reference may be made to various helpful or explanatory observations. For purposes of analysis, Professor R. R. Baxter states that:

international waterways must be considered to be those rivers, canals and straits which are used to a substantial extent by the commercial shipping or warships belonging to states other than the riparian nation or nations.[195]

In its judgement in the Corfu Channel case[196] the International Court of Justice, with reference to the question of whether or not the North Corfu channel belongs to the class of 'international highways, through which a right of passage exists', said:

It may be asked whether the test is to be found in the volume of traffic passing through the strait or in its greater or lesser importance for international navigation. But in the opinion of the Court the decisive criterion is rather its geographical situation as connecting two parts of the high seas and the fact of its being used for international navigation. Nor can it be decisive that this strait is not a necessary route between two parts of the high seas, but only an alternative passage between the Aegean and the Adriatic Seas. It has nevertheless been a useful route for international maritime traffic.[197]

The Court went on to cite statistics and information relating to the amount of traffic in the North Corfu channel.[198]

Professor D. P. O'Connell, in connection with the criterion for determining which straits are international, writes:

A passage of water is a strait in law only if it is a strait geographically, but the converse is not true, for any passage which merits the geographical description 'strait' is not necessarily an international highway.

Professor O'Connell emphasises

When it is said, then, that a strait is a passage of territorial sea linking two areas of high seas this is not to be taken literally, but rather construed as meaning a passage which ordinarily carries the bulk of international traffic not destined for ports on the relevant coastlines.[199]

Finally, reference may be made to Brüel's statement with regard to factors which should be taken into account in considering whether a particular strait is of interest to international sea commerce. Brüel says:

As to this, it would seem that the degree of importance of the particular strait to the international sea-commerce, taken in its broadest sense, concerning the passage of both mercantile ships and warships, must be the decisive factor. How extensive and how deeply rooted this interest should be cannot be determined by any hard and fast rule, but it is a question of fact, depending upon such facts as for instance the number of ships passing through the strait, their total tonnage, the aggregate value of their cargoes, the average size of the ships, and especially, whether they are distributed among a greater or smaller number of nations ... whereby is simply meant that the interest attached to the use of these straits is world wide.[200]

We may now turn to examine the actualities of international use of the Gulf of Aqaba. Captain Morsely, who in 1883 succeeded in surveying the gulf, reported that this part of the Red Sea, 'so little known formerly, has now been found to afford no advantage for a sailing ship' and that 'No native vessels ever navigate the Gulf of A'Kaba, and such a dread have they of this place, that in crossing the Red Sea, near this gulf the Arabs always offer up a prayer for their safety. Numerous vessels have been lost hereabouts and when trying to survey it, four attempts were made before we succeeded.'[201]

In fact through most of history there was so little traffic in the gulf that 'its legal status in the eyes of the riparian states, or other states, was of no moment'.[202] It was not until 1917, when the British government started to supply its troops in Ottoman territory via the Gulf of Aqaba, that this route was used. With the end of World War I the traffic halted and was not resumed until the middle 1930s, when a road was built connecting the then terminal of the Hejaz railway to Maan with Aqaba. However, substantial commercial tonnages were not handled until 1952, when Jordan began to utilise Aqaba.[203] It is also indicated that before 1952 navigation in the gulf was of importance to the riparian Arab States, particularly for pilgrim travel, as foreign powers probably were not interested in the gulf since it apparently had no commercial importance for them.[204]

Between the time of the Israeli occupation of the territory of Eilat in 1949 and the Suez crisis of 1956, fewer than ten ships called at the Israeli port of Eilat—none of them Israeli[205] It has been shown also that between 1951 and 1954 most of the 267 vessels which passed through the Straits of Tiran were headed for the Jordanian port of Aqaba.[206] In the ten years which followed the 1956 Suez crisis, it is claimed, 'the town and port of Eilat gradually grew in size and importance. Israel's political and commercial relations with East African and Asian countries were more vigorously developed, and a 12-inch oil pipeline was constructed between Eilat and Haifa to handle all the country's oil needs.'[207] It is shown, however, that during the same period only five Israeli ships had used the Straits of Tiran, and that the last Israeli ship to do so entered the strait about eighteen months before Egypt announced the blockade against Israeli vessels on 22 May 1967.[208] On the day following the Egyptian announcement the news was published that Israel had a dozen ships trading from Eilat. Most of these were on charter, and there were normally about 100 sailings a year. It was added that, apart from oil, the port handled only 5 per cent of Israel's trade.[209] No official figures are available about oil shipments through Eilat, but in May 1967 one report suggested that 'most of Israel's oil supplies come through Eilat';[210] another report estimated that 'close to 90 per cent of Israel's annual oil requirement is imported (reportedly from Iran) through Eilat'.[211] It was also said that 'oil tankers from Iran only arrive once a fortnight on average'.[212]

Statistics of the United Nations[213] and the Israel government[214] show that up to 1964 no ships entered or left the port, except that, according to the latter, in 1959 forty-five ships moved to and from Eilat. In 1965, 1966 and 1967, excluding petroleum but including traffic between Israeli ports, an annual average of fifty ships moved to and from Eilat.[215] It has been shown that between 1954 and 1967 the number of vessels which annually sailed to and from the Jordanian port of Aqaba averaged between a minimum of 104 and a maximum of 667 vessels.[216]

Following the June 1967 armed conflict, according to Israeli sources, 'Eilat's maritime trade was further developed, its communications link with the northern part of Israel was improved, and its port facilities were expanded'. Consequently, it is added, 'trade through Eilat grew at a rate of more than 15 per cent annually, and by 1972 about nine per cent of Israel's exports and five per cent of its imports passed through its southern port'.[217] However, according to statistics of the United Nations, and the Israel government, between 1969 and 1974 an annual average of 100 ships moved in and out of Eilat, with an annual average of 600 thousand tons loaded and unloaded.[218] During the same period Israel's Mediterranean ports of Ashdod and Haifa each handled an annual average of 1,300 and 1,700 ships respectively, with an annual average of 3,000 and 4,400 thousand tons loaded and unloaded respectively.[219] The port of Ashdod, about twenty miles down the Mediterranean coast of Israel, was projected in 1957 and inaugurated on 23 September 1965 as a natural port for the southern parts of Israel, and is now considered her second major port after Haifa.[220]

During the years 1968 to 1973 Jordan's port of Aqaba handled an annual average of 800 thousand metric tons loaded and unloaded.[221]

It has been observed that Eilat has not developed into a major maritime centre because almost all Israeli maritime traffic can be handled more economically through the ports of Haifa or Tel Aviv/Jaffa than through Eilat. Cargo handled at the latter and destined for the settled portions of Israel has to travel overland a distance exceeding 160 miles at high cost; and, in view of the narrowness of the Gulf of Aqaba, coastal fishing from Israel is in fact restricted to the area close to Eilat, where the prevalence of northerly winds makes for poor fishing.[222] As shown above, with the opening of the Mediterranean port of Ashdod, Eilat has become less important even for the southern part of Israel.

D. CONCLUSION. Having, it is hoped, established that the Straits of Tiran are not an international waterway, and that both the Gulf of Aqaba proper and the straits may under the present circumstances be considered as *territorial waters* to which the rules relating to the traditional right of innocent passage are applicable, it will now be convenient to comment on the question of passage through these waters in the light of the latter rules.

First it will be noted that, under customary international law, the coastal State may take the necessary steps in its territorial sea to prevent passage which is not innocent but 'prejudicial to the peace, good order or security of the coastal state'.[223] The coastal State also may 'suspend temporarily in specified areas of its territorial sea the innocent passage of foreign ships if such suspension is essential for the protection of its security'.[224] The coastal State, at least according to one strong argument, would also be entitled to forbid the passage of foreign warships through its territorial sea.[225]

Having said this, it will now be recalled that Egypt has always made its position clear that it has no intention of preventing 'innocent passage' to the Gulf of Aqaba through the Straits of Tiran.[226] To this end, the Egyptian position appears to be in harmony with the conclusions arrived at in the present study and in conformity with the general principles of international law relating to territorial waters. Egypt, however, has always announced its intention to 'prevent Israeli ships, and other ships carrying strategic cargoes to Israel, from passing through the mouth of the Gulf of Aqaba'.[227] Egypt thus appears to consider that the passage of the latter category of ships through its territorial waters would not be innocent but prejudicial to its 'peace, good order, or security'. It is not proposed, however, to deal with this specific matter, since it is a factual question.[228] But reference may be made to some matters which may have to be taken in consideration in connection with the general problem of defining 'innocence'. McDougal and Burke suggests that Article 14(4) of the 1958 Territorial Sea Convention 'no longer restricts coastal states' competence to prohibit passage to considerations arising from incidents occurring in the territorial sea. It is now open to the coastal state to take other factors into account, including, for example, the purpose of the projected passage, the cargo carried, and destination in a third state'.[229]

In view of Egypt's assertions that Israel's possession of the territory bordering on the Gulf of Aqaba is illegal and that a state of 'war' and 'belligerency' exists between herself and Israel, reference may be made also to the judgement of the International Court of Justice in the Corfu Channel case.[230] But first it should be emphasised that the Court was dealing with a case relating to an international strait, and that the coastal State normally has much wider control over its ordinary territorial waters than that which it has over territorial waters which constitute an international waterway. In its judgement the Court noted that:

... it is a fact that the two coastal States did not maintain normal relations, that Greece had made territorial claims precisely with regard to a part of Albanian territory bordering on the channel, that Greece had declared that she considered herself technically in a state of war with Albania, and that Albania, invoking the danger of Greek incursions, had considered it necessary to take certain measures of vigilance in this region. The Court is of opinion that Albania, in view of these exceptional circumstances, would have been justified in issuing regulations in respect of the passage of warships through the Strait, but not in prohibiting such passage or in subjecting it to the requirement of special authorisation.[231]

4. Israeli withdrawal from the Sinai Peninsula in March 1957 and the right of passage through the Gulf of Aqaba and the Straits of Tiran

As has been noted above, Israel maintains that since the Sinai campaign of 1956 the Straits of Tiran have been free and open to Israel's and to all shipping as a 'provision of the general settlement which led to the withdrawal of the Israel Defence Forces from the Peninsula'.[232] An examination of the history of the development which led to the withdrawal of the Israeli forces does not support this proposition.

On 3 November 1956, as announced by the Ministry for Foreign Affairs of Israel, '... and, for the first time in seven years, navigation through the Straits of Tiran and in the Gulf of Aqaba was free to the ships and cargoes of all nations'.[233] This is correct, but, as rightly observed by the British Prime Minister, it '... does not derive in any sense from the agreement registered by Mr Hammarskjold in 1957, or from anything that was said at the General Assembly in that year'.[234] The latter agreement is the 'Exchange of letters constituting the Status of the United Nations Emergency Force in Egypt' signed between the United Nations and Egypt in New York on 8 February 1957.[235] As the title indicates, this agreement relates only to the status of the United Nations Emergency Force (UNEF) in Egypt. It was signed in compliance with General Assembly Resolution 1125 (XI) of 2 February 1957, which contemplated that 'after full withdrawal of Israel from the Sharm el-sheikh and Gaza areas', units of the UNEF would be placed 'on the Egyptian–Israeli armistice demarcation line ... with a view to assist in achieving situations conducive to the maintenance of peaceful conditions in the area'.[236]

The General Assembly resolution was preceded by Resolution 1124 (XI), adopted on the same day. In the latter the Assembly deplored 'the non-compliance of Israel to complete its withdrawal behind the armistice demarcation line', and called upon 'Israel to complete its withdrawal behind the armistice demarcation line without further delay'.[237]

In an *aide-mémoire* dated 23 January 1957, transmitted to the Secretary General by the Permanent Representative of Israel to the United Nations, the government of Israel considered that 'the United Nations Emergency Force could be a factor in the solution' of the problem of navigation in the Straits of Tiran and the Gulf of Aqaba if, among other things, 'It would be the function of the United Nations Emergency Force to see to it that freedom of navigation was maintained and belligerent acts avoided in the Gulf of Aqaba and the Straits of Tiran'.[238] This proposition was rejected by the Secretary General, who, in a report to the General Assembly in connection with his efforts to secure the complete withdrawal of Israel, stated, *inter alia*:

> In connexion with the question of Israel withdrawal from Sharm el-sheikh area, attention has been directed to the situation in the Gulf of Aqaba and the Straits of Tiran. This matter is of longer duration and not directly related to the present crisis. The concern now evinced in it, however, calls for consideration of the legal aspects of the matter as a problem in its own right. It follows from principles guiding the United Nations that the Israel military action and its consequences should not be elements influencing the solution.
>
> As stated in the previous report (A/3500 and Add. I) the international significance of the Gulf of Aqaba may be considered to justify the right of innocent passage through the Straits of Tiran and the Gulf in accordance with recognised rules of international law. However ... a legal controversy exists as to the extent of the right of innocent passage through these waters.[239]

The Secretary General also noted that 'In accordance with the general legal principles recognised as decisive for the deployment of the United Nations Emergency Force should not be used so as to prejudice the solution of the controversial questions involved'.²⁴⁰

On 4 February 1957 the government of Israel sent the Secretary General another *aide-mémoire* in which a 'clarification' was sought by Israel as to whether:

> Immediately on the withdrawal of Israel forces from the Sharm el-sheikh area, units of the United Nations Emergency Force will be stationed along the Western shore of the Gulf of Aqaba in order to act as a restraint against hostile acts, and will remain so deployed until another effective means is agreed upon between the parties concerned for ensuring permanent freedom of navigation and the absence of belligerent acts in the straits of Tiran and the Gulf of Aqaba.²⁴¹

An additional letter was sent to the Secretary General on 10 February 1957 in which the government of Israel reiterated the request made in its previous *aide-mémoire,* adding that 'The fact that we have not obtained a positive answer on this point has adversely affected the time-schedule for the withdrawal of forces'. It also expressed the opinion that 'In the light of past experience, and of recent Egyptian declarations, my Government must in all prudence', and unless evidence to the contrary became available, hold the assumption that 'Egypt has not agreed that free navigation in the Gulf of Aqaba will be ensured after Israel's withdrawal, or that effective measures such as the stationing of Units of UNEF should be instituted to ensure such continued freedom of navigation'.²⁴² In reply the Secretary General expressed the view that 'the action which the Government of Israel has requested cannot be regarded as properly described in such terms, as it would be an action within the scope of resolution 1125 (XI) and in implementation of this resolution as published, although closely related to resolution 1124 (XI), has, at least, full and unconditional acceptance of the demand in that resolution as its pre-requisite'.²⁴³ On 10 February 1957 also, in reply to a cable dated 3 February, the Prime Minister of Israel, David Ben-Gurion, cabled the President of the United States, General Eisenhower, refusing the latter's request for complete withdrawal and stating that Israel would not evacuate the Gaza strip unless '(*a*) . . . (*b*) Israel had assurances of freedom of passage through the Gulf of Aqaba'.²⁴⁴

Meanwhile the U.S. Department of State, on 11 February 1957, sent the government of Egypt a secret *aide-mémoire,*²⁴⁵ made public on 17 February, which Israel later relied upon in respect of her withdrawal. With respect to the Gulf of Aqaba and access thereto, the *aide-mémoire* said:

> The United States believes that the Gulf comprehends international waters and that no nation has the right to prevent free and innocent

passage in the Gulf and through the Straits giving access thereto ... In the absence of some overriding decision to the contrary, as by the International Court of Justice, the United States, on behalf of vessels of United States registry, is prepared to exercise the right of free and innocent passage and to join with others to secure general recognition of this right.

But on 15 February 1957 the government of Israel sent the government of the United States an *aide-mémoire* 'again refusing to move'.[246] As for Aqaba, Israel supported the replacement of her troops by UNEF provided they stayed there until a peace treaty was agreed with Egypt and permanent arrangements for free navigation were secured. Israel went so far as to envisage settling for 'a precise guarantee ... for the specific protection of Israel-bound shipping'.[247]

In the meantime, President Eisenhower, in a television broadcast focusing on the argument of Israel that it should have 'firm guarantees as a condition to withdrawing its forces of invasion', had asked a 'question of principle':

Should a nation which attacks and occupies foreign territory in the face of United Nations disapproval be allowed to impose conditions on its own withdrawal?

If we agree that armed attack can properly achieve the purposes of the assailant, then I fear we will have turned back the clock of international order.[248]

On 1 March 1957, however, the government of Israel announced in the General Assembly 'its plans for full and prompt withdrawal from the Sharm el-sheikh area and the Gaza strip, in compliance with General Assembly resolution 1124 (XI) of 2 February 1957'.[249] In its announcement Israel invoked various statements and declarations made by U.S. spokesmen as basic guarantees for 'continued freedom of navigation for international and Israel shipping in the Gulf of Aqaba and through the Straits of Tiran' in return for her withdrawal.[250] It referred to the United States *aide-mémoire* of 11 February 1957. It also recalled the statement made by the representative of the United States in the General Assembly on 27 January, and repeated on 2 February, which said:

We believe it is essential that Units of the United Nations Emergency Force be stationed at the Straits of Tiran in order to achieve there the separation of Egyptian and Israel land and sea forces. This separation is essential until it is clear that the non-exercise of any claimed belligerent rights has established in practice the peaceful conditions which must govern navigation in waters having such an international interest. All of this, of course, would be without prejudice to any ultimate determination which may be made of any legal questions concerning the Gulf of Aqaba.[251]

THE GULF OF AQABA AND THE STRAITS OF TIRAN

Although the '*de facto* situation worked to the advantage of Israel',[252] from all the facts and observations mentioned above it is evident that the passage of Israeli ships through the Gulf of Aqaba and the Straits of Tiran was never guaranteed by the United Nations, in spite of repeated requests made by Israel through the Secretary General; or by Egypt, as assumed by the government of Israel. In the event, as Dr Rosalyn Higgins concludes,

Israel appears to have chosen to rely – in respect of her withdrawal from Sharm el-sheikh – on a United States declaration that she regarded the Straits of Tiran as an international waterway, and that it was 'essential that units of the United Nations Emergency Force be stationed at the Straits of Tiran'.[253]

That the United States has no legal authority to guarantee or establish such a principle 'is beyond question'.[254] Even the statements made by the United States representative in the General Assembly clearly reject all stipulations for any kind of guarantee. Following the Israeli announcement of its plans to withdraw from the Sharm-el-sheikh and Gaza areas, the U.S. representative said that 'The United States also takes note of the declarations made in the statement of the representative of Israel. We do not consider that these declarations make Israel's withdrawal "conditional"'.[255] The United States representative also stipulated that UNEF's function in the Straits of Tiran 'of course, would be without prejudice to any ultimate determination of any legal questions concerning the Gulf of Aqaba'.[256] Furthermore, as rightly observed by Kennett Love, the U.S. Representative

emphasised the Administration's often-repeated suggestion that the status of rival claims in the Gulf of Aqaba should be determined by the World Court. He said, 'these views are to be understood in the sense of the relevant portions of the report' of the U.N. International Law Commission's formulations on the law of the sea in the spring and autumn of 1956. It was a particularly interesting remark because those formulations consciously avoided encompassing the Strait of Tiran. And Israel persistently avoided submitting to the World Court the legalities of her cases in both the Gulf of Aqaba and the Suez Canal.[257]

Moreover, at a press conference on 19 February 1957, the United States Secretary of State, John Foster Dulles, in reply to a question regarding the 'guaranty for which Israel has asked of American support over the interests of Aqaba', stated:

Well, a guaranty given to another nation would be something which could not occur without authority from the Congress or by a treaty. The President has inherent power to use the forces of the United States to protect

American ships and their rights all over the world. But he has no power, in my opinion, to use the forces of the United States on behalf of the vessels of another flag unless he is given that authority by some congressional resolution or by a treaty.[258]

5. The 'exceptional—possibly unique' case of the Gulf of Aqaba

As already shown, when the question of passage through the Gulf of Aqaba was raised by the Israeli government in the International Law Commission in 1956 the Commission refused to endorse the Israeli claim that passage in the gulf should be subject to the special regime provided in international law for international straits which connect parts of the high seas. The Commission found that:

the question raised by the Israel Government related to an exceptional case which did not lend itself to the formulation of a general rule.[259]

At the same time Professor François, the Commission's Special Rapporteur, noted that:

[Israel] appeared to have in mind the Gulf of Aqaba, at the head of which Israel had a port to which the only access was through the territorial seas of other coastal states, the width of the Gulf being never more than twice that of the territorial sea. The case was exceptional—possibly unique.[260]

Disagreeing with Professor François, Commander M. Strohl states that:

A study of the world's bays and internal waters discloses that the situation wherein a state has a port in the bay or estuary but does not have possession at the point where the bay connects with the open sea is exceptional—but by no means unique.[261]

In support of his assertion, Commander Strohl refers to three cases from Commander Kennedy's study of bays and estuaries the coasts of which belong to different States.[262] He says:

Such is the situation with respect to the following bays:

a. The Tana Lagoon, shared by Ghana and Ivory Coast. Here the Ivory Coast controls the headlands. [On Commander Kennedy's chart, French West Africa.]
b. The Gulf of Fonseca. The headlands are, respectively, in El salvador and Nicaragua.
c. Chetumal Bay in Central America. The only navigable entrance to the bay, hence the headland of it, are in British Honduras [now known as the British colony of Belize]. The head of the bay is in Mexico.[263]

Commander Strohl also refers to the estuary of the river Scheldt:

both shores of which are in the Netherlands. The highly important Belgian port of Antwerp is just above the point where the Schelde widens into an estuary.[264]

In principle Commander Strohl's observation is correct. But it should be borne in mind that, as viewed by Professor François, the Aqaba case is 'exceptional—possibly unique' not just, as Commander Strohl appears to maintain, because the Gulf of Aqaba represents 'the situation wherein a state has a port in the bay or estuary but does not have possession of the shores at the point where the bay connects with the open sea'. For in his description of the gulf Professor François stressed that *the only access was through the territorial seas of other coastal states, the width of the Gulf being never more than twice that of the territorial sea* (emphasis added). Thus the more significant feature of the Gulf of Aqaba is that it is so narrow that the territorial seas extending from both sides overlap in all its parts. Accordingly, a vessel bound to or from the States which have ports in the Gulf but do not have possession of the shores at the point where it connects with the high seas, i.e. Israel and Jordan, has to traverse not only the territorial waters of the other coastal States, Egypt and Saudi Arabia, at the point where the gulf connects with the high seas, i.e. the Straits of Tiran, but also through the approximately ninety-five mile long territorial sea portions of one and/or both of them in the gulf proper.

Nevertheless, a closer examination of the legal status of the bays and estuaries cited by Commander Strohl and referred to above might be useful, for, as Commander Strohl observed, they represent the 'situation wherein a state has a port in the bay or estuary but does not have possession of the shores at the point where the bay connects with the open sea', and in this, and maybe in other respects, they are similar to the case under consideration.

A. CHETUMAL BAY[265] The penetration of this bay is fifty-seven miles. The general width is about thirteen miles and the maximum width about twenty miles. The width of the entrance is twelve miles, between Ambergris Cay, an island under the sovereignty of Mexico, and the mainland of the British colony of Belize. On 8 July 1893 a boundary treaty was concluded between Mexico and the United Kingdom with regard to the Chetumal Bay, but no specific reference was made to the question of shipping to and from Mexico, which is situated at the head of the bay. A new convention, however, concluded in Mexico City on 7 April 1897, referred specifically to this question. Thus Article 3 *bis* of the new convention read:

> His Britannic Majesty guarantees to Mexican merchant-vessels, in perpetuity, the absolute liberty, as at present enjoyed, of navigating the Strait opening to the south of the Ambergris Cay, otherwise known as the Island of San Pedro, between this Cay and the mainland, as well as of navigating the territorial waters of British Honduras [Belize].

Both the 1893 and 1897 conventions are still in force.

B. THE TANA OR TEUDO LAGOON[266] The River Tana is the boundary between Ghana and the Ivory Coast. On 10 August 1889 a boundary settlement was brought about between the United Kingdom and France at Paris. Under this agreement the frontier follows the Tana river to the Tana or Teudo lagoon, the northern coast of which is the territory of the Ivory Coast, the eastern end of the southern coast the territory of Ghana. The line then crosses the lagoon in a southerly direction to meet the land boundary, which crosses the low spit, about one and a half miles wide, separating the lagoon from the sea, in a southerly direction to reach the coast at a point west of the village of Newtown. Thus it leaves the entrance from the high seas to the lagoon completely under the sovereignty of the Ivory Coast.

Access to the lagoon from the sea is very narrow and is about seven miles west of Assini, situated twelve and a half miles west of Newtown. Under the treaty of 1889, however, 'no special provisions were made by which shipping to Ghana was safeguarded'.[267] The lack of such provisions, it has been observed, perhaps flows from the restricted possibilities of navigation into the lagoon.[268] Owing to the nature of the bar there, passage is only possible during a certain period of the year, the *Harmattan* season.

C. THE ESTUARY OF THE RIVER SCHELDT.[269] There are three channels which connect the river Scheldt with the high seas of the North Sea: Oostgat, Deurloo and Wielingen. There are two riparian States, the Netherlands and Belgium. The Wielingen is the pre-eminently fit channel for navigation to and from the Scheldt, and therefore is of vital interest to Belgium and the Netherlands. Important ports in the Wielingen–Scheldt area are Antwerp and Zeebrugge, both in Belgium, and Flushing in the Netherlands.

The question of sovereignty over the Wielingen arose in the period after the secession of Belgium from the Kingdom of the Netherlands in 1830. The Dutch standpoint was and still is that the

Wielingen is an integral part of Dutch territory. Belgium considers the Wielingen is a part of the Belgium Territorial sea. The claim of the Netherlands is based mainly on historic rights, while the Belgian claim is the immediate consequence of the normal measurement of the territorial sea from the Belgian coast.

This old controversy between Belgium and the Netherlands still flares up occasionally; it became fairly serious in World War I, when Belgium was a belligerent and the Netherlands neutral. In the present-day situation, it has been observed, it is unlikely that problems will arise like those during the First World War because both nations are partners in the North Atlantic Treaty Organisation.[270] Nevertheless, few solutions have been recommended for the settlement of this dispute. Leo J. Bouchez states:

... two solutions recommended themselves: either submission of the dispute to the International Court of Justice or arbitration; or—which is perhaps the best solution—agreement by direct negotiations in which the *Thalweg* will be fixed as the frontier between Belgium and the Netherlands. The latter solution would establish a functional boundary, as navigation is the pre-eminent interest of the two States in this water area. The main consequence of the application of the Thalweg in the Wielingen area would be that both nations will have free and direct communication with the high seas.[271]

Professor J. Verzijl, suggests that a compromise solution might be 'the joint adoption of Belgian sovereignty, subject to a state servitude in favour of the Netherlands'.[272]

D. THE GULF OF FONSECA. The Gulf of Fonseca has been considered earlier in this chapter, and the reader is referred to section D.2d above.

One conclusion significant for the present discussion which might be derived from the cases considered above is that the practice of States does not seem to lend support to the proposition according to which, where a State has a port in a bay or estuary but does not have possession of the shores at the point where the bay connects with the open sea, a right of free passage through the entire waters of the bay may be said to have been given to that State. In the Chetumal Bay, navigation for Mexican ships through British waters was safeguarded by Article 3 *bis* of the 1893 agreement. In the Tana Lagoon case it has been seen that the boundary settlement of 1889 made 'no special provisions ... by which shipping to Ghana was safeguarded'. Thus the lack of such provisions was considered a defect in the agreement. It was, however, attributed to the fact that possibilities of navigation into the Lagoon are restricted. With respect to the Gulf of Fonseca, according to the judgement of the Central American Court of Justice in 1917, every coastal State on the Gulf of Fonseca possesses its own maritime belt, while the remaining waters of the gulf were found to be under the joint sovereignty of the coastal States. In the Gulf of Aqaba the whole waters are claimed to be territorial waters. Rights of sovereignty over the estuary of the river Scheldt are still disputed between Belgium and the Netherlands. But, as shown above, to ensure free and direct communication with the high seas for both nations, various solutions have been suggested.

Thus each of the cases considered above appears to represent a special and distinct situation, and hence the problem arising in each case was solved on its own merits, without reference to any general rule. It is not surprising, therefore, that with regard to the question of passage through the Gulf of Aqaba the International Law Commission in 1956 felt that it 'related to an exceptional case which did not lend itself to the formulation of a general rule'.[273] The Soviet member of the Commission said that the question '... sounded far more like a case for the International Court of Justice than a matter on which the Commission should enunciate a general rule'.[274] In addition, whereas the Secretary General of the United Nations stated that 'The international significance of the Gulf of Aqaba may be considered to justify the right of innocent passage through the Straits of Tiran and the Gulf in accordance with recognised rules of international law', he has expressed the opinion that 'A legal controversy exists as to the extent of the right of innocent passage through these waters'.[275]

More recently Professor Verzijl has expressed the view that 'In order to achieve a satisfactory solution to the controversies which still exist at the present moment about the legal situation an international agreement on the status of the Gulf [of Aqaba] and the Strait [of Tiran] is urgently required'.[276]

E. CONCLUSION

It must be recognised that the present controversy surrounding the Gulf of Aqaba and the Straits of Tiran is, essentially, an outcome of the Palestinian question and probably would not have arisen had the latter issue never existed. However, the main propositions which flow from the above analysis may be formulated as follows.

1. The Gulf of Aqaba is legally a bay which might be fairly dealt with by the littoral States, should they so agree, as a closed bay. But, under the present circumstances, it may be regarded as territorial waters.

2. The last part of Article 16 (4) of the Convention on the Territorial Sea and the Contiguous Zone, 1958, which provides for the right of non-suspendable innocent passage through straits used for international navigation between one part of the high seas and the territorial sea of a foreign State, is not a rule of customary international law.

3. The Straits of Tiran have never been used for international navigation and are not an international strait; they are merely territorial waters.

4. There is a right of innocent passage in favour of foreign ships in the Gulf of Aqaba and the Straits of Tiran, by virtue of general international law as it existed before, and as it was formulated in, the Territorial Sea Convention of 1958.

5. The Israeli withdrawal from the Sinai Peninsula in March 1957 has no bearing on the question of passage through the Straits of Tiran and the Gulf of Aqaba.

6. The Gulf of Aqaba question may be considered an 'exceptional—possibly unique' case.

CHAPTER V

LEGAL ASPECTS OF RED SEA HOT BRINES AND OTHER METALLIFEROUS MUD DEPOSITS

The Red Sea extends in a north-westerly direction from the narrow Straits of Bab El-Mandeb at its southern end to the southern tip of Sinai Peninsula, a distance of about 1,930 km. At its southern end it is connected to the Gulf of Aden, which trends east-north-east—west-south-west, opening into the Indian Ocean and separating the southern part of the Arabian Peninsula from the Somali plateau. At the northern end the Red Sea bifurcates into the Gulfs of Suez and Aqaba, creating the triangular Sinai Peninsula.[1] Physiographically

the bed of the Red Sea is an inner shelf because it is a fault depression in the Arabian–Nubian shield (Drake and Girdler, 1964). The length of the depression at sea level is about 1,875 km from the Sinai Peninsula to the Strait of Bab el-Mandeb. The width of the depression at sea level varies from about 200 km in the north to about 360 km in the south. The width of the Red Sea is substantially the same as the width of the depression, except at the extreme southern end where the sea begins to funnel into the Strait.[2]

A. DISCOVERY AND LOCATION

The existence of metalliferous hot brines in the Red Sea deeps, suspected since the 1880s,[3] was established in 1966 as a result of the investigations carried out by several research vessels, the RV *Discovery*, RV *Meteor*, RV *Atlantis II* and RV *Chain*, during the years 1963–66.[4] The brines are stated to be at a depth of approximately 2,000 metres, as the contact between the upper brine layer and the sea water occurs at about this depth.[5] The main deposits are in the two closely adjacent deeps, the Atlantis II and Discovery, in the central rift valley of the Red Sea. The Atlantis II Deep is about eight miles long and two miles wide, while the Discovery Deep covers an area of about five square miles.[6] An additional small deep, Chain Deep, containing brine is located between these two main deeps.[7] All three are located in a small area of less than ten by ten nautical miles, between Saudi Arabia, west of Jeddah, and the Sudan.[8] A fourth small hole, Oceanographer Deep, possibly also containing brine and situated between the coasts of Egypt and Saudi Arabia, was observed 617 km north-north-west of the original hot brine area by the USC and GSS *Oceanographer* vessel in May 1967.[9] Additional metalliferous precipitates have been recorded in a number of cores from elsewhere; these deposits were referred to as being due to overflows from the Atlantis II deep.[10] It was also reported that several collected cores, from areas approximately as far as 200 miles north and 100 miles south of Atlantis II Deep, had demonstrated the existence of similar brown and red deposits in the calcareous sediments of many other Red Sea deeps; these cores were described as goethite and manganese layers with concentrations of zinc and copper.[11] Moreover it has been indicated that the West German RV *Valdivia*, which carried out prospecting of the Red Sea from March to April 1971, had found scientific evidence of a hydrothermal copper–zinc ore deposit which is still in the making in the central graben of the Red Sea at a depth of 2,200 metres.[12] This deposit, it is added, is about 20,000–30,000 years old, but most of the ooze, which is deposited to a thickness of thirty metres on average, seems to have accumulated in the last 10,000 to 12,000 years.[13]

B. NATURE AND ECONOMIC POTENTIAL

The composition of the Red Sea brines and their associated sediments is stated to be highly variable, but they contain concentrations of sodium, calcium, manganese, magnesium, copper, zinc, iron and other minerals.[14] However, the sediments both in the brine-filled deeps and elsewhere in the median valley of the Red Sea often contain a high percentage of water.[15] Accordingly, it is concluded that the sediments are often in the form of a slurry.[16]

As to the economic potential of the brine deposits, there has been some controversy. In 1969 Bischoff and Manheim concluded that the assayed sediments contain amounts and proportions of metals which would, no doubt, be economically exploitable on land, and that if means for the recovery and separation could be found they represented an attractive prospect, especially since their full potential was still to be explored.[17] Walthier and Schatz agreed that the Red Sea oozes, as now known, are of more academic than economic interest, but observed that the results of some assays were rich enough to warrant attention from the explorationist.[18] In 1970 E. Blissenbach, an authority on exploration, conservatively assumed the development of what he described as 'technically feasible' and 'economically justifiable' means for the extraction of the metallic deposits of the Red Sea in the near to intermediate future.[19] However, commercial companies have expressed considerable interest in obtaining exploration rights and, as mentioned below, Saudi Arabia and the Sudan have already launched a joint venture to develop mineral deposits in the Red Sea between their respective coasts.

C. LEGAL RIGHTS

In 1974 Saudi Arabia and Sudan signed an agreement defining their respective exclusive sea bed zones in the Red Sea and at the same time providing for joint exploitation of the natural resources of the area between the two zones. Before considering the agreement in more detail, it is proposed to the examine the basis of the agreement, which was laid in the 1968 Saudi 'Law relating to the Acquisition of the Red Sea Resources'.

1. The Saudi Arabian Law relating to the Acquisition of the Red Sea Resources[20]

The discovery of the mineral-rich brines in the Red Sea deeps served to highlight the question of sovereignty or sovereign rights over the bed of the Red Sea. Thus in February 1968 an American marine resources firm announced that it had applied to the United Nations for 38·5-square-mile exclusive mineral exploration lease to survey seafloor springs in the middle of the Red Sea. According to the firm, no nation claims sovereignty over the area, and the firm wished to have United Nations approval to sample and map mineral deposits over a three-year period to determine their economic significance. The United Nations replied that it had no authority to grant rights in the Red Sea floor.[21] The American firm considered that no nation claimed sovereignty over the area in question presumably because the depths of the area are well beyond the 200-metre depth-line referred to in Article 1 of the 1958 Geneva Convention on the Continental Shelf.[22] As noted above, the Red Sea brines occur in waters whose depth is approximately 2,000 metres.[23] As has been noted, however, in 1970 E. Blissenbach indicated that the Red Sea brines were exploitable despite the depth of the superjacent waters.[24] It has also been stated that since the maximum breadth of the Red Sea is 340 km—in the vicinity of the brine-filled deeps it is about 225 km wide—any partition would not place the boundary at a point which

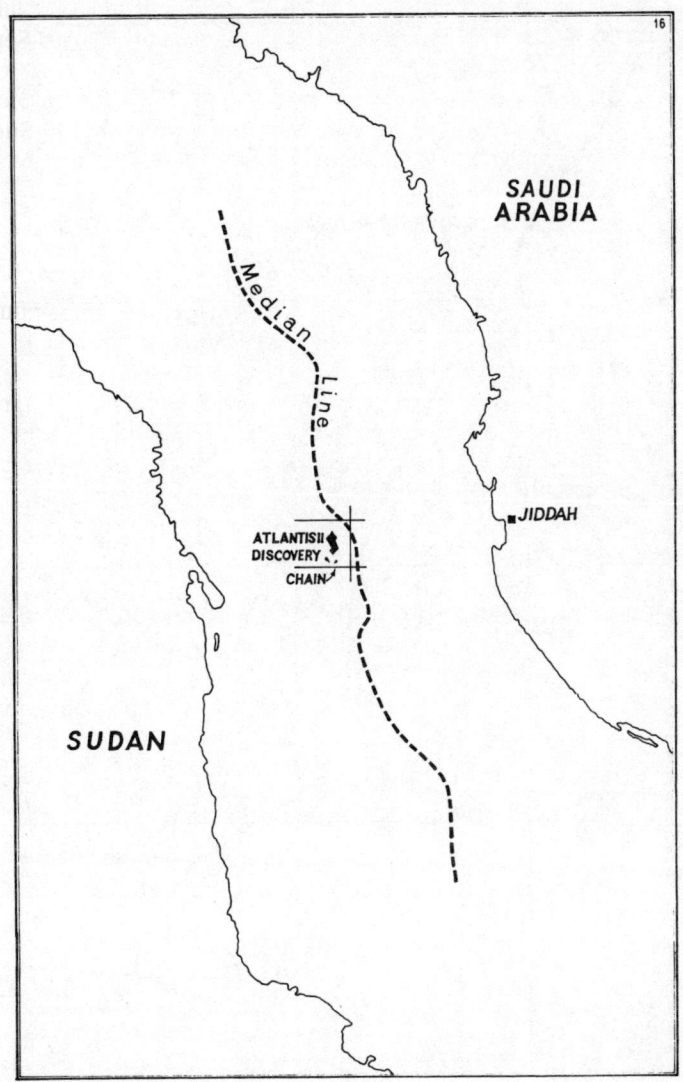

16 Red Sea median line and location of brine deposits. From an *unofficial* map courtesy of the Department of Geology and Mineral Resources, Ministry of Industry and Mining, the Sudan.

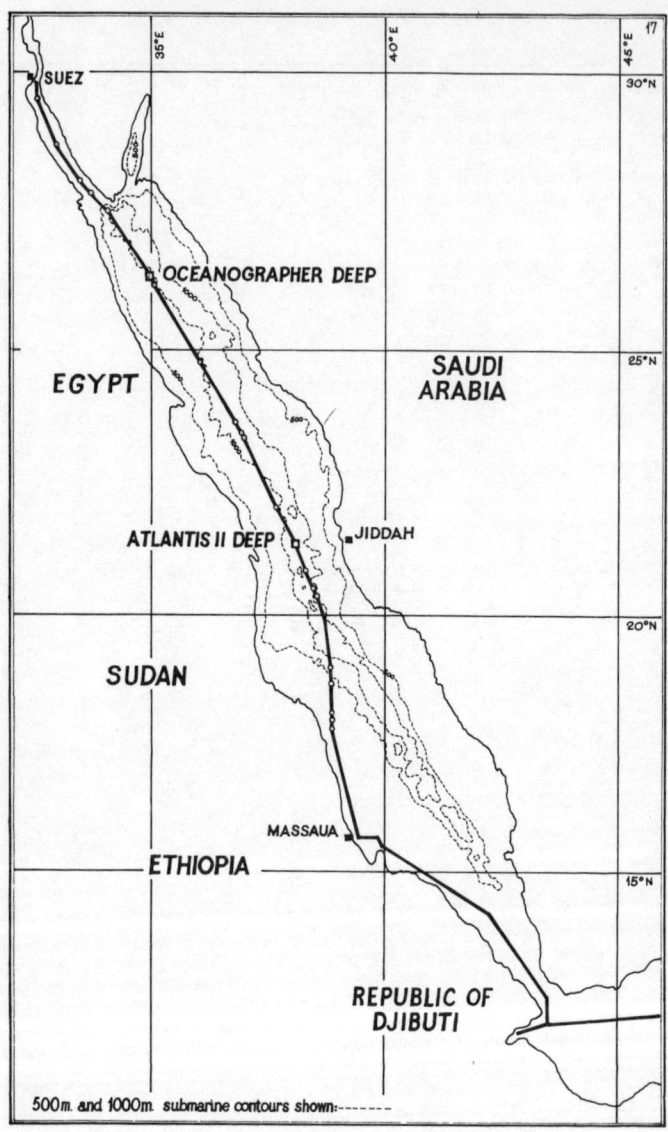

17 Trackline of the *Oceanographer* through the Red Sea, showing geographic locations of Atlantis II Deep and Oceanographer Deep; 500 m and 1,000 m contour lines after Drake and Girdler, 1964. From F. Ostadoff, 'A fourth brine hole in the Red Sea?', in E. T. Degens and D. A. Ross (eds.), *Hot Brines and Recent Heavy Metal Deposits in the Red Sea*, New York, 1969, p. 20.

could be described as not 'adjacent', having regard to distances already covered in the North Sea and on the Australian continental shelf.[25] In addition it may be observed that in accordance with the 200-mile exclusive economic zone concept, which is being discussed at the Third United Nations Conference on the Law of the Sea and which has already been accepted in practice by a large number of States, the States bordering the Red Sea would have, *inter alia*, sovereign rights over the whole bed and subsoil for the purpose of exploring and exploiting its natural resources.[26]

Prompted by the attempts on the part of commercial companies from outside the area to lay claim to Red Sea deposits, on 1 October 1968 Saudi Arabia decreed the 'Law relating to the Acquisition of the Red Sea Resources'. Article 1 of the Saudi law provides that:

> All the hydrocarbon materials and minerals in the Strata of the high sea bottom with respect to an area of the Red Sea extending below the high sea and contiguous to the continental shelf of Saudi Arabia shall appertain to the Kingdom of Saudi Arabia. Such materials and minerals shall hereafter be referred to as 'resources'.

Two matters call for immediate attention. First, by way of implication, the foregoing provision affirms the rights of Saudi Arabia over its continental shelf in the Red Sea, as no reference was made to these rights in the Saudi Sea bed proclamation issued in 1949, which dealt only with the Arabian Gulf coast of Saudi Arabia.[27] Secondly, Saudi Arabia asserts jurisdiction over a sea bed area which it considers as falling beyond the outer limits of its continental shelf. Thus the Saudi claim in this respect is based not on the doctrine of the continental shelf but rather, it may be stated, on what has now crystallised and come to be known as the concept of the 200-mile exclusive economic zone.[28] The Saudi justification for the claim was explained by the Saudi Oil Minister, who, just before the publication of the Saudi law, stated:

> There are vast mineral resources in the Red Sea area west of Jiddah, between Saudi Arabia and the Sudan. This area is not considered as falling within the continental shelf of the Kingdom of Saudi Arabia, and has attracted several companies from distant countries who are now laying claim to the ownership of these resources. The subject of ownership of resources underlying the deep oceans is now pending before the UN General Assembly. Although Saudi ownership of these resources appears both equitable and justified, we have found it necessary to issue a law declaring this ownership. In the meantime, the law does provide for the possibility of joint exploitation of these resources with our neighbour, the Sudan, and we will contact them about this.

This development is analogous to what happened in the US under President Truman's Administration, when the US declared title to the hydrocarbon resources in its offshore areas. Several nations followed the example of the US and it has now become an established international rule that every nation has the right to exercise sovereignty over the subsoil resources of its continental shelf. This time, it is Saudi Arabia that is taking the lead in establishing another fair and equitable rule in international law.[29]

Further justification for the Saudi claim was expressed in an 'Explanatory Note' attached to the law, in which it was indicated that the fact the Red Sea is limited in area, and almost similar in its geographical configuration to 'closed seas', demonstrates the effect which activities in the area might have on the fundamental interests of Saudi Arabia. Saudi Arabia, therefore, found it necessary to issue a law asserting its ownership to the natural resources of the Red Sea.[30]

The Saudi law is silent about the outer limits of the area to which it applies. According to the 'Explanatory Note', the law adopts the approach of the international community in this concern, as reflected in the Truman Proclamation of 1945, the declarations of many other States, and in the 1958 Geneva Convention on the Continental Shelf, which permits the extension of the coastal State's rights to where the depth of the superjacent waters admits of the exploitation of the natural resources of the sea bed. Article 3 of the Saudi law, however, provides some limitation on the seaward limits of the area concerned. Thus, after asserting to the Saudi government alone 'the exclusive right to prospect, explore and exploit the said "resources",' Article 3 goes on to state that:

The Government of Saudi Arabia may exercise its rights to prospect, explore and exploit such 'resources' in participation with neighbouring governments that may have similar right recognised by the Government of Saudi Arabia in any jointly shared areas.

In this regard the 'Explanatory Note' indicates that the term 'neighbouring governments', which appears in the foregoing provision, refers to both the States whose coasts are opposite the coast of Saudi Arabia and the States which are adjacent to Saudi Arabia. The note further states that the Saudi law—seeking further co-operation between the kingdom and its neighbours—allows the Saudi government to exploit the areas in which the legal rights of the kingdom overlap with those of a neighbouring State, in accordance with the principles of co-operation and participation which may be achieved equitably by way of negotiations and agreement.

Finally, the law expressly provides that the implementation of its provisions shall not, to the extent prescribed by the established rules of public international law, result in prejudicing the status of the high seas or disrupting the navigation therein.

2. Agreement between Sudan and Saudi Arabia relating to the Joint Exploitation of the Natural Resources of the Sea Bed and Subsoil of the Red Sea in the Common Zone[31]

The brine deposits of the Atlantis II, Discovery and Chain deeps are located on the Sudanese side of the Red Sea median line.[32] This had led to the suggestion that they must be regarded as being on the legal continental shelf of Sudan. This view, based on the equidistance rule in Article 6 of the 1958 Convention on the Continental Shelf,[33] was made prior to the 1969 decision of the International Court of Justice in the North Sea Continental Shelf cases.[34] This decision dealt with the delimitation of lateral boundaries between adjacent States. The Court found that the notion of equidistance as being logically necessary, in the sense of being 'an inescapable *a priori* accompaniment of basic continental shelf doctrine, is incorrect'.[35] It ruled that delimitation is to be affected 'by agreement in accordance with equitable principles'.[36]

Unlike Saudi Arabia, Sudan did not make any law to deal specifically with the Red Sea deposits, but in 1973 granted exploration licences to Sudanese Minerals Ltd and the West German company Preussag.[37] It is presumed that these licences covered the area of the Atlantis II, Discovery and Chain deeps.

However, as noted earlier, on 16 May 1974 Saudi Arabia and Sudan signed an agreement concerning their respective sovereign rights in the sea bed and subsoil of the submarine areas lying between their coasts in the Red Sea. Under the terms of the agreement, the parties mutually recognised the exclusive sovereign rights of Sudan in the area of the sea bed adjacent to the Sudanese coast and extending eastwards to a line where the depth of the superjacent waters was uninterruptedly 1,000 metres, and those of Saudi Arabia in the area of the sea bed adjacent to the Saudi Arabian coast and extending westwards to a line where the depth of the superjacent waters was uninterruptedly 1,000 metres. Furthermore the two governments recognised that the area falling between the two aforementioned zones was common to both of them, and that they had equal sovereign rights in all the natural resources of the common zone, which rights were exclusive to them. It was also expressly stipulated that no part of the territorial sea of either government should be included in the common zone.

The common zone evidently includes the location of the main

Red Sea brine deposits referred to above, that is, the Atlantis II, Discovery and Chain deeps, for, as already indicated, the brines occur in waters of approximately 2,000 metres depth. To ensure 'the prompt and efficient exploitation' of the natural resources of the common zone, the Saudi–Sudanese agreement stipulated that a joint commission would be established which would undertake, *inter alia,* to survey and delimit the common zone; to carry out the requisite studies concerning the exploration and exploitation of the natural resources there; to encourage specialised bodies to undertake exploration activities in the zone, and to look into applications for licences and concessions concerning exploration and exploitation in the common zone. It was also agreed that the Saudi government would provide the funds required by the joint commission in carrying out its functions, but these would be recovered from future income from the output of the common zone and in a manner to be agreed upon by the two parties.

The agreement took note that the Sudan had concluded on 15 May 1973 an agreement whereby it gave exploration licences to Sudanese Minerals Ltd and Preussag, which agreement created a legal obligation on the Sudan. The two governments, therefore, agreed that the joint commission would decide on this matter in such a manner as to preserve the rights of the Sudan and in the context of the regime established for the common zone.

Article XIV of the agreement provided safeguards against the existence of any accumulation or deposit of a natural resource situated across the boundary of the exclusive sovereign rights area of either government and the common zone. In such an event the joint commission would determine the manner in which the accumulation or deposit was to be exploited, provided that any decision taken should guarantee for the government involved an equitable share in the proceeds of the exploitation of such accumulation or deposit. The agreement also provided that its application should not, to the extent prescribed by the established rules of international law, affect the status of the high seas or obstruct navigation therein.

On the question of settlement of disputes arising from the implementation or interpretation of the agreement, Article XVI provided that any such dispute would be settled by amicable means, but should amicable means fail, the dispute will be submitted to the International Court of Justice. The parties accept the compulsory jurisdiction of the International Court in this respect. Article XVI further stipulated that if one of the two parties takes a measure which is objected to by the other, the objecting government may ask the International Court to indicate interim measures to be taken to stop the measure objected to or to allow its continuance pending the final decision.

In implementation of the provisions of the Saudi Arabian–Sudanese agreement a Saudi–Sudanese Joint Commission for the Exploitation of the Natural Resources of the Common Zone was established, and met for the first time on 10 May 1975 in Khartoum. It decided, in accordance with Article XI of the agreement, to locate the seat of the commission's secretariat in Jeddah. It also decided to proceed with a number of projects, which included studies of the deep sea in the common zone, geological studies of the Red Sea sedimentary basin, aerial magnetometric surveys of the common zone, and investigation of the feasibility of exploiting the mineral-bearing formations in deep waters.[38] More recently it has been reported that the West German company Preussag, referred to above, is understood to be close to signing a $20 million contract with the joint commission for the development of mineral deposits in the common zone.[39]

The Saudi Arabian–Sudanese agreement conforms with the principles of international law since declared by the International Court of Justice in the North Sea Continental Shelf cases, 1969, to be applicable to the delimitation of submarine boundaries, notably the rules that delimitation is to be effected by agreement in accordance with equitable principles, and that if the delimitation leaves to the parties concerned areas that overlap, these are to be divided between them in agreed proportions or, failing agreement, equally, unless they decide on a regime of joint jurisdiction, user, or exploitation for the zones of overlap or any part of them.[40] The agreement also settles one of the main offshore boundaries in the Red Sea, and should help to promote the development of submarine resources between Saudi Arabia and Sudan. The provisions relating to settlement of disputes are also of particular interest. But more than this, the agreement established a valuable precedent for the delimitation of other offshore boundaries in the Red Sea.

3. *Conference of States bordering the Red Sea*
The first Conference of States bordering the Red Sea met in Jeddah on 16–17 July 1972, at the invitation of the government of Saudi Arabia.[41] The following countries were represented: Egypt, Ethiopia, Saudi Arabia, Sudan and the Yemen Arab Republic. The aim of the conference, as explained by its chairman, was to assert the rights of the States bordering the Red Sea over its deep mineral resources and to regulate the use of those rights.[42] At the end of the

conference a joint communiqué was issued in which the States represented expressed the view that the deep resources of the Red Sea are the property of the States bordering it and should remain so. The represented States also agreed to take the necessary measures for the protection of these resources from what they called 'foreign States and/or institutions'. They further stressed the necessity for further co-operation for the exploration and exploitation of the said resources.[43]

The timing of the conference seems to have been directly related to that of the Third United Nations Conference on the Law of the Sea and to the proposed international regime and authority for the sea-bed area beyond national jurisdiction.[44] It has thus been observed that:

> it would be most surprising if the Sudanese or the Saudi Arabian Government were prepared to consider the reservation of the brines, found at a depth of more than 2,000 metres and well beyond the territorial sea claimed by both coastal States, for the proposed international regime. It is difficult to envisage either country giving up minerals having an estimated commercial value of hundreds of millions of dollars.[45]

Sudan has already declared that it

> ... would certainly not view with favour any suggestions that it should renounce its title to that area of the Red Sea in which it had already been carrying out exploratory and prospecting activities for a number of years, since it possessed those rights under existing law.[46]

Similar views had been expressed by the government of Saudi Arabia in a memorandum addressed to the Arab League concerning ownership of the natural resources of the Red Sea.

GENERAL CONCLUSIONS

The aim of the present section is to recapitulate some of the major answers and propositions contained in the preceding chapters, to make a number of observations concerning the Middle Eastern States' attitudes and policies in regard to the law of the sea, and finally to try and ascertain whether such attitudes and policies represent what may be interpreted as being a distinct approach to sea law, and to offer some general proposals.

Even though the twelve-mile territorial sea has been enacted into law by most of the Middle Eastern States, and, in the case of Iran, Democratic Yemen, Oman, Qatar and Saudi Arabia exclusive fishing zones of extent larger than that previously contemplated by international law have been proclaimed, it must be recognised that most Middle Eastern States, unlike some other States, have so far abstained from offshore jurisdictional claims of considerable dimensions. Nevertheless, in the Third United Nations Conference on the Law of the Sea, broadly speaking, with the exception of Kuwait, these States have already shown support for the 200-mile exclusive economic zone concept. At the same time, like most developing countries, they have expressed their belief that the proposed international authority for the exploration and exploitation of the sea bed and ocean floor and subsoil thereof beyond the limits of national jurisdiction, should be essentially an operating rather than a licensing authority.

The questions relating to bays and navigation through straits are of special significance to many Middle Eastern States. This is mainly because their coasts are marked, especially in the case of Egypt, by many bays and embrace important international straits, but partly because of the controversy surrounding the legal status of, and the rules governing the right of passage through, the Gulf of Aqaba and the Straits of Tiran. As proposed above in Chapter IV, and contrary to views suggested by certain countries and writers, the Gulf of Aqaba and the Straits of Tiran do not constitute international waterways or comprehend high seas: they are simply territorial waters in which there is only a right of innocent passage in favour of foreign ships.

Another issue which is especially important to Middle Eastern States, and particularly to those bordering the Arabian Gulf and the

GENERAL CONCLUSIONS

Red Sea, is the problem of offshore boundary delimitations, which had (prior to the discovery of oil in the Arabian Gulf and of mineral-rich deposits in the Red Sea) been of little importance to the governments of the adjacent States. However, in the case of the Arabian Gulf a large number of the required offshore boundary lines and the problems regarding islands of disputed sovereignty have been definitively settled. The various continental shelf boundary agreements so far in existence conform with both the three-point rule concerning delimitation formulated in Article 6 of the Convention on the Continental Shelf of 1958, and the rules and principles laid down by the International Court of Justice in the North Sea Continental Shelf cases, 1969. A successful resolution of the remaining outstanding questions will, no doubt, be of great economic and stabilising importance to the Gulf region. In the Red Sea one of the longest single offshore boundaries, that between Saudi Arabia and Sudan, has been settled by an agreement which provides, *inter alia,* for joint exploitation of part of the sea bed area involved. The agreement established a valuable precedent for the delimitation of other offshore boundaries in the region and should help to promote the orderly development of submarine resources.

The fast-changing law of the sea has to be considered in relation to the past, the present and the future, none of which can be treated in isolation. The past sometimes dictates the tone of the present and the present that of the future. In other words, present attitudes may be a result of our past experiences, and our future attitudes may be the product of our present failures.

In so far as past practice is concerned, it can be seen that in view of their 'recentness' in terms of the existence of Statehood, not much useful analysis can be gained from the previous conduct and legislation of the Middle Eastern States. Much of what could be said of the past is that they 'accepted' subconsciously so-called customary international law.

During what may be called 'the transition from the past to the present' the Middle Eastern States were plagued with a number of problems. Firstly, there was a great lack of international law personnel. Secondly, there was reticence. The Middle Eastern States never really considered themselves as being affected by the esoteric details of the law of the sea. They thought only in terms of their small geographical environment. Thirdly, since their independence most of the States concerned have been engaged in constant, though sporadic, conflict. Lastly, they were economically weak. All these factors militated against the formulation of any concrete and common policies on the law of the sea.

GENERAL CONCLUSIONS

The present attitudes of the Middle Eastern States have been motivated by a reappraisal, or sudden awareness, not only of international affairs and diplomacy but also of the economic importance of the upsurge in the price of oil. International law being an offshoot of international affairs and diplomacy, the Middle Eastern States see a strong connection between their causes and aspirations and those of the other developing Third World countries, even where they are by no means identical. Thus it may be observed that a number, if not all, of the Middle Eastern States are strongly sympathetic towards and are in favour of the 200-mile exclusive economic zone concept or doctrine. They also support a strong international sea-bed authority with functional and supervisory powers.

In so far as the future is concerned, one can only speculate or make tentative forecasts, based firstly on their attitudes and intentions and secondly on the assumption that the present, albeit shaky, 'political' alignments will remain for as long as possible, bearing in mind that 'political solidarity' is likely to alter with changes in economic and socio-economic circumstances. The future of the law of the sea may be of permanent duration only if the developed, industrialised States recognise that the aspirations of the Third World countries (including the Middle Eastern States), are not to be ignored; and if the developing countries acknowledge that political success is of little or no importance without the co-operation of the technologically advanced countries.

Although one cannot discern an exclusively Middle Eastern approach to sea law, it is more correct to say that the Middle Eastern States' policies are varieties of the general 'Developing Third World approach'. Their attitudes to the law of the sea are based essentially on socio-economic, not defence or security considerations. The former have been the basis of most of the claims they have expounded. Thus reference to such considerations was made in the continental shelf proclamations issued by the Gulf States in 1949 and by other Middle Eastern States subsequently. The extension to twelve miles of the territorial sea of many Middle Eastern States was based essentially on economic considerations. These also provided the reasons for the exclusive fishing zones recently claimed by certain Gulf States.

In so far as the region itself is concerned, there is still a great deal to be done by way of pooling arrangements and regional co-operation, and the utilisation of existing international bodies—for example, for scientific research and pollution control. In addition to multilateral instruments, a need arises for the setting up of more

GENERAL CONCLUSIONS

effective regional treaties, based on agreement between all States in the region, irrespective of creed or political views, for the purpose of fish farming and marine education. More specifically, it is of importance to study the issues of scientific research on, and monitoring of, the environment and their relationship with the rationalisation of exploitation and development on a scientific basis of marine natural resources. In the interests of their individual and collective survival Middle Eastern States should accept their responsibility as regards the conservation of environmental conditions from the dangers of pollution and environmental degradation. In view of the special importance of the waters in the area as international trade routes, it is suggested that co-operative efforts be made to achieve some of these objectives: the setting up of a meteorological network for the environment, consisting of national stations run by personnel of the regional States, and maintaining close relations with other similar neighbouring and/or regional networks as well as with the international environmental organisation; the adoption of regional conventions concerning the conservation of the marine ecology and the enforcement of the regulations governing it; the establishment of a regional programme for scientific research and the provision of a special fund, based on defined guidelines, to finance such a programme; the co-ordination of national research stations within the framework of integrated scientific plans. The regional scientific network should have a research centre for marine ecological research work, research vessels for the programme of research and studies, marine biology, reference groups, and the like.

In conclusion, while there is much to be said for regional co-operation and agreements, it is to be hoped that a universally acceptable system of co-operation will supersede those regional arrangements. It can be seen from the foregoing chapters that, in so far as a coherent Middle Eastern point of view emerges, there is great potential for reconciling it with that of the wider international community.

APPENDICES
NOTES
BIBLIOGRAPHY
INDEX

APPENDIX I
NATIONAL LEGISLATION AND INTERNATIONAL AGREEMENTS

I. NATIONAL LEGISLATION

Bahrain
Proclamation with respect to the sea bed and the subsoil of the high seas of the Persian Gulf, 5 June 1949. Text in ST/LEG/Ser.8/1 (1951), pp. 24–5.

Egypt
Royal Decree concerning the territorial waters of the Kingdom of Egypt, 15 January 1951. Text in U.S. Department of State, the Geographer, *Strait Baselines: United Arab Republic, Limits in the Seas,* No. 22, 22 June 1970.

Modification of Egyptian decree on territorial waters, Presidential Decree No. 180, 17 February 1958. For text see *ibid*.

United Arab Republic Decree on the continental shelf, No. 1051, 3 September 1958. Text in 14 *R.E.D.I.* (1958), p. 406.

United Arab Emirates
Abu Dhabi—Proclamation with respect to the sea bed and subsoil of the Persian Gulf, 10 June 1949. Text in ST/LEG/Ser.B/1 (1951), p. 23.
Ajman—Proclamation with respect to the sea bed and the subsoil of the high seas of the Persian Gulf, 20 June 1949. Text in ST/LEG/Ser.B/1 (1951), p. 24.
Dubai—Proclamation with respect to the sea bed and the subsoil of the high seas of the Persian Gulf, 14 June 1949. Text in ST/LEG/Ser.B/1 (1951), pp. 25–6.
Ras al-Khaimah—Proclamation with respect to the sea bed and the subsoil of the high seas of the Persian Gulf, 17 June 1949. Text in ST/LEG/Ser.B/1 (1951), pp. 27–8.
Sharjah—Proclamation with respect to the sea bed and the subsoil of the high seas of the Persian Gulf, 16 June 1949. Text in ST/LEG/Ser.B/1 (1951), pp. 28–9.
—A Decree concerning territorial waters of Sharjah Emirate and its Dependencies and its Islands, 10 September 1969. Text in *Petroleum Legislation, Basic Oil Laws and Concession Contracts: Middle East*, Supplement No. XXXVII, pp. Sharjah A–O.
—Supplementary Decree concerning the territorial sea of the Emirate of Sharjah and its Dependencies, 5 April 1970. For text see *ibid.*, pp. Sharjah B–O.

APPENDIX I

Umm al-Qaiwain—Proclamation with respect to the sea bed and the subsoil of the high seas of the Persian Gulf, 20 June 1949. Text in ST/LEG/Ser.B/1 (1951), pp. 29–30.

Iran
Act on the exploration and exploitation of the natural resources of the Continental Shelf of Iran, 19 June 1955. Text in ST/LEG/Ser.B/16 (1974), p. 151; *Petroleum Legislation, Basic Oil Laws and Concession Contracts: Middle East*, Supplement No. XXXIII, pp. Iran A–I.

Act amending the Act of 15 July 1934 on the territorial waters and the contiguous zone of Iran, 12 April 1959. Text in ST/LEG/Ser.B/16 (1974), p. 10.

Proclamation concerning the outer limit of the exclusive fishing zone of Iran in the Persian Gulf and the Sea of Oman, 30 October 1973. Text in ST/LEG/Ser.B/18 (1976), p. 334.

Iraq
Official proclamation concerning the Continental Shelf of Iraq, 23 November 1957. Text in ST/LEG/Ser.B/15 (1970), p. 368–9.

Supplementary Proclamation concerning the Continental Shelf of Iraq, 10 April 1958. For text see *ibid.*, p. 369.

Law No. 71 of 1958 delimiting the Iraqi territorial waters. For text see *ibid.*, pp. 89–90.

Jordan
Fisheries Act No. 25, December 1943. Text in ST/LEG/Ser.B/6 (1956), p. 522.

Kuwait
Proclamation of the Shaikh of Kuwait with respect to the sea bed and the subsoil of the high seas of the Persian Gulf, 12 June 1949. Text in ST/LEG/Ser.B/1 (1951), p. 26.

Decree regarding the delimitation of the breadth of the territorial sea of the State of Kuwait, 17 December 1967. Text in ST/LEG/Ser.B/15 (1970), p. 96.

Lebanon
Order No. 1104 of the High Commissioner of the French Republic, with respect to the policing of maritime fisheries, 14 November 1921. Text in ST/LEG/Ser.B/1 (1951), p. 83.

Code of customs regulations, adopted by Order No. 137/LR of the High Commissioner of the French Republic, 15 June 1935. For text see *ibid.*, p. 83.

Penal Code, enacted by Legislative Decree No. 340–NT, 1 March 1943. For text see *ibid.*, p. 307.

Libya
Act No. 2 concerning the delimitation of Libyan territorial waters, 18 February 1959. Text in ST/LEG/Ser.B/16 (1974), p. 14.

APPENDIX I

Information concerning the jurisdiction of the Gulf of Surt, 9 October 1973. Text in ST/LEG/Ser.B/18 (1976), p. 26.

Oman
Decree concerning the territorial sea, continental shelf and exclusive fishing zones of the Sultanate of Oman, 17 July 1972. Text in ST/LEG/Ser.B/16 (1974), p. 23; U.S. Department of State, the Geographer, *Strait Baselines (Hypothetical), Limits in the Seas*, No. 61, 4 June 1975.

Decree No. 44 of 15 June 1977 (amending art. 6 of the Decree of 17 July 1972). Text in ST/LEG/SerB/19 (preliminary issue 1978), p. 258.

Marine Pollution Control Law, 1974. Text in ST/LEG/Ser.B/18 (1976), p. 74.

Qatar
Proclamation with respect to the sea-bed and the subsoil of the high seas of the Persian Gulf, 8 June 1949. Text in ST/LEG/Ser.B/1 (1951), p. 27.

Declaration concerning the exclusive sovereign rights of the State of Qatar in the zones contiguous to the territorial sea, 2 June 1974. For text see Appendix IV.

Saudi Arabia
Royal Pronouncement concerning the policy of the Kingdom of Saudi Arabia with respect to the subsoil and sea bed of areas in the Persian Gulf contiguous to the coasts of the Kingdom of Saudi Arabia, 28 May 1949. Text in ST/LEG/Ser.B/1 (1951), p. 22.

Royal Decree concerning the territorial waters of the Kingdom of Saudi Arabia, No. 33, 16 February 1958. Text in ST/LEG/Ser.B/15 (1970), p. 114; U.S. Department of State, the Geographer, *Strait Baselines: Saudi Arabia, Limits in the Seas*, No. 20, 8 June 1970.

Saudi Royal Decree relating to the acquisition of the Red Sea Resources No. M/27, dated 9–7–1388 (1 October 1968). Text in Organisation of Petroleum Exporting Countries (OPEC), *Selected Documents of the International Petroleum Industry, 1968* (Vienna, 1969), pp. 33–4; 8 *I.L.M.* (1969), p. 606.

Declaration concerning the limit of the exclusive fishing zones of Saudi Arabia in the Red Sea and the Arabian Gulf, 1974. For text see Appendix V.

Sudan
The Sudan territorial waters and continental shelf Act, No. 106 of 1970. Text in Special Supplement to the Democratic Republic of the Sudan *Gazette* No. 1112, 31 December 1971, Supplement No. 1: General Legislation, p. 478.

The Convention on the Continental Shelf (Ratification) Act, No. 62 of 1970. Text in Legislative Supplement to the Democratic Republic of the Sudan *Gazette* No. 1107, 15 July 1970, Supplement No. 1: General Legislation, p. 306.

APPENDIX I

Syria
Legislative Decree No. 304 concerning the territorial sea of the Syrian Arab Republic, 28 December 1963. Text in U.S. Department of State, the Geographer, *Strait Baselines: Syria, Limits in the Seas,* No. 53, 10 December 1973.

Yemen Arab Republic
Decree No. 15 concerning the territorial waters of the Yemen Arab Republic, 30 April 1967. For text see Appendix VI(A).
Decree No. 16 concerning the Continental Shelf of the Yemen Arab Republic, 30 April 1967. For text see Appendix VI(B).

Democratic Yemen
Act No. 45 of 1977 concerning the territorial sea, exclusive economic zone, Continental Shelf and other marine areas (entry into force on 15 January 1978 pursuant to article 25). Text in ST/LEG/Ser.B/19 (preliminary issue 1978), p. 53.

II. INTERNATIONAL AGREEMENTS

Bahrain–Saudi Arabia Boundary Agreement, done on 22 February 1958, signed and ratified 26 February 1958. Text in ST/LEG/Ser.B/16 (1974), p. 409; U.S. Department of State, the Geographer, *Continental Shelf Boundary: Bahrain–Saudi Arabia, Limits in the Seas*, No. 12, 10 March 1970.

Agreement concerning the Sovereignty over the Islands of al-'Arabiyah and Farsi and the Delimitation of the Boundary Line separating the Submarine Areas between the Kingdom of Saudi Arabia and Iran. Done at Tehran on 24 October 1968 and ratified on 29 January 1969. Text in ST/LEG/Ser.B/18 (1976), p. 403; U.S. Department of State, the Geographer, *Continental Shelf Boundary: Iran–Saudi Arabia, Limits in the Seas*, No. 24, 6 July 1970; 69 *U.N.T.S.*, p. 212.

Agreement for Settlement of the Offshore Boundary and Ownership of Islands between Abu Dhabi and Qatar, signed and ratified on 20 March 1969. Text in ST/LEG/Ser.B/16 (1974), p. 403; U.S. Department of State, the Geographer, *Continental Shelf Boundary: Abu Dhabi–Qatar, Limits in the Seas,* No. 18, 29 May 1970.

Offshore Boundary Agreement between the Amirates of Abu Dhabi and Dubai, signed 18 February 1968. Text in *Petroleum Legislation, Basic Oil Laws and Concession Contracts–Middle East*, Suppl. XXI, pp. Abu Dhabi A–O; Organisation of Petroleum Exporting Countries (OPEC), *Selected Documents of the International Petroleum Industry, 1968* (Vienna, 1969), p. 367.

Agreement concerning the Boundary Line dividing the Continental Shelf between Iran and Qatar. Done at Doka on 20 September 1969 and ratified on 10 May 1970. Text in ST/LEG/Ser.B/16 (1974), p. 416; 787 *U.N.T.S.*, No. 11197; U.S. Department of State, the Geographer, *Continental Shelf Boundary: Iran–Qatar, Limits in the Seas,* No. 25, 9 July 1970.

APPENDIX I

Agreement concerning Delimitation of the Continental Shelf between Bahrain and Iran, signed at Bahrain on 17 June 1971, and entered into force on 14 May 1972. Text in ST/LEG/Ser.B/16 (1974), p. 428; U.S. Department of State, the Geographer, *Continental Shelf Boundary: Bahrain–Iran, Limits in the Seas*, No. 58, 13 September 1974.

Agreement concerning the Boundary Line dividing Parts of the Continental Shelf between Iran and the United Arab Emirates (Dubai), signed on 13 August 1974. Text in U.S. Department of State, the Geographer, *Continental Shelf Boundary: Iran–United Arab Emirates (Dubai), Limits in the Seas*, No. 63, 30 September 1975.

Agreement concerning Delimitation of the Continental Shelf between Iran and Oman. Signed on 25 July 1975 and ratified on 28 May 1975. Text in U.S. Department of State, the Geographer, *Continental Shelf Boundary: Iran–Oman, Limits in the Seas*, No. 67, 1 January 1976.

Documents on the Understanding concerning the Island of Abu Musa; for text see Appendix VII.

Agreement between Sudan and Saudi Arabia relating to the Joint Exploitation of the Natural Resources of the Sea Bed and Subsoil of the Red Sea in the Common Zone. Done at Khartoum on 16 May 1974. Text in ST/LEG/Ser.B/18 (1976), p. 452.

APPENDIX II
LIMITS OF NATIONAL CLAIMS TO OFFSHORE JURISDICTIONS
(ALL FIGURES ARE NAUTICAL MILES UNLESS OTHERWISE STATED)

	Territorial sea	Exclusive fishing zone	'Pollution-free zone'	Security, sanitary and fiscal	Immigration	Customs	Penal	Navigation	Continental shelf
Bahrain	3								A
Egypt*	12			6				6	B
United Arab Emirates	3 (except Sharjah, 12)								
Iran	12	38 (Gulf of Oman). Correspond to continental shelf limits in Arabian Gulf							A
Iraq	12								A
Jordan*	No specific claim	3 from low-water line							A
Kuwait*	12								D
Lebanon*	No specific claim	6 measured from the coast				20 km from coast	20 km from coast		A
Libya*	12								D
Oman	12	188	38						A
Qatar	3								B
Saudi Arabia*	12	Correspond to limits of the continental shelf							A
Sudan†	12	Correspond to limits of the continental shelf		6		6		6	A
Syria*	12			6	6	6			B
Yemen Arab Republic	12			6				6	B
Democratic Yemen*	12	188 (exclusive economic zone)		12		12			C

Key to column 10
A Adopted continental shelf concept without precise definition of outer limits.
B 200 m depth and exploitability criteria.
C To the outer limit of the continental margin, or to a distance of 200 n.m.
D No express claim.

* These States are party to the International Convention for the Prevention of Pollution of the Sea by Oil, 12 May 1954, as amended 13 April 1962. Egypt, Lebanon, Libya and Saudi Arabia have also ratified the 1969 amendments. IMCO Document MP/Conf./Inf.10, 2 October 1973.
† Sudan is a party to the 1958 Convention on the Continental Shelf.

APPENDIX III

LETTER FROM THE POLITICAL AGENT TO SHAIKH SAQR, RULER OF SHARJAH
(ARABIC TRANSLATION OMITTED)[1]

SECRET

No. C/S–76

Political Agency,
BAHRAIN
2 June 1949

To
    Shaikh Sultan bin Saqr Al Qasim
    Ruler of Sharjah

After compliments,
    I have the honour to refer to the Political Officer, Trucial Coast's, conversation with you on the subject of the Continental Shelf and to say that His Excellency the Political Resident has directed me to ask you now to issue a proclamation claiming jurisdiction and control over the sea bed and subsoil adjacent to the coasts of your State, the area of which is to be more precisely determined on justifiable principles.

2 I now enclose two copies of a draft proclamation which has been drawn up by legal experts and which would give you the necessary jurisdiction and control. One copy you should sign (or seal) and issue publicly and the other copy you should retain.

3 I should be grateful for confirmation from you that you have made the proclamation as drafted.

                                      Usual ending

                        HIS BRITANNIC MAJESTY'S
                            POLITICAL AGENT

---

[1] *Source.* Reproduced from 'Trucial States Mediation', *op. cit.*, vol. II, Doc. No. 4, p. 5.

APPENDIX IV

DECLARATION CONCERNING THE EXCLUSIVE SOVEREIGN RIGHTS OF THE STATE OF QATAR IN THE ZONES CONTIGUOUS TO THE TERRITORIAL SEA, 2 JUNE 1974[1]

No doubt that the fish resources, as well as the natural resources and other marine resources, have always in the past been, and are at present, and shall remain in the future to be considered to the State of Qatar an essential factor for the development and a principal factor for its social and economic progress;

And considering that other States in the area have recently issued declarations confirming their exclusive jurisdiction and sovereignty with regard to the fish resources and all the natural resources and other marine resources in the areas adjacent to their territorial seas and continental shelves;

And since the State of Qatar is very determined to fully protect all its rights, and to exercise its jurisdiction and authority in all fields;

And according to the resolutions of the United Nations which affirm the right of every State in the exercise of its complete and permanent sovereignty over its natural wealth and economic resources, particularly those which concern the welfare of its people;

For all these reasons, the State of Qatar, while reaffirming what it declared in its proclamation of June 1949 with respect to its sovereignty and the exercise of its jurisdiction over all its natural resources and marine wealth in its continental shelf, and asserting all its rights in the maritime area subject to its sovereignty in accordance with international law, declares the following rules:

1. The State of Qatar alone has the exclusive sovereign rights over the natural resources and the marine resources and fishing, in the zones contiguous to the territorial sea of its coasts and the coasts of its islands, and without prejudice to the freedom of international navigation, maritime and aerial, in accordance with the established rules of international law.

The outer limits of these zones shall be defined according to bilateral agreements already concluded or to be concluded. Where no such agreement exists, the limits shall be defined by reference to the outer limits of the continental shelf of Qatar or to the median line every point of which is equidistant from the baselines from which the territorial seas of Qatar and

---

[1] *Source*. Translated by the present writer from a copy of the original Arabic text acquired by courtesy of His Excellency the Ambassador of Kuwait in London, Sheikh Saud Nasir Al-Sabah.

APPENDIX IV

the states concerned are measured in accordance with the rules of international law.

2. The State of Qatar alone has, in the aforementioned Qatari Zone, the right of prospecting, exploration, exploitation, development, fishing, construction of installations and safety and control zones, and the conservation of the marine wealth and natural resources, whether situated on, under or over the sea bed.

3. Fishing and all related activities, exploitation of the marine wealth and natural resources, and the undertaking of any type of research by non-Qataris in the aforementioned zone are prohibited unless by prior permission from the Government of Qatar in accordance with the regulations that might be established in this regard.

4. The rights or the exercise of any of the activities mentioned in this declaration do not depend on occupation, effective or notional, or on the issue of special declarations or permits.

The outer limits of the zones provided for in this declaration shall be drawn on the official maritime charts of the State of Qatar.

APPENDIX V

DECLARATION CONCERNING THE LIMITS OF THE EXCLUSIVE FISHING ZONES OF SAUDI ARABIA IN THE RED SEA AND THE ARABIAN GULF, 1974[1]

The Foreign Ministry issued a declaration concerning the policy of the Kingdom of Saudi Arabia in relation to the fishing zones in the Red Sea and the Arabian Gulf adjacent to the coasts of the Kingdom of Saudi Arabia. The following is the text of the declaration:

Whereas the fish resources are considered a principal diet for the people of the Kingdom of Saudi Arabia and a vital factor for its social and economic progress; and recognising that jurisdiction over those fish resources is required for their protection and prudent exploitation; and in affirmation of the provisions of Article 9 concerning fishing of the Royal Decree No. 33 of 27 Rajab 1372 A.H. (corresponding to 16 February 1958) concerning the territorial waters; and considering that other States have at present affirmed their jurisdiction over the fish resources in the areas adjacent to their territorial seas; therefore, the Kingdom of Saudi Arabia declares the following policy for the protection of the exclusive fishing rights of the Kingdom in the areas adjacent to its coast and the coasts of its islands in the Arabian Gulf and the Red Sea:

Article 1. The exclusive fishing zones of the Kingdom of Saudi Arabia are those areas contiguous to the coasts of the Kingdom and the coasts of its islands, from the coastal sea of the Kingdom towards the high seas; if the fishing zones, measured from the baselines referred to in Article 5 of the Royal Decree concerning the territorial waters referred to above, be overlapped with those of another Coastal State, the boundary shall be the median line every point of which is equidistant from the baselines from which the territorial seas is measured.

Article 2. Fishing and all related activities by non-Saudis in the exclusive fishing zone are prohibited unless prior permission is obtained from the Government of the Kingdom of Saudi Arabia.

Article 3. The implementation of this declaration shall not prejudice the status of the fishing zones as high seas in accordance with the established principles of international law.

Article 4. The outer limits of the exclusive fishing zones of Saudi Arabia in the Arabian Gulf and the Red Sea shall be drawn on maritime charts.

---

[1] *Source.* Translated by the present writer from a copy of the original Arabic text acquired by courtesy of His Excellency the Ambassador of Kuwait in London, Sheikh Saud Nasir Al-Sabah.

APPENDIX VI

A. DECREE NO. 15 CONCERNING THE TERRITORIAL WATERS OF THE YEMEN ARAB REPUBLIC, 30 APRIL 1967[1]

The President of the Republic,
Having seen the Constitution,
Article 1. Are meant by the terms appearing in this Resolution the following:
   a. The 'nautical mile' is the equivalent of 1,852 (one thousand, eight hundred and fifty two) metres.
   b. The 'bay' is every inlet, lagoon or other arm of the sea.
   c. The 'island' is every islet, reef, rock, or permanent artificial structure not submerged at lowest low tide.
   d The 'shoal' is every area covered by shallow water, a part of which is not submerged at lowest low tide.
   e. The 'coast' refers to the coast of the Red Sea.

Article 2. The territorial waters of the Yemen Arab Republic, the air space over them and the land beneath them and the subsoil under them are under the sovereignty of the Republic, with due consideration of the rules of international law relating to the innocent passage of vessels of other nations in the coastal sea.

Article 3. The territorial waters of the Yemen Arab Republic include the inland waters and the coastal sea of the Republic.

Article 4. The inland waters of the Republic include:
   a. The waters of the bays along the coasts of the Republic.
   b. The waters over the land from any shoal not more than twelve nautical miles from the mainland or from a Yemeni island, and the waters between such a shoal and the land.
   c. The waters between the mainland and any Yemeni island not more than twelve miles from the mainland.
   d. The waters between the Yemeni islands which are not farther apart than twelve nautical miles.

Article 5. The coastal sea of the Yemen Arab Republic lies outside the inland waters of the Yemen Arab Republic and extends seaward for a distance of twelve nautical miles.

Article 6. The determination of the baselines from which the coastal sea of the Republic is measured shall be made according to the following:
   a. If the mainland or the shore of the island is fully exposed to the sea, the lowest low-water mark on the shore.

---

[1] *Source.* Translated by the present writer from a copy of the original Arabic text acquired from the League of Arab States.

APPENDIX VI

    b. In case of the existence of a bay facing the sea, lines drawn from headland to headland across the mouth of the bay.
    c. In case of the existence of a shoal not more than twelve nautical miles from the mainland or from a Yemeni island, lines drawn from the mainland or the island and along the outer edge of the shoal.
    d. In case of the existence of a wharf or port facing the sea, lines drawn along the seaward side of the outermost works of the wharf or port and between such works.
    e. In case of the existence of an island not more than twelve miles from the mainland, lines drawn from the mainland along the outer shores of the island.
    f. In case of the existence of an island group which may be linked together by lines not more than twelve nautical miles long, lines drawn along the shore of all the islands of the group if the islands form a chain, or along the outer shores of the outermost islands of the group if the islands do not form a chain.

Article 7. If the measurement of the territorial waters in accordance with the provisions of this resolution leaves an area of high sea wholly surrounded by territorial waters and extending not more than twelve nautical miles in any direction, such area shall form part of the territorial waters. The same rule shall apply to a pronounced pocket of high sea which may be wholly enclosed by drawing a single straight line not more than twelve nautical miles long.

Article 8. In the event of waters of another State overlapped with the internal waters or the coastal sea of the Yemen Arab Republic the boundaries will be determined in agreement with the State concerned in accordance with the principles observed in international law or by mutual agreement.

Article 9. To enforce the laws and regulations relating to security, navigation, fiscal and sanitary purposes, maritime surveillance covers an area falling next to the coastal sea and contiguous to it, to a distance of six nautical miles in addition to the twelve nautical miles measured from the baselines of the coastal sea. This order shall not affect the rights of the Yemen Arab Republic with respect to fishing.

Article 10. This decree shall be published in the *Official Gazette* and take effect from date of its issue. Our Ministers, each in so far as he is concerned, are charged with the execution of this decree.

The Presidency   *President of the Republic*
Dated 20 Moharam 1387
Corresponding to 30 April 1967

APPENDIX VI

B. DECREE NO. 16 CONCERNING THE CONTINENTAL SHELF OF THE YEMEN ARAB REPUBLIC, 30 APRIL 1967[1]

The President of the Republic
Having seen the Constitution and the Decree of the President of the Republic No. 15 of 1967 Concerning the Territorial Waters of the Yemen Arab Republic,

Decreed:

Article 1. The Yemen Arab Republic enjoys sovereign rights over the sea bed and the subsoil of the continental shelf beyond the territorial waters of the Republic to a depth of 200 metres or, beyond that limit, to where the depth admits of the exploitation of the natural resources which exist in the sea bed. The Yemen Arab Republic furthermore enjoys sovereign rights over similar continental shelf in the case of islands belonging to the Yemen Arab Republic.

The foregoing do not affect the status of the superjacent waters of the said areas as being high seas or the freedom of navigation within the sea waters and in the air space above.

Article 2. The Yemen Arab Republic has alone the right of prospect, exploration and exploitation of all the natural mineral resources and other non-living resources together with living organisms belonging to sedentary species which exist on or under the sea bed of the regions mentioned in Article 1. To this end it has the right to construct, maintain and operate the installations necessary for this purpose, and to establish, for a distance of 500 metres around such installations, safety zones and to take in those zones measures necessary for their protection.

Article 3. The rights referred to in the two preceding articles, or their exercise, do not depend on occupation, effective or notional, of the said regions or on any special declarations.

Article 4. It is forbidden for any foreign, natural or artificial, person to undertake the exploitation of any of the natural resources in the continental shelf except by a decree from the President of the Republic.

Article 5. This decree shall be published and take effect from date of its issue.

President of the Republic

The Presidency
Dated 20 Moharam 1387
Corresponding 30 April 1967

---

[1] *Source.* Translated by the present writer from a copy of the original Arabic texts acquired from the League of Arab States.

APPENDIX VII

DOCUMENTS ON THE UNDERSTANDING CONCERNING THE ISLAND OF ABU MUSA[1]

(A) 'MEMORANDUM OF UNDERSTANDING' BETWEEN IRAN AND SHARJAH, NOVEMBER 1971.

Neither Iran nor Sharjah will give up its claim to Abu Musa nor recognise the other's claim. Against this background the following arrangements will be made:

1. Iranian troops will arrive in Abu Musa. They will occupy areas the extent of which have been agreed on the map attached to this memorandum.
2. *(a)* Within the agreed areas occupied by Iranian troops, Iran will have full jurisdiction and the Iranian flag will fly.
   (b) Sharjah will retain full jurisdiction over the remainder of the island. The Sharjah flag will continue to fly over the Sharjah police post on the same basis as the Iranian flag will fly over the Iranian military quarters.
3. Iran and Sharjah recognise the breadth of the island's territorial sea as twelve nautical miles.
4. Exploitation of the petroleum resources of Abu Musa and the sea bed and subsoil beneath its territorial sea will be conducted by Buttes Gas & Oil Company under the existing agreement, which must be acceptable to Iran. Half the governmental oil resources hereafter attributable to the said exploitation shall be paid direct by the Company to Iran and half to Sharjah.
5. The nationals of Iran and Sharjah shall have equal rights to fish in the territorial sea of Abu Musa.
6. A financial assistance agreement will be signed between Iran and Sharjah.

---

[1] *Source. M.E.E.S.*, Supplement to vol. xv, No. 28, 5 May 1972.

APPENDIX VII

(B) CORRESPONDENCE BETWEEN SHARJAH, BRITAIN AND IRAN

Khalid bin Muhammad Al Qasimi
Ruler of Sharjah and its Dependencies
Date: 18 November 1971
Secretary of State for Foreign and Commonwealth Affairs,
The Foreign and Commonwealth Office
London

After greetings,
With reference to our discussions about the arrangements between Sharjah and Iran on the Abu Musa question, I confirm that I accept the arrangements set out in the Memorandum of Understanding annexed to this letter. I should be grateful for confirmation that the Iranian Government for its part accepts the arrangements.
Finally, please accept our highest regards and respects.

Khalid BIN MUHAMMAD ALQASMI
Ruler of Sharjah and its Dependencies

Foreign and Commonwealth Office
London, S.W.1.
26 November 1971

Your Highness:
I refer to your Highness's letter of 18 November in which you ask for confirmation that the Iranian Government, for its part, accepted the arrangements for Abu Musa set out in the Annex to your letter. I enclose copies of correspondence between myself and the Iranian Minister for Foreign Affairs in which the Iranian Government's acceptance is given.

Yours sincerely,
[*Alec Douglas-Home*]

His Highness
Shaikh Khalid bin Muhammad al Qasimi,
Ruler of Sharjah

Imperial Ministry
of Foreign Affairs

Tehran, 25 November 1971
M/21282

Your Excellency:
I confirm that my Government accepts the arrangements for Abu Musa as set out in the enclosure of 24 November 1971.

APPENDIX VII

A copy of the Memorandum of Understanding in which the arrangements are set out is annexed to this letter,

Abbas Ali Khalatbari
Minister for Foreign Affairs

Principal Secretary of the Foreign and Commonwealth Affairs Office
London

(C) CORRESPONDENCE BETWEEN BUTTES AND NATIONAL IRANIAN OIL COMPANY

Buttes Gas & Oil Co.
1970 Broadway
Oakland, California 94612

26 November 1971

Dr M. Eghbal
Chairman of the Board and General Managing Director
National Iranian Oil Company
Post Office Box No. 1863
Tehran, Iran

Your Excellency:

1. The Buttes Gas and Oil Co. understands that certain arrangements have been made relating to Abu Musa and its territorial sea, which provide, *inter alia*, that:
   A. Neither Iran nor Sharjah would give up its claim to Abu Musa and its twelve mile territorial sea, nor recognise the other's claim;
   B. Exploitation of the petroleum resources of Abu Musa and of the sea bed and subsoil beneath its territorial sea will be conducted by Buttes Gas and Oil Co. under the existing agreement which must be acceptable to Iran. Half of the governmental oil resources hereafter attributable to the said exploitation shall be paid directly by the Company to Iran.
2. The Company hereby agrees to make the payment under paragraph 1(B) above directly to the Government of Iran, and has taken the necessary measures in accordance with the preceding paragraph.
3. The Company further agrees that the terms of the Tehran Oil Price Agreement of February 14, 1971, will be adhered to.
4. Our Company would be grateful for confirmation that National Iranian Oil Company on behalf of the Government of Iran accepts that pur-

APPENDIX VII

suant to the acceptance of the arrangements our Company or its subsidiaries can proceed with operations under the terms of this letter.

Yours sincerely,
John Boreta
President

National Iranian Oil Company
Central Office
Ave. Takhte. Jamshid
Tehran, 27 Nov. 1971

Gentlemen:

Pursuant to the acceptance of certain arrangements with respect to Abu Musa and its territorial sea, I confirm that National Iranian Oil Company on behalf of the Government of Iran accepts that your company or its subsidiaries can proceed with operations under the terms of your letter of 26 November 1971.

Dr Eghbal
Chairman of the Board

Buttes Gas and Oil Company

NOTES

CHAPTER I

[1] E. D. Brown, 'Maritime zones: a survey of claims', in R. Churchill, K. Simmonds and J. Welch (eds.), *New Directions in the Law of the Sea,* Collected papers, vol. III (BIICL, London and New York, 1973), p. 157, at p. 159.
[2] *Ibid.* See Chapter II below.
[3] As to the attitudes of the Middle Eastern States in the Third Conference on the Law of the Sea, see Chapter II below.
[4] See the Sudanese (Ratification) Act, 1970, text in Special Supplement to the Sudan Gazette, No. 1112, 31 December 1971, p. 478. For texts of the 1958 Conventions, namely *Convention on the Territorial Sea and the Contiguous Zone* (A/Conf. 13/L. 52), *Convention on the Continental Shelf* (A/Conf. 13/L. 55), *Convention on Fishing and Conservation of the Living Resources* (A/Conf. 13/L. 54), *Convention on the High Seas* (A/Conf. 13/L. 53 and Corr. 1), see Cmnd 584 (1958); Special Supplement to 7 *I.C.L.Q.* (1958). The following Middle Eastern States participated in the First (in 1958) and Second (in 1960) Geneva Conferences on the Law of the Sea: Iran, Iraq, Jordan, Lebanon, Saudi Arabia, Sudan (not in the 1960 conference), United Arab Republic (then Egypt and Syria), and the Yemen Arab Republic (though it appeared at the First Conference, it did not vote). At that time the other Middle Eastern States were not fully independent countries. The United Kingdom's ratification of the four 1958 Geneva Conventions did not extend to the Trucial States of the Arabian Gulf, which at that time were under British protection. This is in accordance with the declaration made by H.M. Government on depositing its instrument of ratification; see 516 *U.N.T.S.*, p. 278. As to the policies of the Middle Eastern States in the Third United Nations Conference on the Law of the Sea, see below, Chapter II.
[5] See Cmnd 584 (1958).
[6] See below, Chapter IV.
[7] E. D. Brown, *The Legal Regime of Hydrospace* (London, 1971), p. 16. Brown indicates that Iran had ratified the 1958 Convention on the Continental Shelf, which is an error. See *ibid.,* pp. 64–5.
[8] LSCOR (1st), vol. VI, p. 14, para. 23. See further below, notes 157–9.
[9] Texts of these laws can be found in references indicated in Appendix I and, unless otherwise indicated, all information in the present chapter regarding existing offshore jurisdictional claims of the Middle Eastern States is derived therefrom. For a summary of the existing offshore jurisdictional claims of the Middle Eastern States see Appendix II.
[10] See below, in Chapter II.
[11] This was in accordance with the revoked Saudi Royal Decree No. 6/4/5/3711 of 28 May 1949 and the Egyptian Royal Decree of 15 January 1951, which has now been amended. For text of the 1949 Saudi decree see 5 *R.E.D.I.* (1949), p. 343. For texts of the Egyptian decree of 1951 and its amendment see U.S. Department

NOTES

of State, the Geographer, *Straight Baselines: United Arab Republic,* Limits in the Seas No. 22, 22 June 1970.

[12] See, e.g., A. Dean, 'The Geneva Conference on the Law of the Sea: what was accomplished', 52 *A.J.I.L.* (1960), p. 751, at pp. 767-8. However, see below, Chapter II, note 31.

[13] G. Lenczowski, *Oil and State in the Middle East* (New York, 1960), p. 133.

[14] This agreement is considered below in Chapter III.

[15] Note of 2 February 1956 from the Foreign Ministry of Iraq to the United Nations, ST/LEG/Ser.B/6 (1957), p. 26.

[16] 12 *Encyclopaedia Britannica,* 1966, p. 527.

[17] Before 1959 the territorial sea of Libya was fixed at six miles, but for customs control purposes the jurisdiction of Libya extended to a distance of ten miles from the coast; see ST/LEG/Ser.B/6 (December 1956), p. 32. And when the 1959 law extended the territorial sea of Libya to twelve miles, an oral protest was made by the United Kingdom ambassador on 11 March 1959; see E. Lauterpacht, 'The contemporary practice of the U.K. in the field of international law', 9 *I.C.L.Q.* (1960), p. 278.

[18] LSCOR (1st), vol. III, p. 53. M. McDougal and W. Burke, however, state that, judging from some United Nations reports, the reference in the statement of the Libyan speaker at the 1958 conference to fish and sponges as valuable exports and the alleged wrongful exploitation by foreign fishermen 'appear similarly unrealistic'. M. McDougal and W. Burke, *The Public Order of the Oceans* (New Haven, 1961), pp. 550-2. The Libyan argument was reiterated at the Third Conference on the Law of the Sea in support of Libya's stand in favour of the exclusive economic zone concept, see below, in Chapter II.

[19] The recommendation was made under Resolution 1579 of 26 March 1959 adopted during the League's thirty-first session, in Cairo.

[20] Resolution No. 1047 of 2 August 1960 of the Council of Ministers of the Sudan, pertaining to the territorial sea, ST/LEG/Ser.B/15 (April 1970), p. 119.

[21] It may be observed that, at the 1958 Law of the Sea Conference, the Yemen Arab Republic told the conference that 'The territorial sea of Yemen was twelve nautical miles broad', LSCOR (1st), vol. III, p. 16.

[22] See 'Explanatory Note' attached to the 1967 Kuwaiti decree on the territorial sea. See also Ministry of Finance and Oil of Kuwait, *The Oil of Kuwait—Facts and Figures* (Kuwait, August 1970, 3rd edn.).

[23] 'Explanatory Note' attached to the 1967 Kuwaiti decree on territorial sea.

[24] A. F. Kassim, 'Conflicting claims in the Persian Gulf', IV *Journal of Law and Economic Development,* No. 2, fall 1969, p. 282, at p. 300.

[25] See below in Chapter III.

[26] ST/LEG/Ser.B/6 (December 1956), p. 522. Jordan's only outlet to the sea is the Gulf of Aqaba. According to an agreement signed on 10 August 1965 between Saudi Arabia and Jordan, the two countries agreed on a small exchange of land to their mutual benefit; this lengthened Jordan's coastline down the Gulf of Aqaba from four to about fifteen miles in return for territory lying between two Saudi villages farther east. Saudi Arabia and Jordan also agreed to share equally any oil or other natural resources which may be discovered in the future in the exchanged areas. See 'Agreement for the Determination of Boundaries between Hashemite Kingdom of Jordan and the Kingdom of Saudi Arabia'; for full text see XXII *Middle East Journal* (1968), p. 346.

[27] ST/LEG/Ser.B/1 (1951), p. 83.

[28] *Ibid.,* p. 307.

[29] *Ibid.,* p. 83.

[30] In his award in the *Matter of an Arbitration between Petroleum Development (Trucial Coast) Ltd and the Sheikh of Abu Dhabi,* 1952, Lord Asquith said: 'If I

think of the three-mile limit and the Territorial Maritime Belt interchangeably, this is only for brevity. I am aware that some States claim more than a three-mile belt, but about 80 per cent of the merchant shipping in the world is registered in 'three-mile' countries; and this is the width of the territorial waters on the Persian Gulf'; 1 *I.C.L.Q.* (1952), p. 247, at p. 254, note 2. However, a commentary on Lord Asquith's statement observed that 'The latter part of his statement may be true with respect to Abu Dhabi, although it is questionable whether the Sheikh is bound, for any purpose except the allocation of concession rights, to accept Lord Asquith's views. It is certainly erroneous with respect to the Persian Gulf in general, where the two principal coastal States, Iran and Saudi Arabia, have each expressly declared their adherence to a six-mile limit'; R. Young, 'Lord Asquith and the continental shelf', 46 *A.J.I.L.* (1951), p. 512, at pp. 514–5.

[31] Within the United Arab Emirates the power to define the territorial sea is expressly conferred on the Federal authorities by Article 121 of the Constitution of 18 July 1971. For English translation of the constitution see 26 *Middle East Journal* (1971), p. 307.

[32] It has been said that the ruler of Sharjah made this decree subsequent to receiving a report on the law of the sea prepared by his principal legal adviser—Judge Yusri Dweik—upon the ruler's request in the summer of 1969 after the Iranian claim to Abu Musa (and the similar claim to the islands of Tumb belonging to Ras al Khaimah) had become more insistent. M. E. Bathurst, R. Y. Jennings and Northcutt Ely, 'Trucial States (Ajman, Sharjah, Umm Al Qaiwain) Mediation', unpublished dossier submitted on behalf of His Highness Shaikh Khalid Bin Mohamed Al Qasimi, Ruler of Sharjah and its Dependencies, to Sir Gawain Bell, Mediator appointed by Her Majesty's Government in the United Kingdom, August 1970 (hereinafter 'Trucial States Mediation'), vol. I, pp. 36–7. Copies of the two volumes of the dossier were examined by courtesy of Professor R. Y. Jennings. The questions relating to Abu Musa and the Tumb Islands are considered in Chapter III.

[33] It has been stated that in issuing the supplementary decree, the ruler acted upon advice by his special counsel at that time—Mr Northcutt Ely—'in order to forestall a U.S. protest about the September Decree', and 'in view of the known attitude of the U.S. Government towards claims to a twelve-mile territorial sea without guaranteeing to other States innocent transit and overflight', 'Trucial States Mediation', *op. cit.*, vol. I, p. 43. However, on 24 July 1970, the embassy of the United States in London delivered a note to H.M. Government referring to Sharjah's decrees of September 1969 and April 1970, reserving the rights of the U.S. and its nationals 'in all areas of superjacent waters referred to in the September 10 and April 5 Decrees seaward of the traditional three-mile limit'. The note was stated to be 'without comment on the existing dispute with respect to sovereignty over the island of Abu Musa to which the subject Decrees also apply, and without prejudice to the sovereign rights of the coastal state to explore and exploit the natural resources of the continental shelf extending from its coast'. For full text see 'Trucial States Mediation', *op. cit.*, vol. II, p. 133.

[34] Prior to this date and in accordance with the Iranian Act of 15 July 1934 the territorial sea of Iran was fixed at six nautical miles; see ST/LEG/Ser.B/6 (December 1956), p. 24.

[35] E. D. Brown, 'Maritime zones: a survey of claims', *op. cit.*, p. 160.

[36] With further elaboration these rules are embodied in the Informal Composite Negotiating Text of the Third Law of the Sea Conference.

[37] *Anglo-Norwegian Fisheries case*, I.C.J. Reports, 1951, p. 116.

[38] Although Kuwait is not a party to the 1958 Territorial Sea Convention, the Preamble to the Kuwaiti decree on the territorial sea of 1967, as well as the 'Explanatory Note' attached to it, express that the provisions of the convention

were the guiding principles in drafting the Kuwaiti decree. The 'Explanatory Note' also expresses Kuwait's intention to accede to the 1958 convention.

[39] For text of the Saudi royal decree of 1949 see 5 *R.E.D.I.* (1949), p. 343. On 19 December 1949 the government of the United States of America addressed to the government of the Saudi Arabia a 'Note' taking exception to certain provisions of the Saudi territorial sea decree of 1949, namely: '1. All provisions to the effect that the inland waters of the Kingdom include waters outside of ports, harbors, bays and other enclosed arms of the sea along its coast, and 2. All provisions to the effect that the coastal sea, i.e., the marginal sea of the Kingdom extends seaward of a belt of three nautical miles along its coast or around its islands.' The full text of the 'Note' is reprinted in *Anglo-Norwegian Fisheries Case,* I.C.J. Pleadings, 1951, vol. IV, p. 601.

[40] Similarly, the Omani decree on territorial sea, in establishing the baseline for the measurement of the breadth of the territorial sea, permits the use of submerged features—some rocks, reefs and shoals.

[41] It may be observed also that the Kuwaiti territorial sea decree has considered the Bay of Kuwait to be purely internal waters.

[42] 7 *R.E.D.I.* (1951), p. 91; 11 *R.E.D.I.* (1955), p. 206. Notes of protest against the Egyptian decree of 1951 and in particular against those provisions dealing with bays were made by the United Kingdom and the United States, on 28 May 1951 and 4 June 1951 respectively. For full texts see *Anglo-Norwegian Fisheries Case,* I.C.J. Pleadings, 1951, vol. IV, pp. 578–80 and 603; 7 *R.E.D.I.* (1951), pp. 91, 94.

[43] 13 *R.E.D.I.* (1957), pp. 70–1. See also editorial comment in 14 *R.E.D.I.* (1958), p. 173. See further in this regard M. P. Strohl, *The International Law of Bays* (The Hague, 1962), pp. 258–61. For further analysis of the baseline system created by the territorial sea legislation of Saudi Arabia, Egypt, Syria and Oman see U.S. Department of State, the Geographer, *Straight Baselines: Saudi Arabia,* Limits in the Seas, No. 20. 8 June 1970, *Straight Baselines: United Arab Republic,* Limits in the Seas, No. 22, 22 June 1970, *Straight Baselines: Syria,* Limits in the Seas, No. 53, 10 October 1973, and *Straight Baselines: Oman (Hypothetical),* Limits in the Seas, No. 61, 4 June 1975, respectively.

[44] In a protest dated 11 February 1974 against the Libyan declaration, the United States of America characterised the Libyan claim to the Gulf of Surt as 'unacceptable as a violation of international law'. The protest further noted that 'Under international law, as codified in the 1958 Convention on the Territorial Sea and the Contiguous Zone, the body of water enclosed by this line (a line approximately 300 miles long at a latitude of 32 degrees 30 minutes) cannot be regarded as the juridical internal or territorial waters of the Libyan Arab Republic. Nor does the Gulf of Sirte meet the international law standards of past open, notorious and effective exercise of authority, continuous exercise of authority, and acquiescence of foreign nations necessary to be regarded historically as Libyan internal or territorial waters ...'. The protest was sent to the embassy of the Libyan Arab Republic in Washington. For full text see Arthur W. Rovine, *Digest of United States Practice in International Law, 1974* (Department of State Publication 8809, released 9 July 1975), p. 293. The criteria referred to in the final paragraph of the American protest were set out in a study by the United Nations Secretariat of the 'Juridical Regime of Historic Waters, including Historic Bays', A/CN.4/143 (1962).

[45] A similar provision has been included in the Informal Composite Negotiating Text adopted during the sixth session of the Third Law of the Sea Conference.

[46] See below, in Chapter II.

[47] See further discussion below, in Chapter II.

[48] As regards the Gulf of Aqaba and the Straits of Tiran see below, Chapter IV.

[49] R. H. Kennedy, 'A Brief geographical and hydrographical study of straits which constitute routes for international traffic', in LSCOR (1st), vol. 1—

NOTES

Preparatory Documents, Document No. 6 (A/Conf. 13/6) (hereinafter 'R. H. Kennedy "A brief study of straits"'), p. 114, at p. 115. See also map 2.

[50] Democratic Yemen, under the 'Territorial Waters and the Continental Shelf of the People's Republic of Southern Yemen Law, 1970' which was rescinded by Act No. 45 of 1977. French Territory of Afars and Issas (now Djibouti) by virtue of French Law 71–1060 of 24 December 1971, which extended the territorial sea of France and its overseas territories to twelve nautical miles.

[51] *Corfu Channel Case, judgement,* of 5 April 1949, p. 4, at p. 28.

[52] See below, in Chapter II.

[53] See Jean-Pierre Queneudec, 'France', in R. Churchill, K. Simmonds, and J. Welch (eds.), *New Directions in the Law of the Sea,* vol. III, *op. cit.,* p. 257, at pp. 259–60.

[54] 282 *H. L. Deb,* cols, 1073–4, 4 May 1967. The reference in Lord Beswick's statement to 'international Convention', is clearly to the 1958 *Territorial Sea Convention.* See also statement by the British Foreign Secretary in the House of Commons on 29 November 1967, 755 *H. C. Deb.,* col. 438, 29 November 1967.

[55] *The Economist,* 10 November 1973. According to various reports published there the blockade was lifted in late October 1973. For further comments on this incident see D. P. O'Connell, *The Influence of Law on Sea Power* (Manchester University Press, 1975), pp. 101–2.

[56] *The Guardian,* 31 October 1974.

[57] *An-Nahar* (Arabic daily, Beirut), 6 October 1974.

[58] In the early part of the sixteenth century the Portuguese gained control of the Iranian island of Hormuz on the Strait of Hormuz, and with their naval power were able to close trading with the Gulf States to ships from other countries. England and Persia joined forces against this intervention and succeeded in driving the Portuguese out of Hormuz in 1622. During the First World War the British made use of this area, which strategically is the key to almost the whole of the Middle East. See 21 *Encyclopedia Americana* (1956 edn.), p. 628; M. T. Sadik and W. P. Snavely, *Bahrain, Qatar and the United Arab Emirates; Colonial Past, Present Problems, and Future Prospects* (Toronto and London, 1972), p. 3.

[59] *Washington Post,* 23 March 1973.

[60] R. H. Kennedy, 'A brief study of straits', *op. cit.,* at p. 130. See further map 3.

[61] See below, in Chapter II.

[62] In the Arabian Gulf there are many islands whose sovereignty has been, or in some cases is still, in dispute. This question is considered below in Chapter III.

[63] See 'Memorandum of Agreed Points relating to Independence for South Arabia (The People's Republic of Southern Yemen)', Cmnd 3504, Southern Yemen No. 1 (1968), 'The Aden, Perim and Kuria Muria Islands Act, 1967 (Appointed Day) Order 1967', S.I. 1967, No. 1761, 28 November 1967. The withdrawal of all British forces from Aden was completed on 29 November 1967. At midnight Aden Colony and the Protectorate of South Arabia, together with the islands of Perim and Kamaran, became the People's Republic of Southern Yemen. For an account of the events which led to the proclamation of Southern Yemen see *Keesing's Contemporary Archives,* 1967–68, pp. 22411–15.

[64] For full test of the 'Consensus' resolution see *Yearbook of the United Nations,* 1967, p. 653.

[65] For full text see *Yearbook of the United Nations,* 1966, p. 568.

[66] *Yearbook of the United Nations,* 1967, p. 653. Similar statements were made by the British Foreign Secretary in the House of Commons, see 755 *H.C. Deb.,* Written Answers, cols. 167–8, 30 November 1967, and 765 *H.C. Deb.,* Written Answers, col. 23, 11 December 1967.

[67] 'Treaty of Cession between Her Majesty in respect of the United Kingdom of Great Britain and Northern Ireland and the Sultan of Muscat and Oman, relating to

the Kuria Muria Islands', 8 *U.K.T.S.* (1968); Cmnd 3505 (1968).

[68] For text of the 1854 agreement see 10 Hertslet, *Treaties*, p. 938, 'Act of Cession, 14 July 1854'. It has been shown that the Kuria Muria islands were ceded to Britain in 1854 to enable her to build a cable station there, and although the High Commissioner in Aden had legislative power over the islands during the period of British rule, administration has been the responsibility of the Political Resident in the 'Persian Gulf', *Keesing's Contemporary Archives*, 1967–68, p. 22415. See also 'The Kuria Muria Islands Order in Council, 1963', S.I., 1963, No. 86.

[69] See *GAOR*, 22nd session, Fourth Committee, 1730th and 1731st meetings, 29 November 1967.

[70] *Keesing's Contemporary Archives*, 1967–68, p. 22415.

[71] *Ibid.*

[72] Kuria Muria and the island of al Ghanam (or Umm al-Ghanam), which lies off the Musandam peninsula near the Straits of Hormuz and also belongs to the Sultanate of Oman, were reportedly occupied by Iran in the early 1972 (*Assayad* (Arabic weekly, Beirut), No. 1489, 29 March–5 April 1973). This, however, was denied by Sultan Qabus of Oman, who also affirmed that al-Ghenam and the Kuria Muria islands were under his 'Sultanate Sovereignty'; *Al-Hawadess* (Arabic weekly, Beirut), No. 900, 8 February 1974.

[73] Kamaran's adjacent islets include: Kadaman Saghir, Kadaman Kabir, Shab Bodinjan, Okban, El Bodli, Okban Saghir, Jureb, Risha and Arab Shoal.

[74] 'Treaty of Peace', signed at Lausanne, 24 July 1923, 28; 29 *L.N.T.S.*, No. 701.

[75] S.I., 1963, No. 85.

[76] 'A Proclamation terminating Her Majesty's Power and Jurisdiction in Kamaran', S.I., 1967, Part III, Section 2, p. 5456.

[77] 551 *H.C. Deb.*, Written Answers, col. 146, 25 April 1956.

[78] [1967] *A.S.C.L.*, p. 715.

[79] Robert R. Robbins, 'The legal status of Aden Colony and the Aden Protectorate', 33 *A.J.I.L.* (1939), p. 700, at p. 701.

[80] See 'The Perim Order in Council, 1963', S.I., 1963, No. 87.

[81] See 748 *H.C. Deb.*, cols. 1274, 1287, 1294–5, 1264, 19 June 1967, and 749 *H.C. Deb.*, cols. 597–8, 626, 633–6, 641–56, 28 June 1967. See also 282 *H.L. Deb.*, cols. 1073–4, 4 May 1967.

[82] 755 *H.C. Deb.*, Written Answers, col. 168, 30 November 1967.

[83] *Ibid.* Humphrey Trevelyan wrote: 'We conducted our referendum on Perim one afternoon and it passed peacefully to South Arabia'. *The Middle East in Revolution* (Boston; Mass., 1970), p. 261.

[84] S.I., 1967, No. 1961.

[85] E. D. Brown, 'Maritime zones: a survey of claims', *op. cit.*, p. 165.

[86] See U.S. Department of State, the Geographer, *National Claims to Maritime Jurisdictions*, Limits in the Seas, No. 36 (3rd revision), 23 December 1975.

[87] See below, in Chapter II.

[88] But see the position of these States as to the contiguous zone concept at the Third Conference on the Law of the Sea, below, in Chapter II.

[89] II *Yearbook of the ILC* (1956), p. 295.

[90] See *Proposal for an additional Special Area, submitted by the Imperial Government of Iran* to the International Conference on Marine Pollution, 1973, MP/Conf/C.2/WP.28 (17 October 1973), p. 2.

[91] *Ibid.* In March 1973 it was estimated that one oil tanker passes through the Strait of Hormuz every fourteen minutes: *Washington Post*, 23 March 1973.

[92] *The Times*, 8 June 1973.

[93] *Ibid.*

NOTES

[94] IMCO (Intergovernmental Maritime Consultative Organization) Doc. MP/Conf./C.2/WP.28 (17 October 1973), p. 3.

[95] See *Proposal concerning the Provisions for 'Special Areas'*, submitted jointly by the Delegations of Cyprus, Egypt, France, Greece, Italy, Monaco, Spain and Tunisia, to the *International Conference on Marine Pollution*, 1973, MP/Conf./C.2/WP.22/Rev. 2 (17 October 1973), p. 1. See also United Nations press release HE/318 (30 January 1976), p. 2.

[96] IMCO Doc. MP/Conf./Inf.10 (2 October 1973), Egypt, Libya, Saudi Arabia and Lebanon have also ratified the 1969 amendments. For text of the 1954 convention see 327 *U.N.T.S.*, p. 3. For a composite text of the convention as amended in 1962 and 1969 see IX *I.L.M.* (1970), p. 1.

[97] For text see ST/LEG/Ser.B/16 (New York, 1974), p. 464.

[98] For text see 12 *I.L.M.* (1973), p. 1319.

[99] Upon its entering into force, the 1973 Convention supersedes the International Convention for the Prevention of Pollution of the Sea by Oil, 1954, as amended. According to Annex I of the new convention, which in principle applies to all ships, any discharge into the sea of 'oil' or 'oily mixtures' shall be prohibited except when the specific conditions set out in the annex are satisfied. According to the same annex, a 'Special area', means 'a Sea area where for recognised technical reasons in relation to its oceanographic and ecological condition and to the particular character of its traffic the adoption of special mandatory methods for the prevention of sea pollution by oil is required'. In so far as the Mediterranean Sea, Black Sea and Baltic Sea areas are concerned, Regulation 10(7) of Annex I requires, *inter alia*, that 'The Government of each Party of the Convention, the coastline of which border on any given special area undertakes to ensure that not later than 1 January 1977 all oil loading terminals and repair ports within the special area are provided with facilities adequate for the reception and treatment of all the dirty ballast and tank washing water from oil tankers. In addition all ports within the special area shall be provided with adequate facilities for other residues and oily mixtures from all ships. Such facilities shall have adequate capacity to meet the needs of the ships using without causing undue delay.' A similar requirement is provided for with regard to the Red Sea and the 'Gulfs area'. Annex I also required that all new and existing oil-carrying ships and tankers must be fitted with new gear, including an oil discharge monitoring and control system. In addition, an International Oil Pollution Prevention Certificate (1973) shall be issued after special survey to any tanker of 150 tons gross tonnage and above, and any ships of 400 tons gross tonnage and above which are engaged in voyages to ports or offshore terminals under the jurisdiction of other parties to the convention.

[100] This conference followed preliminary meetings held earlier in Kuwait and Bahrain in co-operation with the United Nations Environment Programme and U.N. specialised agencies.

[101] Both the convention and the protocol were signed on 24 April 1978 by all participating States, with the exception of Oman, which signed them on 22 May 1978. Kuwait ratified these instruments under Law No. 45 of 1978, dated 7 December 1978. The Arabic texts of the two instruments are published in the Kuwaiti official gazette, *Kuwait Al-Yom*, No. 1220, 19 November 1978. These developments took place after the present work went to press, therefore it has not been possible to elaborate on them.

[102] The Arabic text of the agreement is published in *Al-Naft Wa Al-Alam (Oil and the World)*, No. 20, December 1974, p. 8 (an Arabic monthly magazine published by Iraq National Oil Company).

[103] For texts of the Final Act of the Conference on the Protection of the Mediterranean Sea, the conventions, the protocols, and resolutions adopted by the conference, see xv *I.L.M.* (1976), pp. 285–318; ST/LEG/Ser.B/19 (preliminary issue 1978), pp. 438–46.

NOTES

[104] Algeria and Albania did not attend the Barcelona conference. Yugoslavia, Libya, Syria and Tunisia, though they attended, did not sign the convention; see *The Times*, 13 and 17 February 1976. The Barcelona conference was convened by the United Nations Environment Programme (UNEP).

[105] In co-operation with the World Health Organisation, the United Nations Environment Programme convened in Athens from 7 to 11 February 1977 an International Consultation concerning a *Draft Protocol for the Protection of the Mediterranean Sea against Pollution from Land-based Sources*. For text of the Draft Protocol see XVI *I.L.M.* (1977), pp. 964–9.

[106] The law entered into force on 1 January 1975. For full text see ST/LEG/Ser.B/18 (New York, 1976), p. 74.

[107] Unlike the Canadian Arctic Waters Pollution Act of 1970, the Omani law does not give the government powers to prescribe standards for the construction of vessels exercising a right of passage through the pollution zone, to control standards of navigation and operation, or to prohibit, if deemed necessary, the passage of vessels in those waters. For full text of the Canadian Act see ST/LEG/Ser.B/16 (1974), p. 183.

[108] For full text see *Petroleum Legislation, Basic Oil Laws and Concession Contracts—Middle East*, Suppl. No. XXIX, p. Iraq A–O.

[109] For full text of the Iranian Petroleum Act of 1974 see *Petroleum Legislation, Basic Oil Laws and Concession Contracts—Middle East*, Suppl. No. 44, p. 3.

[110] *The Times*, 29 April 1971.

[111] *Ibid*.

[112] For full text of the 1964 Kuwaiti law and its annexes see ST/LEG/Ser.B/15 (April 1970), p. 281.

[113] See Albert E. Utton, 'A survey of national laws on the control of pollution from oil and gas operations on the continental shelf', 9 *Columbia Journal of Transnational Law*, No. 2, fall 1970, p. 331, at p. 343; Michael Hardy, 'Offshore development and marine pollution', 1 *Ocean Development* (1973–4), p. 239, at p. 258.

[114] Offshore Concession Agreement between the Government of Kuwait and Arabian Oil Co. (July 1958), Article 3(c). For full text of the agreement see *Petroleum Legislation, Basic Oil Laws and Concessions Contracts—Middle East*, vol. II (1959), p. Neutral Zone B–I.

[115] *Ibid.*, Article 3(d).

[116] U.S. Department of State, the Geographer, *National Claims to Maritime Jurisdictions, op. cit.*, pp. 12–15. The thirty-six States referred to by the Geographer do not include Saudi Arabia and Qatar, which were listed under the twelve- and three-mile fishery limit respectively, although, as will be shown below, in 1974 these States formally claimed exclusive fishing zones whose limits were not specifically stated, but presumed to be each in excess of twelve nautical miles. Probably these claims were not yet known or available to the Geographer of the U.S. Department of State at time of the publication of the study in December 1975.

[117] The Iranian proclamation does not apply to the sea adjacent to the Iranian coast on the Caspian Sea. Fishing in this sea is regulated by the USSR–Iran Treaty of Commerce and Navigation of 25 March 1940 according to which each party has reserved a ten-mile fishing zone adjacent to its coasts for its own flag vessels; beyond the ten-mile zone, fishing may be pursued exclusively by Soviet and Iranian nationals. W. E. Butler, *The Soviet Union and the Law of the Sea* (Baltimore and London, 1971), p. 102.

[118] See Iranian delegate's remarks at the Third Law of the Sea Conference, LSCOR (3rd), vol. I, 1974 (1 July), p. 72.

[119] Fishing has always been a major occupation in Oman, and contributes significantly to its gross domestic product. In 1975 a report on fisheries, submitted to the government of Oman by Mardela International, an American marine and

fisheries research corporation, showed that, off the coast of the sultanate, most fishing operations by foreign interests were carried out in an area south of Ras al Hadd, particularly in Kuria Muria Bay. Mardela judged that to date the catch of sardines by Omani fishermen using beach seines and cast nets had been in the region of 40,000 metric tons per year. With proper methods and an expanded fisheries programme this could, it was estimated, be increased to something like 600,000 tones. Tuna resources, at present hardly utilised, it was added, could produce anything between 10,000 and 60,000 metric tones per year. One of the principal recommendations of Mardela was the development of trawling. See Ministry of Information and Culture, Sultanate of Oman, *Sultanate of Oman, Agriculture and Fisheries* (1975).

[120] At the Second Conference on the Law of the Sea in 1960, the Iranian delegation said that 'All the living resources of the Persian Gulf belonged by historic right to all the coastal states thereof, that right having been expressly laid down in article 7 of the Iranian Law of 1959 on the territorial sea', LSCOR (2nd), (A/Conf.19/8), p. 104.

[121] *Echo of Iran* (daily news bulletin, Tehran), 31 October 1973.

[122] As the texts show, the drafting of some provisions of these declarations, particularly the Saudi declaration, is obscure. See Appendices IV and V.

[123] See further the discussion in Chapter II below of the position of these and the other Middle Eastern States towards the exclusive economic zone concept, which is now being discussed at the Third Law of the Sea Conference.

[124] See Iranian delegate's remarks at the Third Conference on the Law of the Sea, LSCOR (3rd), vol. I, 1974 (1 July), p. 72.

[125] In 1973 a study carried out by the United Nations Food and Agriculture Organisation (FAO) estimated that, with proper development, fish production in the Arabian Gulf could rise from the then annual level of about 100,000 metric tons to about six times that figure. In April 1975 a conference attended by representatives of the eight Gulf littoral States decided to launch the second stage of a fisheries survey and development scheme which could result in a ten fold increase in the region's fishing catch. The main aim of the project, it was stated, was to carry out a systematic survey of Gulf waters to identify the species of fish present, determine their quality and seasonal distribution, and calculate their potential annual yield. Recommendations would then be made to the States involved on ways of developing their national industries on a scientific basis, with due regard to conservation of resources. According to the report, Iran was to provide one-third of the costs involved, with another $1·5 million coming from the United Nations Development Programme (UNDP). Qatar, which has already financed preparatory studies carried out by FAO, would provide headquarters for the survey—which was expected to take three and half years—while an associated fisheries training centre is to be established in Kuwait. Each of the States involved is expected to contribute a research vessel for the project. *M.E.E.D.*, 30 March 1973, p. 359, and 18 April 1975, p. 38.

[126] See *Kayhan International* (daily newspaper, Tehran), 13 May 1970.

[127] These views were expressed in a decision adopted by the Kuwaiti Cabinet in 1971; text supplied by courtesy of His Excellency the Ambassador of Kuwait in London, Sheikh Saud Nasir Al-Sabah. Fishing was a traditional activity in Kuwait prior to the discovery of oil and offers one of the brightest prospects for the future of the non-oil sector in Kuwait. Alongside fishing, shrimping is becoming a thriving business, with a lucrative world market. In April 1972 the three major fisheries companies of Kuwait (Kuwait National Fisheries Company, Gulf Fisheries Company and International Fisheries Company) merged to form the Kuwait United Fisheries Company (KUFC), with a capital of KD10 million, 47 per cent of which is owned by the government of Kuwait. The new company operates eighty-two vessels from Kuwait and eighty-eight vessels from its bases elsewhere. It has fishing

NOTES

agreements with the Yemen Arab Republic, the People's Democratic Republic of Yemen, Madagascar, New Guinea, Mauritania, Pakistan and Saudi Arabia, and KUFC boats operate in the waters off these States. Agreements were also reached early in 1973 for setting up joint fishing ventures with Senegal and Nigeria. The new ventures, to be run by KUFC, would carry out the preservation and canning of fish, in addition to ordinary fishing operations. The agreements also mean that Kuwait can fish in waters off the coasts of Senegal and Nigeria without having to pay duties. In addition a modern fishing port is being built at Shuaiba, and a shrimp and fish processing and freezing plant has been opened. The majority of the products are exported to the United States and Japan. The Kuwait Sea Foods Company was set up to import and freeze fish and shrimps for the local market. See *M.E.E.D.*, 30 March 1973, p. 359.

[128] Presidential proclamation No. 2667, 'Policy of the United States with respect to the National Resources of the Subsoil and Sea Bed of the Continental Shelf'. For texts of the proclamation and the related Executive Order and White House press release issued on the same day, 28 September 1945, see ST/LEG/Ser.B/1(1951), p. 38.

[129] *North Sea Continental Shelf, Judgement*, I.C.J. Reports, 1969, p. 3, at pp. 32–3.

[130] See, e.g., H. Lauterpacht, 'Sovereignty over submarine areas', 27 *B.Y.I.L.* (1950), p. 376.

[131] *North Sea Continental Shelf, Judgement, op. cit.* p. 39.

[132] The rules enshrined in Articles 2 and 3 of the 1958 convention, it is expected, will be retained without change in the convention the Third Law of the Sea Conference is expected to adopt. The definition of the continental shelf as enunciated in Article 1, however, will be revised, mainly because it is open to varying interpretations and because the rapid technological advance of the last decade made the exploitability criterion impracticable. See Informal Composite Negotiating Text, Article 76. See also below, in Chapter II. In the North Sea Continental Shelf cases, 1969, the International Court of Justice said that the continental shelf is 'the natural prolongation or continuation of the land territory or domain, or land sovereignty of the coastal State, into and under the high seas, via the bed of its territorial sea which is under the full sovereignty of that State.' *North Sea Continental Shelf, Judgement, op. cit.*, p. 31. Article 76 of the Informal Composite Negotiating Test states that 'The continental shelf or a coastal state comprises the sea bed and subsoil of the submarine areas that extend beyond its territorial sea throughout the natural prolongation of its land territory to the outer edge of the continental margin, or to a distance of 200 nautical miles from the baselines from which the breadth of the territorial sea is measured where the outer edge of the continental margin does not extend up to that distance'.

[133] This Saudi pronouncement dealt only with the continental shelf of Saudi Arabia in the Arabian Gulf. A Saudi law issued in 1968, discussed below in Chapter V, dealt with the sea bed claims of Saudi Arabia in the Red Sea.

[134] The proclamations of the Trucial States are identical except for minor variations, some of which at least appear to be owing to clerical oversight rather than intentional changes. The similarity indicates the common origin of the proclamations, which were drawn up apparently by the United Kingdom government, then the protecting power, and then issued publicly, on the advice of the latter, by the rulers of the various Trucial States. See, e.g., text of letter dated 2 June 1949 from His Britannic Majesty's Political Agent in Bahrain to the Ruler of Sharjah concerning the issue of a continental shelf proclamation, below, Appendix III.

[135] Fujairah's continental shelf proclamation is not available, but it has been indicated that it adopts the continental shelf concept without a precise definition; see U.S. Department of State, *National Claims to Maritime Jurisdictions, op. cit.*, p. 206.

NOTES

[136] *North Sea Continental Shelf, Judgement, op. cit.*, p. 22. It has been observed that in the Truman Proclamation of 1945 the United States was careful not to claim any 'sovereign rights' over the continental shelf and instead used the terms 'jurisdiction and control', taking the position that under such decisions as the *Island of Palmas Arbitration*, 1928, there can be no sovereignty without effective occupation or control. A. H. Dean, 'The Geneva Conference on the Law of the Sea: what was accomplished', 52 *A.J.I.L.* (1958), p. 607, at p. 620.

[137] *North Sea Continental Shelf, Judgement, op. cit.*, p. 46.

[138] *Ibid.*

[139] *Ibid.*, pp. 53–4.

[140] See below, Chapter III. Article 83 (1) of the Informal Composite Negotiating Text (A/Conf.62/WP.10, 15 July 1977), provides that 'The delimitation of the continental shelf between adjacent or opposite states shall be effected by agreement in accordance with equitable principles, employing, where appropriate, the median or equidistance line, and taking account of all the relevant circumstances'. See also below, in Chapter II. In connection with the sea bed proclamation of the Trucial States and the question of delimitation reference may be made also to the problem brought about by the proclamations of Abu Dhabi and Qatar. The problem was raised in two cases, when the rulers of Qatar and Abu Dhabi, whose territories were already covered by oil concession agreements with the IPC group signed in 1935 and 1939 respectively, following the issue of their respective sea bed proclamations, decided to grant separate oil concessions in respect of their submarine areas to other companies. The original oil concessionaries considered that the continental shelf was already within the terms of their oil concessions, which referred to the 'territorial waters and islands' and 'the whole extent of the Ruler's dominions'. The rulers, on the other hand, argued that the terms of the original concessions were not comprehensive enough to include the sea bed of the continental shelf, since this had not been in contemplation when the concession agreements were signed. The disputes were submitted to arbitration in accordance with the provisions of those agreements. In the first case, between Petroleum Development (Qatar) and the ruler of Qatar, Lord Radcliffe, in 1950, decided in favour of the ruler of Qatar and said that 'The concession does not include the sea bed and subsoil or any part there of beneath the high seas of the Persian Gulf contiguous with [the territorial] waters'. In the second case, between Petroleum Development (Trucial Coast) Ltd and the ruler of Abu Dhabi, Lord Asquith of Bishopstone, in August 1951, decided that Petroleum Development's concession extended to the subsoil of the territorial waters, including those of the islands, but not to the subsoil of the continental shelf, which he defined as the submarine areas contiguous to Abu Dhabi outside its three-mile territorial zone. Lord Asquith opposed the view that claims to the continental shelf were recognised by customary international law at that time; he said that the continental shelf doctrine 'cannot claim as yet to have assumed hitherto the hard lineaments of the definitive status of an established international law'. See *Petroleum Development (Qatar) Ltd* v. *Ruler of Qatar*, 1950, and *The Matter of an Arbitration between Petroleum Development (Trucial Coast) Ltd and the Sheikh of Abu Dhabi*, in Sir H. Lauterpacht (ed.), *International Law Reports*, 1951 (London, 1957), p. 161 and p. 144 respectively. See also R. Young, 'Lord Asquith and the continental shelf', 46 *A.J.I.L.* (1951), p. 512.

[141] In 1953, in a commentary on the 1951 ILC's draft articles on the continental shelf and related subjects (A/CN.4/49, 31 July 1951), the Egyptian government considered that 'the concept of "control and jurisdiction for the purpose of exploring [the continental shelf] and exploiting its natural resources" contained in article 2 might be replaced by the well-known concept of "Sovereignty", which there is no good reason for rejecting, and which presents definite advantages from the point of view of practical interpretation. The continental shelf would simply be subject to the sovereignty of the coastal state. There is no reason to fear that the concept of

sovereignty would be criticised on the grounds that it might give rise to an extension of the power and control of the coastal state, since articles 3, 4 and 5, which the Egyptian Government supports in principle, seem to offer assurances which could logically be accepted'. II *Yearbook of the ILC* (1953), p. 200, at p. 249. Articles 3, 4 and 5 referred to in the Egyptian statement reserve the character of the superjacent waters and the air space above the continental shelf as high seas and allow the establishment, or maintenance of submarine cables on the continental shelf.

[142] H. J. Liebesny, 'Legislations on the sea bed and territorial waters of the Persian Gulf', 4 *Middle East Journal* (1950), p. 94. Similarly, it has been stated that 'In so far as the [continental shelf] claims apply to submarine areas, it would seem unprofitable to speculate on possible shades of meaning in the various phrases used. All have in common a minimum intent to control exclusively the resources of certain areas of sea bed and subsoil, and as a practical matter it would seem impossible to control these resources *in situ* without controlling the sea bed and subsoil which contain them', R. Young, 'Legal status of submarine areas beneath the high seas', 45 *A.J.I.L.* (1951), p. 225.

[143] B. Auguste, *The Continental Shelf: the Practice and Policy of the Latin American States* (Geneva, 1960), p. 95, note 274.

[144] See report of the ILC on its draft articles on the continental shelf, II *Yearbook of the ILC* (1955), pp. 296–7.

[145] The Sea bed Proclamation of Abu Dhabi omitted the assurance regarding the unchanged status of the air space above the continental shelf; this, however, might have been owing to clerical oversight. It may, however, be indicated also that notwithstanding the fact that Article 5 of the 1955 Iranian Act on the Continental Shelf provides that 'This law shall not contravene status governing superjacent waters in so far as same apply to the rights of free navigation and the installation of submarine cables', on signing the 1958 Convention on the Continental Shelf and the Convention on the High Seas Iran made reservations which run counter to this provision. With regard to the former convention the Iranian government reserved its right to allow or not to allow the laying of submarine cables and pipelines on its continental shelf. With respect to Article 2 of the latter convention, which dealt with the freedom of the high seas and provided that 'no state may validly purport to subject any part of them to its sovereignty', Iran maintained, in a reservation, that this prohibition did not apply to the continental shelf. See Cmnd 584 (reprinted 1968), p. 47. So far, however, Iran has not ratified any of the 1958 conventions. On 14 June 1965 France, on the occasion of its accession to the 1958 Convention on the Continental Shelf, made an objection against the Iranian reservation. See 538 *U.N.T.S.*, p. 338. Similar objections were made by the United States and the Netherlands. See *North Sea Continental Shelf*, I.C.J. Pleadings, 1968, vol. I, pp. 230–1.

[146] See texts of the agreements.

[147] Emphasis added. Article 121 of the Informal Composite Negotiating Text provides that 'Rocks which cannot sustain human habitation or economic life of their own shall have no exclusive economic zone or continental shelf'.

[148] As stated at the outset, Sudan is the only Middle Eastern State party to the 1958 Continental Shelf Convention.

[149] For full text of the Libyan petroleum law see *Petroleum Legislation, Basic Oil Laws and Concession Contracts—North Africa*, vol. I, p. Libya A-I.

[150] *Petroleum Economist*, vol. XLII, No. 2, February 1975, p. 50.

[151] *Ibid.* See also *M.E.E.S.*, No. 33, 7 June 1976, pp. 5–6.

[152] *M.E.E.S.*, No. 33, 7 June 1976, pp. 5–6.

[153] For full text of the agreement see *Petroleum Legislation, Basic Oil Laws and Concession Contracts—Middle East*, vol. I (1959), p. Iran D-I.

[154] Iraq has unilaterally delimited her continental shelf boundary on the basis of the equidistance principle, but no agreement in this regard has yet been concluded

NOTES

with either of the States adjacent to her, Kuwait and Iran. See below, in Chapter III.

[155] The Act provides that 'In respect of the Caspian Sea, the principles of International Law relating to closed seas shall remain applicable'. It has been stated that a recent Soviet international law manual has observed that the resources of the continental shelf in the Caspian Sea belong to the USSR and Iran, each within the limits of its respective area of the sea. W. E. Butler, *The Soviet Union and the Law of the Sea, op. cit.*, pp. 101, 119 and 136. The Caspian, with an average depth of 180 m. ranges from an average of 6·2 m in the northern portion to 325 m in the southern portion. The greatest depth is about 1,000 m. *Ibid.*

[156] LSCOR (1st), vol. VI, p. 14.

[157] *Ibid.*, p. 92.

[158] *Ibid.*

[159] *Ibid.* It has been indicated, however, that on the Iranian side of the Arabian Gulf the low-water line had been mapped in the 1950s and 1960s with a high degree of accuracy as an incident of determining the boundaries between on-shore and offshore oil concessions; and that a new map of the Arabian Gulf area, showing with a high degree of precision the relationship of the Saudi Arabian and Iranian coastlines to the low-water lines and the position of islands located between the two coastlines was used in preparing the 1968 continental shelf agreement between Iran and Saudi Arabia. R. Young 'Equitable solutions for offshore boundaries: the 1968 Saudi Arabia–Iran agreement', 69 *A.J.I.L.* (1970), p. 152, at p. 156.

[160] LSCOR (1st), vol. VI, p. 92.

[161] *Ibid.*, p. 96.

[162] *Ibid.*, p. 142 (A/Conf.13/C.4/L.60). Iran also expressed its belief that 'the most convenient and most equitable solution was that proposed by Mr Kennedy (U.K. delegation) . . . namely, not to permit islands situated much further out than the territorial sea to have any influence on the boundary'. *Ibid.*, p. 96. At the conference Italy suggested a similar proposal, but the representative of the United States, Miss Whiteman, opposed it, as she found that 'in view of the great variety of size, grouping and position of islands, it would be impossible either to include or exclude all islands on the continental shelf, and that each case should be considered on its merits'. Miss Whiteman suggested that very small islands or sand cays on a continuous continental shelf and outside the belt of territorial sea might be neglected as base points for measurement and have only their own appropriate territorial sea. *Ibid.*, p. 96.

[163] *Ibid.*, p. 98.

[164] See Cmnd 584 (reprinted 1968), p. 47. As noted above, however, so far Iran has not ratified any of the 1958 Geneva conventions on the Law of the Sea, including that on the continental shelf.

[165] E. D. Brown, *The Legal Regime of Hydrospace, op. cit.*, p. 59.

[166] A. Dean, 'The Law of the Sea Conference, 1958–60, and its aftermath', in L. M. Alexander, *The Law of the Sea* (Ohio State University Press, 1967), p. 244, at p. 251.

[167] John Christopher Dewdney, 'Persian Gulf', in 17 *Encyclopaedia Britannica* (1973 edn.), p. 649.

[168] A. Dean, 'The Law of the Sea Conference, 1958–60, and its aftermath', *op. cit.*, p. 251.

[169] D. J. Padwa 'Submarine boundaries', 9 *I.C.L.Q.* (1960), p. 628, at p. 643, note 51.

[170] This treatment of islands follows the proposal made at the 1958 Conference on the Law of the Sea by the representative of the United States, Miss Whiteman, and referred to above in note 162.

[171] 14 *Encyclopaedia Britannica* (15th edn., 1974), p. 106.

[172] In its commentary on what later became Article 1 of the 1958 Geneva Con-

NOTES

vention on the Continental Shelf the International Law Commission pointed out that 'while adopting, to a certain extent, the geographical test for the "Continental Shelf" as the basis of the juridical definition of the term, the Commission therefore in no way holds that the existence of a continental shelf, is essential for the exercise of the rights of the coastal state as defined in these articles. Thus if, as in the case of the Persian Gulf, the submarine areas never reach to a depth of 200 metres, that fact is irrelevant for the purposes of the present article.' II *Yearbook of the ILC* (1956), p. 297, para. 7. Article I of the 1958 convention defines the continental shelf as referring '*(a)* to the sea bed and subsoil of the submarine areas adjacent to the coast but outside the area of the territorial sea, to a depth of 200 metres or, beyond that limit, to where the depth of the superjacent waters admits of the exploitation of the natural resources of the said areas; *(b)* to the sea bed and subsoil of similar submarine areas adjacent to the coasts of islands'. For the definition of the continental shelf as stated by the International Court of Justice in the North Sea Continental Shelf cases, 1969, and as used in the Informal Composite Negotiating Text prepared at the Third Conference on the Law of the Sea in 1977, see above, note 132.

[173] R. Young, 'Saudi Arabian offshore legislation', 43 *A.J.I.L.* (1949), p. 530, at p. 533.

[174] *Ibid.*, p. 531. Elsewhere R. Young states that the Arabian Gulf as a whole is clearly continental shelf in the legal sense: 'Equitable solutions for offshore boundaries: the 1968 Saudi Arabia–Iran agreement', 64 *A.J.I.L.* (1970), p. 152.

[175] H. Lauterpacht, 'Sovereignty over submarine areas', 27 *B.Y.I.L.* (1950), p. 376, at p. 384. As shown earlier above, the 600 ft (200 m) figure was referred to first in the White House press release which accompanied the Truman Proclamation of 1949, and subsequently in the definition of the continental shelf enshrined in Article 1 of the 1958 Convention on the Continental Shelf.

[176] *Ibid.* To the same effect see J. L. Brierly, *The Law of Nations* (6th edn. by Sir Humphrey Waldock, Oxford, 1963), p. 211; H. M. Al-Baharna, *The Arabian Gulf States, op. cit.*, p. 279; J. Y. Brinton, 'Jurisdiction over sea bed resources and recent developments in the Persian Gulf area', 5 *R.E.D.I.* (1949), p. 131, at p. 137; Bernard H. Oxman, 'The preparation of Article 1 of the Convention on the Continental Shelf', 3 *J. Mar. L. and Comm.* (1971–72). p. 245, at pp. 254 and 265.

[177] This argument was developed in an unpublished paper delivered to a conference on 'Legal Problems of the Continental Shelf', held in Cambridge in April 1967, under the auspices of the British Institute of International and Comparative Law and the Cambridge Faculty of Law. A copy of the paper was acquired by courtesy of Mr E. Lauterpacht.

[178] *Ibid.* Similarly Bernard H. Oxman concludes that 'while there was unanimous agreement (during the debate of the question of the continental shelf in the International Law Commission) that the coastal state would have exclusive rights to the natural resources of the sea bed and subsoil in relatively shallow areas such as the Persian Gulf which were not believed to compromise part of a geological continental shelf, this conclusion is not necessarily compelled by the text of the Commission's final draft articles on the Convention itself. Yet from the first report the Commission issued on this subject until the final report in 1956 which explicitly refers to the Persian Gulf in this context, the rejection of the need for a continental shelf in a strict geological sense is apparent.' Oxman, 'The preparation of Article 1 of the Convention on the Continental Shelf', 3 *J. Mar. L. and Comm.* (1971–72), p. 245, at p. 246.

[179] E. D. Brown, *The Legal Regime of Hydrospace, op. cit.*, p. 8, note 18.

[180] II *Yearbook of the ILC* (1951), p. 141.

[181] II *Yearbook of the ILC* (1953), p. 212.

[182] *Ibid.*

[183] II *Yearbook of the ILC* (1956), pp. 269–97.

NOTES

[184] *Ibid.*

[185] Reproduced in I *Yearbook of the ILC* (1956), p. 131, and in UNESCO Secretariat memorandum on 'Scientific considerations relating to the continental shelf', LSCOR (1st), vol. I, p. 39. Similar definitions were proposed by a group of geologists in 1970 to a symposium on the international regime of the sea bed; see Jerzy Sztucki (ed.), *Symposium on the International Regime of the Sea Bed* (Rome, 1970), p. 33.

[186] B. Auguste, *The Continental Shelf: the Practice and Policy of the Latin American States* (Geneva, 1960), p. 31.

[187] UNESCO Secretariat memorandum on 'Scientific considerations relating to the continental shelf', *op. cit.*, p. 40, para. 12.

[188] Aaron L. Shalowitz (U.S. Department of Commerce), *Shore and Sea Boundaries* I (Washington, D.C., 1962), p. 190, note 20.

[189] In his discussion of the question of protection of sedentary fisheries, C. J. Colombos states: 'Vattel has already asked himself the question "Who can doubt that the pearl fisheries of Bahrain and Ceylon can lawfully fall under ownership?".' Colombos adds, 'at the time Vattel wrote his famous book the doctrine of the freedom of the seas had not as yet been generally acknowledged as a principle of international law. More modern writers have rested the justification of the British claims on the occupation of the bed of the sea which, it is contended, is capable of being subjected to a State's ownership. Such occupation of the bed of the high seas is liable to interfere with the freedom of the high seas and it is submitted that the better view is to base the exclusive rights of the British Government to the pearl fisheries off Ceylon and the Persian Gulf on their effective occupation extending over several centuries and implicitly accepted by other States.' C. J. Colombos, *The International Law of the Sea* (6th revised edn., London, 1967), p. 404.

[190] A/CN.4/42, p. 59.

[191] J. G. Lorimer, C.I.E., *Gazetteer of the Persian Gulf, Oman, and Central Arabia* (reprinted in 1970, London; hereinafter *Lorimer's Gazetteer of the Persian Gulf*), vol. I, p. 2244. The *Gazetteer*, in two volumes, vol. I, *Historical* (3 parts), and vol. II, Geographical and Statistical (2 parts), was first published by Calcutta Superintendent, Government Printing, India, in 1915 and 1908 respectively.

[192] *Ibid.*, p. 2245.

[193] *Ibid.*, pp. 2248–9.

CHAPTER II

[1] United Nations press release SG/SM/1289 (29 June 1970), p. 3.

[2] G. A. Res. 2750C (XXV), 17 December 1970; full text in 10 *I.L.M.* (1971), p. 220.

[3] The preparatory work for the Third Conference was entrusted to the Committee on the Peaceful Uses of the Sea Bed and the Ocean Floor, beyond the Limits of National Jurisdiction (hereinafter the Sea Bed Committee), which was first established, in response to a Maltese proposal (A16695, 17 August 1967), under General Assembly Resolution 2340 (XXII), 18 December 1967, as an *ad hoc* committee 'to study the peaceful uses of the Sea Bed and the ocean floor beyond the limits of national jurisdiction'. Under Resolution 2467A (XXIII), 21 December 1968, the *ad hoc* committee was transformed into a standing committee with forty-two members, expanded to eighty-six members and converted to a preparatory committee by Resolution 2750 (XXV), 17 December 1970. The Sea Bed Committee did not succeed in completing draft articles for the Third Conference, but at the end of its meetings in 1973 it adopted a report in six volumes (A/9021, 1973), containing

texts of working papers and other numerous proposals and amendments which were submitted to it, plus texts illustrating areas of agreement and disagreement on some items of its programme of work. The Sea Bed Committee was dissolved, in accordance with General Assembly Resolution 3067 (XXVIII), 16 November 1973, prior to the inaugural session of the Third Conference in December 1973. The Middle Eastern States of Egypt, Iraq, Kuwait, Lebanon, Libya, Sudan and the Yemen Arab Republic had been members of the Sea Bed Committee.

[4] A/Conf.62/WP.8/Parts I, II and III (May 1975); text in LSCOR (3rd), vol. IV, pp. 137 et seq.

[5] A/Conf.62/WP.9 (21 July 1975); text in LSCOR (3rd), vol. V, pp. 115–25.

[6] A/Conf.62/WP.8./Rev. 1/Parts I, II and III (May 1976), and A/Conf.62/WP.9/Rev. 1 (May 1976); texts in LSCOR (3rd), vol. V, pp. 125–201.

[7] A/Conf.62/WP.10, 15 July 1977. This text, like its two predecessors, according to its Preamble, has no other status than that of serving as a basis for continued negotiation without prejudice to the right of any delegation to move any amendments or to introduce any new proposals.

[8] The Committee of Arab Experts on the Law of the Sea (hereinafter 'Committee of Arab Experts') was first established in 1957 under a resolution adopted by the Council of the Arab League on 17 November 1957 to consider the ILC's draft articles concerning the law of the sea (A/3159), which were prepared for the 1958 Law of the Sea Conference. See *Report of the Committee of Arab Experts on the Law of the Sea,* League of Arab States, the Secretariat, Legal Department (January 1958). Recently the Committee of Arab Experts was re-established under Resolution 2677 of 15 September 1970 of the Council of the Arab League. The latter report of the Committee of Arab Experts and all its other reports and documents which will be referred to in this volume, as well as the resolutions of the Council of the Arab League, are published in Arabic, and the English translation is provided by the present writer. Where the reference number and/or date of the document concerned are available they will be indicated, otherwise only the title will be given.

[9] The drafting of the recommendation is rather obscure and the reference to 'straits and gulfs' in one and the same context is confusing. However, in a resolution adopted during the Arab League's sixty-third ordinary session in 1975, the Council of the Arab League reaffirmed its recommendation referred to above but with more precision, as the resolution stated that '... Straits used for international navigation are those which link between one part of the high seas and another part of the high seas and thus do not include those which link between high seas and territorial waters of a foreign state ...'.

[10] But see below, in Chapter IV.

[11] Memorandum N.S/9/1 of 21 February 1972 from the Embassy of Iraq in Cairo to the Arab League; Embassy of the Republic of Iraq, Cairo, Arab Department, Doc. No. N/9/6/370, 9 July 1970. The first of these two memoranda has been referred to in the Preamble to Resolution 2978, 13 September 1972, of the Arab League's Council.

[12] For description and a consideration of the legal status of the Strait of Hormuz see above, in Chapter I.

[13] *Corfu Channel case,* I.C.J. Reports, 1949, p. 1, at p. 28.

[14] Such attitudes have been expressed at the Third Law of the Sea Conference, see below, p. 52.

[15] See *Report of the Secretary General of the Arab League to the Council of the Arab League,* during the League's fifty-eighth ordinary session, 1972. Dossier No. 21/2/1 old, 21/2/21 new, Cairo, 30 August 1973 (League of Arab States, the Secretariat, Legal Department).

[16] The three sessions were convened in accordance with resolutions of the Council of the Arab League Nos. 2978 of 13 September 1972, 3035 of 7 April 1973, and 3097 of 15 September 1973 respectively. They were held at the headquarters of the

NOTES

Arab League in Cairo; the first met from 10 to 15 February 1973, the second from 4 to 14 June 1973 and the third from 2 to 10 March 1974. Two more sessions were held in January 1975 and in January 1976 respectively. The Committee of Arab Experts also held informal meetings in Caracas and Geneva during the second and third sessions of the Third Conference on the Law of the Sea, for the purpose of co-ordinating policies of the Arab States inside the conference towards new developments and proposals. The States of Jordan, the United Arab Emirates, Tunis, Saudi Arabia, Sudan, Syria, Iraq, Qatar, Kuwait, Lebanon, Libya, Egypt, the Yemen Arab Republic and Democratic Yemen were represented at the first session of the Committee of Arab Experts. At its second session representatives from all member States of the Arab League were present, while at the third session only the following were not represented: Bahrain, Tunisia, Lebanon, Morocco and the Islamic Republic of Mauritania.

[17] See statement by Mr Azzam (League of Arab States), LSCOR (3rd), vol. I, 1974 (4 July), pp. 119-20.

[18] A/AC.138/89 (2 July 1973). This declaration, adopted by the Council of Ministers of the OAU in Addis Ababa in 1973, was reaffirmed during their meeting in Mogadiscio in 1974; see A/Conf. 62/33 (19 July 1974), in LSCOR (3rd), vol. III, p. 63.

[19] Mauritania claims thirty miles in accordance with a decree issued on 31 July 1972; Somalia claims 200 miles in accordance with Law No. 37 of 20 December 1973. See U.S. Department of State, the Geographer, *National claims to Maritime Jurisdictions, op. cit.*, pp. 127 and 172 respectively. Article 1 of the Somali law of 1973 prohibits innocent passage for ships of nationality not recognised by Somalia. The Somali law brought an Israeli protest, which was made in a letter dated 19 March 1974 transmitted to the Secretary General of the United Nations, who in turn communicated it to members of the United Nations in a note dated 29 March 1975. Reference LE113 (3-3) Somal. Somalia borders the Gulf of Aden, which leads to the Straits of Bab el-Mandeb and the Red Sea.

[20] At the Third Conference many Arab States supported the idea of a 'contiguous zone' but made no reference to 'security' matters; see below at pp. 52-53.

[21] The Iraqi representative on the Committee of Arab Experts made a formal reservation with respect to the breadth of the exclusive economic zone. As will be shown, Iraq considers that the concept of an exclusive economic zone should not be applied to semi-enclosed seas such as the Arabian Gulf, which it borders.

[22] This recommendation was adopted as a draft resolution, by the drafting Committee of the Committee of Arab Experts, in March 1974.

[23] See above, in Chapter I, and below, in Chapter IV.

[24] Recommendation I (b) of the *Conclusions in the General Report of the African States' Regional Seminar on the Law of the Sea held in Yaounde*, 20-30 June 1972, provides: 'On "Historic Rights" and "Historic Bays": (1) That the "historic rights" acquired by certain neighbouring African States in a part of the sea which may fall within the exclusive jurisdiction of another State should be recognised and safeguarded. (2) The impossibility for an African State to provide evidence of an uninterrupted claim over a historic bay should not constitute an obstacle to the recognition of the rights of that State over such a bay'. The Yaounde conclusions were adopted by sixteen African States, including Egypt; for full text see ST/LEG/Ser.B/16 (1974), p. 601, (A/AC.138/79, 21 July 1972).

[25] Representatives from the League of Arab States and the Palestine Liberation Organisation are attending as observers, the former as an intergovernmental organisation, the latter in accordance with the decision of the conference on 12 July 1974 that had subsequently been endorsed by the General Assembly in Resolution 3334 (XXIX) of 17 December 1974, and later formulated into a new rule of procedure and inserted into the *Rules of Procedure* (A/Conf. 62/30/Rev.1 and Add.1) as rule 63. The latter was originally proposed by the representative of Senegal on behalf of

the OAU and the Arab League. The new rule was adopted by consensus, in spite of strong objections by the representative of Israel, who opposed an invitation to the P.L.O. but did not call for a vote on this additional rule of procedure (see LSCOR (3rd), vol. I, pp. 165–76). Article 63 reads: '1. National liberation movements in their respective regions recognized by the Organization of African Unity or by the League of Arab States may designate representatives to participate as observers, without the right to vote, in the deliberations of the Conference, the Main Committees and, as appropriate, the subsidiary organs. 2. Written statements of such observers shall be distributed by the Secretariat to the delegations of the Conference.'

[26] Hawwar, a group of sixteen islands, is nearer to the coast of Qatar than to Bahrain, but sovereignty over the islands is disputed between these two States. See below, in Chapter III. At the Third Conference the representative of Bahrain stated: 'Consisting as it did of an archipelago, Bahrain supported the right of archipelagic States to draw straight baselines which safeguarded their territorial, political, economic and national unity and within which they might exercise their sovereignty, subject to the right of innocent passage.' LSCOR (3rd), vol. I, 1974 (12 July), p. 174.

[27] Data taken from U.S. Department of State, the Geographer, *National Claims to Maritime Jurisdictions*, Limits in the Seas, No. 36 (3rd revision), 23 December 1975, p. 8. Lebanon has no territorial sea legislation yet.

[28] Article 3 of the Informal Composite Negotiating Text (A/Conf.62/WP.10, 15 July 1977) gives each State the right to establish the breadth of its territorial sea up to a limit not exceeding twelve nautical miles.

[29] Delegate of the United States in the Sea Bed Committee, A/AC.138/SC.II/SR.48–62 (16 May 1973), pp. 129–30. See also his statement at the Third Conference, LSCOR (3rd), vol. I, 1974 (11 July), p. 160.

[30] For discussion on policies of the States advocating a territorial sea of 200 miles see, e.g., E. D. Brown, 'Maritime zones', *op. cit.*, especially pp. 165–9; F. V. Garcia-Amador, 'The Latin American contributions to the development of the law of the sea', 68 *A.J.I.L.* (1974), p. 33.

[31] At the First and Second United Nations Conferences on the Law of the Sea the Arab States and Iran were in favour of the twelve-mile limit for the territorial sea. Israel, on the other hand, favoured a maximum of six miles. It has been stated that the position of the Arab States at the 1958 and 1960 conferences was strongly affected by the issue of the passage of Israeli vessels through the Gulf of Aqaba and the Straits of Tiran (see, e.g., A. H. Dean, 'The Geneva Conference on the Law of the Sea: what was accomplished', 52 *A.J.I.L.* (1958), p. 607, at pp. 608–9). This was 'emphatically denied' by the Egyptian delegate at the 1960 conference, who also observed that the small and economically less developed countries, including the Arab States, were in favour of a twelve-mile limit to secure broader exclusive fishing zones and to ensure that foreign warships and military aircraft were unable to pass through or over areas closely adjacent to their coasts. LSCOR (2nd), p. 102.

[32] LSCOR (3rd), vol. I, 1974 (11 July), p. 155. Similar views were expressed by the Yemen Arab Republic, *ibid.* (4 July), p. 116; Democratic Yemen, *ibid.* (8 July), p. 125; Lebanon, *ibid.* (9 July), p. 135; Libya, *ibid.* (9 July), p. 133; Bahrain, *ibid.* (12 July), p. 174; and Saudi Arabia, *ibid.* (10 July), p. 144.

[33] *Ibid.*, 1974 (9 July), p. 141.

[34] See statements made by the representatives of Egypt and Oman, *ibid.* (1 July), p. 75, and (9 July), p. 152 respectively.

[35] AALCC, *Report of the Twelfth Session*, Colombo, January 1971, p. 298. A similar view was expressed in statements made by the Libyan delegate in the Sea Bed Committee, A/AC.138/SC.II/SR.10 (10 August 1971) and A/AC.138/SCII/SR.40 (4 August 1972).

[36] A/A.138/SC.II/SR.10 (10 August 1971).

[37] LSCOR (3rd), vol. I, 1974 (1 July), p. 71.

[38] On signing the 1958 Territorial Sea Convention the Soviet Union and several other States entered reservations requiring the coastal State's permission for the passage of warships through the territorial sea; other States, such as the Sudan, Democratic Yemen and Syria, made similar limitations in their national laws. For further discussion on the right of innocent passage of warships through the territorial sea see, e.g., O. G. de Vries Reilingh, 'Warships in territorial waters, their right of innocent passage', II *Netherlands Y.I.L.* (1971), p. 29.

[39] Malaysia, Morocco, Oman and Yemen: *Draft articles on navigation through the territorial sea, including Straits used for international navigation,* A/Conf.62/C.2/L.16 (22 July 1974).

[40] Part II, Section 3 of the *ICNT* contains draft articles relating to innocent passage through the territorial sea which are based, for the most part, on the provisions of the 1958 convention and partly on proposals initially presented by Fiji A/Conf.62/C.2/L.3 (3 July 1974) those provisions which suggested that the right of L.3 (3 July 1974). The draft articles enumerate twelve activities which if committed in the territorial sea by foreign ships render the passage of the ships non-innocent; these include 'any act of wilful and serious pollution . . .', but it is not clear whether the list is exhaustive or illustrative. The draft articles also make it clear that warships have the same rights of innocent passage through territorial waters as merchant ships. Tankers and ships carrying nuclear and other inherently dangerous or noxious substances may be required to navigate through designated sea lanes.

[41] See U.S. Department of State, the Geographer, 'World straits affected by a twelve-mile territorial sea' (map, 510376 2–71); R. H. Kennedy, 'A brief study of straits'. See also U.S. Department of State, the Geographer, *Sovereignty of the Sea* (Geographic Bulletin No. 3, revised October 1969), Table III, 'Widths of selected straits and channels'.

[42] For a very representative statement on the view of the United States see the reply of the Acting Legal Adviser of the Department of State in response to the question 'Why is the concept of free transit so important to our national interest?', made during a hearing on United States oceans policy before the Sub-committee on Oceans and International Environment of the Senate Foreign Relations Committee, in Arthur W. Rovine, *Digest of United States Practice in International Law, 1973* (Department of State Publication 8756, released July 1974), p. 273.

[43] Colin Warbrick, 'The regulation of navigation', in R. Churchill, K. R. Simmond, and Jane Welch (eds.), *New Directions in the Law of the Sea,* vol. III, *op. cit.,* p. 137 at p. 146.

[44] The articles in Part III of the ICNT concerning straits used for international navigation, are largely based on proposals submitted by the United Kingdom (A/Conf.62/C.2/L.3, 3 July 1974). These Articles provide, *inter alia,* that the right of 'transit passage' applies to 'straits which are used for international navigation between one area of the high seas or an exclusive economic zone and another area of the high seas or an exclusive economic zone'. The right of non-suspendable innocent passage, however, would apply to straits which are used for international navigation between one area of the high seas or an exclusive economic zone and the territorial sea of a foreign State. The strait State may make laws and regulations regarding, *inter alia,* the prevention, reduction and control of pollution by giving effect to 'applicable international regulations.' For further discussion on the general question of free or transit passage through international Straits see, e.g., Manjula Shyam, 'International straits and ocean law', 15 *Indian J.I.L.* (1975), p. 17; R. P. Anand, 'Freedom of navigation through territorial waters and international straits', 6 *J. Mar. L. & Comm.* (1974–75), p. 175.

[45] See statements made by Iranian delegation, LSCOR (3rd), vol. I, 1974, (1 July), p. 71, and vol. II, 1974 (22 July), pp. 123–4. See also statement made by the representative of Iran before the Asian–African Legal Consultative Committee in

1972, AALCC, *Report of the Thirteenth Session*, Lagos, January 1972, p. 271.

[46] LSCOR (3rd), vol. II, 1974 (22 July), p. 124.

[47] LSCOR (3rd), vol. V, 1976 (26 April), p. 66.

[48] Statement made by delegate of Kuwait on behalf of Iraq, the United Arab Emirates, the Libyan Arab Republic, Saudi Arabia, Qatar and Kuwait, LSCOR (3rd), vol. II, 1974 (23 July), p. 139. See also Algeria, Bahrain, Iraq, Kuwait, Libyan Arab Republic, Qatar, Saudi Arabia, Syrian Arab Republic, Tunisia and United Arab Emirates, *Draft article on definition of Straits used for international navigation*, A/Conf.62/C.2/L.44 (7 August 1974). The draft article provides: 'In the context of this Convention, the term "Straits used for international navigation" means any Strait connecting two parts of the high seas and customarily used for international navigation'. The rule that there should be no suspension of innocent passage between straits used for international navigation between one part of the high seas and the territorial sea of a foreign State, and the assertion that this rule is applicable to the Gulf of Aqaba, are considered in more detail in Chapter IV below.

[49] LSCOR (3rd), vol. II, 1974 (23 July), p. 139. See also statement made by Kuwaiti representative before the Asian–African Legal Consultative Committee in 1971, AALCC, *Report of the Twelfth Session*, Colombo, January 1971, pp. 278–9.

[50] A/Conf.62/C.2/L.6 (10 July 1974).

[51] See Statements made by the delegate of Iraq, LSCOR (3rd), vol. II, 1974 (23 July), p. 140, and vol. I, 1974 (10 July), p. 148. See also statement of representative of Iraq at the Asian–African Legal Consultative Committee, AALCC, *Report of the Twelfth Session*, Colombo, January 1971, p. 303. At the Third Conference the representative of Iraq spoke in favour of Article 1 of the Draft on Straits submitted by the six East European States (A/Conf.62/C.2/L.11, 17 July 1974) and said that it 'was a safeguard and ensured freedom of navigation through straits linking two parts of the high seas while taking account of the interests of coastal states'. Nevertheless he appealed to these States and also to the United Kingdom to delete from their respective draft articles which dealt with the question of straits (U.K., A/Conf.62/C.2/L.3, 3 July 1974) those provisions which suggested that the right of non-suspendable innocent passage should be maintained in straits linking high seas to the territorial sea of a foreign State. Delegate of Iraq, LSCOR (3rd), vol. II, 1974 (23 July), p. 140.

[52] LSCOR (3rd), vol. I, 1974 (1 July), p. 75. See also *ibid.*, vol. II, 1974 (23 July), pp. 131, 135.

[53] Delegate of Egypt, AALCC, *Report of the Thirteenth Session*, Lagos, January 1972, p. 320.

[54] A/Conf.62/C.2/L.16 (22 July 1974).

[55] *Corfu Channel case, judgement* of 9 April 1949, I.C.J. Reports 1949, p. 4.

[56] LSCOR (3rd), vol. II, 1974 (23 July), p. 136.

[57] For further information on the attitudes of Oman and the Yemen Arab Republic see statements made by the representative of Oman, LSCOR (3rd), vol. I, 1974 (10 July), p. 152, and vol. II, 1974 (23 July), p. 135; and statements made by the representative of the Yemen Arab Republic, LSCOR (3rd), vol. I, 1974 (4 July), pp. 116–17, and vol. II, 1974 (23 July), p. 134. The Yemen Arab Republic was one of the sponsors of the proposals of the eight powers of the 'Straits States group' which were submitted to the Sea Bed Committee in 1973. A/AC.138/5C.II/L.18 (27 March 1973).

[58] LSCOR (3rd), vol. I, 1974 (8 July), p. 125.

[59] See statements made by the representatives of Lebanon and the United Arab Emirates, *ibid.* (9 July), pp. 135 and 141 respectively. See also statement of the Lebanese delegate at the Sea Bed Committee, A/AC.138/SC.I/SR.17 (9 August 1974).

[60] LSCOR (3rd), vol. I, 1974 (11 July), p. 155.

NOTES

[61] A/AC.138/5C.II/SR.40 (4 August 1972).

[62] See the statement made by the representatives of Lebanon, LSCOR (3rd), vol. II, 1974 (22 July), pp. 121–3.

[63] See, e.g., statements by representatives of Iraq, Bahrain, and Kuwait, *ibid.*, pp. 121–4. See also statement made by the representative of Bahrain on 7 August 1974 where he said, *inter alia*, that 'The contiguous zone was very important to coastal states, particularly in areas where there were wide divergences in the prices of commodities and precious materials or where foreign labour was attracted by the better pay or working conditions. Many developing states did not possess the modern technical equipment or the large coastal fleets to protect the whole of their territorial belt from smugglers and infiltrators and to intercept suspicious vessels before they broke through into the territorial zone'; *ibid.* (7 August), pp. 234–5.

[64] A/Conf.62/WP.10 (15 July 1977), Article 33.

[65] Article 2, *Convention on the Continental Shelf*, 1958.

[66] The overwhelming majority of States exercise exclusive fisheries jurisdiction up to twelve miles from their coast, either by virtue of a twelve-mile territorial sea claim embracing such jurisdiction, or specification of a contiguous fisheries zone. In some cases claims up to 200 miles were made. For further details on State practice see U.S. Department of State, the Geographer, *National Claims to Maritime Jurisdictions, op. cit.*

[67] *Fisheries Jurisdiction (United Kingdom* v. *Iceland), Merits, Judgement*, I.C.J. Reports, 1974, pp. 3 and 23.

[68] *Ibid.*, pp. 23, 24. For analysis of the Court's judgement see R. R. Churchill, 'The fisheries jurisdiction cases: the contribution of the International Court of Justice to the debate on coastal States' fisheries rights', 24 *I.C.L.Q.* (1975), p. 82; Rahmetullah Khan, 'The fisheries jurisdiction case—a critique', 15 *Indian J.I.L.* (1975), p. 1.

[69] The term 'patrimonial sea' has been introduced by Latin American States, whilst the expression 'exclusive economic zone' has been introduced, mainly by African States. The concept of the exclusive economic zone or patrimonial sea has been expressed chiefly in four documents: (i) *Declaration of Santo Domingo* approved by the meeting of Ministers of the Specialised Conference of the Caribbean Countries (including Mexico) on Problems of the Law of the Sea held in June 1972, A/AC.138/80 (26 July 1972). (ii) *Conclusions in the General Report of the African States' Regional Seminar on the Law of the Sea held in Yaounde*, 20–30 June 1972, A/AC.138/79 (21 July 1972). (iii) Kenya: Draft Articles on Exclusive Economic Zone, A/AC.138/SC.II/L.10 (7 August 1972), and (iv) Addis Ababa Declaration of May 1973, adopted by the Council of Ministers of the Organisation of African Unity, and reaffirmed at their meeting at Mogadiscio in June 1974, *Declaration of the Organization of African Unity on the Issues of the Law of the Sea*, A/Conf.62/33 (19 July 1974). For detailed analysis and discussion of the exclusive economic zone concept see, e.g., Douglas M. Johnston and Edgar Gold, *The Economic Zone in the Law of the Sea: Survey, Analysis and Appraisal of Current Trends* (Law of the Sea Institute, University of Rhode Island, Occasional Paper No. 17, June 1973); L. D. M. Nelson, 'The patrimonial sea', 22 *I.C.L.Q.* (1973), p. 668; E. D. Brown, 'Maritime zones', *op. cit.*; Karin Hjertonsson, *The New Law of the Sea: Influence of the Latin American States on Recent Development of the Law of the Sea* (Leiden, 1973); Ralph Zacklin, 'Latin America and the Development of the Law of the Sea', 4 *Annals of International Studies* (1973), p. 31.

[70] See, e.g., statements made at the Caracas session of the Third Conference by the delegates of the United States, the United Kingdom and the Soviet Union, LSCOR (3rd), vol. II, 1974 (1 August), p. 190 (5 August), p. 200, and (6 August), p. 221, respectively. A large number of States have already made unilateral claims based on the exclusive zone concept, including Costa Rica, Bangladesh, Mexico, the United States of America, the United Kingdom, Canada, Iceland, Colombia,

NOTES

India, Sri Lanka, the Soviet Union, the Faroes, Norway, Mozambique, Bahamas, Japan, Senegal, Angola and Cuba. For a brief survey of these claims see 25 *I.C.L.Q.* (1976), pp. 685–8, *Keesing's Contemporary Archives* (1976), p. 27999, and (1977), pp. 28233, 28252, 28292, 28564 and 28600.

[71] LSCOR (3rd). vol. II, 1974 (24 August), p. 302.
[72] See Articles 55 and 57 of the *ICNT*.
[73] *Ibid.*, Article 56.
[74] *Ibid.*, Article 62(2).
[75] *Ibid.*, Article 69(1). Developed landlocked States shall, however, be entitled to exercise their rights only within the exclusive economic zones of adjoining developed coastal States. *Ibid.*
[76] Data from L. M. Alexander, 'Regionalism and the law of the sea: the case of semi-enclosed seas', 2 *Ocean Development and International Law Journal* (1974), p. 151, at pp. 176, 180, 181 (appendix). It may be noted also that with respect to the Gulf of Aden, on which Democratic Yemen has borders, 35 per cent of the water area of this sea would be closed off by forty-mile limits, 100 per cent by 200-miles limits, and there would be 93 per cent of sea bed beyond a 200 m depth. *Ibid.*, p. 164. The Gulf of Oman, on which Iran, Oman and the United Arab Emirates (Sharjah and Fujairah) have borders, would be in a situation similar to that of the Gulf of Aden because they are nearly equal in width; the Gulf of Aden and Oman have maximum widths of 335 and 330 km respectively.
[77] *North Sea Continental Shelf, Judgement,* I.C.J. Reports, 1969, p. 3 at p. 22.
[78] This proposal is considered further below in the next section.
[79] On the Red Sea brines see Chapter V below.
[80] Delegate of Sudan at the Sea Bed Committee, A/AC.138/SC.I/SR.18 (9 August 1971). See also statement by the Sudanese representative in the Sea Bed Committee in 1972, A/AC.138/SR.85 (14 August 1972), p. 12.
[81] LSCOR (3rd), vol. II, 1974 (5 August), p. 204. See also statement made by the Egyptian delegate before the Asian–African Legal Consultative Committee, AALCC, *Report of Fourteenth Session,* New Delhi, January 1973, pp. 114–16. A similar view was expressed by representatives of Oman, LSCOR (3rd), vol. I, 1974 (10 July), p. 152. See also statements by representative of Democratic Yemen, *ibid.* (8 July), p. 125, and vol. II, 1974 (5 August), p. 209, and by the delegate of the Yemen Arab Republic in the Sea Bed Committee, A/AC.138/SR.65 (18 August 1971).
[82] LSCOR (3rd), vol. II, 1974 (5 August), p. 214. A similar argument was advanced by the Libyan representative at the 1958 Law of the Sea Conference in support of his argument for a twelve mile territorial sea; LSCOR (1st), vol. III, p. 53; see above, Chapter I, note 18.
[83] LSCOR (3rd), vol. I, 1974 (9 July), p. 141.
[84] Iraq, *ibid.* (10 July), p. 148. Similarly see statement by Bahrain, *ibid.* (7 August), p. 235. The issue of semi-enclosed seas and Iraq's proposals in this regard are considered below.
[85] Delegate of Iraq at the Asian–African Legal Consultative Committee, AALCC, *Report of the Thirteenth Session,* Lagos, January 1972, pp. 292–5.
[86] Iraq was among the twenty-two landlocked and other geographically disadvantaged States which sponsored the *Draft articles on participation of landlocked and other geographically disadvantaged states in the exploration and exploitation of the living and non-living resources in the area beyond the territorial sea,* A/Conf.62/C.2/L39 (5 August 1974). See also statement by Iraqi delegate, LSCOR (3rd), vol. II (6 August 1974), p. 225.
[87] LSCOR (3rd), vol. II, 1974 (6 August), p. 225, para. 25.
[88] See Chapter I above.
[89] Delegate of Iran, AALCC, *Report of the Thirteenth Session,* Lagos, January 1972, pp. 270–1.

[90] Delegate of Iran, LSCOR (3rd), vol. II, 1974 (8 August), p. 244.

[91] *Ibid.*, p. 243. At the Third Conference Iran submitted a draft article on the continental shelf which read: 'The sovereign rights of the coastal state over its continental shelf are exclusive. The revenues derived from the exploitation of the natural resources of the continental shelf shall not be subject to any revenue sharing.' A/Conf.62/C.2/L.84 (27 August 1974). See also statement by delegate of Iran, LSCOR (3rd), vol. II, 1974 (27 August), p. 296.

[92] See statement by delegate of Afghanistan, LSCOR (3rd), vol. II, 1974 (8 August), p. 248.

[93] *Ibid.*, p. 244. Elsewhere Iran stated that 'The rights of the coastal states over the living resources of the coastal zone must be exclusive and not preferential. However, if a coastal state was unable to exploit the size of catch scientifically justifiable, it would be in its own interest to permit others to exploit the surplus on terms to be fixed by itself.' *Ibid.*, vol. I, 1974 (1 July), p. 72.

[94] LSCOR (3rd), vol. II, 1974 (6 August). p. 221. In a statement made before the Sea Bed Committee in 1971, in connection with the claims to a 200-mile territorial sea, the Lebanese delegate said: 'The territorial sea should not exceed a breadth of twelve miles, since territorial sovereignty presupposed a minimum of effective control. What effective control could a state claim over the sea areas several times longer than its own territory? If his country extended its territorial sea to 200 miles and Cyprus did the same they would have to share the sea area between them in accordance with the principle of the median line. The Lebanese would hardly be in a position to exercise effective control over such a large sea area.' A/AC.138 SC.I/SR.17 (8 August 1971).

[95] LSCOR (3rd), vol. II, 1974 (22 July), p. 122, and (6 August), p. 222.

[96] LSCOR (3rd), vol. I, 1974 (11 July), p. 156.

[97] See above, Chapter I, note 127.

[98] *Ibid.*

[99] The contention of these States is partly based on the argument that such rights are already vested in coastal States under the adjacency criterion of the 1958 Convention on the Continental Shelf, and the theory of 'natural prolongation' put forward by the International Court of Justice in the North Sea Continental Shelf cases, 1969. For the views in support of this approach see, e.g., statements made by the representatives of Australia, Venezuela, the Soviet Union and Indonesia, LSCOR (3rd), vol. II, pp. 146, 150, 152, 160 and 169 respectively. The Declaration of Santo Domingo (A/AC.138/80, 26 July 1972) does not rule out the possibility of a continental shelf extending beyond the 200-mile limit, for, in this concern, it provides that 'in that part of the continental shelf covered by the patrimonial sea, the legal regime provided for this area [that is, the patrimonial sea] shall apply. With respect to the part beyond the patrimonial sea, the regime established for the continental shelf by international law shall apply.'

[100] ICNT, Articles 76 and 82. Article 76 states that 'The Continental Shelf of a coastal state comprises the sea bed and subsoil of the submarine areas that extend beyond its territorial sea throughout the natural prolongation of its land territory to the outer edge of the continental margin, or to a distance of 200 nautical miles from the baselines from which the breadth of the territorial sea is measured where the outer edge of the continental margin does not extend up to that distance'.

[101] See above, Table 1.

[102] On the general question of the interests of shelf-locked States see, e.g., Vladimir Ibler, 'The interests of shelf-locked States and the proposed development of the law of the sea', 11 *Indian J.I.L.* (1971), p. 389.

[103] LSCOR (3rd), vol. I, 1974 (11 July), p. 156.

[104] See statements expressed by Iraq, *ibid.*, vol. II, 1974 (30 July), p. 156, and Iran, *ibid.*, vol. I, 1974 (10 July), p. 172. See also statement made by the representative of Iran at the Asian–African Legal Consultative Committee in 1973,

NOTES

AALCC, *Report of the Fourteenth Session,* New Delhi, January 1973, p. 50, where the Iranian representative stated, *inter alia,* that 'it is tempting to retain the 200-metres isobath criterion for countries endowed with a large shelf. But taking into account the geophysical characteristics as a whole, I think a combination criterion of depth and distance would be suitable for us all'.

[105] LSCOR (3rd), vol. I (12 July 1974), p. 174. Bahrain has concluded continental shelf boundary agreements with both Saudi Arabia and Iran; see Chapter III below.

[106] LSCOR (3rd), vol. II, 1974 (29 July), pp. 148–9. Similar views were expressed by Libya, *ibid.* (26 July), p. 145; Egypt, *ibid.* (29 July), p. 147; Saudi Arabia, LSCOR (3rd), vol. I, 1974 (10 July), p. 144; and Oman, *ibid.* (10 July), p. 152. It might be recalled that at the 1958 conference Lebanon had favoured deletion of the exploitability criterion from the definition of the continental shelf, in the interests of the high seas, LSCOR (1st), vol. VI, pp. 14, 34, 38 and 129. At the same conference Egypt proposed that exclusive rights in the continental shelf should be limited by a fixed distance from the coast, whatever the depth of the sea, in order that consideration be given 'to the desire of countries without a continental shelf'. *Ibid.,* p. 27.

[107] See Chapter III below.
[108] See Chapter IV below.
[109] See above, p. 34.
[110] *North Sea Continental Shelf, Judgement,* I.C.J. Reports, 1969, p. 3.
[111] See Iraq, LSCOR (3rd), vol. I, 1974 (10 July), p. 148, and vol. II, 1974 (30 July), p. 159; Israel, *ibid.,* vol. II, 1974 (26 July), p. 144; Libya, *ibid.,* p. 145, and (5 August), p. 204; Democratic Yemen, *ibid.* (5 August), p. 209; Bahrain, *ibid.,,* vol. I, 1974 (12 July), p. 174; United Arab Emirates, *ibid.* (9 July), p. 141; Iran, *ibid.* (1 July), p. 72; Yemen Arab Republic, *ibid.* (4 July), p. 117; and Kuwait, *ibid.* (11 July), p. 156, and vol. II, 1974 (13 August), p. 273.
[112] ICNT, Article 83 (1).
[113] *Ibid.,* Article 121.
[114] A/Conf.62/C.2/L.42/Rev.1 (13 August 1974).
[115] ICNT, Article 79 (3).
[116] The Iranian government reserved its right to allow or not to allow the laying or maintenance of submarine cables or pipelines on its continental shelf, see *Report on the First United Nations Conference on the Law of the Sea,* Cmnd 584 (November 1958), p. 47.
[117] *State of Multilateral Conventions,* ST/LEG/3.
[118] Iran, LSCOR (3rd), vol. II, 1974 (13 August), p. 273. Similar statements were made by representatives of Denmark, Thailand, Iraq and the German Democratic Republic, *ibid.,* pp. 273–6.
[119] These seas, together with other twenty-two seas, including the Gulf of Aden, the Baltic Sea, the Black Sea, the Caribbean, Hudson's Bay and the South China Sea, are classified by Professor L. M. Alexander as 'semi-enclosed seas'. According to Professor Alexander, for the purposes of analysis, 'a semi-enclosed sea must have an area of at least 50,000 square nautical miles and be a "primary" sea, rather than an arm of a larger semi-enclosed water body. At least 50 per cent of its circumference should be occupied by land, and the width of the connector between the sea and the open ocean must not represent more than 20 per cent of the sea's total circumference.' Professor Alexander envisages that at some future time either of two categories of special regimes might be adopted for the semi-enclosed seas. One type is 'exclusionary', that is, the littoral States would exclude outsiders from certain types of activities within the sea, such as military vessels and potential pollutant; a second category of regime would be 'developmental' in nature, in the sense that all or most of the coastal States on the semi-enclosed sea would join together to invest in improving the environment and the use of the sea's resources.

L. M. Alexander, 'Regionalism and the Law of the Sea: the case of semi-enclosed seas', 2 *Ocean Development and International Law Journal* (1974), p. 151, at pp. 155–7, 159–61.

[120] Iran: *Draft articles on enclosed and semi-enclosed seas*, A/Conf.62/C.2/L.72 (21 August 1974). According to the delegate of Iran, who introduced these draft articles, the draft articles are 'preliminary in nature', LSCOR (3rd), vol. II, 1974 (23 August), p. 295.

[121] Delegate of Iran, *ibid.*, pp. 295–6. In a statement made before the introduction of the Iranian proposals, the representative of Iran referred to the 'Persian Gulf' as a 'semi-enclosed sea' (*ibid.*, p. 273). This demonstrates that the description of an enclosed or a semi-enclosed sea remains highly arbitrary.

[122] LSCOR (3rd), vol. II, 1974 (13 August), p. 273.

[123] Iraq: *Draft articles on enclosed and semi-enclosed seas*, A/Conf.62/C.2/L.71. And Add. 1 and 2 (21 August 1974). Though the title of the draft refers to both enclosed and semi-enclosed seas, there is no reference to or definition in the body of the draft of the former category.

[124] On the ownership of these islands see below, in Chapter III.

[125] LSCOR (3rd), vol. II, 1974 (13 August), p. 276.

[126] *Ibid.*, p. 277.

[127] LSCOR (3rd), vol. I, 1974 (4 July), p. 116.

[128] *Ibid.* (9 July), p. 133.

[129] Soviet delegate, LSCOR (3rd), vol. II, 1974 (13 August), p. 277.

[130] See W. E. Butler, *The Soviet Union and the Law of the Sea* (Baltimore and London, 1971), p. 132.

[131] ICNT, Article 122.

[132] *Ibid.*, Article 130.

[133] See, e.g., statements made by the representatives of France and the Soviet Union, LSCOR (3rd), vol. II, 1974 (13 August), pp. 276 and 277 respectively.

[134] A/6695.

[135] G. A. Res. 2340 (XXII); text in 7 *I.L.M.* (1968), p. 174. See also Goldberg, 'U.N. establishes ad hoc committee to study the use of ocean floor', 58 *Dept. of State Bull.* (1968), p. 125. The ad hoc committee was later converted to a standing committee and eventually into a preparatory committee for the Third Conference, see above, note 3.

[136] This resolution was opposed by most of the technologically developed nations, including the United States, the Soviet Union, the United Kingdom, Japan, France, Italy, Norway and Denmark. Many of these nations doubted the usefulness of a 'freeze' on exploration and exploitation of the sea bed beyond the limits of national jurisdiction. (Of the Middle Eastern States, only Iraq, Jordan, Kuwait, Democratic Yemen and the Yemen Arab Republic voted in favour of the resolution, all the others abstained.) For complete list of voting and views of different countries on the resolution see *Year Book of the United Nations*, 1969, pp. 66–70. In 1972 Kuwait placed before the Sea Bed Committee a new draft decision on a moratorium on exploration and exploitation of the deep sea bed area. Introducing the draft to the Sea Bed Committee on 14 August 1972, on behalf of the twelve sponsors, the Kuwaiti representative explained that in submitting the text his delegation and the other sponsors had been motivated by evidence that certain States were engaged in operational activities in the sea bed area beyond the limits of national jurisdiction, in defiance of the provisions of the moratorium resolution 2574D (XXIV), and the *Declaration of Principles* resolution 2749 (XXV), in addition to the UNCTAD moratorium resolution 52 (III) adopted in Santiago. Statement by delegate of Kuwait, A/AC.138/SR.84, pp. 79–80. The draft resolution was sponsored by Algeria, Brazil, Chile, China, Iraq, Kenya, Kuwait, the Libyan Arab Republic, Mexico, Venezuela, the Yemen Arab Republic and Yugoslavia, A/AC.138/L.11/Rev.1 (9 August 1972). The draft was rejected by many

developed countries and was not adopted. Kuwait and many developing countries have been disturbed particularly by the Bills which were introduced in the United States ninety-second Congress and reintroduced in the ninety-third Congress. The Bills would enable the Government of the United States to issue licences to operate in the international sea bed area to its own nationals and, on a reciprocal basis, to nationals of other States engaged in similar operations. See, e.g., Donald L. Humphreys, 'An international regime for the exploration and exploitation of the resources of the deep sea bed—the United States hard mineral industry position', 5 *N.R.L.* (1972), p. 731; Louis Henkin, 'The changing law of sea-mining', 4 *Annals of International Studies* (1973), p. 281, at pp. 302–4.

[137] For further discussion on the *Declaration of Principles* and its legal effect see, e.g., E. D. Brown, 'The 1973 Conference on the Law of the Sea: the consequences of failure to agree', in L. M. Alexander (ed.), *Law of the Sea: a New Geneva Conference*, Proceedings of the Sixth Annual Conference of the Law of the Sea Institute, University of Rhode Island, 21–24 June 1971 (January 1972), p. 1, especially pp. 9–47; Atwood C. Wolf, 'The U.N. Declaration of Principles Governing the Deep Sea Bed', in N. Rodley and C. Ronning (eds.), *International Law in the Western Hemisphere* (The Hague, 1974), p. 70; Neil Faris, 'The Declaration of Principles Governing the Sea Bed and the Ocean Floor, and the Subsoil Thereof, beyond the Limits of National Jurisdiction, G.A. Res. 2749 (XXV)—an examination of its legal effects', unpublished dissertation submitted for the Diploma in International Law in the University of Cambridge, 1974 (deposited in the Squire Law Library, Cambridge). H. Gary Knight concludes that 'In spite of the overwhelming support for Resolution 2749 in the voting, its value as evidence of customary international law is greatly reduced by the compromise nature of most of its operative provisions'. H. Gary Knight, 'Issues before the Third United Nations Conference on the Law of the Sea', 34 *Louisiana L. Rev.* (1974), p. 155, at p. 162, note 23.

[138] ICNT, Article 1 (1) (2).

[139] For further discussion on the concept of the 'common heritage of mankind' see R. P. Arnold, 'The common heritage of mankind as a legal concept', 9 *Int. Lawyer* (1975), p. 153; Louis Sohn, *The United Nations and the Oceans: Current Issues in the Law of the Sea*, 23 Report, Commission to Study the Organisation of Peace (1973), pp. 11–12; see also references cited in note 137 above.

[140] See Article 9, alternatives A, C, and D, *Draft Articles considered by the Committee at its informal meetings* (Articles 1–21), A/Conf.62/C.1/L.3 (5 August 1974). See also United States of America: *Draft appendix to the Law of the Sea Treaty concerning mineral resources development in the international sea bed area*, A/Conf.62/C.1/L.16 (13 August 1974); Belgium, Denmark, France, Germany (Federal Republic), Italy, Luxembourg, Netherlands, United Kingdom of Great Britain and Northern Ireland: *Working Paper*, A/Conf.62/C.1/L.8 (16 August 1974); and Japan: *Working Paper on Conditions of Exploration and Exploitation*, A/Conf.62/C.1/L.9 (19 August 1974).

[141] The name 'Group of Seventy-seven' was first used at the First United Nations Conference on Trade and Development (UNCTAD) in 1964 to refer to the seventy-seven countries from the developing world. The name is now widely used in United Nations circles, but its numbers are now over 100 developing countries. By 1975 the number of the 'Group of Seventy-seven' was 105. See *Keesing's Contemporary Archives*, 1972, p. 25377, and 1975, pp. 27010 and 27163.

[142] See Article 9, alternative B, *Draft Articles considered by the Committee at its informal meetings* (Articles 1–21), A/Conf.62/C.1/L.3 (5 August 1974). See also *Text on conditions of exploration and exploitation prepared by the Group of Seventy-seven*, A/Conf.62/C.1/L.7 (16 August 1974); *Resolution concerning the Law of the Sea, passed by the Fourth Conference of Heads of State or Government of Seventy-five Non-aligned Countries at Algiers*, 9 September 1973.

NOTES

[143] See statements by the representatives of Kuwait, A/C.1/PV.1780 (25 November 1970), p. 31, and A/AC.138/SC.1/SR.38 (14 March 1972); Iran, A/C.1/PV.1854, pp. 3–5, and A/C.1/PV.1911 and A/AC.138/SC.1/SR.18 (10 August 1971), p. 227; Yemen Arab Republic, A/AC.138/SR.46 (15 March 1971), p. 24; Iraq, A/AC.138/SC.1/SR.7 (23 July 1971), and A/AC.138/SR.55 (22 March 1971), p. 130; Sudan, A/AC.138/SC.1/SR.17; Egypt, A/AC.138/SC.1/SR.20 (13 August 1971); Libya, A/AC.138/SRT.53 (19 March 1971), p. 93.

[144] LSCOR (3rd), vol. II, 1974 (17 July), p. 37.

[145] *Ibid.*, p. 32. In 1971 the delegate of Kuwait in the Sea Bed Committee, in connection with the United States proposal for an 'International Trusteeship Area', said that 'The experience of the oil-producing countries, including Kuwait, with the concession-holding companies revealed only too clearly the dangers of that course'. A/AC.138/SC.1/SR.4 (25 March 1971). At the Caracas session of the Third Conference on the question 'who has jurisdiction over the Area', Kuwait proposed that 'The Authority shall act as the Administrator of a trust for the benefit of mankind as a whole. Its powers shall be coexistence with the regime and shall form an integral part of it.' The proposal, however, has not dealt with the question of who may exploit the area or how the area is to be exploited. A. O. Adede, 'The System for exploitation of the "common heritage of mankind" at the Caracas conference', 69 *A.J.I.L.* (1975), p. 31, at p. 36. The Kuwaiti proposal is contained in *Informal Working Paper* No. C.1/CRP 1 (22 July 1974).

[146] LSCOR (3rd), vol. I, 1974 (1 July), p. 72. Similarly, see statement by the representative of Oman, *ibid.* (10 July), p. 152.

[147] LSCOR (3rd), vol. II, 1974 (17 July), p. 43.

[148] *Ibid.* (27 August), p. 89. See also statement made by delegate of Egypt in April 1975, LSCOR (3rd), vol. IV, 1975 (28 April), p. 67.

[149] For further general discussion on the international regime and authority for the exploration and exploitation of the area beyond national jurisdiction see, e.g., C. F. Amerasinghe, 'Basic principles relating to the international regime of the oceans at the Caracas session of the U.N. Law of the Sea Conference', 6 *J. Mar. L. & Comm.* (1975), p. 213; V. S. Mani, 'Resources of the sea bed beyond national jurisdiction: who shall exploit and how?' 14 *Indian J.I.L.* (1974), p. 245; A. O. Adede, 'The system for exploitation of the "common heritage of mankind" at the Caracas conference', 69 *A.J.I.L.* (1975), p. 31; Johnathan I. Charney, 'The international regime fort the deep sea bed: past conflicts and proposals for progress', 17 *Har. I.L.J.* (1976), p. 1; L. M. Alexander, 'Future regimes: a survey of proposals', in R. Churchill, K. R. Simmonds and Jane Welch (eds.), *New Directions in the Law of the Sea*, vol. III, *op. cit.*, p. 119; Mrs S. K. Kuba, 'The conditions of exploration and exploitation of the sea bed activities in the proposed "area"', 15 *Indian J.I.L.* (1975), p. 216; R. Y. Jennings, 'Jurisdictional adventures at sea—who has jurisdiction over the natural resources of the sea bed?' 4 *N.R.L.* (1971), p. 829, and 'A changing international law of the sea', 31 *C.L.J.* (1972B), p. 32; D. W. Bowett 'Deep sea bed resources: a major challenge', 31 *C.L.J.* (1972B), p. 50; F. M. Auburn, 'The international sea bed area', 20 *I.C.L.Q.* (1971), p. 173; Krishna Rao, 'The legal regime of the sea bed and ocean floor', 9 *Indian J.I.L.* (1969), p. 1; L. F. E. Goldie, 'A general international law doctrine for sea bed regimes', 7 *Intl. Lawyer* (1973), p. 796; Shigeru Oda, 'Towards a new regime for ocean development', 1 *Ocean Development* (1973–74), p. 291.

[150] 'Possible impact of sea bed mineral production in the area beyond national jurisdiction on world markets, with special reference to the problems of developing countries: a preliminary assessment', *Report of the Secretary General*, A/AC.138/36 (28 May 1971).

[151] See A/Conf.62/C.1/L.2 (26 July 1974). This document is a note, prepared by the chairman of the first committee at the Caracas session, containing the major summaries and conclusions of the pertinent documents presented to the conference

in order to assist in the consideration of questions relating to economic implications of sea bed mining. See also report of the Secretary General on the 'Economic significance in terms of sea bed mineral resources of the various limits proposed for national jurisdiction', A/AC.138/87 (June 1973) (this document is summarised by Gunnar G. Schram in 2 *Ocean Management* (1974), p. 249); 'Economic implications of sea bed mining in the international area: report of the Secretary General', A/Conf.62/37 (18 February 1975).

[152] Chairman of the first committee, Mr P. B. Engo, LSCOR (3rd), vol. II (8 August 1974), p. 68.

[153] See, e.g., United States of America, *Working paper on the economic effects of sea bed exploitation*, A/Conf.62/C.1/L.15 (8 August 1974). For further general discussion on the economic implications of deep sea bed exploitation see, e.g., P. Diebold, 'The richness of the sea: minerals', in L. J. Bouchez and L. Kaijen (eds.), *The Future of the Law of the Sea* (The Hague, 1973), p. 51; Giulio Pontecorvo, 'Reflections on the economics of the common heritage of mankind: the organisation of deep-sea mining industry and the expected benefits from resource exploitation', 2 *Ocean Development and International Law Journal* (1974), p. 203.

[154] ICNT, Article 162(3).

[155] Kuwait, LSCOR (3rd), vol. II, 1974 (17 July), p. 32. Similar statements were made by Iraq (*ibid.*, p. 37) and Iran (see above, note 146). During the debate on Resolution 2750 A(XXV), referred to above, in the General Assembly's first committee, the representative of Kuwait, who together with the representatives of Iraq, Lebanon and Libya was among the seventeen members which sponsored this resolution, stated that international commodity agreements such as those concluded within the framework of UNCTAD, had proved to be an effective method of avoiding fluctuation in the prices of raw materials produced on land and in the continental shelf. It was inevitable that the projected international machinery should impose a ceiling on the production of similar resources from the sea bed. This was a matter of vital concern to developing countries, whose economics were still dependent on a limited number of agricultural and mineral commodities. A/AC.1/PV.1780 (25 November 1970), pp. 36–7.

[156] Concerning this, Article 208 of the ICNT provides, *inter alia*, that States shall establish national laws and regulations and take such other measures as may be necessary to prevent, reduce and control pollution of the marine environment from land-based sources. It also says that 'States shall endeavour to harmonise their national policies at the appropriate regional level'. Other provisions deal with the prevention of marine pollution from dumping of wastes and other matter at sea. They provide, *inter alia*, that 'National Laws, regulations and measures shall be no less effective in preventing, reducing and controlling pollution from dumping than global rules and standards'. *Ibid.*, Article 211.

[157] Article 209 of the ICNT suggests that coastal States should establish national laws and regulations and take any other measures as may be necessary 'to prevent, reduce and control pollution of the marine environment arising from or in connexion with sea bed activities, subject to their jurisdiction and from artificial islands, installations and structures under their jurisdiction'. Such laws, regulations and measures 'shall be no less effective than generally accepted international rules, standards and recommended practices and procedures', and States 'shall endeavour to harmonise their national policies at the appropriate regional level'.

[158] In this regard Article 145 of the ICNT proposes that the international authority shall adopt appropriate rules, regulations and procedures for, *inter alia*, the prevention of pollution and contamination, and other hazards to the marine environment and the protection and conservation of the natural resources of the area.

[159] Text in 12 *I.L.M.* (1973), p. 1319.

[160] Text in ST/LEG/Ser.B/16 (1974), p. 464.

[161] Article 212 of the ICNT provides that 'States acting through the competent

international organisation or by general diplomatic conference, shall establish international rules and standards for the prevention, reduction and control of pollution of the marine environment from vessels'. It also proposes that 'States shall establish laws and regulations for the prevention, reduction and control of pollution of the marine environment from vessels flying their flag or vessels of their registry'. In addition, 'coastal states may, in the exercise of their sovereignty within their territorial sea, establish national laws and regulations for the prevention, reduction and control of marine pollution from vessels'. For further general discussion on the question of marine pollution see, e.g., Churchill, Simmonds and Welch (eds.), *New Directions in the Law of the Sea*, Vol. III, *op. cit.*, pp. 73 *et seq.* (Part III—Pollution); M. Waldichuk, 'International approach to the marine pollution problem', 1 *Ocean Management* (1973), p. 211; Aaron L. Danzig 'Marine pollution: a framework for international control', 1 *Ocean Management* (1973) p. 347; E. D. Brown, *The Legal Regime of Hydrospace* (London, 1971), pp. 127 *et seq.*

[162] LSCOR (3rd), vol. I, 1974 (11 July), p. 156.

[163] LSCOR (3rd), vol. II, 1974 (16 July), p. 316.

[164] *Ibid.* See also statements made by delegate of Egypt during the third session of the Third Conference, LSCOR (3rd), vol. IV, 1975 (10 April), p. 91.

[165] LSCOR (3rd), vol. II, 1974 (17 July), pp. 333–4.

[166] See above, pp. 64–66.

[167] Canada, Fiji, Ghana, Guyana, Iceland, India, Iran, New Zealand, the Philippines and Spain: *Draft articles on zonal approach to the preservation of the marine environment*, A/Conf.62/C.3/L.5 (29 July 1974). See also statements made by representatives of Iran, ISCOR (3rd), vol. II, 1974 (5 August), p. 360, and vol. IV, 1975 (10 April), p. 90.

[168] ICNT, Article 247(2).

[169] *Ibid.*, Article 143(1).

[170] ICNT, Article 267(2).

[171] LSCOR (3rd), vol. II, 1974 (18 July), p. 337.

[172] *Ibid.* Similarly see, Egypt, LSCOR (3rd), vol. I, 1974 (1 July), p. 76, and vol. IV, 1975 (7 May), p. 114. See also Kuwait, LSCOR (3rd), vol. I, 1974 (11 July), p. 156.

[173] LSCOR (3rd), vol. II, 1974 (19 July), p. 347.

[174] *Ibid.* Similarly see Lebanon, LSCOR (3rd), vol. I, 1974 (9 July), pp. 135, 136.

[175] LSCOR (3rd), vol. II, 1974 (19 July), p. 350. See also draft articles on scientific research and transfer of technology submitted by Iraq on behalf of the 'Group of Seventy-seven', Iraq: *Revised draft articles on scientific research*, A/Conf.62/C.3/L.13/Rev.2 (21 April 1975); and Iraq: *Revised draft articles on transfer of technology*, A/Conf.62/C.3/L.12/Rev.1 (24 April 1975).

[176] LSCOR (3rd), vol. II, 1974 (19 July), p. 353.

CHAPTER III

[1] J. C. Dewdney, 'Persian Gulf', in 17 *Encyclopaedia Britannica* (1973 edn.), p. 649. See also map 4. About the ports of the 'Persian Gulf', Dewdney writes: 'No part of the Gulf coast is particularly favourable for port development. Natural harbours are rather more common on the Iranian side, but even they have little shelter from the prevailing wind. Bander Abbas, on the Strait of Hormuz, and Bushire are connected by road to the interior. Bandar-e Shahpur, however, is the chief port of Iran. Standing at the head of the Gulf, it is connected to the Iranian rail system. Abadan, forty miles up the Shatt al Arab, is of more recent origin and owes its existence to the oil traffic. Apart from the oil terminal at Al Faw on the

coast, the only other Iraqi port is Basra, located on the inland side of the marsh zone.

'On the Arabian side, ports are of two kinds: the older are small centres of trade, fishing, and pearling; the newer are large oil terminals constructed at points suitable for tanker access. In the first category are Al Manamah (Manama) in Bahrain, Ad Dawhah (Doha) in Qatar, Dhahran (Az Zahran) and Ad Dammam in Saudi Arabia, and Ash Sharigh (Sharjah) and Dubai (Dhubai) in the United Arab Emirates. The new oil terminals are at Mina' al Ahmadi and Mina' 'Abd Allah in Kuwait, Mina' Su'ad (until December 1969 in the neutral zone) and Ras Tanura both in Saudi Arabia, Bahrain, Musay'id in Qatar, and Das Island and Jebel Dannah in the United Arab Emirates.' *Ibid.*, p. 652.

[2] See above, Chapter I, note 172.

[3] Oman borders the Strait of Hormuz, but not the Gulf proper. The major territorial segment of Oman is situated along the shores of the Gulf of Oman and the Arabian Sea. The former has an average depth of 490 m and reaches 3,474 m, whereas the latter has a mean depth of 2,734 m.

[4] 'Before oil was discovered [in the Gulf], many . . . rocks and sand-banks were ownerless—the resort of a few stray fisher-folk and cormorants. Recently, however, there has been great competition to prove ownership and, as in the case of such islands it is often impossible to prove any constructive act of sovereignty in the past, there was at one time an epidemic of establishing on them marks with inscriptions asserting ownership. These were removed as soon as they had been put up. Attempts had been made to convert shoals, which appear only at low tide, into islands by erecting cairns on them.' Sir R. Hay, 'The Persian Gulf States and their boundary problems', 120 *Geographical Journal* (1954), p. 431, at p. 441.

[5] It has been indicated that about 300–400 sea oil wells are in operation in the Arabian Gulf and that about 'one-tenth of the total production of crude oil in the Gulf comes from these sea wells; some of the oilfields have been proved to extend across the boundaries of the jurisdiction of neighbouring or facing States'. Working paper submitted by the Imperial Government of Iran to the International Conference on Marine Pollution, 1973, MP/Conf./C.2/WP.28 (17 October 1973), p. 2.

[6] It has been noted that more than 200 islands are subject to the sovereignty of the United Arab Emirates alone. Delegate of the United Arab Emirates, LSCOR (3rd), vol. I, 1974 (9 July), p. 141. The presence of numerous islands on a continuous continental shelf, as in the case of the Arabian Gulf, creates a difficult problem with reference to the delimitation of continental shelf boundaries. The problem is briefly and clearly described by Miss J. A. Gutteridge in connection with Article 6 of the 1958 Geneva Convention on the Continental Shelf, see J. A. Gutteridge, 'The 1958 Convention on the Continental Shelf', 35 *B.Y.I.L.* (1959), p. 102, at p. 120. Commander R. H. Kennedy, who also stated that the presence of islands may complicate some sea boundary problems and form real difficulties, has referred to some of these difficulties and made interesting suggestions for their solution, see R. H. Kennedy, 'Brief remarks on median lines and lines of equidistance, and on the methods used in their construction' (distributed at First Law of the Sea Conference on 2 April 1958).

[7] The agreement was made on 22 February 1958, and signed and ratified on 26 February 1958. For full text, see reference in note 10 below. See also map 5. Though at the time of signing the agreement Bahrain was still under British protection, the agreement appears to have been concluded without the direct participation of the British government, which at that time did not maintain diplomatic relations with Saudi Arabia. However, in a letter dated 21 April 1958 H.M. Political Agent in Bahrain informed the ruler of Bahrain that Her Majesty's government were prepared formally to waive the provisions of the 1880 and 1892 Special Treaty Relations Agreement between the U.K. and Bahrain in so far as the Bahrain–Saudi Arabia agreement was concerned, and that, so far as H.M. Gov-

NOTES

ernment were concerned, the agreement was thereupon given international validity. E. Lauterpacht, 'Contemporary practice of the United Kingdom in the field of international law', 7 *I.C.L.Q.* (1958), p. 514, at p. 518.

[8] Article 1(1) of the Bahrain–Saudi Arabia agreement.
[9] Article 1 of the Bahrain–Saudi Arabia agreement.
[10] U.S. Department of State, the Geographer, *Continental Shelf Boundary: Bahrain–Saudi Arabia*, Limits in the Seas, No. 12, 10 March 1970, p. 3.
[11] *Ibid.*
[12] *Cf.* agreement between Iran–Saudi Arabia, Abu Dhabi–Qatar and Iran–United Arab Emirates (Dubai), below, pp. 94, 97 and 103.
[13] H. Al-Baharna, *op. cit.*, pp. 308–9.
[14] U.S. Department of State, the Geographer, *Continental Shelf Boundary: Iran–Saudi Arabia*, Limits in the Seas, No. 24, 6 July 1970, p. 4; R. Young, 'Equitable solutions for offshore boundaries: the 1968 Saudi Arabia–Iran agreement', 64 *A.J.I.L.* (1970), p. 152, at p. 153. Iran had claimed Bahrain until 1970. Speaking to press correspondents on 10 March 1958, the Iranian Foreign Minister stated that the Bahrain Islands 'are an indivisible and integral part of Iran' and that, therefore, Iran considered the agreement between Bahrain and Saudi Arabia as 'null and void and with no legal grounds'. As regards its future utilisation he said that 'If any Government or foreign company obtains concessions in accordance with this agreement, or takes any action regarding exploitation and extraction, this act will be considered as an aggressive and illegal one against Iran's territory and rights'. He added that the Iranian government 'reserves its rights as regards the fixing of frontier boundaries and territorial waters and any loss resulting from this agreement'. *M.E.E.D.*, 14 March 1958, p. 2.
[15] See below, p. 100.
[16] D. J. Padwa, 'Submarine boundaries', 9 *I.C.L.Q.* (1960), p. 628, at p. 630.
[17] E. Lauterpacht, 'Contemporary practice of the United Kingdom in the field of international law', 7 *I.C.L.Q.* (1958), p. 514, at p. 519; A. H. Dean, 'The Law of the Sea Conference, 1958–60, and its aftermath', in L. M. Alexander (ed.), *The Law of the Sea* (Ohio State University Press, 1967), p. 244, at p. 251; M. M. Whiteman, 4 *Digest of International Law, op. cit.*, p. 331; R. Young, 'Equitable solutions for offshore boundaries: the 1968 Saudi Arabia–Iran agreement', *op. cit.*, p. 153; E. D. Brown, *The Legal Regime of Hydrospace, op. cit.*, p. 60; U.S. Department of State, the Geographer, *Continental Shelf Boundary: Iran–Saudi Arabia, op. cit.*, p. 5.
[18] See *North Sea Continental Shelf, Judgement*, I.C.J. Reports, 1969, p. 3, at p. 39.
[19] *Ibid.*
[20] *Ibid.*, p. 53.
[21] *Ibid.*, pp. 53, 54.
[22] *Ibid.*, pp. 37, 49.
[23] *Ibid.*, pp. 36, 37.
[24] See *ibid.*, para. 79, p. 45.
[25] Such suggestion has been made by Northcutt Ely, 'Sea bed boundaries between coastal States: the effect to be given islets as "special circumstances"', 6 *International Lawyer* (1972), p. 219, at p. 224.
[26] *North Sea Continental Shelf, op. cit.*, p. 46.
[27] It has been observed that this treatment of these islands involved 'a desire for simplification of alignment ... The result was a simpler boundary.' R. D. Hodgson, *Islands: Normal and Special Circumstances* (Research Study, the Geographer, Bureau of Intelligence and Research, U.S. Department of State, RGES-3, 10 December 1973), p. 60.
[28] See, e.g., H. Lauterpacht, 'Sovereignty over submarine areas', 27 *B.Y.I.L.* (1950), p. 376, at p. 410; M. W. Mouton, 'The continental shelf', 85 *Hague Recueil*

(1954–I), p. 420; D. J. Padwa, 'Submarine boundaries', *op. cit.*, p. 654; Aaron L. Shalowitz, II *Shore and Sea Boundaries* (U.S. Department of Commerce, 1964), p. 232, note 55; M. McDougal and W. Burke, *The Public Order of the Oceans* (New Haven, 1962), pp. 436, 437; J. A. C. Gutteridge, 'The 1958 Geneva Convention on the Continental Shelf', 35 *B.Y.I.L.* (1959), p. 102, at p. 120; Lars Delin, 'Shall islands be taken into account when drawing the median line according to Art. 6 of the Convention on the Continental Shelf?', 41 *Nordish Tidsskrift for International Ret.* (1971), p. 205, especially pp. 214, 218.

[29] *North Sea Continental Shelf, op. cit.*, p. 36.

[30] *Ibid.*, pp. 53, 54.

[31] *Ibid.*, p. 52.

[32] Separate opinion, *ibid.*, p. 149. To the same effect see D. J. Padwa, 'Submarine boundaries', *op. cit.*, p. 645.

[33] E. D. Brown, *The Legal Regime of Hydrospace, op. cit.*, p. 67 where it is also stated that 'It goes without saying that the parties [to a delimitation] are free, on a consensual basis, to make whatever provision they please for the economic or convenient exploitation of a common deposit, either by joint exploitation or otherwise.' See further W. T. Onorato, 'Apportionment of an international common petroleum deposit', 17 *I.C.L.Q.* (1968), p. 85.

[34] *Cf.* agreements on the continental shelf concluded between Iran and Qatar, Abu Dhabi and Qatar, Bahrain and Iran, Iran and the United Arab Emirates (Dubai), and Iran and Oman, below, pp. 91, 95 and 103.

[35] See M. W. Mouton, 'The continental shelf', *op. cit.*, pp. 420–2. See also remarks made at the 1958 Conference on the Law of the Sea by Commander Kennedy (united Kingdom) and Mr Carbajal (Uruguay), LSCOR (1st), vol. VI, pp. 93 and 95 respectively.

[36] The agreement was signed at Tehran, 24 October 1968, and ratified on 29 January 1969. For full text see reference in note 43 below. See also map 6.

[37] R. Young, 'Equitable solutions for offshore boundaries: the 1968 Saudi Arabia–Iran agreement', *op. cit.*, p. 152.

[38] *M.E.E.S.*, No. 33, 21 June 1963.

[39] *Petroleum Legislation, Basic Oil Laws and Concession Contracts—Middle East*, vol. I—1959, p. Iran B–1.

[40] Pre-announcement of National Iranian Oil Company concerning Offshore Exploration, No. 228/15, 1 April 1958; see *ibid.*, Suppl. No. 5, p. Iran A–1.

[41] *Ibid.*, vol. I, p. Saudi Arabia A–53.

[42] *M.E.E.D.*, vol. XII, No. 35, 30 August, p. 837.

[43] U.S. Department of State, the Geographer, *Continental Shelf Boundary: Iran–Saudi Arabia*, Limits in the Seas, No. 24, 6 July 1970, p. 3.

[44] *Ibid.*

[45] R. Young, 'Equitable solutions for offshore boundaries: the 1968 Saudi Arabia–Iran agreement', *op. cit.*, p. 155.

[46] U.S. Department of State, the Geographer, *Continental Shelf Boundary: Iran–Saudi Arabia, op. cit.*, p. 4, note 4.

[47] Article 1, Iran–Saudi Arabia agreement.

[48] U.S. Department of State, the Geographer, *Continental Shelf Boundary: Iran–Saudi Arabia, op. cit.*, p. 4.

[49] See *ibid.*, p. 5, Table 1, 'Physical characteristics of the Iran–Saudi Arabia continental shelf boundary'.

[50] See above, p. 88 and below, p. 100.

[51] This solution, following suggestions made by R. H. Kennedy (see above, note 6), is similar to the one employed by Italy and Yugoslavia concerning offshore islands in the Adriatic Sea; see U.S. Department of State, the Geographer, *Continental Shelf Boundary: Italy–Yugoslavia, Limits in the Seas*, No. 9, 20 February 1970. The same solution has also been employed in later agreements in the Ara-

bian Gulf area between Abu Dhabi and Qatar (with regard to the Abu Dhabi island of Dayyinah) and Iran and the United Arab Emirates (Dubai) (with regard to the Iranian island of Sirri). See below, pp. 97, 103. On the Iranian view regarding the question of islands and its relevance to continental shelf delimitation as expressed at the 1958 Geneva Conference on the Law of the Sea; see above, in Chapter I.

[52] R. Young, 'Equitable solutions for offshore boundaries: the 1968 Saudi Arabia–Iran agreement', *op. cit.*, p. 153.

[53] See map 6.

[54] U.S. Department of State, the Geographer, *Continental Shelf Boundary: Iran–Saudi Arabia, op. cit.*, p. 5. For the geographical location of Kharg see map 12. Elsewhere it is indicated that Kharg (Khark) lies about twenty-five or thirty miles from the Iranian mainland. It is also stated that Kharg gained importance as a result of the expansion of Iran's oil industry on the shore and offshore, and it is now considered the world's largest oil export terminal. Iran's chief oilfields are connected with the island terminal through four 30 in. diameter pipelines laid along the sea bottom. R. K. Ramazani, *The Persian Gulf: Iran's Role* (Charlottesville, Va., 1972), p. 75; Alvin J. Cottrell, 'Iran, the Arabs and the Persian Gulf', XVII *Orbis* (1973), p. 978, at p. 980.

[55] U.S. Department of State, the Geographer, *Continental Shelf Boundary: Iran–Saudi Arabia, op. cit.*, p. 3, note 1.

[56] This interpretation of Article 4 is made in two exchanges of notes which accompanied the principal agreement and were dated the same day as the agreement. For full text of the two notes see *Petroleum Legislation, Basic Oil Laws and Concession Contracts—Middle East,* Suppl. No. XXXIII, pp. Saudi Arabia A–4 to A–11.

[57] See above, p. 91.

[58] R. D. Hodgson, *Islands: Normal and Special Circumstances, op. cit.*, pp. 61–2. It has been stated that the Iran–Saudi Arabia boundary line 'was actually drawn near the coast of Saudi Arabia in favour of Iran's claim. This was hardly a geographical median line, but it represented a solution based on the economic realities of equitable distribution of resources.' Shigeru Oda, 'International law of the resources of the sea', 127 *Hague Recueil* (1969–II), p. 355, at p. 445.

[59] See map 6.

[60] This decree is considered above in Chapter I.

[61] For text see reference in note 68 below. See also map 7.

[62] *Lorimer's Gazetteer of the Persian Gulf, op. cit.*, vol. II, p. 617.

[63] *Ibid.* Lorimer adds that 'the pearl divers and fishermen both of Qatar and of Trucial Oman are in the habit of resorting to [Halul], and, so far as can be learnt, no exclusive or preferential rights are claimed by any of the classes who use it, or by any territorial chief.'

[64] Sir R. Hay, *The Persian Gulf States* (Washington, D.C., 1959), p. 115.

[65] The British government, with the approval of Abu Dhabi and Qatar, chose Mr Charles Goult, former British Political Agent in Bahrain, and Professor J. N. D. Anderson, Professor of Islamic Law in the University of London, to examine and report on the shaikhdoms' claims over the disputed islands. Reference to the findings of the experts on the issue was made in the *Daily Telegraph,* 26 April 1962. But no mention was made of the names of the other two smaller islands referred to above. The award has not been published by the British government. For commentary on the historical and legal bases of the experts verdict see H. M. Al-Baharna, *The Arabian Gulf States* (2nd edn., Beirut, Lebanon, 1975), p. 304.

[66] The decree was issued on 10 March 1962. For text see Qatar government's *Official Gazette,* No. 2, 27 Shawwal 1381, corresponding to 2 April 1962.

[67] Articles 1 and 2 of the Qatar–Abu Dhabi agreement. See also map 7. Daiyinah is 'An island off the coast of the Abu Dhabi principality in Trucial Oman near its western end, and about twenty-nine miles north by east of Dalmah island. Daiyinah

NOTES

is low, flat and sandy, bearing scanty grass; the highest part is a black detached rock at the north end—rising about 9 ft above high water. The length of the island is 1½ miles from north-north-west to south-south-east and the breadth about 600 yards. A fair anchorage in a Shamal exists close to the south of Daiyinah, Daiyinah belongs to the Shaikh of Abu Dhabi.' *Lorimer's Gazeteer of the Persian Gulf, op. cit.,* vol. II, p. 361.

[68] U.S. Department of State, the Geographer, *Continental Shelf Boundary: Abu Dhabi–Qatar, Limits in the Seas,* No. 18, 29 May 1970, p. 2.

[69] See map 7. As shown in Chapter I above, Abu Dhabi and Qatar still adhere to the three-mile limit. The treatment accorded to Dayyinah is similar to that given to the islands of Farsi and Al'Arabiyah in the agreement concluded between Iran and Saudi Arabia. See above, pp. 92 and 94.

[70] The treatment accorded to Dayyinah has been categorised as an illustration of the situation where islands, generally small and uninhabited and falling in the rock and islet categories, situated in the middle of restricted water bodies, i.e. semi-enclosed or enclosed seas, are disregarded in the construction of equidistance shelf boundaries because they have the effect of 'displacing (assuming a position near mid-point or an opposite situation) the boundary approximately a quarter of the width of the body of water, they may continue to influence a displacement along the water body's length for a maximum distance equal to the width of the body. The inequity would be obvious'. R. D. Hodgson, *Islands: Normal and Special Circumstances, op. cit.,* pp. 58–9. See also above, p. 90.

[71] U.S. Department of State, the Geographer, *Continental Shelf Boundary: Abu Dhabi–Qatar, op. cit.,* p. 3.

[72] It has been observed that the co-ordinates given in the agreement (point D) place the intersection point 1·25 nautical miles inside the actual three-mile limit. Therefore the correct location of the landward terminus of the continental shelf boundary should be point D', as reflected on map 7. *Ibid.*

[73] *Ibid.,* p. 2. See also map 8.

[74] It is pointed out that the geographical co-ordinates in the agreement do not locate point B precisely on the al-Bunduq oil well, but rather at a site 0·5 nautical miles south-west. This discrepancy, it is added, could be the result of map distortion. *Ibid.,* p. 2. See also map 7.

[75] *Ibid.,* p. 3.

[76] *North Sea Continental Shelf, Judgement, op. cit.*

[77] *Ibid.,* p. 52, para. 99.

[78] See map 5.

[79] M. W. Mouton, 'The continental shelf', *op. cit.,* p. 421.

[80] For full text see references indicated in Appendix I.

[81] See below, p. 103.

[82] H. Al Baharna, *The Arabian Gulf States, op. cit.,* p. 303. See also *M.E.E.S.,* No. 32, 10 June 1966.

[83] The four agreements were signed on 20 September 1969, 17 June 1971, 13 August 1975 and 25 July 1974 respectively; and ratified on 10 May 1970, 14 May 1972, 15 March 1975 (by Iran only) and 28 May 1975 respectively. For full texts see respectively references in notes 85, 89, 93 and 100 below. See also maps 8–11. According to the Geographer of the U.S. Department of State, on 30 September 1975 the agreement between Iran and the United Arab Emirates had not yet been ratified by the latter party. U.S. Department of State, the Geographer, *Continental Shelf Boundary: Iran–United Arab Emirates (Dubai), Limits in the Seas,* No. 63, 30 September 1975, p. 1.

[84] The agreement between Bahrain and Iran, originally initialled during the official visit of the ruler of Bahrain to Iran during December 1970, came shortly after Iran's decision to relinquish its long-standing claim to Bahrain. The Iranian claim had consistently overshadowed the relations between the two countries and

because of it Bahrain was excluded from the negotiations held towards the end of 1965 between Iran and the United Kingdom for the delimitation of the submarine boundaries between Iran and the Trucial States, which were then under British protection. Iran has also protested to Saudi Arabia and to Britain over the conclusion of the 1958 continental shelf agreement between Saudi Arabia and Bahrain. See above, note 14. Iran dropped its historic claim to Bahrain in 1970, upon the recommendations made by Vittorio Winspeare Guicciardi—the U.N. Secretary General's personal representative—who paid a twenty-day fact-finding visit to Bahrain during April 1970. His report was accepted by the U.N. Security Council on 11 May 1970. Britain and Iran, the two outside parties who were most intimately involved, had agreed in advance to accept the findings and to act on them. In his report Mr Winspeare said that the overwhelming majority of the people of Bahrain wish to gain recognition of their identity in a fully independent and sovereign State. Bahrain is now fully independent and has joined the United Nations and the Arab League. See 7 *U.N. Monthly Chronicle* (1970), No. 6, p. 3; H. M. Al-Baharna, 'The fact-finding mission of the United Nations Secretary General and the settlement of the Bahrain–Iran dispute, May 1970', 22 *I.C.L.Q.* (1970), p. 541, and *The Arabian Gulf States, op. cit.*, pp. 315–26; E. Gordon, 'Resolution of the Bahrain dispute', 65 *A.J.I.L.* (1971), p. 561.

[85] U.S. Department of State, the Geographer, *Continental Shelf Boundary: Iran–Qatar, Limits in the Seas*, No. 25, 9 July 1970, p. 2.

[86] See maps 8 and 9.

[87] See map 8.

[88] See, U.S. Department of State, the Geographer, *Continental Shelf Boundary: Iran–Qatar, op. cit.*, p. 3, 'Physical characteristics of the Iran–Qatar continental shelf boundary'.

[89] U.S. Department of State, the Geographer, *Continental Shelf Boundary: Bahrain–Iran, Limits in the Seas*, No. 58, 13 September 1974, p. 3.

[90] See above, p. 88.

[91] See U.S. Department of State, the Geographer, *Continental Shelf Boundary: Bahrain–Iran, op. cit.*, pp. 3, 4. See also map 9.

[92] H. Al-Baharna, *The Arabian Gulf States, op. cit.*, pp. 355–6, where it is also disclosed that prior to the conclusion of the agreement between Bahrain and Iran experts from the British Foreign Office had advised the Bahrain government that the Bahrain–Iran shelf boundary should basically be drawn on the principle of equidistance from both coasts, using mainland low-water as the baseline. Accordingly the Foreign Office experts suggested that al Muharrag should be considered as part of the Bahraini mainland. As regards 'other islands or offshore islands', so the suggestion ran, they should not be given effect in drawing the Bahrain–Iran median line.

[93] U.S. Department of State, the Geographer, *Continental Shelf Boundary: Iran–United Arab Emirates (Dubai), Limits in the Seas*, No. 63, 30 September 1975, p. 3.

[94] See above, p. 99. See also map 10.

[95] In 1963–64 a series of sea boundaries between the Trucial States were determined by the British government, as protecting power, and proposed to the rulers of the Trucial States. The sea boundary between Dubai and Sharjah was defined as a line at 90° to the coastline, running between Manzer and Abu Hail (Abu Hayl). The starting point on the coast of this line was then disputed by Dubai though accepted by Sharjah. Dubai claimed a starting point two miles farther north-east. See also map 10.

[96] See below, p. 127.

[97] The ruler of Abu Dhabi claims that the island of Sir Bani Yas constitutes part of Abu Dhabi's coastline. The ruler felt strongly about his claim and in 1966 announced his willingness 'to go to arbitration with the Persians on this matter'.

NOTES

M.E.E.S., No. 14, 4 February 1966. More recently, however, it was reported that an offshore boundary line between Abu Dhabi and Iran was initialled in 1971. R. Young, 'The Persian Gulf', in R. Churchill, K. R. Simmonds and Jane Welch (eds.), *New Directions in the Law of the Sea*, vol. III (London and New York, 1973), p. 231, at p. 233.

[98] See map 9.

[99] See above, pp. 92 and 97.

[100] U.S. Department of State, the Geographer, *Continental Shelf Boundary: Iran–Oman, Limits in the Seas*, No. 67, 1 January 1976, p. 4. See also map 11.

[101] See U.S. Department of State, the Geographer, *Continental Shelf Boundary: Iran–Oman, op. cit.*, pp. 6–7, 'Physical characteristics of the Iran–Oman continental shelf boundary'. See also map 11.

[102] U.S. Department of State, the Geographer, *Continental Shelf Boundary: Iran–Oman, op. cit.*, p. 5.

[103] See map 11.

[104] *North Sea Continental Shelf, Judgement, op. cit.*, pp. 51–2, para. 97.

[105] For texts of these agreements see ST/LEG/Ser.B/15 (April 1970), pp. 775, 778 and 755 respectively. See also the agreement of 3 March 1966 between the United Kingdom and Norway relating to the delimitation of the continental shelf between the two countries, *ibid.*, p. 781.

[106] See 'Agreement between the State of Kuwait and the Kingdom of Saudi Arabia relating to Partition of the Neutral Zone', (hereinafter referred to as the 'Partition Agreement'). The agreement was signed on 7 July 1965 and ratified by Saudi Arabia and Kuwait on 11 July 1965 and 25 July 1965 respectively; 4 *I.L.M.* (1965), pp. 1134–7; ST/LEG/Ser.B/15 (April 1970), p. 760. See also M. T. El-Ghoneimy, 'The legal status of the Saudi–Kuwaiti neutral zone', 15 *I.C.L.Q.* (1966), p. 690; S. M. Hosni, 'The partition of the neutral zone', 60 *A.J.I.L.* (1966), p. 735.

[107] *Supplemental Agreement approving the Demarcation of the Median Line of the Saudi–Kuwait Neutral Zone*, ratified by Saudi Arabia under Royal Decree No. M/28 of 12/11/1389H. and by Kuwait under an Amiri decree dated 21 January 1970. For English translation of the text see *M.E.E.S.*, Supplement to No. 32, 5 June 1970; *Petroleum Legislation, Basic Oil Laws and Concession Contracts: Middle East*, Supp. No. XXVII, p. Kuwait–Saudi Arabia A–0.

[108] S. M. Hosni, *op. cit.*, p. 743.

[109] R. Young, 'The Persian Gulf', *op. cit.*, p. 233. In 1964 it was reported that 'A permanent government committee is to be established to govern oil production from Safaniya field (in Saudi Arabia's offshore) and Khafji (Neutral Zone field of Arabian Oil Co.). The two fields are tapping the same oil reservoir, according to [Saudi] Oil Minister Yamani...'; *Petroleum Legislation, Basic Oil Laws and Concession Contracts: Middle East Report*, vol. 2, No. 1, January 1964 (review of 1963), p. 8.

[110] The question concerning the offshore boundary between Iran and the partitioned zone is considered separately below.

[111] M. T. El-Ghoneimy, *op. cit.*, p. 711; S. M. Hosni, *op. cit.*, p. 740.

[112] *Lorimer's Gazetteer of the Persian Gulf, op. cit.*, vol. II, p. 1061. The full statement of *Lorimer* is quoted below at note 160. For geographical location of the two islands see map 12.

[113] E. H. Brown, *The Saudi Arabia–Kuwait Neutral Zone* (1963), p. 107.

[114] M. T. El-Ghoneimy, *op. cit.*, pp. 706–11.

[115] Kuwait, Ministry of Finance and Oil, General Oil Affairs, *The Oil of Kuwait–Facts and Figures* (3rd edn., August 1970), p. 46.

[116] El-Ghoneimy, *op. cit.*, p. 706; *Petroleum Legislation, Basic Oil Laws and Concession Contracts, Middle East Report, Review and Summary of Year 1964*, pp. 7–8.

NOTES

[117] *The Oil of Kuwait—Facts and Figures, op. cit.,* p. 48.

[118] See M. El-Sahily and A. F. El-Massaeed, *A Collection of Laws and Legislations of the State of Kuwait,* (1963), p. 7.

[119] 'Explanatory Note' attached to Kuwaiti decree of 1967 concerning the determination of the extent of the territorial waters of the State of Kuwait.

[120] See *M.E.E.S.,* 13 December 1963 and 14 February 1964; *Petroleum Legislation, Basic Oil Laws and Concession Contracts, Middle East Report,* vol. 2, No. 1, January 1964, pp. 5–6.

[121] *M.E.E.S.,* Supplement to vol. VI, No. 11, 18 January 1963.

[122] A. F. Kassim, 'Conflicting claims in the Persian Gulf States', IV *Journal of Law and Economic Development* (1969), p. 282, at p. 328.

[123] Article 2 of the agreement defines the concession area to include 'all that offshore area outside the territorial waters limit of the Saudi Arabia–Kuwait Neutral Zone over which the Government has or may hereafter, during the period of this agreement, have right, title or interest. It is understood that such offshore area extends to the delimitation in the middle of both mean low water coastlines of the Saudi Arabia–Kuwait Neutral Zone and of Iran on the Persian Gulf and that such offshore area shall include shoals, reefs, waters, wholly or partly submerged lands and submarine areas, sea bed and subsoil.' For full text of the agreement see *Petroleum Legislation, Basic Oil Laws and Concession Contracts, Middle East,* Supp. No. III, p. Kuwait A–1.

[124] E. H. Brown, *op. cit.,* p. 108.

[125] *Ibid.*

[126] See above, p. 108.

[127] See *M.E.E.S.,* No. 36, 8 July and No. 37, 15 July 1966.

[128] See above, note 54.

[129] See above, pp. 109–10. See also map 12.

[130] For text of NIOC pre-announcement see *Petroleum Legislation, Basic Oil Laws and Concession Contracts, Middle East,* Suppl No. 5, p. Iran A–1.

[131] *M.E.E.S.,* No. 27, 10 May 1963.

[132] *M.E.E.S.,* No. 31, 7 June, No. 32, 14 June, and No. 33, 21 June 1963.

[133] *Ibid.*

[134] *Ibid.*

[135] *Ibid.,* No. 51, 15 October 1963. Towards the end of 1966 it was reported that the Kuwait government has authorised Kuwait Shell to proceed with its drilling operations in the disputed area, apparently after the failure of the trilateral talks between the governments of Saudi Arabia, Kuwait and Iran at Tehran on 27 August 1966 concerning their respective continental shelf boundaries. These talks were first started in Copenhagen on 10 July 1966. See *M.E.E.D.,* No. 28, 22 July 1966, pp. 333–4, No. 32, 2 September 1966, p. 391, and No. 47, 16 December 1966, p. 639.

[136] For an account of these negotiations see *M.E.E.S.,* No. 51, 25 October 1963, No. 3, 22 November 1963, No. 24, 17 April 1964, No. 20, 18 March 1966, No. 22, 1 April 1966, No. 28, 22 July 1966, No. 32, 2 September 1966, and No. 38, 17 July 1970. See also *Petroleum Legislation, Basic Oil Laws and Concession Contracts, Middle East Report,* vol. 2, No. 1, January 1964, pp. 1–2; *Petroleum Legislation, Basic Oil Laws and Concession Contracts, Oil and Gas Report, Year's Summary, 1965,* p. 6.

[137] See map 12. Kharg was given half effect in delimiting the offshore boundary between Iran and Saudi Arabia; see above, p. 94. Failka (Failaka) or Failakah, 'To British mariners formerly known as "Phelechi", from the local pronunciation, which is Failachah. An island seven miles in length with a maximum breadth of three miles, lying on the north side of the entrance to Kuwait Bay; its western end, the nearest to Kuwait Town, is about ten miles east-north-east of Ras-al-Ardh,

NOTES

while its northern end is about seven miles south-east of the mouth of Khor-as-Sabiyah.' *Lorimer's Gazetteer of the Persian Gulf, op. cit.,* vol. II, p. 512.

[138] *M.E.E.S.*, 16 February 1968.

[139] *Information concerning the Sovereignty over Iraq's Territorial Waters and its Continental Shelf,* provided by the Deputy Permanent Representative of Iraq to the United Nations in a *note verbale* of 15 May 1973, ST/LEG/Ser.B/18 (New York, 1976), p. 25.

[140] *M.E.E.S.*, No. 38, 17 July 1970, p. 7.

[141] *Ibid.*

[142] D. J. Padwa, 'Submarine boundaries', *op. cit.,* p. 644, note 52.

[143] For texts of the 1937 treaty and the document of abrogation and other relevant documents see 8 *I.L.M.* (1969), pp. 478–92. On the dispute which erupted between Iran and Iraq in 1969 see *Keesing's Contemporary Archives,* 1969, p. 23544A. For comments and views concerning the Shutt al-Arab frontier see *Facts about the Shatt-al-Arab issue,* a booklet issued by Iran in 1969; *Comment on the Iranian Claims concerning the Iraqi-Iranian Frontier Treaty of 1937 and the Legal Status of the Frontier between the two Countries,* a booklet issued by the Iraqi Ministry of Foreign Affairs (Baghdad, July 1969); Khalid Al-izzi, *The Shatt al-Arab River Dispute in Terms of Law* (Baghdad, 1972). See also E. Lauterpacht, 'River boundaries: legal aspects of the Shatt Al-Arab frontier', 9 *I.C.L.Q.* (1960), p. 208. The Shutt al-Arab, which gives access to the Iraqi port of Basra and several Iranian ports, especially Abadan and Khorramshahr, 'is a large river combining the waters of the Rivers Tigris and Euphrates, which enter the head of the Persian Gulf. Near its mouth, its eastern bank forms the boundary between Iraq to the west and Iran to the east . . . The amount of coastline at the river mouth appertaining to Iraq and Iran is about equally divided . . .' R. H. Kennedy, 'A brief study of bays', *op. cit.,* p. 209.

[144] See 'Iran–Iraq: treaty on international borders and good neighbourly relations', XIV *I.L.M.* (1975), p. 1133. For an account of the meetings and negotiations which preceded the signing of the agreement see, e.g., *Keesing's Contemporary Archives,* 1975, 27053A and 27284A (27285).

[145] *M.E.E.S.*, 20 June 1975, p. 2; *Quarterly Economic Review,* Iraq, No. 3, 1975, p. 3.

[146] As shown below, reference to these indications or unilateral actions was made in the pleadings in the North Sea Continental Shelf cases, 1969, among other reasons because the geographical configuration at the northern end of the Arabian Gulf to some extent resembles the situation in that area of the North Sea between Denmark, the Federal Republic of Germany and the Netherlands, in the sense that 'a number of States on the same coastline are grouped around a sharp curve or bend of it'. *North Sea Continental Shelf, Judgement,* I.C.J. Reports, 1969, p. 3, at p. 45, para. 79.

[147] For full text see *Petroleum Legislation, Basic Oil Laws and Concession Contracts–Middle East,* Suppl. No. III, p. Kuwait A-1. See also map 12.

[148] *North Sea Continental Shelf cases,* I.C.J. Pleadings, 1968, vol. I, p. 439. It is presumed that the Federal Republic meant to refer to the 'land frontier' between Kuwait and Iraq. According to the Iraq-Kuwait Convention on Boundaries, 1932, the boundary between Kuwait and Iraq ends in Khor Abdullah on the coast and has not been prolonged offshore. See maps 12 and 14.

[149] *Ibid.,* pp. 500–1.

[150] See below, p. 117.

[151] See map 13.

[152] 'Information concerning the Boundary of the Continental Shelf', provided by the Permanent Mission of the State of Kuwait to the United Nations in a *note verbale* of 12 July 1971, ST/LEG/Ser.B/16 (New York, 1974), p. 152.

NOTES

[153] *North Sea Continental Shelf cases*, I.C.J. Pleadings, 1968, vol. I, pp. 501, 574. See also map 13.

[154] *Ibid.*, p. 501, para. 72. In its supplementary proclamation concerning the continental shelf dated 10 April 1958 the Iraqi government declared 'its adherence to international practice in this respect and to the principles of equidistance . . .'. In his separate opinion in the North Sea Continental Shelf cases, Judge Ammoun declined to accept the view expressed in the rejoinder, noting that 'the declaration of Iraq was made on 10 April 1958, i.e. before the signature of the Geneva Convention; the reference to Article 6 thereof is consequently out of place. The Iraqi declaration can nevertheless be taken into consideration, like the Truman Proclamation, as starting a trend towards a new custom.' *North Sea Continental Shelf, Judgement*, I.C.J. Reports, 1969, p. 3, at p. 129.

[155] *Ibid.*

[156] *Ibid.*, pp. 37 (para. 58), 49 (para. 89).

[157] *Ibid.*, pp. 53, 54.

[158] On this question see also H. Al-Baharna, *The Arabian Gulf States, op. cit.*, p. 330.

[159] See map 14.

[160] *Lorimer's Gazetteer of the Persian Gulf, op. cit.*, vol. II, p. 1061.

[161] The contents of the letter of the Iraqi Prime Minister were also indicated in a letter, No. 5405, dated 19 April 1923, from His Excellency the High Commissioner in Iraq to the Political Agent in Kuwait. Arabic texts of this letter, the letters of the Prime Minister of Iraq and the ruler of Kuwait, and of the 1963 agreement were acquired by courtesy of the Kuwait Foreign Ministry. For English translation of the 1932 letters of the Prime Minister of Iraq and the ruler of Kuwait see H.M. al-Baharna, *The Arabian Gulf States, op. cit.*, p. 383.

[162] For a summary of this agreement see *Petroleum Legislation, Basic Oil Laws and Concession Contracts–Middle East*, vol. II, p. Kuwait A–1.

[163] See *The Oil of Kuwait: Facts and Figures, op. cit.*, p. 76.

[164] *M.E.E.S.*, No. 22, 23 March 1973. The occupation of the Kuwait frontier post by Iraqi troops ended on 5 April 1973. *The Times*, 6 April 1973.

[165] *M.E.E.S.*, No. 22, 23 March 1973.

[166] *Ibid.*, No. 23, 30 March 1973, where it was also stated that the Iraqi draft agreement provided, *inter alia*, for the granting by Kuwait to Iraq of a ninty-nine year lease allowing the Iraqis the right to build, operate, maintain and manage one or more pipelines in Kuwait territory and to construct a deep-water terminal in the Kuwaiti offshore together with the ancillary installations needed for this purpose.

[167] *M.E.E.S.*, No. 22, 23 March 1973. The official statements were issued on 20 March 1973 by the Kuwait government and the National Assembly of Kuwait.

[168] *Ibid.*, No. 24, 6 April 1973.

[169] See *M.E.E.S.*, No. 44, 24 August 1973; *Daily News* (Kuwait), 8 April 1973; *Alrai Alam* (Arabic daily, Kuwait), 23 August 1973.

[170] *Al-Hawadess* (Arabic weekly, Beirut), No. 981, 29 August 1975, pp. 21–2. According to earlier reports Kuwait was willing to lease certain territory, which was described to be in a commanding position opposite the expanding Iraqi port of Umm Qasr, to Iraq to enable it to assure for itself the approaches to the latter port, in return for water-bearing Iraqi territory adjacent to its dry interior. *The Guardian*, 17 May 1975; *Keesing's Contemporary Archives*, 1975, 27284A (p. 27285).

[171] *Keesing's Contemporary Archives*, 1975, 27284A (p. 27285).

[172] See, *M.E.E.S.*, No. 6, December 1965. See also *Petroleum Legislation, Basic Oil Laws and Concession Contracts, Middle East, Oil and Gas Reports, Year's Summary, 1965*, p. 13.

[173] H. Al-Bahrana, *The Arabian Gulf States, op. cit.*, p. 302.

[174] On the Zubarah dispute see H. Al-Bahrana, *The Arabian Gulf States, op. cit.*, p. 247; J. B. Kelly, 'Sovereignty and jurisdiction in Eastern Arabia', 34 *Interna-*

tional Affairs (1958), p. 16, at pp. 17–8.

[175] Sir R. Hay, *The Persian Gulf States, op. cit.*, p. 88.

[176] H. Al-Bahrana, *The Arabian Gulf States, op. cit.*, p. 303.

[177] *An-Nahar* (Arabic daily, Beirut), 22 September 1974.

[178] *Al-Hawadess* (Arabic weekly, Beirut), No. 939, 8 November 1974.

[179] *Ibid.*

[180] See map 4.

[181] 'Sharjah's memorandum to Arab States on Abu Musa', 23 August 1971, *M.E.E.S.*, No. 6, 3 December 1971. For Arabic text of the memorandum see *Al-Anwar* (daily, Beirut), 30 November 1971.

[182] *M.E.E.S.*, No. 14, 4 February 1966. See also Sir R. Hay, *The Persian Gulf States, op. cit.*, p. 148.

[183] *M.E.E.S., loc. cit.*

[184] 'Sharjah's memorandum to Arab States on Abu Musa', *op. cit.*

[185] See *Buttes Gas & Oil Company* v. *Armand Hammer and Occidental Petroleum Corporation* and *Occidental Petroleum Company* v. *Buttes Gas & Oil Company and John Boreta, Judgement,* 5 December 1974 (Court of Appeal) (hereinafter 'Buttes v. Occidental (C.A.)').

[186] For full text of the two letters see 'Trucial States Mediation', *op. cit.*, vol. II, documents, Nos. 43 and 49, pp. 121 and 128 respectively.

[187] 'Sharjah's memorandum to Arab States on Abu Musa', *op. cit.*

[188] *Ibid.* Abu Musa was included in the concession area granted in 1969 by Sharjah to Buttes Gas & Oil Company, see below. According to Lorimer 'The maritime possessions of Sharjah are the islands of Bu Musa and Sir Bu Na'air, which are associated with the district of Sharjah proper; and the island of Tumb, and probably that of Nabiyu Tumb, which are attached to Ras-al-Khaimah district'. *Lorimer's Gazetteer of the Persian Gulf, op. cit.*, vol. I, p. 1758. Similarly Sir R. Hay states that 'The islands of Bu Musa and Sir bu Na'ir, about forty-five and sixty-five miles from Sharjah respectively, are included in the Shaikhdom [of Sharjah]'. Sir R. Hay, *The Persian Gulf States, op. cit.*, pp. 123–4. See also 'Sharjah's title to Abu Musa', Interim Report to His Highness the Ruler of Sharjah, prepared by Coward Chance & Associates, London, 23 July 1971 (unpublished). For excerpts from the report see H. Al-Baharna, *The Arabian Gulf States, op. cit.*, pp. 343–5.

[189] For the full text of the agreement between Sharjah and Buttes Gas & Oil Company see *Petroleum Legislation, Basic Oil Laws and Concession Contracts–Middle East,* Suppl. No. 44, p. 44.

[190] In a letter dated 16 May 1970 addressed by H.M. Political Agent in Dubai to the ruler of Sharjah it was stated, *inter alia,* that 'Until a few weeks ago none of us had had any reason to suppose that the breadth of the territorial waters of Sharjah was other than it has always been, that is to say three nautical miles. Her Majesty's Government and each of the Persian Gulf States in special treaty relation with the United Kingdom have always worked on this basis in awarding oil concessions, fixing operating limits and so on. Sea charts were drawn up on this basis. And, in particular, the Concession Agreements which you concluded with Buttes Gas and Oil Company last year and which His Highness the Ruler of Umm al-Qaiwain concluded with Occidental of Umm al-Qaiwain must have proceeded on the same basis and were certainly approved by Her Majesty's Government on that basis. As a matter of international law, it is not right for a state simply to extend its territorial waters regardless of the consequences on its neighbours: if there are agreements or settled legal situations with neighbours, or if vested rights have been acquired in the area, account must be taken of these agreements, situations and rights. In the case of Sharjah, for example, there is a particular problem arising in relation to Umm al-Qaiwain, where there is an agreed sea boundary of 1964 between Sharjah and Umm al-Qaiwain and approved by Her Majesty's Government on the basis of that sea boundary. It is not right simply to ignore the existence of the sea boundary and

NOTES

the Concession Area of Occidental of Umm al-Qaiwain.' 'Trucial States Mediation', *op. cit.*, vol. II, Document No. 37, p. 105. According to the 1964 sea boundary agreement between Sharjah and Umm al-Qaiwain, 'the sea bed boundary between Sharjah and Umm al-Qaiwain shall be a line starting from a point on the coast near the site of the dead well Miradar Bu Salaf and going out to the sea on a bearing of 312°'. The boundary was agreed on by parallel instruments signed by the rulers of Umm al-Qaiwain and Sharjah. For the text of the two instruments see *ibid.*, Documents No. 11 and 12, pp. 13 and 14 respectively. It has been observed that in establishing the sea boundary between Sharjah and Umm al-Qaiwain the equidistance principle was applied. Full weight, however, was given to the island of Abu Musa, and the boundary line therefore 'followed the three-mile territorial water limits of Abu Musa where it intersected those limits'. Letter dated 21 May 1970 from Mr M. A. Holding of the Arabian Department, Foreign and Commonwealth Office, to Mr W. H. Smith, manager of Buttes Gas & Oil Company, Sharjah's oil concessionaire. For full text see *ibid.*, Document No. 39, p. 110.

[191] See *M.E.E.S.*, No. 32, 5 June 1970, p. 2.

[192] *Sunday Times*, 31 May 1970, where it was also reported that on 29 May the police chief of Sharjah served a notice on Occidental considering that any drilling operations in the disputed site would be treated as an act of trespass.

[193] *Quarterly Economic Review, The Arabian Peninsula and Jordan*; No. 3, 1970, where it was also stated that 'it seems that British intervention came only after considerable pressure had been applied by Iran ... Iran feels that Abu Musa and the two Tumb islands should be ceded to it following its generous abandonment of its claim to Bahrain'. See also writ issued in the High Court of Justice between Occidental of Umm al-Qaiwain Inc and Lt George S. Pearson and others, 'Trucial States Mediation', *op. cit.*, vol. II, Document No. 45, p. 123.

[194] See *M.E.E.S.*, No. 41, 7 August 1970, p. 5.

[195] 'Trucial States Mediation', *op. cit.*, vol. I, pp. 13, 40, 77–80.

[196] *Ibid.*, pp. 51–93. Sharjah's decrees on the territorial sea are considered in Chapter I above.

[197] *M.E.E.S.*, vol. XV, No. 6, 3 December 1971, p. 2.

[198] *Quarterly Economic Review*, 'The Arabian peninsula: shaikhdoms and republics', No. 2 (1972), p. 20. See also *M.E.E.S.*, 28 April 1972.

[199] *Occidental Petroleum Corp.* v. *Buttes Gas & Oil Co.*, 331 F. Suppl 92 (C.D. Cal. 1971). See also 12 *Virginia Journal of International Law*, No. 3, April 1972, p. 413; 7 *Texas International Law Journal*, No. 2, winter 1972, p. 247.

[200] *Occidental Petroleum Corp.* v. *Buttes Gas & Oil Co.*, 461 F. 2nd 1261 (1972).

[201] 409 US. 950, 34 L, Ed. 2d. 221 (1972). See also *M.E.E.S.*, 27 October 1972.

[202] *Petroleum Times*, volume 79, Number 2011, September 5, 1975, p. 33.

[203] *Buttes Gas & Oil Company* v. *Armand Hammer and Occidental Petroleum Corporation, Occidental Petroleum Corporation* v. *Buttes Gas & Oil Company and John Boreta, Judgement*, 31 May 1974 (Queen's Bench Division) [1975] Q.B. 557.

[204] *Buttes Gas & Oil Company* v. *Armand Hammer and Occidental Petroleum Corporation, Occidental Petroleum Corporation* v. *Buttes Gas & Oil Company and John Boreta, Judgement*, 5 December 1974 (Court of Appeal). See also *The Times*, 6 December 1974.

[205] See *M.E.E.S.*, No. 6, 3 December 1971, p. 4. See also statement on the 'Gulf' made by the Foreign Secretary in the House of Commons on 6 December 1971, 827 *H.C. Deb.* (5th Series), col. 945, 6 December 1971; 827 *H.C. Deb.*, Written Answers, col. 189, 3 December 1971; *Keesing's Contemporary Archives*, 1971–72, 25010A. For text of the memorandum, the correspondence relating to confirmation and acceptance of the memorandum exchanged between Sharjah and Iran through the British Foreign Secretary, and the correspondence relating to the memorandum exchanged between National Iranian Oil Company and Buttes Gas & Oil Company, see Appendix VII.

NOTES

[206] For full text of Iranian Premier's statement on Abu Musa and the two Tumbs see *FBIS, Daily Report, Middle East and Africa,* v, No. 230 (30 November 1971). The question of the two Tumbs is discussed separately below. The Iranian landing of troops on the islands was criticised by a number of Arab States. The then ruler of Sharjah, Shaikh Khaled Ibn Muhammed al-Qasimi, was attacked by Kuwait for what it called his 'compromise formula over Abu Musa', *Quarterly Economic Review, Arabian Peninsula: Shaikhdoms and Republics,* Review No. 4, 1971, p. 9. In an official statement Iraq declared that the Iranian occupation of the islands would constitute 'a grave threat to peace and international navigation in the whole area'. On 30 November 1971 Iraq decided to break off diplomatic relations with both Iran and Britain—with Iran in protest at what was described as 'flagrant aggression in collusion with Britain', and with Britain on the grounds that that country had the obligation to preserve the 'Arab character' of the islands. *Keesing's Contemporary Archives,* 1971–72, 25010A. On 9 December 1971 the Iraqi representative told the United Nations Security Council that 'the alleged agreement between Iran and the Sheikh of Al-Sharjah regarding the island of Abu Musa is not valid for a number of reasons. It was concluded when the Sheikh was bound by the terms of the exclusive Agreement of 1892 with the United Kingdom and had no power to "enter into any agreement or correspondence with any Power other than the British Government" ... It was concluded under duress.' *SCOR*, Twenty-sixth Year, 1971, 1610th meeting: 10 December 1971, para. 105, p. 10. Libya announced the nationalisation of British Petroleum (BP) properties in that country, allegedly in retaliation for Britain's failure to resist the Iranian move. *Ibid.,* para. 237, p. 20. In a statement issued on 2 December 1971 the Council of Ministers of the United Arab Emirates criticised the Iranian landing and said that the UAE 'repudiates the principle of the use of force, rejects Iran's occupation of a part of the cherished Arab homeland, and advocates the need to respect legitimate rights and discuss any difference that may occur among states through internationally agreed methods'. *Arab Reports and Records,* 1971, p. 627. In a statement Umm al-Qaiwain demanded the cancellation of Sharjah's agreement with Iran on the grounds that the Sharjah authorities were not competent to sign such an agreement. *M.E.E.S.,* No. 6, 3 December 1971, p. 2.

[207] After the Iranian landing on Abu Musa and the Tumb islands it was reported that the Iranians had made the first step in an attempt to control all the traffic in the Gulf by naval gun emplacements on Abu Musa and Greater Tumb from which they made spot radio checks on passing vessels. *Newsweek,* 21 May 1973.

[208] See the correspondence between the National Iranian Oil Company and Buttes Gas & Oil Company, Appendix VI(c). For text of the agreement between Sharjah and Buttes see *Petroleum Legislation, Basic Oil Laws and Concession Contracts–Middle East,* Suppl. No. 44, p. 44.

[209] See 827 *H.C. Deb.* (5th series), Written Answers, col. 189, 3 December 1971; *Keesing's Contemporary Archives,* 1971–72, 25010A.

[210] It has been observed that the memorandum makes no provision for the use of Abu Musa's coast as a baseline for a median line against either the Arabian or Iranian coast. Northcutt Ely, 'Sea bed boundaries between coastal States: the effect to be given to islets as "special circumstances"', *op. cit.,* p. 230.

[211] See above, note 206.

[212] *M.E.E.S.,* No. 15, 5 February 1972, p. 4.

[213] H. Al-Baharna, *The Arabian Gulf States, op. cit.,* p. 348.

[214] See map 4.

[215] According to *Lorimer,* 'Tunb, in English formerly "Tomb", an island in the Persian Gulf, lying twelve miles off the south-west of Qishm island and forty-six miles north-west of Jazirat-al Hamra, which is the nearest point on the coast of Trucial Oman. Tunb belongs to the Sheikh of Sharjah, and is connected with the Ras al-Khaimah District of his principality.' Tunb (Nabiy or Nabi) , 'An island in

NOTES

the Persian Gulf eight miles west of the island of Tunb . . . The island is uninhabited, the ownership is presumably determined by that of Tunb.' *Lorimer's Gazetteer of the Persian Gulf,* vol. I, *op. cit.,* pp. 1908–9. Similarly Sir R. Hay states that 'The islands of Tamb and Nabiyu, or little Tamb, are under the rule of Ras al-Khaimah, from which they are about sixty miles distant. The main island contains a lighthouse manned by the Persian Gulf Lighting Service and a village where the representative of the Ruler resides.' Sir R. Hay, *The Persian Gulf States, op. cit.,* p. 126. It may be observed also that the two Tumbs were specifically included in the concession area granted by the government of Sharjah to Vital Exploration B.V. of the Netherlands under the agreement signed on 23 May 1973. For full text see *Petroleum Legislation, Basic Oil Laws and Concession Contracts—Middle East,* Suppl. No. 42, p. 2.

[216] E.g. see Sir R. Hay, *The Persian Gulf States, op. cit.,* p. 148.

[217] See statements by Secretary of State for Foreign and Commonwealth Affairs (Sir Alec Douglas Home), 827 *H.C. Deb.,* cols. 945 *et seq.,* 6 December 1971; United Kingdom Representative, *SCOR,* Twenty-sixth Year, 1971, 1610th meeting, 9 December 1971, para. 228, p. 20.

[218] *Ibid.*

[219] Representative of Iran, *SCOR,* Twenty-sixth Year, 1971, 1610th meeting, 9 December 1971, paras. 212, 215, p. 18.

[220] See above, note 193, and below, note 228.

[221] Letter to the President of the Security Council dated 3 December 1971, S/10409, printed in *SCOR,* Twenty-sixth Year, 1971, Supplement for October, November and December 1971, p. 78.

[222] *SCOR,* Twenty-sixth Year, 1610th meeting, 9 December 1971, para. 266, p. 23.

[223] *Ibid.,* para. 271.

[224] *Ibid.,* para. 101, p. 9. In an editorial in *The Times* it was stated that 'Iraq . . . argued that Britain had guaranteed to preserve the "Arab character" of the [Tumb] islands and was guilty of collusion with Iran's "flagrant aggression". This was denied by the Foreign Office, but was arguably true in spirit if not in the letter, since the neighbouring island of Abu Musa was ceded to Iran by Sharjah with British approval, and Britain repeatedly urged the Ruler of Ras al-Khaimah to settle his dispute on the same lines, warning him that Iran would seize the islands in any case.' *The Times,* 10 April 1974.

[225] *SCOR,* Twenty-sixth Year, 1971, 1610th meeting, 9 December 1971, para. 134, 135, p. 12.

[226] On 8 January 1972 the Iranian Foreign Minister announced that Iran had 'absolutely no more territorial claims' in the Gulf and would not use its strategic position to block transit in the Gulf. 26 *Middle East Journal* (1972), p. 167.

[227] Article 2(4) of the Charter of the United Nations reads: '4. All Members shall refrain in their international relations from the threat or use of force against the territorial integrity or political independence of any State, or in any other manner inconsistent with the purposes of the United Nations'. As to the effect of modern law on territorial acquisition by use or threat of force see R. Y. Jennings, *The Acquisition of Territory in International Law* (Manchester University Press, 1963).

[228] *The Economist,* 31 October 1970. Similarly the Prime Minister of Iran is reported to have stated that 'Iran needed these islands [Abu Musa and the Tumbs] for "its security and prosperity", a general goal for whose attainment Iran would fight with all its might should it fail to settle this problem by peaceful means'. Rouhallah K. Ramazani, *The Persian Gulf: Iran's Role, op. cit.,* p. 60. For further similar statements by Iranian officials see *Keesing's Contemporary Archives,* 1971–72, 25010A.

[229] For further discussion on the question of the Tumbs and Abu Musa islands see H. M. Al-Baharna, *The Arabian Gulf States, op. cit.,* pp. 339–48; Mohammed Aziz

Shukri, *The Problem of the Islands in the Arabian Gulf and International Law* (in Arabic, 1972); Rouhallah K. Ramazani, *The Persian Gulf: Iran's Role, op. cit.,* pp. 56–68. It has recently been reported that Iran has proposed to withdraw from the islands of Abu Musa and the Tumbs and that the Iranian proposal has already been conveyed to a number of Arab States. See *New Horizon* (London), vol. 3, No. 29, 28 August–3 September 1976, p. 1, quoting *As-Siyasah* (Arabic daily, Kuwait). On 31 March 1979 officials of the new Iranian regime expressed the intention of returning the three islands to their Arab owners. See *As-Siyasah*, 1 April 1979.

[230] It may be recalled that Article 6 of the Geneva convention stipulates that the delimitation of the boundary of the continental shelf, where it is shared between opposite or adjacent States, is to be determined, in the first place, by agreement between these States, but in the absence of agreement, or unless another boundary line is justified by 'special circumstances' the boundary is the median line or the line of equidistance between the baselines of territorial seas. It may be recalled also that in the North Sea Continental Shelf cases, 1969, the International Court found that the use of the equidistance method of delimitation was not obligatory as between the parties because it was not a mandatory Rule of customary international law. *North Sea Continental Shelf, Judgement,* I.C.J. Reports, 1969, p. 3, at pp. 46, 53.

[231] *North Sea Continental Shelf, Judgement, op. cit.*
[232] *Ibid.,* p. 53, para. 101.
[233] *Ibid.,* p. 52, para. 99.

CHAPTER IV

[1] International Association of Democratic Lawyers, *The Middle East Conflict, Notes and Documents,* 1915–67 (Belgium, 1967), p. 113.

[2] See map 15.

[3] 'The depths in the Gulf of 'Akabah are greater than those in the Gulf of Suez [the north-western fringe of the Red Sea], no bottom being found at 130 fathoms in the former; the shores are steep too. The bottom of the Gulf of 'Akabah is a continuation of the valley in which lie the Dead Sea and river Jordan, both of which are much more below the level of the Mediterranean.' British Admiralty, *Red Sea Pilot* (2nd edn., 1873), p. 133.

[4] R. H. Kennedy, 'A brief geographical and hydrographical study of bays and estuaries the coasts of which belong to different States', in LSCOR (1st), vol. I, Preparatory Documents, Doc. No. 12, p. 198 (A/Conf.13/15), at p. 208.

[5] The only islets inside the gulf are Humaidha, off the Saudi coast, and the Egyptian island of Pharoun (Gezirat Firoun in Arabic), both close inshore, the former off the eastern side, twenty and a half miles from the head of the gulf, and the latter off the western side, seven and a half miles from the head.

[6] As to the question of sovereignty over these two main islands see below, p. 137.

[7] For detailed information concerning islets and dangers in the entrance of the Gulf of Aqaba see British Admiralty, Hydrographic Department, *Red Sea and Gulf of Aden Pilot* (11th edn., 1967), p. 286.

[8] Charles B. Selak, 'A consideration of the legal status of the Gulf of Aqaba', 52 *A.J.I.L.* (1958), p. 660, at 662. For further historical literature regarding the Gulf of Aqaba see, e.g., M. Burhan Hammad, 'The right of passage in the Gulf of Aqaba', 15 *R.E.D.I.* (1959) p. 118, especially pp. 123–8; Commander Malcolm W. Cagle, 'The Gulf of Aqaba—Trigger for conflict', 85 *U.S. Naval Institute Proceedings,* January 1959, p. 75, especially pp. 76–7; Alexander Melamid, 'The political geography of the Gulf of Aqaba', 47 *Annals of the Association of American Geographers* (1957), p. 231; Walter H. Dixon, 'The Gulf of Aqaba: history, geography and law', unpublished Ph.D. thesis, Johns Hopkins University, 1970; Naval Intelligence Division, British Admiralty, *Palestine and Transjordan,* Geographical

NOTES

handbook, series B.R. 514 (December 1943), pp. 521–4, 'The port of Akaba and the adjacent coasts of Palestine and Transjordan'.

[9] Before 1965 only about four miles of the Gulf's coastline were in Jordan's territory, but in accordance with the 1965 border agreement signed between Jordan and Saudi Arabia, Jordan's coastline was lengthened to about fifteen miles in return for territory lying between two Saudi villages farther east. Saudi Arabia and Jordan also agreed to share equally any oil or other natural resources that might be found in the future in the exchanged areas. See 'Agreement for the Determination of Boundaries between the Hashemite Kingdom of Jordan and the Kingdom of Saudi Arabia', XXII *Middle East Journal* (1968), p. 346.

[10] This chapter is not the place for a full discussion of Israeli disputed statehood or of the position of Israel on the Gulf of Aqaba. In one view, Israel has no right to any part of the coast of the gulf, so that on this view there is really no issue. However, for the sake of analysis of Israel's arguments, one must assume that Israel is a coastal State on the gulf, and it is for this purpose only that the assumption is made in this chapter.

[11] This is in accordance with the 'Modification of Egyptian Decree on Territorial Waters', Presidential Decree No. 180, 17 February 1958; 'Territorial Waters Law' of Israel, 23 October 1956; Jordanian 'Fisheries Act No. 25', 2 December 1943; and 'Royal Decree No. 33 (concerning the Territorial Waters of the Kingdom of Saudi Arabia', 16 February 1958, respectively. See further discussion in Chapter I above.

[12] See L. M. Bloomfield, *Egypt, Israel and the Gulf of Aqaba in International Law*, (Toronto, 1957), p. 4.

[13] 42 *U.N.T.S.*, No. 654, p. 251.

[14] *Ibid.*, No. 656, p. 303.

[15] About the occupation of Umm Rashrash, Kenneth Love writes: 'The Palestine war stopped with Arab grievances unredressed and Israeli geographical objectives unfulfilled. Thus there were motives on both sides for the renewals of the war that came in 1956 and 1967. One of the bones of contention in all three rounds of the war was the Gulf of Aqaba. Israel, in fact, did not acquire her foothold there, which later became the port of Eilat, until after the end of the first round. Israel and Egypt accepted a cease-fire on 7 January 1949. They began armistice talks on the Island of Rhodes on 12 January but did not conclude the armistice until 24 February, by which time Israel still had not reached Eilat. 'After the fighting had ceased,' Ben-Gurion reminded the Knesset in 1957, 'our forces were unable to reach Eilat because this was a death trap, being a narrow triangle whose sides were occupied by enemies. Only after we signed an armistice with Egypt and ensured ourselves of one free flank were we able to send the Israel Defence Forces to occupy the Gulf of Eilat without shedding one drop of blood.' Actually, it was not until after the Jordanian delegation had also come to Rhodes for the next set of truce parleys that Israel was able to dispatch two columns southward with tongue-in-cheek orders to "defend yourselves all the way to Eilat".' Kenneth Love, *Suez: the Twice-fought War* (London, 1970), p. 42.

[16] Cablegram from the United Nations Acting Mediator on Palestine to the Security Council, dated 11 March 1949; see SCOR Fourth year, 1949, Supplement for March 1949, pp. 41–4 (Document S/1285).

[17] *Ibid.* In 1948 the Security Council of the United Nations adopted several resolutions regarding the situation in Palestine and calling for a truce. In Resolution 61(1948) of 4 November 1948 the Security Council called upon the governments, *inter alia*, '(i) To withdraw those of their forces which have advanced beyond the positions held on 14 October, the Acting Mediator being authorised to establish provisional lines beyond which no movement of troops shall take place'. *Resolutions and Decisions of the Security Council, 1948, SCOR,* Third year, 1948, pp. 13–31.

NOTES

[18] Article II(2). A similar provision is contained in Article V(2) of the Egyptian–Israeli armistice agreement of 24 February 1949, about which the late Secretary General Dag Hammarskjold in a report to the General Assembly noted: '10. Article V of the General Armistice Agreement between Egypt and Israel of 24 February 1949 provides that the armistice line established in article VI "is not to be construed in any sense as a political or territorial boundary, and is delineated without prejudice to the rights, claims, and positions of either party to the Armistice as regards ultimate settlement of the Palestine Question". It goes on to say that "the basic purpose of the Armistice Demarcation Line is to delineate the line beyond which the armed forces of the respective parties shall not move . . .". '11. Although the armistice line thus does not create any new rights for the parties on either side, it resulted in a *de facto* situation by leaving the "control" (see article VII) of the territory in the hands of the Government, the military forces of which were there in accordance with the stipulations of the Armistice. Control in this case obviously must be considered as including administration and security.' Document A/3512 (24 January 1957), in *GAOR*, Eleventh session, 1956–57, Annexes, Agenda item 66, p. 47, at p. 48.

[19] Charles B. Selak, *op. cit.*, p. 697.

[20] The text is quoted in, L. M. Bloomfield, *op. cit.*, p. 9. Arabic text published in *Al-Ahram* (daily newspaper, Cairo), 24 May 1967, p. 7. Excerpts from the Egyptian *aide-mémoire* were contained in an *aide-mémoire* handed to the Israeli ambassador on 11 February 1957 by the United States Secretary of State, J. F. Dulles; 36 *Dept. of State Bull.* (1957), p. 392.

[21] *SCOR,* Ninth year, 1954, 659th meeting, para. 132, p. 25, and para. 60, p. 10.

[22] Charles B. Selak, *op. cit.,* p. 666, where it was also stated that 'Egypt does not appear to have questioned this Saudi claim of sovereignty'.

[23] 'Memorandum registering the Saudi Arabia Government's legal and historical rights in the Straits of Tiran and the Gulf of Aqaba', A/3575 (15 April 1957).

[24] This was stated in a meeting of the Egyptian Society of International Law in 1967 for the discussion of the 'Problem of the Gulf of Aqaba and the Straits of Tiran', 23 *R.E.D.I.* (1967), Arabic part, pp. 34, 39 and 43. In 1957 Paul A. Porter, a former U.S. representative on the United Nations Palestine Conciliation Commission, wrote: 'In law the status of Tiran and Sanafir is undetermined. Unoccupied since medieval times, no evidence of sovereignty by any power in modern times exists. Geographically, they appear as an offshoot from the Saudi Arabian coastline. Not until April 1957 did Saudi Arabia make formal claim to them. Nor is there any evidence that these islands ever belonged to Egypt.' Paul A. Porter, *The Gulf of Aqaba: an International Waterway—its Significance to International Trade* (Washington, D.C., 1957), p. 2.

[25] Carl F. Salens, 'Gulf of Aqaba and Straits of Tiran—troubled waters', 94 *U.S. Naval Institute Proceedings,* December 1968, p. 54, at p. 57, where it was also stated that 'while the U.S. Government did not recognise the validity of the Egyptian position or the Egyptian instructions for notification of passage through the Straits of Tiran, these instructions were printed in the *Sailing Directions for the Red Sea and the Gulf of Aden* issued by the U.S. Hydrographic Office as instructions to U.S. masters and shipping companies. And presumably ships complied with these instructions on many occasions.'

[26] The letters, exchanged between the British ambassador in Cairo and the Egyptian Minister for Foreign Affairs on 29 July 1951 and 30 July 1951 respectively, were read by the delegate of Egypt into the records of the Security Council on 29 May 1967. *SCOR,* Twenty-second year, 1967, 1343rd meeting, 29 May 1967, para. 102, pp. 9–10.

[27] Secretary of State for Foreign Affairs, 491 *H.C. Deb.* (5th Ser.), 30 July 1951, col. 976. When asked in the House of Commons late in February 1956 'why Her Majesty's Government continue to acquiesce in an arrangement under which Brit-

ish ship owners are required to notify the Egyptian Government of their intention to sail their ships to the Red Sea port of Eilat', the Secretary of State for Foreign Affairs, Selwyn Lloyd, replied: 'Her Majesty's Government have never accepted the contention of the Egyptian Government that they are entitled at the present time to belligerent rights with regard to shipping going to the Gulf of Aqaba. They have, however, accepted these arrangements, initiated by the right hon. gentlemen opposite, on practical grounds preceding a wider settlement.' 549 *H.C. Deb.* (5th Ser.), 22 February 1956, col. 362. For further comments made in the House of Commons about the Anglo-Egyptian arrangement see M. M. Whiteman, 4 *Digest of International Law* (U.S. Department of State Publication 7825, April 1965), pp. 479–80. See also comments by British delegate in the Security Council, *SCOR*, Ninth year, 1954, 663rd meeting, 25 March 1954, para. 29.

[28] See 'The *Empire Roche* incident', in *Documents on International Affairs, 1951* (Royal Institute of International Affairs, London), p. 448.

[29] M. Burhan Hammad, *op. cit.*, p. 120.

[30] 'Notice to Mariners No. 40' of 1 October 1955. See L. M. Bloomfield, *op. cit.*, p. 15.

[31] Commander Malcom W. Gagle, *op. cit.*, p. 79.

[32] *Ibid.*

[33] 'Ports and Lighthouses Administration Circular to Shipping No. 4 of 1955'. This Egyptian circular, together with a circular issued by the United States Navy Hydrographic Office on 29 October 1955, 'Notice to Mariners No. 44', based upon the Egyptian circular, were circulated on 5 June 1957 by the Department of State to United States shipping companies in the Red Sea area. 37 *Dept. of State Bull.* (1957), pp. 112–3. As to the regulations imposed by Egypt regarding air traffic over the Gulf of Aqaba see L. M. Bloomfield, *op. cit.*, p. 10.

[34] See L. M. Bloomfield, *op. cit.*, chapter 3, 'Incidents arising out of the Egyptian regulations'.

[35] On the Sinai campaign see, e.g., Robert R. Bowie, *Suez, 1956: International Crisis and the Role of the Law* (London, 1974).

[36] *Egypt's Unlawful Blockade of the Gulf of Aqaba,* a background paper issued by the Israeli Ministry for Foreign Affairs, Information Division (1967), p. 5.

[37] For text see *GAOR*, Eleventh Session, 1956–57, Supplement No. 17 (A/3752), p. 62. See also Walid Abi-Mershed, *Israeli Withdrawal from Sinai* (Institute for Palestine Studies, Beirut).

[38] 42 *U.N.T.S.*, No. 654, p. 251.

[39] *Special Report of the Secretary General*, A/6669 (1967), p. 1. This document and others relating to the same matter are published as Doc. A/6730 and Add. 1–3 in *GAOR*, Fifth Emergency Special Session, Annexes, 17 June–18 September 1967. For comments on the acceptance of the Secretary General to withdraw UNEF from Egypt see, e.g., Rosalyn Higgins, *United Nations Peacekeeping, 1946–67*, vol. I, *The Middle East* (London, 1969), chapter 9; 'The June war: the United Nations and legal background', 3 *Journal of Contemporary History* (1968), p. 253; D. W. Bowett, 'The United Nations and peaceful settlement', in *International Disputes: the Legal Aspects* (London, 1972), p. 201; Tandon, 'UNEF, War', 22 *Int. Organisation* (1968), p. 529; N. Ache, 'The termination of the mandate of the United Nations Emergency Force, dissertation submitted for the Diploma in International Law in the University of Cambridge, 1969 (Squire Law Library, Cambridge). See also discussion in the Security Council, *SCOR*, Twenty-second year, 1967, 1343rd meeting, 29 May 1967.

[40] *New York Times,* 23 May 1967, p. 1. See also *Sunday Times,* 28 May 1967, p. 11. For further details see *Keesing's Contemporary Archives,* 1967–68, pp. 22063–103; Arthur Lall, *The UN and the Middle East Crisis, 1967* (New York and London, 1968). For a selection of readings and documents on the Arab–Israeli conflict and international law see John Norton Moore (ed.), *The Arab–Israeli*

NOTES

Conflict, vols. I–III (Princeton, N.J., 1974). For further discussions on the announcement of the President of Egypt on 22 May 1967 and on the incident involving the Israeli destroyer *Eilat* which took place on 21 October 1967 see D. P. O'Connell, *The Influence of Law on Sea Power, op. cit.,* pp. 110–13 and pp. 127–9 respectively.

[41] The partial withdrawal of Israeli forces from Egyptian territories in accordance with the 1975 agreement between Egypt and Israel has not affected this position. For text of the agreement see *The Times,* 3 September 1975.

[42] The controversy was discussed in the Security Council in February and March 1954, and in May and June 1967. It was also discussed in the General Assembly during its eleventh session in 1956–57, and again during its Fifth Emergency Special Session in 1967.

[43] Delegate of Egypt, *SCOR,* Twenty-second year, 1967, 1343rd meeting, 29 May 1967, para. 78, p. 7.

[44] See, e.g., *ibid.*; Delegate of Egypt, *SCOR,* Ninth year, 1954, 661st meeting, 12 March 1954, and 662nd meeting, 23 March 1954; *GAOR,* Fourteenth session, Sixth Committee, 644th meeting, 2 December 1959, p. 232. Similarly see statements expressed by Saudi Arabia and Jordan, *GAOR,* Fourteenth session, 1959, Sixth Committee: Legal Questions, 643rd and 644th meetings 30 November and 2 December 1959, and 646th meeting, 4 December 1959 respectively. See also *Memorandum registering the Saudi Arabia Government's Legal and historical rights in the Straits of Tiran and the Gulf of Aqaba,* letter dated 12 April 1957 from the permanent representative of Saudi Arabia to the United Nations, addressed to the Secretary General (A/3575, 5 April 1957).

[45] Delegate of Egypt, *SCOR,* Twenty-second year, 1967, 1343rd meeting, 29 May 1967, paras. 87 and 92.

[46] *Ibid.,* para. 78.

[47] *Republic of El Salvador* v. *Republic of Nicaragua, Central American Court of Justice,* opinion and discussion of the Court, 11 *A.J.I.L.* (1917), p. 644.

[48] *Ibid.,* p. 693. This case is considered further, below, in this chapter.

[49] See delegate of Egypt, *SCOR,* Twenty-second year, 1967, 1343rd meeting, 29 May 1967, paras. 80–7.

[50] *The Palestine Question,* Seminar of Arab Jurists on Palestine, Algiers, 22–27 July 1967 (Institute for Palestine Affairs, Beirut, 1968), p. 164. This view has also been expressed in two documents, produced in Arabic, submitted to the Committee of Arab Experts on the Law of the Sea during its meetings in Cairo in 1972 and 1973. One is document No. N/9/6/370, 9 July 1972, submitted by Iraq, the other is a study of 'The enclosed and semi-enclosed seas' prepared by the delegation of Qatar in the committee.

[51] Egypt, *SCOR,* Twenty-second year, 1967, 1343rd meeting, 29 May 1967, paras. 87 and 92.

[52] *Ibid.,* paras. 93 *et seq.*

[53] For text see above, note 20.

[54] Egypt, *SCOR,* Twenty-second year, 1967, 1343rd meeting, 29 May 1967, para. 102, p. 9. This Egyptian view finds support in a statement by Professor R. R. Baxter, who, with regard to the Egyptian *aide-mémoire,* expresses the opinion that 'In light of what international practice has hitherto been established, this statement did not constitute the assumption of any responsibility to grant to enemy vessels or to permit the free passage of vessels carrying contraband'. R. R. Baxter, *The Law of International Waterways, with Particular Regard to Interoceanic Canals* (Harvard, 1964) (hereinafter, 'R. R. Baxter, *The Law of International Waterways*'), p. 24.

[55] Announcement of the President of Egypt on 22 May 1967. *New York Times,* 23 May 1967, p. 1.

[56] Statement read to the press by the Egyptian press attaché in Washington on 29 May 1967 in connection with the announcement of the Egyptian President on 22

May 1967. Quoted in C. Ernest Dawn, 'The Egyptian remilitarisation of Sinai, May 1967', 3 *Journal of Contemporary History* (1968), p. 201, at p. 219. See also the Egyptian *aide-mémoire* of 1950, above, note 20. It may be observed also that in a statement in reply to Mr Wilson's declaration in 1967 that the Strait of Tiran was an international waterway, the Egyptian Foreign Minister announced that '"innocent passage" would be allowed [through the Strait of Tiran], but that strategic goods would first be removed'. *The Times,* 27 May 1967, p. 1. The 1975 agreement between Egypt and Israel on partial withdrawal of Israeli forces from Sinai, which provides, *inter alia,* that 'Non-military cargoes destined for or coming from Israel shall be permitted through the Suez Canal', is not relevant to the problem under consideration. For text of the agreement see *The Times,* 3 September 1975.

[57] Delegate of Israel, LSCOR (1st), vol. III, p. 35, where the Israeli representative also stated that 'whatever might be decided about extending the territorial sea', in a bay having more than one coastal State, no extension could ever justify the appropriation by one coastal State of waters which constituted the only access to a harbour belonging to another State.

[58] Israel, *GAOR,* Eleventh session, 1956–57, Plenary Meetings, vol. II, 666th meeting, 1 March 1957, paras. 10–11, p. 1276.

[59] *Ibid.*

[60] Israel, *SCOR,* Ninth year, 1954, 659th meeting, 15 February 1954, para. 99. See also delegate of Israel, *SCOR,* Twenty-second year, 1967, 1342nd meeting, 24 May 1967.

[61] For text of the provisional articles see II *Yearbook of the ILC* (1955), pp. 1 *et seq.* (Doc. A/2934).

[62] II *Yearbook of the ILC* (1956), p. 53, at pp. 56 and 59.

[63] *Israel Government Yearbook,* 5728 (1967–68), p. 170. See also *Egypt's Unlawful Blockade of the Gulf of Aqaba, op. cit.,* at p. 12.

[64] *Israel Government Yearbook,* 5728 (1967–68), p. 170. See also delegate of Israel, *GAOR,* Fifth Emergency Special Session, 17 June–18 September 1967, Plenary Meetings, 1526th meeting, 19 June 1967, para. 129, p. 11.

[65] Israel, *SCOR,* Ninth year, 1954, 659th meeting, 15 February 1954, paras. 102–4, p. 19; *Egypt's Unlawful Blockade of the Gulf of Aqaba, op. cit.,* pp. 3–4; see also Robert J. Eckert, 'The Straits of Tiran: innocent passage or endless war', 22 *University of Miami Law Review* (1967–68), p. 873, at p. 883.

[66] On the first question see, e.g., Leo Gross, 'Passage through the Straits of Tiran and in the Gulf of Aqaba', 33 *Law and Contemporary Problems* (1968), p. 125, at pp. 129–33; Pritam T. Merani and Jimmie L. Sterling, 'Legal consideration of the Israeli–Egyptian dispute involving the right of innocent passage through the Straits of Tiran', 11 *Indian J.I.L.* (1971), p. 411, especially pp. 419–23; Charles B. Selak, *op. cit.* On the claim that a continuing state of 'war' and 'belligerency' exists between Egypt and Israel see, e.g., Colonel H. S. Levie, 'The nature and scope of the armistice agreement', 50 *A.J.I.L.* (1956), p. 880; Leo Gross, 'Passage through the Straits of Tiran and in the Gulf of Aqaba', *op. cit.,* especially pp. 133–9; 'Passage through the Suez Canal of Israel-bound cargo and Israeli ships', 51 *A.J.I.L.* (1957), p. 530; Majid Khaddouri, 'Closure of the Suez Canal to Israeli shipping', 33 *Law and Contemporary Problems* (1968), p. 147; L. M. Bloomfield, *op. cit.,* especially chapter 8; Charles B. Selak, *op. cit.,* pp. 681–4; Rosalyn Higgins, 'The June war: the United Nations and legal background', 3 *Journal of Contemporary History* (1968), p. 253, especially pp. 267–9; R. R. Baxter, *The Law of International Waterways,* p. 209 *et. seq.*; 'The definition of war', 16 *R.E.D.I.* (1960), p. 1; Robert H. Foreward *et al.,* 'The Arab–Israeli war and international law', 9 *Har. I.L.J.* (1968), p. 232, especially pp. 248–52.

[67] R. R. Baxter, *The Law of International Waterways, op. cit.,* p. 4, note 7.

[68] 'A passage of water is a Strait in law only if it is a Strait geographically', D. P. O'Connell, 1 *International Law* (2nd edn., London, 1970), p. 497. Similarly see R.

NOTES

R. Baxter, *The Law of International Waterways, op. cit.*, pp. 159–60.

[69] *Corfu Channel case, judgement* of 5 April 1949: I.C.J., Report, 1949, p. 4, at p. 28.

[70] R. R. Baxter, *The Law of International Waterways, op. cit.*, pp. 3–4.

[71] A/Conf.62/WP.10, 15 July 1977. See further above, in Chapter II.

[72] One of the Red Sea littoral States, Saudi Arabia, has already claimed a considerable exclusive fishing zone, but this, however, is without prejudice to the freedom of navigation. See above, in Chapter I.

[73] See above, in Chapter I.

[74] D. P. O'Connell, 1 *International Law* (2nd edn.), p. 487. See also Leo Bouchez, *The Regime of Bays in International Law* (Leyden, 1964), p. 17.

[75] Leo Bouchez, *op. cit.*, pp. 16–17.

[76] D. P. O'Connell, 1 *International Law, op. cit.*, p. 494.

[77] See above, note 4.

[78] '*Strait Gulf,* an arm of the sea running into the land through a narrow entrance, as the Gulf of Venice.' *Oxford English Dictionary* (1933).

[79] Leo Bouchez, *op. cit.*, note 72, pp. 143–4.

[80] *Ibid.*

[81] J. H. Verzijl, III *International Law in Historical Perspective* (Leyden, 1970), p. 602.

[82] *Corfu Channel case, Judgement* of 5 April 1949: I.C.J. Report, 1949, p. 4.

[83] As to the view that the Gulf of Aqaba is an Arab 'historic' bay see, e.g., Zaki Hashim, 'Rationale of the theory of historic bays with special reference to the international status of the Gulf of Aqaba', 25 *R.E.D.I.* (1969), p. 1; M. Burham Hammad, *op. cit.*, especially pp. 123–40; Ahmad Shukairy, chairman of the Saudi Arabia delegation to the United Nations, 'On the question of the regime of historic waters, including historic bays', *GAOR*, Fourteenth session, 1959, Sixth Committee: Legal Questions, 643rd and 644th meetings, 30 November and 2 December 1959; for full text of this address see Ahmad Shukairy, *Territorial and Historical Waters in International Law* (Palestine Monograph No. 24, published by the Research Centre, Palestine Liberation Organisation, Beirut), pp. 171 *et seq.*; *Memorandum registering Saudi Arabia Government's Legal and historic rights in the Straits of Tiran and the Gulf of Aqaba,* Doc. A/3575 (15 April 1957); P. Merani and J. Sterling, *op. cit.,* especially pp. 416–23; B. S. N. Murti, 'The legal status of the Gulf of Aqaba', 7 *Indian J.I.L.* (1967), p. 201, especially pp. 203–4; J. H. W. Verzijl, III *International Law in Historical Perspective,* p. 602. For a contrary view see, e.g., Mitchell P. Strohl, *The International Law of Bays* (The Hague, 1963), pp. 389–97; Charles B. Selak, *op. cit.*; Leo J. Bouchez, *op. cit.*, especially pp. 222–3; Rosalyn Higgins, 'The June war: the United Nations and legal background', *op. cit.*; Leo Gross, 'The Geneva Conference on the Law of the Sea and the right of innocent passage through the Gulf of Aqaba', 53 *A.J.I.L.* (1959), p. 564, especially pp. 566–72.

[84] Statement by the Secretary of State for Foreign Affairs, Selwyn Lloyd, in the House of Commons on 13 May 1957 in response to a question whether Her Majesty's Government recognised the waters of the Gulf of Aqaba as Arab territorial waters. 570 *H.C. Deb.* (5th Ser.), 13 May 1957, col. 12. Similarly see statements made by the United States Secretary of State, J. F. Dulles, 37 *Dept. of State Bull.* (1957), 5 August 1957, p. 232, and by the representatives of Israel, the United States, the United Kingdom, Australia, Denmark, Belgium, Norway and New Zealand in the United Nations, *GAOR,* Eleventh session, 1956–57, Plenary Meetings, vol. II, 666th, 667th and 668th meetings, 1, 4 and 8 March 1957 respectively.

[85] See, e.g., Leo Gross, 'Passage through the Straits of Tiran and in the Gulf of Aqaba', *op. cit.,* p. 141. See also statement by Professor François, Special Rapporteur of the International Law Commission, below, p. 152. Dr Y. Blum, however,

seems to believe that the territorial waters of the littoral States of the Gulf of Aqaba overlap only 'in certain parts of the Gulf'. Y. Blum, *Historic Titles in International Law* (The Hague, 1965), p. 275.

[86] *Corfu Channel case, Judgement* of 5 April 1949: I.C.J., Report, 1949, p. 4, at p. 28.

[87] See, e.g., statements made by France and the Netherlands, *GAOR*, Eleventh session, 1956–57, Plenary Meetings, vol. II, 666th and 667th meetings, 1 and 4 March 1957 respectively; United States, *SCOR*, Twenty-second year, 1967, 1343rd meeting, 29 May 1967, para. 31, p. 4. See also Charles B. Selak, *op. cit.*, p. 276; Paul A. Porter, *op. cit.*, p. 17; 'Gaza and the Gulf—what international law has to say', by a 'Special Correspondent', *The Times*, 8 March 1971, p. 11. Aaron L. Shalowitz, 'Straits of Tiran and the law', letter to the editor, *Washington Post*, 4 June 1967.

[88] L. Oppenheim, I *International Law* (1st edn., 1905), pp. 247–8.

[89] Gilbert Gidel, III *Le Droit International Public de la Mer* (1934), pp. 593–608.

[90] *Ibid.*, p. 601. Passage translated into English by courtesy of Dr G. Marston, University of Cambridge.

[91] L. Oppenheim, I *International Law* (1st edn., 1905), pp. 247–8. The same proposition is substantially retained in subsequent editions, including the fourth edition, edited by Arnold McNair in 1928, and the eighth edition, edited by Sir H. Lauterpacht in 1955. To the passage quoted above Arnold McNair adds a footnote to the effect that 'This is not contested. A few writers—see, for instance, Twiss, i, Sect. 181—assert that narrow gulfs and bays surrounded by the land of two different States are territorial, the central line dividing the territorial portions. However, the majority of writers do not accept this opinion, and it would seem that the practice of States likewise rejects it, except in the case of such bays as possess the characteristics of a closed sea. Thus, in the case of *San Salvador* v. *Nicaragua*, the International Court of the Central American Republics decided in 1917 that, taking into consideration its geographical and historical conditions, as well as its situation, extend, and configuration, the Gulf of Fonseca must be regarded as "an historic bay possessed of the characteristics of a closed sea", and that it therefore was part of the territories of San Salvador, Honduras, and Nicaragua.' L. Oppenheim, I *International Law* (4th edn., 1928), note 5, pp. 409–10. Arnold McNair also points out that: 'The expression "territorial bay" must not be allowed to obscure the facts (1) that the waters contained in territorial bays, and in the territorial portions of bays not wholly territorial, are not territorial waters and part of the maritime belt, but national waters, and (2) that the limit of the national waters is the datum line for the measurement of the maritime belt'. *Ibid.*, note 1, p. 407.

[92] See L. Oppenheim, 1 *International Law* (1st edn., 1905), pp. 241–2. See also *ibid.*, 4th edn., ed. Arnold McNair, 1928, pp. 396–7, and 8th edn., ed. Sir H. Lauterpacht, 1955), pp. 490–2.

[93] C. C. Hyde, 1 *International Law, Chiefly as Interpreted and Applied by the United States* (2nd rev. edn., Boston, Mass., 1945), p. 475.

[94] *Ibid.*, p. 476.

[95] 23 *A.J.I.L.* Spec. Supp. (1929), p. 274. The 1929 Harvard draft convention was prepared in anticipation of the First Conference on the Codification of International Law, The Hague, 1930.

[96] P. Jessup, *The Law of Territorial Waters and Maritime Jurisdiction* (1927), p. 476.

[97] Commander M. Strohl, *op. cit.*, p. 375.

[98] *Ibid.*, pp. 375–6.

[99] J. H. W. Verzijl, III *International Law in Historical Perspective, op. cit.*, p. 593.

[100] Commentary to Article 7 of the 1956 ILC's draft articles on the law of the sea, II *Yearbook of the ILC* (1956), p. 296. At the 365th meeting of the ILC in 1956 the

Special Rapporteur of the Commission pointed out that 'The Israeli Government inquired, *inter alia*, what was the position of bays whose coastline are shared by more than one State. That problem was one of many which the Commission, aware that it was making the first effort to codify the matter, had deliberately refrained from attempting to solve.' I *Yearbook of the ILC* (1956), p. 190.

[101] Article 7(1), *Convention on the Territorial Sea and the Contiguous Zone*, 1958.

[102] Thus Article 10, concerning bays, of the Informal Composite Negotiating Text of the Third United Nations Conference on the Law provides that its provisions relate only 'to bays the coasts of which belong to a single state' (A/Conf.62/WP.10, 15 July 1977).

[103] Commander M. Strohl, *op. cit.*, p. 376.

[104] C. C. Hyde, *op. cit.*, p. 476.

[105] D. H. N. Johnson, 'Some legal problems of international waterways, with particular reference to the Straits of Tiran and the Suez Canal', 31 *Modern Law Review* (1968), p. 158, at p. 162; Charles B. Selak, *op. cit.*, p. 697; J. H. W. Verzijl, III *International Law in Historical Perspective, op. cit.*, p. 602. Although Professor Leo Gross ('The Geneva Conference on the Law of the Sea and the right of passage through the Gulf of Aqaba', *op. cit.*, p. 570), argues that the Gulf of Aqaba can be transformed into a closed sea by agreement amongst the littoral States, he also suggests that this is dependent on 'recognition by other nations'. In the present submission the latter suggestion hardly seems tenable, for, as concluded above, the Gulf of Aqaba does not constitute part of the high seas and, as will be shown, foreign nations had no corresponding record of shipping practice in that gulf because it apparently had no commercial or strategic importance to them; foreign States, therefore, had no vested interest in the Gulf of Aqaba and its legal status in their eyes, as Commander M. Strohl finds, 'was of no moment'. Commander M. Strohl, *op. cit.*, p. 387. It may be observed that the United States and Canada exercise dominion over, and regard as territorial, the waters of the Straits of Juan de Fuca, which separate Canada on the north from the United States on the south; the breadth of Juan de Fuca, at the narrowest part, is about ten marine miles. In the course of a communication of 22 May 1891 to the United States Secretary of the Treasury, Dr Wharton, Acting Secretary of State, adverted to the circumstances that these Straits were 'not a great natural thoroughfare or channel of navigation in an international sense' and stated that 'in view of this situation, it is not apprehended that any other nation can make reasonable objection to the jurisdiction of the Government of the United States and of Great Britain over their entire areas'. C. C. Hyde, *op. cit.*, p. 488.

[106] In 1957 John Foster Dulles, then United States Secretary of State, declared that 'If the four littoral States which have boundaries upon the Gulf [of Aqaba] should all agree that it should be closed it could be closed.' News conference, 19 February 1957, 36 *Dept. of State Bull.* (1957), p. 404.

[107] Professor J. H. W. Verzijl states that 'Although other juridical constructions are possible, the Gulf of Aqaba must in my opinion be considered to be a bay of the Red Sea, divided mainly into four zones of territorial sea, respectively belonging to Egypt and Saudi Arabia from the Straits of Tiran at its entrance inward, and to Israel and Jordan at its far end.' J. H. W. Verzijl, III *International Law in Historical Perspective, op. cit.*, p. 602. As already stated, the territorial seas of the littoral States overlap in all parts of the Gulf of Aqaba; there has not been, however, any agreement between these States for the delimitation of boundaries. According to Article 12(1) of the 1958 *Convention on the Territorial Sea and the Contiguous Zone*, 'Where the coasts of two States are opposite or adjacent to each other, neither of the two States is entitled, failing agreement between them to the contrary, to extend its territorial sea beyond the median line every point of which is equidistant from the nearest points on the baselines from which the breadth of the

territorial seas of each of the two States is measured...'.

[108] *Republic of El Salvador* v. *Republic of Nicaragua, op. cit.,* p. 674.
[109] *Ibid.,* p. 706. See also R. H. Kennedy, 'A brief study of bays', *op. cit.,* p. 203.
[110] *Republic of El Salvador* v. *Republic of Nicaragua, op. cit.,* p. 674.
[111] *Ibid.,* especially pp. 693-4.
[112] See above, notes 48 and 83.
[113] *Republic of El Salvador* v. *Republic of Nicaragua, op. cit.,* p. 689.
[114] *Ibid.,* pp. 677-9.
[115] *Ibid.,* p. 693.
[116] Italy claims a territorial sea of six nautical miles, while Yugoslavia claims ten nautical miles; FAO Fisheries Circular No. 127, Rev. 1 (FID/C/127, Rev. 1, Rome, 1973), pp. 6, 19.
[117] Leo Bouchez, *op. cit.,* p. 138. See also R. H. Kennedy, 'A brief study of bays', *op. cit.,* p. 214.
[118] *Corfu Channel case, Judgement* of 5 April 1949: I.C.J., Report, 1949, p. 4. For analysis of this judgement see G. C. Fitzmaurice, 'The law and procedure of the International Court of Justice: general principles and substantive law', 27 *B.Y.I.L.* (1950), pp. 3, 27-31.
[119] *Corfu Channel case, Judgement* of 5 April 1949: I.C.J., Report, 1949, p. 4, at p. 28.
[120] From an *aide-mémoire* handed to the Israeli ambassador, Abba Eban, on 11 February 1957 by the United Stated Secretary of State, J. F. Dulles, 36 *Dept. of State Bull.* (1957), p. 393. See also above, note 84.
[121] I *Yearbook of the ILC* (1956), p. 202.
[122] *Ibid.*
[123] See above, note 62.
[124] I *Yearbook of the ILC* (1956), p. 202.
[125] *Ibid.*
[126] *Ibid,* p. 203.
[127] *Ibid.*
[128] *Ibid,* p. 202.
[129] *Ibid,* p. 203.
[130] II *Yearbook of the ILC* (1955), p. 39.
[131] I *Yearbook of the ILC* (1956), p. 203.
[132] *Ibid.*
[133] II *Yearbook of the ILC* (1956), p. 258.
[134] See above, note 57.
[135] See A/Conf.13/C.1/L.3 (United Kingdom); A/Conf.13/C.1/L.51 (Netherlands); A/Conf.13/C.1/L.47 (Portugal); A/Conf.13/C.1/L.56. These documents are printed in LSCOR (1st), vol. III, pp. 218, 224, 223 and 226 respectively.
[136] Article 16(4) was based on the 'new three-power proposal' submitted to the conference by the Netherlands, Portugal and the United Kingdom, A/Conf.13/C.1/L.71 as amended. See LSCOR (1st), vol. III, pp. 231 and 100.
[137] Leo Gross, 'Passage through the Strait of Tiran and in the Gulf of Aqaba', *op. cit.,* p. 141.
[138] *Ibid.* See also A. Dean, 'The Geneva Conference on the Law of the Sea: what was accomplished', 52 *A.J.I.L.* (1958), p. 607, at pp. 621-3; J. H. W. Verzijl, III *International Law in Historical Perspective, op. cit.,* p. 28, where Professor Verzijl says, with reference to Article 16(4), 'a provision which in its final words clearly covers situations such as that of the Gulf of Aqaba'. Elsewhere, however, Professor Verzijl expresses the view that 'In order to achieve a satisfactory solution to the controversies which still exist at the present moment about the legal situation, an international agreement on the status of the Gulf [of Aqaba] and the Strait [of Tiran] is urgently required.' J. H. W. Verzijl, IV *International Law in Historical Perspective,* p. 138. As chairman of the Netherlands delegation at the 1958 Law of

NOTES

the Sea Conference, Professor Verzijl was one of the sponsors of the last part of Article 16(4) and played an active role in its adoption.

[139] See above, p. 142.

[140] In a statement before the Security Council the U.K. representative, *inter alia*, stated that '. . . In addition there is one most urgent and most dangerous issue of all—the question of the right of passage for shipping of all nationalities through the Straits of Tiran. The maintenance of the provisions of the Geneva Convention on the Territorial Sea dealing with international navigation between the high seas and territorial waters is of the greatest concern to my Government, as it must be to all engaged in international trade.' SCOR, Twenty-second Year, 1967, 1342nd meeting, 24 May 1967, para. 36. See also statement by the British Prime Minister in the House of Commons on 31 May 1967, 747 *H.C. Deb.* (5th Ser.), cols. 205–6.

[141] See U.S. representative, *SCOR,* Twenty-second year, 1967, 1343rd meeting, 29 May 1967, para. 30. See also statement by the late President Johnson on 23 May 1967, *Keesing's Contemporary Archives,* 1967, p. 22066. See also statement by the Prime Minister of Canada in the Canadian House of Commons on 24 May 1967, quoted in *Egypt's Unlawful Blockade of the Gulf of Aqaba, op. cit.,* pp. 27–8.

[142] This view is taken, e.g., by Professor D. H. Johnson, *op. cit.*, pp. 160–1. See also the view expressed by Sir Gerald Fitzmaurice, above, notes 128 and 129. Professor Johnson also notes that, though R. H. Kennedy had conducted, as preparatory documents for the purposes of the 1958 Conference on the Law of the Sea, separate studies on . . . Straits which constitute Routes for International Traffic' and on '. . . Bays and Estuaries the Coasts of which belong to Different States', the description of the Straits of Tiran and the Gulf of Aqaba is a combined description appearing in the latter study (*ibid.*, p. 159). This is significant because, in other instances, such as the 'Persian Gulf' and its entrance the 'Hormuz Strait', Kennedy had treated each of the two elements under a different study. For texts of the two studies, see LSCOR (1st), vol. I, Preparatory Documents, Documents No. 6 (A/Conf.13/6) and No. 12 (A/Conf.13/15), pp. 114 and 198, respectively. Besides, it may be observed that a list of 137 selected straits and channels drawn up by the Geographer of the U.S. Department of State in 1969 does not include or refer to the Straits of Tiran. See U.S. Department of State, the Geographer, *Sovereignty of the Sea,* Geographic Bulletin No. 3 (revised October 1969), p. 22, Table III.

[143] LSCOR (1st), vol. III, p. 100.

[144] Max Sorenson, *Law of the Sea,* 520 *Intl. Conc.* (1958), p. 236.

[145] LSCOR (1st), vol. III, p. 100.

[146] *Ibid.*, p. 96. The Saudi delegate also declared that 'His government's participation in the final act of the Conference would be conditional, among other things, on the rejection of the amendments' to the original text of para. 4. *Ibid.*, p. 100.

[147] LSCOR (1st), vol. II, p. 65.

[148] *Ibid.* For further discussion on the adoption of Article 16(4) see, e.g., J. H. W. Verzijl, 'the United Nations Conference on the Law of the Sea, Geneva, 1958', VI *Netherlands International Law Review* (1959), p. 1, especially at pp. 30–2; IV *International Law in Historical Perspective, op. cit.*, pp. 184–6; Max Sorenson, *op. cit.*, p. 236.

[149] LCSOR (1st), vol. II, p. 65.

[150] D. H. N. Johnson, *op. cit.*, p. 157. Under para. 1 of Resolution 1759 of the League of Arab States, adopted on 26 March 1959 during the League's thirty-first session in Cairo, member States were urged to postpone their adherence to the 1958 Convention on the Territorial Sea and the Contiguous Zone. This recommendation was reaffirmed in the League's Resolution 2978 of 13 September 1972.

[151] See, e.g., J. H. W. Verzijl (chairman of the Netherlands delegation), 'The United Nations Conference on the Law of the Sea, Geneva, 1958', *op. cit.*, p. 32.

[152] See 516 *U.N.T.S.*, p. 271. Israel, Australia, Madagascar, the United Kingdom

NOTES

and the United States made formal objections to the reservation of Tunisia; see *ibid.*, pp. 280–2.

[153] The fact that the Arab States had not acceded to the Convention on the Territorial Sea and the Contiguous Zone, 1958, because they opposed the interpretation of the concept in Article 16, para. 4, of the convention, which treated all straits alike, has been emphasised again at the second session of the Third United Nations Conference on the Law of the Sea in 1974 by the Arab States, which in addition have reiterated the view that the term 'Straits used for international navigation' should be strictly confined to straits which connected two parts of the high seas. See above, in Chapter II.

[154] See *LSCOR* (1st), vol. II, p. 71.

[155] The Indian proposal was adopted by a majority of forty-three to sixteen, with eight abstentions. *Ibid.* It may be observed that the Convention on the Fishing and Conservation of the Living Resources of the High Seas, and the Convention on the Continental Shelf, contain clauses allowing reservations to be made with respect to specified articles.

[156] H. G. Schermers, 'The suitability of reservations to multilateral treaties', VI *Netherlands International Law Review* (1959), p. 350, at p. 353.

[157] *Reservations to the Convention on Genocide,* Advisory Opinion, I.C.J. Report, 1951, p. 15.

[158] See LSCOR (1st), vol. II, pp. 71–2. For further discussion and comments on the decision of the conference see, e.g., J. H. W. Verzijl, 'The United Nations Conference on the Law of the Sea, Geneva, 1958', *op. cit.*, pp. 4, 10–11; H. G. Schreiber, *op. cit.*, especially pp. 352–3; Kaye Holloway, *Modern Trends in Treaty Law* (London, 1967), pp. 622–6. Since the 1958 Law of the Sea Conference the problem of reservations to international treaties has developed further. The admissibility and effect of reservations were among the main controversial issues during the preparation of the draft convention on treaties by the International Law Commission and the deliberations at the two sessions of the United Nations Conference on the Law of Treaties held in Vienna in 1968 and 1969, and resulted in the adoption of the Vienna Convention on the Law of Treaties, 1969 (A/Conf.39/27, 22 May 1969). Article 19 of that convention, the basic article on the formulation of reservations, provides that a State may, when signing, ratifying, accepting, approving or acceding to a treaty, formulate a reservation unless the reservation is prohibited by the treaty, or the treaty itself provides that only specified reservations which do not include the reservation in question may be made, or in other cases the reservation 'is incompatible with the object and purpose of the treaty'. The latter criterion, originally laid down by the International Court of Justice in the Genocide case, 1951, has been invoked in the Israeli objection, referred to earlier, to the reservation made by Tunisia with regard to Article 16(4) of the Territorial Sea Convention on the occasion of signature. On the Vienna Convention on the Law of Treaties see I. M. Sinclair, *The Vienna Convention on the Law of Treaties* (Manchester University Press, 1973); T. O. Elias, *The Modern Law of Treaties* (New York, 1974); J. H. W. Verzijl, VI *International Law in Historical Perspective*, chapter V.

[159] See 516 *U.N.T.S.*, pp. 206 *et seq*.

[160] J. H. W. Verzijl, 'The United Nations Conference on the Law of the Sea, Geneva, 1958', *op. cit.*, p. 10.

[161] Zaki Hashim, 'Some international law aspects of the Palestine question', 23 *R.E.D.I.* (1967), p. 63.

[162] A. H. Dean, 'The Geneva Conference on the Law of the Sea: what was accomplished', *op. cit.*, pp. 621.

[163] *Ibid.*, 621–3.

[164] See Leo Gross, 'Passage through the Strait of Tiran and in the Gulf of Aqaba', *op. cit.*, p. 143.

NOTES

[165] *Corfu Channel case, Judgement* of 5 April 1949: I.C.J., Report, 1949, p. 4, at p. 28.

[166] Leo Gross, 'Passage through the Strait of Tiran and in the Gulf of Aqaba', *op. cit.*, p. 143. Similarly see Leo Gross, 'The Geneva Conference on the Law of the Sea and the right of passage through the Gulf of Aqaba', *op. cit.*, pp. 594–5; Quincy Wright, 'the Middle East crisis', in Isaac Shapiro (ed.), *The Middle East: Prospects for Peace* (background papers and proceedings of the thirteenth Hammarskjold Forum, New York, 1969), p. 1, at p. 28.

[167] Leo Gross, 'Passage through the Strait of Tiran and in the Gulf of Aqaba', *op. cit.*, p. 143.

[168] *North Sea Continental Shelf, Judgement*, I.C.J. Reports, 1969, p. 3.

[169] *Ibid.*, p. 42, para. 73; emphasis added. See also R. R. Baxter, 'Multilateral treaties as evidence of customary international law', 41 *B.Y.I.L.* (1965–66), p. 275, at p. 291, where he states that 'Except in the case of the Geneva Convention on the High Seas, the preponderance of the evidence is thus weighted against the "codification" conventions concluded under United Nations auspices being declaratory of customary international law . . . It may be possible through an examination of the *travaux préparatoires* to demonstrate that a particular article was intended to be declaratory of customary law but this will be possible only in those exceptional cases in which the path was well marked and clear.'

[170] See Lay, Churchill and Nordiquist (eds.), II *New Directions in the Law of the Sea* (London, 1973), p. 43.

[171] J. H. W. Verzijl, 'The United Nations Conference on the Law of the Sea, Geneva, 1958', *op. cit.*, pp. 31–2, also in IV *International Law in Historical Perspective, op. cit.*, p. 185.

[172] Y. Blum, *op. cit.*, p. 275.

[173] L. Oppenheim, 1 *International Law* (8th edn., 1955), p. 512.

[174] Dr Blum's suggestion has been criticised also by Ruth Lapidoth, who stated that 'As far as the last words of [Article 16(4)] are concerned ('. . . or the territorial sea of a foreign state'), this suggestion would perhaps have merited some further discussion.' 1 *Israel Law Review* (1966), p. 508, 'Book reviews', at p. 510.

[175] Y. Blum, *op. cit.*, p. 275. See also above, note 85.

[176] This view has been expressed by various writers; see, e.g., Solomon Slonim, 'The right of innocent passage and the 1958 Geneva conference', 5 *Columbia Journal of Transnational Law* (1966), p. 96, at pp. 112–15; Robert J. Eckert, *op. cit.*, p. 882; Kenneth Levan, 'Justification for the opening of hostilities in the Middle East', 26 *R.E.D.I.* (1970), p. 88, at p. 100; Robert H. Forward *et al.*, *op. cit.*, p. 247; Zaki Hashim, 'Some international aspects of the Palestine question', *op. cit.*, p. 88; G. I. A. Draper, letter to *The Times*, 31 May 1967, p. 11; Roger Fisher, 'Legality of the Arab position', letter to the *New York Times*, 11 June 1967, section 4, p. 13; Henry Cattan, *Palestine and International Law* (London, 1973), p. 133. See also Aaron L. Shalowitz, I *Shore and Sea Boundaries* (publication 10–1, U.S. Department of Commerce, 1962), p. 238, where it is stated: 'The Convention adopted at Geneva goes further than the Corfu Channel case and the ILC draft. It incorporates in Article 16, Paragraph 4, the new concept that innocent passage should also include straits that connect the high seas with the territorial sea of another state. This is a distinct broadening of the existing rule and in the direction of greater freedom of the seas.' Elsewhere, however, Mr Shalowitz expresses the view that 'the Strait of Tiran would be an international waterway under Article 16(4)'; *Washington Post*, 4 June 1967, 'The Strait of Tiran and the law'.

[177] C. C. Hyde, *op. cit.*, pp. 487–8. To the same effect see A. Pearce Higgins and John Colombos, *The International Law of the Sea* (London, 1943), p. 126.

[178] R. R. Baxter, *The Law of International Waterways*, *op. cit.*, p. 3.

[179] *Corfu Channel case*, Pleadings, Oral Arguments, Documents, I.C.J., 1949, p. 548.

NOTES

[180] *Corfu Channel case*, Pleadings, Oral Arguments, Documents, I.C.J., 1950, p. 278.

[181] *Corfu Channel case, Judgement* of 9 April 1949; I.C.J. Reports, 1949, p. 4, at p. 28.

[182] *Ibid*.

[183] Professor D. P. O'Connell emphasises that both tests of the Court are 'interrelated'; D. P. O'Connell, 1 *International Law op. cit.*, p. 497.

[184] L. Oppenheim, 1 *International Law* (8th edn., 1955), p. 512. Similarly see, R. R. Baxter, *The Law of International Waterways, op. cit.*, pp. 3–4; D. P. O'Connell, 1 *International Law, op. cit.*, p. 493.

[185] A. H. Charteris, 'Territorial jurisdiction in wide bays', in *International Law Association, Report of the Twenty-third Conference, Berlin, 1906*, p. 103, p. 107.

[186] See above, note 153 and Chapter II, note 48.

[187] LSCOR (3rd), vol. II, 1974 (23 July), p. 137.

[188] A/Conf.138/SC.II/L.4 and Corr.1 (3 August 1971).

[189] A/Conf.62/C.2/L.3 (3 July 1974). The United Kingdom considered that the interests of the international community in free navigation in straits used for international navigation between one part of the high seas and the territorial sea of a foreign State was not so strong as in the case of straits linking two parts of the high seas. See LSCOR (3rd), vol. II, 1974 (11 July), p. 102, and (22 July), p. 125.

[190] A/Conf.62/C.2/L.II (26 August 1974). It has been stated that by providing for the right of non-suspendable innocent passage in straits which connect the high seas with the territorial waters of a foreign State the draft of the socialist States takes into account the interests of the States which have coasts in respective straits and also 'the position of the Arab countries with regard to the Strait of Tiran'. V. Yaroslavtsev, 'The world ocean and international law', *International Affairs* (Moscow), 1975, 2 February, p. 61, at p. 68.

[191] See statement by Israel's delegate, LSCOR (3rd), vol. II, 1974 (23 July), p. 137.

[192] A/Conf.62/WP.10, 15 July 1977. See further above, in Chapter II.

[193] LSCOR (3rd), vol. II, 1974 (9 August), p. 255.

[194] *Ibid*.

[195] R. R. Baxter, *The Law of International Waterways, op. cit.*, p. 3.

[196] *Corfu Channel case, Judgement*, of 5 April 1949, I.C.J. Reports, 1949, p. 4.

[197] *Ibid.*, p. 28.

[198] Concerning this, the Court said: 'The following is the total number of ships putting in at the port of Corfu after passing through or just before passing through the Channel. During the period of one year nine months, the total number of ships was 2,884. The flags of the ships are Greek, Italian, Romanian, Yugoslavia, French, Albanian and British. Clearly, very small vessels are included, as the entries for Albanian vessels are high, and of course one vessel may make several journeys, but 2,884 ships for a period of one year nine months is quite a large figure. These figures relate to vessels visited by the customs at Corfu and so do not include the large number of vessels which went through the strait without calling at Corfu at all. There were also regular sailings through the strait by Greek vessels three times weekly, by a British ship fortnightly, by two Yugoslav vessels weekly and by two others fortnightly. The Court is further informed that the British Navy has regularly used this channel for eighty years or more and that it has also been used by the navies of other States.' *Ibid.*, pp. 28–9.

[199] D. P. O'Connell, I *International Law, op. cit.*, p. 497.

[200] Erik Brüel, I *International Straits: a Treatise on International Law* (1947), pp. 43–5.

[201] *Red Sea Pilot* (British Admiralty Publication, 2nd edn., 1873), p. 133.

[202] Mitchell P. Strohl, *op. cit.*, p. 397.

NOTES

[203] Alexander Melamid, 'Legal status of the Gulf of Aqaba', 53 *A.J.I.L.* (1959), p. 412, at p. 413, and *id.*, 'The political geography of the Gulf of Aqaba', *op. cit.*, p. 235.

[204] Charles B. Selak, *op. cit.*, p. 692.

[205] Malcolm W. Gagle, *op. cit.*, p. 77.

[206] Of the 267 vessels, 214 were British, thirty-five German, five American, three Greek, two Syrian, three Norwegian, one Turkish, one Panamanian, one Pakistani, one Italian, and one Danish. See Egypt, *SCOR*, Ninth year, 1954, 659th meeting, 15 February 1954, para. 58, p. 10; L. M. Bloomfield, *op. cit.*, p. 3. See also Alexander Melamid, 'The political geography of the Gulf of Aqaba', *op. cit.*, p. 235. According to the *New York Times* (9 December 1955), since the establishment of the State of Israel and up to the year 1955 'only four or five ships sailing to or from the Israeli port of Elath have passed through the Gulf' of Aqaba.

[207] Mordechai Abir, *Sharm-el-Sheikh–Bab al-Mandeb: the strategic balance and Israel's southern approaches'*, Jerusalem Papers on Peace Problems, No. 5, March 1974 (Leonard Davis Institute for International Relations–Hebrew University of Jerusalem), pp. 12–13.

[208] Arthur Lall, *op. cit.*, p. 37. During the crisis which followed the Egyptian announcement of 22 May 1967, Harold Wilson, the British Prime Minister, said that it was a fact that no great number of Israeli vessels actually used the Straits of Tiran and he therefore hoped that 'a compromise settlement can be reached which would ensure that Israel would get all the "essential cargo" through the Straits of Tiran. The problem of the passage of ships flying the Israeli flag would remain in abeyance'. *Sunday Times*, 4 June 1967, p. 1. See also Walter Laqueur, *The Road to War, 1967* (London, 1968), p. 172.

[209] *The Times*, 23 May 1967, p. 8. See also *Middle East Record*, vol. 3, 1967 (Jerusalem 1971), p. 195. It is stated that according to the *Statistical Bulletin of Israel, 1966*, seven per cent of all Israeli exports passed through Eilat during 1966. Approximately a quarter of that was carried aboard Israeli ships. Imports through Eilat constituted two per cent of total imports. About half of that was transported on Israeli ships. Kenneth Levan, *op. cit.*, p. 88.

[210] *The Times*, 23 May 1967, p. 8.

[211] Anthony S. Reyner, 'The Strait of Tiran and the Sovereignty of the sea', XXI *Middle East Journal* (1967), p. 403, at p. 405.

[212] *Sunday Times*, 28 May 1967, p. 11.

[213] *United Nations Statistical Yearbook*, 1973 (ST/ESA/STAT/Ser.S/1), Table 151, p. 540, and 1974 (ST/ESA/STAT/Ser.S/2), Table 156, pp. 464–5.

[214] *Israel Government Yearbook*, 1968, p. 435; *Statistical Abstract of Israel*, No. 26 (1975), p. 496.

[215] *Israel Government Yearbook*, 1968, p. 435.

[216] *The Hashemite Kingdom of Jordan Statistical Yearbook*, No. 9 (1958), p. 111; No. 15 (1964), p. 561; and No. 21 (1970), pp. 128–31.

[217] Mordechai Abir, *op. cit.*, p. 13.

[218] *United Nations Statistical Yearbook*, 1974 (ST/ESA/STAT/Ser.S/2), Table 156, pp. 464–5; *Statistical Abstract of Israel*, No. 26 (1975), p. 496.

[219] *Ibid.*

[220] See *Keesing's Contemporary Archives*, 18289A (1961) and 21050B (1965).

[221] *United Nations Statistical Yearbook*, 1974 (ST/ESA/STAT/Ser.S/2), Table 156, pp. 464–5.

[222] Alexander Melamid, 'The political geography of the Gulf of Aqaba', *op. cit.*, pp. 237–8. See also Mitchell P Strohl, *op. cit.*, p. 391, where he expresses the view that even if the Suez Canal were opened to Israeli ships and ships bound for Israel 'it is unlikely that many ships would proceed to the poorly equipped port of Elath in preference to Israel's Mediterranean ports, which are tied to the country by adequate lines of communication'. Indeed, following the 1975 Egyptian-Israeli agreement

which provides that 'Non-military cargoes destined for or coming from Israel shall be permitted through the Suez Canal', oil tankers bound for Israel from Iran have started to use the Mediterranean ports of Israel instead of Eilat. The first oil tanker for Israel passed through the Suez Canal on 9 March 1976. See *The Times*, 10 March 1975, p. 9. For the text of the 1975 Israel–Egypt agreement see *The Times*, 2 September 1975, p. 6.

[223] *Convention of the Territorial Sea and the Contiguous Zone*, 1958, Article 14 (4).

[224] *Ibid.*, Article 16 (3).

[225] See, e.g., O. G. de Vries Reilingh, 'Warships in territorial waters: their right of innocent passage', II *N.Y.I.L.* (1971), p. 29; Solomon Slonim, 'The right of innocent passage and the 1958 Geneva Conference on the Law of the Sea', 5 *Columbia Journal of Transnational Law* (1966), p. 96. The Informal Composite Negotiating Text, which was prepared after the sixth session of the Third Conference on the Law of the Sea in 1977, makes it clear that warships have the same rights of innocent passage through the territorial sea as merchant ships. See A/Conf.62/WP.10, 15 July 1977. See also above, in Chapter II.

[226] See above, pp. 137 and 141.

[227] See above, notes 55 and 56.

[228] It might be recalled also that Egypt considers herself in a state of 'war' and 'belligerency' with Israel and further asserts that Israel's possession of the territory of Eilat is not lawful. As stated at the outset, however, these questions are not issues for full analysis or conclusions here. It has been stated that innocent passage 'is a function of normal', and that the term 'normal' as used here refers to the circumstances prevailing most of the time in regard to navigation in most areas of the world; and that the 'word "normal"', which has in this sense the connotation "peaceful", cannot be applied to the situation in the Gulf of Aqaba, which is still legally linked to the Egypt–Israel belligerancy'. (Walter Herbert Dixon, *The Gulf of Aqaba: History, Geography, and Law, op. cit.*, p. 471, note 1).

[229] M. McDougal and W. Burke, *The Public Order of the Oceans* (New Haven, 1962), p. 258. This view is shared by Max Sorensen, *The Law of the Sea, op. cit.*, p. 234. For further discussion on the meaning of 'innocent passage' see, e.g., Sir Gerald Fitzmaurice, 'Some results of the Geneva Conference on the Law of the Sea', 8 *I.C.L.Q.* (1959), 92; O. G. de Vries Reilingh, 'Warships in territorial waters: their right of innocent passage', *op. cit.*, p. 29; Solomon Slonim, *op. cit.* In the above proposition McDougal and Burke contest Leo Gross's contention, which they found to be 'unfortunately without supporting explanation', (*ibid.*, note 221). Professor Leo Gross contends that 'the text as adopted clearly puts the burden on the coastal state to show that the passage itself rather than the passage of a particular ship, its purpose or cargo, was prejudicial to the stated values of the coastal state'. Leo Gross, The Geneva Conference on the Law of the Sea and the right of passage through the Gulf of Aqaba', *op. cit.*, p. 582. Elsewhere Professor McDougal, with reference to the territorial sea, states that 'The ships of other states are said to have a right of innocent passage, but within this geographic zone the burden is put upon such ships of proving their innocence'. M. McDougal, 'International law and the law of the sea', in L. M. Alexander (ed.), *The Law of the Sea* (Ohio State University Press, 1967), p. 3, at p. 17.

[230] *Corfu Channel case, Judgement* of 9 April 1949; I.C.J. Reports, 1949, p. 4.

[231] *Ibid.*, p. 29.

[232] *Israel Government Yearbook* 5728 (1967/68), p. 170.

[233] *Egypt's Unlawful Blockade of the Gulf of Aqaba, op. cit.*, p. 5.

[234] Mr Harold Wilson, the British Prime Minister, in a debate in the British House of Commons on the Middle East, 747 *H.C. Deb.*, col. 204, 31 May 1967.

[235] 260 *U.N.T.S.*, No. 3704 (1957).

[236] For full text of the resolution see *GAOR,* Eleventh Session, 1956–57, Supple-

ment No. 17 (A/3572), p. 62.
[237] *Ibid.*
[238] *Note by the Secretary General Transmitting an aide-mémoire on the Israel position on the Sharm el-sheikh area and the Gaza strip* (A/3511, 24 January 1957), printed in *GAOR,* Eleventh Session, 1956–57, Annexes, Agenda item 66, p. 45.
[239] *Report of the Secretary General in Pursuance of General Assembly Resolution 1123 (XI)* (A/3512, 24 January 1957), printed in *GAOR,* Eleventh Session, 1956–57, Annexes, Agenda item 66, p. 47, at p. 49.
[240] *Ibid.,* p. 50.
[241] *Report of the Secretary General in Pursuance of General Assembly Resolutions 1124 (XI) and 1125 (XI)* (A/3527, 11 February 1957), Annex 1, printed in *GAOR,* Eleventh Session, 1956–57, Annexes, Agenda item 66, p. 60.
[242] *Ibid.,* Annex IV.
[243] *Ibid.,* p. 58, para. 10.
[244] Dwight D. Eisenhower, *Waging Peace, 1956–61* (London, 1965), p. 184.
[245] *Ibid.* For text of U.S. *aide-mémoire* see *ibid.,* Appendix J; 36 *Dept of State Bull.* (1957), p. 392.
[246] D. Eisenhower, *op. cit.,* p. 185.
[247] Kennett Love, *op. cit.,* pp. 666–7.
[248] D. Eisenhower, *op. cit.,* p. 188.
[249] Mrs Meir (Israel), *GAOR,* Eleventh Session, 1956–57, Plenary Meetings, vol. II, Meeting 661, 1 March 1957, para. 1.
[250] *Ibid.,* para. 16.
[251] Mr Lodge (U.S.A.), *GAOR,* Eleventh Session, 1956–57, Plenary Meetings, vol. II, Meetings 645, 28 January 1957, and 650, 2 February 1957, paras. 4 and 55 respectively.
[252] D. Eisenhower, *op. cit.,* p. 130.
[253] Rosalyn Higgins, *United Nations Peacekeeping, 1946–67, Documents and Commentary, I, The Middle East* (London, 1969), p. 480.
[254] M. Burhan Hammad, 'The Right of passage in the Gulf of Aqaba', 15 *R.E.D.I.* (1959), p. 118, at p. 121.
[255] Mr Lodge (U.S.A.), *GAOR,* Eleventh Session, 1956–57, Plenary Meetings, vol. II, Meeting 666, 1 March 1957, para. 28.
[256] *Ibid.,* para. 32.
[257] Kennett Love, *op. cit.,* pp. 669–70. See also U.S. representative, Mr Lodge, *GAOR,* Eleventh Session, 1956–57, Plenary Meetings, vol. II, Meeting 666, 1 March 1957, para. 33.
[258] Secretary Dulles's news conference of 19 February 1957, 36 *Dept. of State Bull.* (1957), p. 404.
[259] I *Yearbook of the ILC* (1956), pp. 202–3.
[260] *Ibid.,* p. 202.
[261] Commander M. Strohl, *The International Law of Bays, op. cit.,* p. 375.
[262] R. H. Kennedy, 'A brief study of bays', *op. cit.*
[263] Commander M. Strohl, *The International Law of Bays, op. cit.,* p. 375.
[264] *Ibid.*
[265] The information regarding this bay is derived from: Leo J. Bouchez, *op. cit.,* pp. 158–9; R. H. Kennedy, 'A brief study of bays', *op. cit.,* p. 204.
[266] The information relating to this lagoon is derived from: Leo J. Bouchez, *op. cit.,* pp. 139–40; R. H. Kennedy, 'A brief study of bays', *op. cit.,* p. 200.
[267] Leo J. Bouchez, *op. cit.,* p. 140.
[268] *Ibid.*
[269] The information concerning this estuary is derived mainly from Leo J. Bouchez, *op. cit.,* pp. 130–5.
[270] *Ibid.,* p. 134.
[271] *Ibid.,* p. 135.

NOTES

[272] J. H. W. Verzijl, III *International Law in Historical Perspective—State Territory* (Leyden, 1970), p. 598.

[273] I *Yearbook of the ILC* (1956), p. 203.

[274] *Ibid.* A similar view was expressed by Mr Spiropoulous, another member of the International Law Commission, who said, 'The right of access to a port such as that mentioned [i.e. Eilat] could be based on international agreement or on a long usage. Strictly speaking, however, such a consideration was irrelevant, since the Commission was concerned with establishing general rules.' *Ibid.*

[275] A/3512, p. 8, para. 24; reproduced in *GAOR,* Eleventh Session, 1956–57, Annexes, Agenda item 66, p. 47.

[276] J. H. W. Verzijl, IV *International Law in Historical Perspective* (Leyden, 1971), p. 138.

CHAPTER V

[1] Monem Abdel-Gawad, 'Geological structure of the Red Sea area inferred from satellite pictures', in E. Degens and D. Ross (eds.), *Hot Brines and Recent Heavy Metal Deposits in the Red Sea* (New York, 1969), p. 25.

[2] William L. Griffin, 'International Legal Rights to Minerals in the Red Sea Deposits', in *ibid.*, p. 550, at p. 551. For a detailed discussion on the structure and origin of the Red Sea area see N. L. Falcon *et al.*, 'A discussion of the Red Sea, Gulf of Aden and Ethiopia Rift junction', 267 *Philosophical Transactions of the Royal Society of London,* Series A, No. 1181, October 1970.

[3] E. Degens and D. Ross, 'The Red Sea hot brines', 22 *Scientific American*, No. 4, April 1970, p. 32.

[4] For an account of the exploration and discovery see E. Degens and D. Ross (eds.), *Hot Brines and Recent Heavy Metal Deposits in the Red Sea, op. cit.*, pp. 3–17; *id.*, 'The Red Sea hot brines', *op. cit.*

[5] See, J. S. Tooms, 'Metal deposits in the Red Sea . . .', *Underwater Science and Technology Journal,* March 1970, p. 28; F. M. Auburn, 'The 1973 Conference on the Law of the Sea', 1 *Canadian Bar Review,* No. 1, 1972, p. 87, at p. 101; D. W. Bowett, 'Deep-sea-bed resources: a major challange', 31 *C.L.J.* [1972B], p. 50, at p. 51.

[6] J. S. Tooms, *op. cit.* According to E. Degens and D. Ross, the Atlantis II Deep embraces about thirty square miles of bottom and the Discovery Deep covers an area of nine square miles. E. Degens and D. Ross, 'The Red Sea hot brines', *op. cit.*, p. 36.

[7] Feodor Ostapoff, 'A fourth brine hole in the Red Sea?', in E. Degens and D. Ross, *Hot Brines and Recent Heavy Metal Deposits in the Red Sea, op. cit.*, p. 18.

[8] *Ibid.* See also map 16.

[9] *Ibid.* See also map 17.

[10] J. S. Tooms, *op. cit.*, p. 13.

[11] *Ibid.*

[12] 'Red Sea exploration', in *Mining Magazine,* November 1971, pp. 401–3.

[13] *Ibid.* 'Red Sea-like metals' have also been found in the Atlantic Ocean about 300 miles south-west of New York City. The metals have been found in one hole of fifteen drilled in the north-west Atlantic during leg XI of a series of two-month-long cruises of the RV *Glomar Challenger. Christian Science Monitor,* 14 August 1970, p. 7, 'Red Sea and Atlantic more alike than not'. In 1971, with the approval of the coastal States, the Democratic Republic of Somalia and the People's Democratic Republic of Yemen, two commercial exploration expeditions were undertaken to investigate the possibility of similar brines in the Gulf of Aden. F. M. Auburn, 'The 1973 Conference on the Law of the Sea', *op. cit.*, p. 101.

NOTES

[14] J. S. Tooms, *op. cit.*, p. 21. See also Peter A. Rona, 'New evidence for sea bed resources from global tectonics', 1 *Ocean Management* (1973), p. 145, at pp. 149–50. F. M. Auburn states that high concentrations of iron, silver, copper, gold and other minerals have been found in brine-bearing thermal seafloor springs at a depth of 7,000 ft in international waters in the Red Sea. F. M. Auburn, 'The international sea bed Area', 20 *I.C.L.Q.* (1971), p. 173, at p. 175. The metallic content of one of the Red Sea sites, the Atlantis II Deep, has been estimated as follows: copper, 0·9 per cent; zinc, 2·6 per cent; silver, 0·008 per cent; lead, 0·10 per cent; tin, 0·002 per cent; and gold, 0·0001 per cent. Vincent E. McKelvey, 'Mineral potential of the submerged parts of the U.S.', III *Ocean Industry*, No. 9, p. 41.

[15] J. S. Tooms, *op. cit.*, p. 29, where Tooms also indicates that 'Bischoff reports interstitial brine contents of more than 80 per cent in some samples from outside the Atlantis II and Discovery Deeps ... Results as high as 97 per cent brine in some cores in the Atlantis Deep are recorded.'

[16] *Ibid.*

[17] J. Bischoff and F. Manheim, 'Economic potential of the Red Sea heavy metal deposits', in E. Degens and D. Ross (eds.), *Hot Brines and Recent Heavy Metal Deposits in the Red Sea, op. cit.*, p. 535, at p. 541.

[18] T. Walthier and C. Schatz, 'Economic significance of minerals deposited in the Red Sea Deeps', in *ibid.*, p. 542.

[19] E. Blissenbach, 'Metalliferous deposits of the Red Sea bottom and development aspects', a paper presented to the World Peace through Law Conference, Belgrade, July 1970, cited by F. M. Auburn, 'The 1973 Conference on the Law of the Sea', *op. cit.*, p. 102.

[20] The Saudi law was ratified by Saudi Royal Decree No. M/27, dated 9–7–1388 (1 October 1968). For full text see references indicated in Appendix I.

[21] William L. Griffin, 'International legal rights to minerals in the Red Sea deeps', in E. Degens and D. Ross, *Hot brines and Recent Heavy Metal Deposits, op. cit.*, p. 550. It has been recorded that about the same time, February 1968, International Geomarine Corporation, a Los Angeles firm, demonstrated to the government of Sudan that the mineralised belt lay within the area of Sudanese jurisdiction. They then applied, successfully, to the Sudanese government for exclusive rights of exploration. Later a third company, Red Sea Enterprise Inc, an international consortium, with Seaonics Inc, of Los Angeles, made public claim through a London newspaper to 270 square miles of the Red Sea floor, including that claimed by IGC. 'Marine minerals exploration and speculative leasing continue world-wide', *Under Sea Technology*, January 1969, p. 63.

[22] Article 1 of the 1958 Convention on the Continental Shelf provides that 'For the purpose of these articles, the term "Continental Shelf" is used as referring *(a)* to the sea bed and subsoil of the submarine areas adjacent to the coast but outside the area of the territorial sea, to a depth of 200 metres or, beyond that limit, to where the depth of the superjacent waters admits of the exploitation of the natural resources of the said areas; *(b)* to the sea bed and subsoil of similar submarine areas adjacent ot the coasts of islands'. Article 2(1) of the same convention states that 'The Coastal State exercises over the Continental Shelf sovereign rights for the purpose of exploring it and exploiting its natural resources'.

[23] The Red Sea has an average depth of 490 m and reaches 2,359 m.

[24] E. Blissenbach, *Bulletin C.N.E.X.O.* (December 1970), p. 21, at p. 22, cited by F. M. Auburn, 'The 1973 Conference on the Red Sea', *op. cit.*, p. 104.

[25] F. M. Auburn, 'The 1973 Conference on the Law of the Sea', *op. cit.*, p. 104. Northcutt Ely considers it possible to regard the Red Sea as a special case from the point of view of the continental shelf doctrine of a 'semi-enclosed sea'. Northcutt Ely, 'Legal problems in undersea mineral development', *J. Petroleum Technology* [1970], p. 237, at p. 239.

[26] See above, in Chapter II.

NOTES

[27] See above, in Chapter I.

[28] But unlike the exclusive economic zone, which relates to the living and non-living resources of the zone, the Saudi claim is concerned only with non-living resources. In the course of his separate opinion in the North Sea Continental Shelf cases, 1969, Judge Ammoun referred to the 1968 Saudi law as one of two fresh facts which have reinforced the position taken by a number of Latin American States, particularly Peru, Chile and Ecuador, between 1946 and 1950 to the effect that each of them possesses sole sovereignty and jurisdiction over the area of sea adjacent to its coast of and extending not less than 200 nautical miles from the said coast. The other fact referred to by Judge Ammoun is the Italian–Yugoslav agreement of 8 January 1968 delimiting the whole breadth of the Adriatic Sea between the two parties. The depths of the area delimited, on average about 800 m, in fact attain 1,589 m. *North Sea Continental Shelf, Judgement,* I.C.J. Reports, 1969, p. 3, at pp. 107–10.

[29] *M.E.E.S.*, No. 50 11 October 1968, pp. 1–2.

[30] A copy of the original Arabic text of the 'Explanatory Note' was acquired from the League of Arab States.

[31] The agreement was made at Khartoum on 16 May 1974 and ratified on 24 August 1974. For full text see ST/LEG/Ser.B/18 (New York, 1976), p. 452.

[32] See map 16. It has been indicated that it has been scientifically established that these brine deposits are located in an area of the Red Sea whose north-western corner lies 85 km from the Sudanese coastline and 116 km from the Saudi coastline, whose south-eastern corner lies 95 km from the Sudanese coastline and 106 km from the Saudi coastline, and whose centre coincides with the co-ordinates lat. 21°N, long. 38°E. *M.E.E.S.*, No. 31, 24 May 1974, p. 2.

[33] According to Article 6 of the Geneva Convention on the Continental Shelf, the boundary of the continental shelf between adjacent or opposite States is, in the absence of agreement on a specific boundary, and unless there are special circumstances, the line of equidistance or the median line between the baselines of territorial seas. It may be recalled that Sudan acceded to the 1958 Continental Shelf Convention in 1970, but Saudi Arabia has so far not acceded to the Convention. See Chapter I.

[34] *North Sea Continental Shelf, Judgement,* I.C.J. Reports, 1969, p. 3.

[35] *Ibid.*, p. 32.

[36] *Ibid.*, p. 53. See also further discussion on the judgement above, pp. 89–90.

[37] This is indicated in Article XIII of the Saudi-Sudanese agreement concerning the resources of the Red Sea.

[38] *M.E.E.S.*, No. 30, 16 May 1975, p. 5.

[39] *M.E.E.D.*, 21 May 1976, p. 26.

[40] *North Sea Continental Shelf, Judgement, op. cit.,* p. 53.

[41] *Alam Al-Naft* (an Arabic weekly periodical on oil, Cairo), vol. 4, No. 49, 22 July 1972, p. 3.

[42] *Ibid.*

[43] *Ibid.*, No. 50, 29 July 1972, p. 3.

[44] See above, in Chapter II.

[45] F. M. Auburn, 'The 1973 Conference on the Law of the Sea', *op. cit.,* p. 104.

[46] Statement made by the Sudanese representative in the Sea Bed Committee on 9 August 1971, A/AC.138/SC.I/SR.18 (9 August 1971).

SELECTED BIBLIOGRAPHY

Note is made, mainly, of books and articles. Full bibliographical references of official (including United Nations) documents and publications, general sources of State practice and press reports and articles will be found in the notes to each chapter. Abbreviations are listed at pages xvii–xviii.

Abi-Mershed, Walid, *Israeli Withdrawal from Sinai* (Beirut).
Abir, Mordechai, *Sharm el-Sheikh–Bab el-Mandeb: the Strategic Balance and Israel's Southern Approaches,* Jerusalem Papers on Peace Problems, No. 5 (March 1974).
Adede, A. O. 'The system for exploitation of the "common heritage of mankind" at the Caracas conference', 69 *A.J.I.L.* (1975), p. 31.
Alexander, L. M. (ed.), *The Law of the Sea* (Ohio, 1967).
— 'Future regimes: a survey of proposals', in Churchill, R., Simmonds, K. R., and Welch, Jane (eds.), *New Directions in the Law of the Sea,* vol. III (London and New York, 1973).
— 'Indices of national interest in the oceans', 1 *Ocean Development* (1973–74), p. 21.
— 'Regionalism and the law of the sea: the case of semi-enclosed seas', 2 *Ocean Development* (1974), p. 151.
Al-Baharna, H. M., *The Arabian Gulf States* (1st edn., Manchester University Press, 1968; 2nd edn., Beirut, 1975).
— 'The fact-finding mission of the United Nations Secretary General and the settlement of the Bahrain–Iran dispute, May 1970', 22 *I.C.L.Q.* (1970), p. 541.
Al-Izzi, Khalid, *The Shatt Al-Arab River Disputed in Terms of Law* (2nd edn., Baghdad, 1972).
Amerasingh, C. F., 'Basic principles relating to the international regime of the oceans at the Caracas session of the U.N. Law of the Sea Conference', 6 *J. Mar.L. and Comm.* (1975), p. 213.
Amerasinghe, H. S., 'The Third United Nations Conference on the Law of the Sea', in *UN and the Sea, UNITAR News,* vol. 6, No. 1, 1974, p. 2.
Anand, R. P., 'Interests of the developing countries and the developing law of the sea', in 4 *Annals of International Studies* (Geneva, 1973), p. 13.
Andrassy, Juraj, *International Law and the Resources of the Sea* (London and New York, 1970).
Anthony, John Duke, *Arab States of the Lower Gulf: People, Politics, Petroleum* (Washington, D.C., 1975).

SELECTED BIBLIOGRAPHY

Arab Jurists on Palestine, Seminar of (Algiers, 22–27 July 1967), *The Palestine Question* (Beirut, 1968).
Arnold, Rudalph, P., 'The common heritage of mankind as a legal concept', 9 *Int. Lawyer* (1975), p. 153.
Asamoah, O. Y., *The Legal Significance of the Declarations of the General Assembly* (The Hague, 1966).
Auburn, F. M., 'The international sea-bed area', 20 *I.C.L.Q.* (1971), p. 173.
— 'The 1973 Conference on the Law of the Sea', 1 *Canadian Bar Review* (1972), p. 87.
Auguste, B. *The Continental Shelf: the Practice and Policy of the Latin American States* (Geneva, 1960).
Bathurst, M. E., Jennings, R. Y., and Ely, Northcutt, 'Trucial States (Ajman, Sharjah, Umm Al Qaiwain) Mediation', unpublished dossier submitted on behalf of His Highness Sheikh Khalid Bin Mohamed Al Qasimi, Ruler of Sharjah and its Dependencies, to Sir Gawain Bell, Mediator appointed by Her Majesty's Government in the United Kingdom, 2 vols. (August, 1970). Copies of the two volumes were examined by courtesy of Professor R. Y. Jennings.
Baxter, R. R., 'Passage of ships through international waterways in time of war', 31 *B.Y.I.L.* (1954), p. 187.
— 'The definition of war', 16 *R.E.D.I.* (1960), p. 1.
— *The Law of International Waterways, with Particular Reference to Interoceanic Canals* (Harvard, 1964).
— 'Multilateral treaties as evidence of customary international law', 41 *B.Y.I.L.* (1965–66), p. 275.
— 'Treaties and custom', 129 *Hague Recueil* (1970–1), p. 25.
Becker, Gordon L., 'A short cruise on the good ships TOVALOP and CRISTAL', 5 *J. Mar.L. and Comm.* (1973–74), p. 609.
Blissenbach, E., 'Metalliferous deposits of the Red Sea bottom, and development aspects', in *World Peace through Law Conference* (Belgrade, July 1970).
Bloomfield, L. M., *Egypt, Israel and the Gulf of Aqaba in International Law* (Toronto, 1957).
Blum, Y. Z., *Historic Titles in International Law* (The Hague, 1965).
Bouchez, Leo J., *The Regime of Bays in International Law* (Leyden, 1964).
Bowett, D. W., 'The Second United Nations Conference on the Law of the Sea', 9 *I.C.L.Q.* (1960), p. 415.
— *The Law of the Sea* (Manchester, 1967).
— 'The United Nations and peaceful settlement', in Report of a Study Group of the David Davies Memorial Institute of International Studies, *International Disputes: the Legal Aspects* (London, 1972), p. 201.
— 'Deep sea-bed resources: a major challenge', 31 *C.L.J.* (1972 B), p. 50.
Bowie, Robert R., *Suez, 1956: International Crisis and the Role of Law* (Oxford, 1974).
Brierly, J. L., *The Law of Nations,* 6th edn., ed. Sir Humphrey Waldock (Oxford, 1963).
Brinton, J. Y., 'Jurisdiction over sea-bed resources and recent developments in the Persian Gulf area', 5 *R.E.D.I.* (1949), p. 131.

SELECTED BIBLIOGRAPHY

British Admiralty, *Red Sea Pilot* (2nd edn., 1873).
— *Palestine and Transjordan* (December, 1943).
— *Red Sea and Gulf of Aden Pilot* (11th edn., 1967).
Brown, E. D., *The Legal Regime of Hydrospace* (London, 1971).
— 'The 1973 Conference on the Law of the Sea: the consequences of failure to agree', in Alexander, L. M. (ed.), *Law of the Sea: a New Geneva Conference*, Proceedings of the Sixth Annual Conference of the University of Rhode Island Law of the Sea Institute, 21–24 June 1971 (January, 1972), p. 1.
— 'Maritime zones: a survey of claims', in Churchill, R., Simmonds, K. R., and Welch, Jane (eds.), *New Directions in the Law of the Sea*, vol. III (London and New York, 1973), p. 157.
Brown, E. H., *The Saudi Arabia–Kuwait Neutral Zone* (Beirut, 1963).
Brownlie, Ian, *Principles of Public International Law* (2nd edn., Oxford, 1973).
Brüel, Erik, I *International Straits: a Treatise on International Law* (London, 1947).
Burger, W., 'Treaty provisions concerning marine research', 1 *Ocean Development* (1973–74), p. 159.
Burke, William T., *Scientific Research Articles in the Law of the Sea Informal Single Negotiating Text*, University of Rhode Island Law of the Sea Institute Occasional Paper No. 25 (June 1975).
Butler, W. E., *The Soviet Union and the Law of the Sea* (Baltimore and London, 1971).
— 'Union of Soviet Socialist Republics', in Churchill, R., Simmonds, K. R., and Welch, Jane (eds.), *New Directions in the Law of the Sea*, vol. III (London and New York, 1973), p. 271.
Cagle, M. W., 'The Gulf of Aqaba—trigger for conflict', 85 *U.S. Naval Institute Proceedings*, January, 1959, p. 75.
Castaneda, J., *Legal Effects of United Nations Resolutions* (New York, 1969).
— 'The concept of the patrimonial sea in international law', 72 *Indian J.I.L.* (1972), p. 535.
Cattan, H., *Palestine and International Law* (London, 1973).
Chandler, Albert T., 'Boundary demarcation of offshore concession areas', in *Proceedings of the Fourth Seminar on Petroleum Legislation, with Particular Reference to Offshore Operations*, Bangkok, 18–25 October 1971, Mineral Resources Development Series, No. 40 (Economic Commission for Asia and the Far East (ECAFE), Doc. E/CN.11/1052, 1973). p. 44, Chapter VII (ECAFE Doc. 1 and NR/PL/11).
Charney, J. I., 'The international regime for the deep sea bed: past conflicts and proposals for progress', 17 *Har.I.L.J.* (1976). p. 1.
Charteris, A. H., 'Territorial jurisdiction in wide bays', in International Law Association, *Report of the Twenty-third Conference*, Berlin, 1906, p. 103.
Churchill, R., Simmonds, K. R., and Welch, Jane (eds.), *New Directions in the Law of the Sea*, vol. III, *Collected Papers* (London and New York, 1973).
Churchill, R., 'The Fisheries Jurisdiction cases: the contribution of the

SELECTED BIBLIOGRAPHY

International Court of Justice to the debate on coastal States' fisheries rights', 24 *I.C.L.Q.* (1975), p. 82.

Colombos, C. J., *The International Law of the Sea* (6th edn., London, 1967).

Cottrell, Alvin J., 'Iran, the Arabs and the Persian Gulf', XVII *Orbis*, No. 3, 1973, p. 978.

Danzing, Aaron L., 'Marine pollution: a framework for international control', 1 *Ocean Management* (1973), p. 347.

Dawn, C. Ernest, 'The Egyptian remilitarization of Sinai, May 1967', 3 *Journal of Contemporary History* (1968), p. 201.

Dean, A. H., 'The law of the Sea', 38 *United States Department of State Bulletin* (1958), p. 574.

— 'Freedom of the seas', 37 *Foreign Affairs* (1958), p. 83.

— 'The Geneva Conference on the Law of the Sea: what was accomplished', 52 *A.J.I.L.* (1958), p. 607.

— 'The Second Geneva Conference on the Law of the Sea: the fight for freedom of the seas', 54 *A.J.I.L.* (1950), p. 751.

— 'The Law of the Sea Conference, 1958–60, and its aftermath', in Alexander, L. M. (ed.), *The Law of the Sea* (Ohio, 1967), p. 244.

Degens, E. T., and Ross, D. A. (eds.), *Hot Brines and Recent Heavy Metal Deposits in the Red Sea* (New York, 1969).

— 'The Red Sea hot brines', 222 *Scientific American*, No. 4, April 1970, p. 32.

Delin, Lars, 'Shall islands be taken into account when drawing the median line according to Art. 6 of the Convention on the Continental Shelf?', 41 *Nordisk Tidsskrift for International Ret* (1971), p. 205.

Democratic Lawyers, International Association of, *The Middle East Conflict: Notes and Documents, 1915–67* (Belgium, 1967).

Diebold, P., 'The richness of the sea: minerals', in Bouchez, L. J., and Kaijen, L. (eds.), *The Future of the Law of the Sea* (The Hague, 1973), p. 51.

Dixit, R. K., 'Freedom of scientific research in and on the high seas', II *Indian J.I.L.* (1971), p. 1.

Dixon, Walter H., 'The Gulf of Aqaba: history, geography and law' (unpublished Ph.D. thesis, Johns Hopkins University, 1970).

Eckert, Robert J., 'The Straits of Tiran: innocent passage or endless war', 22 *University of Miami Law Review* (1967–68), p. 873.

Elias, T. O., *The Modern Law of Treaties* (New York, 1974).

Eisenhower, Dwight D., *Waging Peace, 1956–61* (London, 1965).

El-Ghoneimy, T., 'The legal status of the Saudi–Kuwaiti neutral zone', 15 *I.C.L.Q.* (1966), p. 696.

El-Sahily, M., and El-Massaeed, A. F., *A Collection of Law and Legislation of the State of Kuwait* (1963).

Ely, Northcutt, 'A case for the administration of mineral resources underlying the high seas by national interests', 1 *N.R.L.* (1968), p. 78.

— 'Legal problems in undersea mineral development', *Journal of Petroleum Technology* (1970), p. 237.

— 'Sea-bed boundaries between coastal States: the effect to be given islets as "special circumstances"', 6 *Int. Lawyer* (1972), p. 219.

SELECTED BIBLIOGRAPHY

Falcon, N. L., *et al.*, 'A discussion of the structure of the Red Sea, Gulf of Aden and Ethiopia rift junction', *Philosophical Transactions of the Royal Society of London,* Series A, vol. 267, No. 1181, October 1970.

Faris, Neil, 'The Declaration of Principles Governing the Sea Bed and the Ocean Floor, and the Subsoil thereof, beyond the Limits of National Jurisdiction, G.A. Res. 2749 (XXV)—an examination of its legal effects' (dissertation submitted for the Diploma in International Law, University of Cambridge, 1974).

Fenelon, K. G., *The United Arab Emirates* (London, 1973).

Fereydon, Adamiyat, *Bahrain Islands—a legal and Diplomatic Study of the British–Iranian Controversy* (New York, 1955).

Fisher, Roger, 'Legality of the Arab position', *The New York Times,* 11 June 1967, Section 4, p. 13.

Fitzmaurice, Sir Gerald, 'The law and procedure of the International Court of Justice: general principles and substantive law', 27 *B.Y.I.L.* (1950), p. 3.

— 'Some results of the Geneva Conference on the Law of the Sea', 8 *I.C.L.Q.* (1959), p. 3.

Forward, Robert H., *et al.*, 'The Arab–Israeli war and international law', 9 *Har. I.L.J.* (1968), p. 232.

Franklin, Carl M., *The Law of the Sea: Some Recent Developments (with Particular Reference to the United Nations Conference of 1958),* International Law Studies, U.S. Naval War College, Rhode Island, III (1959–60).

Friedmann, Robert L., *Understanding the Debate on Ocean Resources,* Social Science Foundation and Graduate School of International Studies, University of Denver, Monograph Series in World Affairs, vol. 6, Monograph No. 3, 1968–69.

Friedmann, Wolfgang, *The Future of the Oceans* (London, 1972).

Ganz, D. L., *The United Nations and the Law of the Sea,* 26 *I.C.L.Q.* (1977), p. 1.

Ghanem, M. H., 'United Arab legislation on the continental shelf', 15 *R.E.D.I.* (1955), p. 163.

Garcia-Amador, F. V., *Latin America and the Law of the Sea,* University of Rhode Island Law of the Sea Institute, Occasional Paper No. 14 (July, 1972).

— 'The Latin American contribution to the development of the law of the sea', 68 *A.J.I.L.* (1974), p. 33.

Ghobsy, Omar, 'The Gulf of 'Aqaba and the Strait of Tiran', 3 *Egyptian Economic and Political Review,* Nos. 7 and 8, March 1957, also in 45 *Islamic Review* (Woking, Berks.), December 1957, p. 31.

Gidel, Gilbert, III *Le Droit international de la mer* (1934).

Goldberg, A. J., 'U.N. establishes *ad hoc* committee to study the use of ocean floor', 58 *Dept. of State Bull.* (1968), p. 125.

Goldie, L. F. E., 'A lexicographical controversy—the word "adjacent" in Article 1 of the Continental Shelf Convention', 66 *A.J.I.L.* (1972), p. 829.

— 'A general international law doctrine for sea-bed regimes', 7 *Int. Lawyer* (1973), p. 796.

Gordon, E., 'Resolution of the Bahrain dispute', 65 *A.J.I.L.* (1971), p. 651.
Gross, Leo, 'Passage through the Suez Canal of Israel-bound cargo and Israeli ships', 51 *A.J.I.L.* (1957), p. 530.
— 'The Geneva Conference on the Law of the Sea and the right of passage through the Gulf of Aqaba', 53 *A.J.I.L.* (1959), p. 564.
—'Passage through the Strait of Tiran and in the Gulf of Aqaba', 33 *Law and Contemporary Problems* (1968), p. 125.
Groustra, Fenrke, 'Legal problems of scientific research in the oceans', 1 *J. Mar.L. and Comm.* (1970), p. 603.
Gutteridge, J. A. C., 'The 1958 Convention on the Continental Shelf', 35 *B.Y.I.L.* (1959), p. 102.
— 'The U.N. and the law of the sea', in Churchill, R., Simmonds, K. R., and Welch, Jane (eds.), *New Directions in the Law of the Sea,* vol. III (London and New York, 1973), p. 313.
Hammad, M. Burhan, 'The right of passage in the Gulf of Aqaba', 15 *R.E.D.I.* (1959), p. 118.
Hashim, Zaki, 'Some international aspects of the Palestine question', 23 *R.E.D.I.* (1967), p. 63.
— 'Rationale of the theory of historic bays, with special reference to the international status of the Gulf of Aqaba', 25 *R.E.D.I.* (1969), p. 1.
Hay, Sir R., 'The Persian Gulf States and their boundary problems', 120 *Geographical Journal* (1954), p. 431.
— *The Persian Gulf States* (Washington, D.C., 1959).
Hardy, Michael, 'Offshore development and marine pollution', 1 *Ocean Development* (1973–74), p. 239.
Hawley, Donald, *The Trucial States* (London, 1970).
Henkin, Louis, 'The changing law of the sea—mining', 4 *Annals of International Studies* (Geneva, 1973), p. 281.
— 'Old politics and new directions', in Churchill, R., Simmonds, K. R., and Welch, Jane (eds.), *New Directions in the Law of the Sea,* vol. III (London and New York, 1973), p. 3.
Higgins, A. Pearce, and Colombos, C. J., *The International Law of the Sea* (London, 1943).
Higgins, Rosalyn, 'The June war: the United Nations and legal background', 3 *Journal of Contemporary History* (1968), p. 253.
— *United Nations Peace-keeping, 1946–67,* vol. I, *The Middle East* (Oxford, 1969).
Hjertonsson, Karin, *The New Law of the Sea: Influence of the Latin American States on Recent Developments of the Law of the Sea* (Leyden, 1973).
Hodgson, R. D., *Islands: Normal and Special Circumstances,* U.S. Department of State, the Geographer, Research Study—RGES—3 (10 December 1973).
Holloway, Kaye, *Modern Trends in Treaty Law* (London, 1967).
Hosni, S. M., 'The partition of the neutral zone', 60 *A.J.I.L.* (1966), p. 735.
Humphrey, Donald L., 'An international regime for the exploration and exploitation of the resources of the deep sea bed—the United States hard mineral industry position', 5 *N.R.L.* (1972), P. 731.
Hyde, C., 1 *International Law, Chiefly as Interpreted and Applied by the United States* (Boston, Mass., 1945).

SELECTED BIBLIOGRAPHY

Ibler, Vladimir, 'The interests of shelf-locked States and the proposed development of the law of the sea', 11 *Indian J.I.L.* (1971), p. 389.

Iran, Government of, *Facts about the Shatt al-Arab Issue* (1969).

Iraq, Ministry of Foreign Affairs, *Comment on the Iranian Claims concerning the Iraqi–Iranian Frontier Treaty of 1937 and the Legal Status of the Frontier between the two Countries* (July, 1969).

Israel, Ministry for Foreign Affairs, *Egypt's Unlawful Blockade of the Gulf of Aqaba* (1967).

Jennings, R. Y., *The Acquisition of Territory in International Law* (Manchester, 1963).

— 'The limits of the continental shelf: some possible implications of the North Sea case judgement', 18 *I.C.L.Q.* (1969), p. 819.

— 'Jurisdictional adventures at sea—who has jurisdiction over the natural resources of the sea bed?', 4 *N.R.L.* (1971), p. 829.

— 'A changing international law of the sea', 31 *C.L.J.* (1972 B), p. 32.

— 'The Santiago conference and the future', in Churchill, R., Simmonds, K. R., and Welch, Jane (eds.), *New Directions in the Law of the Sea*, vol. III (London and New York, 1973), p. 12.

Jessup, P. C., *The Law of Territorial Waters and Maritime Jurisdiction* (New York, 1972).

— 'The International Law Commission's 1954 report on the regime of the territorial sea', 49 *A.J.I.L.* (1955), p. 221.

— 'The United Nations Conference on the Law of the Sea', 59 *Columbia Law Review* (1959), p. 234.

Johnson, D. H. N., 'Rights of sea passage', in *Sunday Times,* 4 June 1967, p. 10.

— 'Some legal problems of international waterways, with particular reference to the Straits of Tiran and the Suez Canal', 31 *M.L.R.* (1968), p. 158.

Johnston, Douglas M., and Gold, Edgar, *The Economic Zone in the Law of the Sea: Survey, Analysis and Appraisal of Current Trends,* University of Rhode Island Law of the Sea Institute, Occasional Paper No. 17 (June, 1973).

Kassim, A. F., 'Conflicting claims in the Persian Gulf', IV *Journal of Law and Economic Development,* No. 2, Fall 1969, p. 288.

Kelly, J. B., 'The Persian claim to Bahrain', 33 *International Affairs* (1957), p. 51.

— 'Sovereignty and jurisdiction in eastern Arabia', 34 *International Affairs,* (1958), p. 16.

Kennedy, R. H., 'A brief geographical and hydrographical study of straits which constitute routes for international traffic', in LSCOR (1st), vol. 1, Preparatory Documents, Document No. 6 (A/Conf.13/6 and Add. 1, 23 October 1957), p. 114.

— 'A brief geographical and hydrographical study of bays and estuaries the coasts of which belong to different States', *ibid.,* Document No. 12 (A/Conf.13/15), p. 198.

— 'Brief remarks on median lines and lines of equidistance, and on the methods used in their construction' (distributed at First United Nations Conference on the Law of the Sea, 12 April 1958).

SELECTED BIBLIOGRAPHY

Khadduri, Majid, 'Iran's claim to the sovereignty of Bahrayn', 45 *A.J.I.L.* (1951), p. 63.
— 'Closure of the Suez Canal to Israeli shipping', 33 *Law and Contemporary Problems* (1968), p. 147.
— (ed.), *Major Middle Eastern Problems in International Law* (Washington, D.C., 1972).
Khan, Rahmatullah, 'The Fisheries Jurisdiction case—a critique', 15 *Indian J.I.L.* (1975), p. 1.
Knight, H. Gary, 'Issues before the Third United Nations Conference on the Law of the Sea', 34 *Louisiana L. Rev.* (1974), p. 155.
Kuba, S. K., 'The conditions of exploration and exploitation of the sea-bed activities in the proposed "area"', 15 *Indian J.I.L.* (1975), p. 216.
Kuwait, Ministry of Finance and Oil, *The Oil of Kuwait—Facts and Figures* (3rd edn., August, 1970),
Lall, Arthur, *The UN and the Middle East Crisis, 1967* (London and New York, 1968).
Laqueur, Walter, *The Road to War, 1967* (London, 1968).
Lauterpacht, E., 'The contemporary practice of the United Kingdom in the field of international law', 6 *I.C.L.Q.* (1957), p. 506; 7 *I.C.L.Q.* (1958), p. 514; 9 *I.C.L.Q.* (1960), p. 278.
— *British Practice in International Law*, 1963.
— 'River boundaries: legal aspects of the Shatt al-Arab frontier', 9 *I.C.L.Q.* (1960), p. 208.
— 'Legal problems of the continental shelf', unpublished paper submitted to a conference on 'Legal Problems of the Continental Shelf' held in Cambridge in April 1967 under the auspices of the BIICL and the Faculty of Law, Cambridge University. Copy supplied by courtesy of Mr E. Lauterpacht.
Lauterpacht, Sir H., 'Sovereignty over submarine areas', 27 *B.Y.I.L.* (1950), p. 376.
— (ed.), *International Law Reports, 1951* (London, 1957).
Lay, S. Houston, Churchill, R., and Nordquist, M., *New Directions in the Law of the Sea*, vol. II (London and New York, 1973).
Leczowski, G., *Oil and State in the Middle East* (New York, 1960).
Levan, Kenneth M., 'Justification for the opening of hostilities in the Middle East', 26 *R.E.D.I.* (1970), p. 88.
Levie, Colonel H. S., 'The nature and scope of the armistice agreement', 50 *A.J.I.L.* (1956), p. 880.
Liebesny, H. J., 'Legislation on the sea bed and territorial waters of the Persian Gulf', 4 *Middle East Journal*, (1950), p. 94.
Longrigg, S. H., *Oil in the Middle East—its Discovery and Development* (3rd edn., Toronto, 1968).
Lorimer, J. G., *Gazetteer of the Persian Gulf, 'Oman and Central Arabia*, vol. I, *Historical* (1915), vol. II, *Geographical and Statistical* (1908); (reprinted, 1970).
Mabruk, E. A., 'Offshore oil concession agreements in OPEC member countries', Conference on Petroleum and the Sea, 1965, Paper No. 508; printed in *La Revue Petrolière*, No. 1.072, May 1965.

SELECTED BIBLIOGRAPHY

Mani, V. S., 'Resources of the sea bed beyond national jurisdiction: who shall exploit and how?', 14 *Indian J.I.L.* (1974), p. 245.

McDougal, M., 'International law and the law of the sea', in Alexander, L. M. (ed.), *The Law of the Sea* (Ohio, 1967).

McDougal, M., and Burke, W., *The Public Order of the Ocean* (New Haven, 1962).

McNees, Richard B., 'Freedom of transit through international straits', 6 *J. Mar. L. and Comm.* (1974–75), p. 175.

Melamid, Alexander, 'The political geography of the Gulf of Aqaba', 47 *Annals of the Association of American Geographers* (1957), p. 231.

— 'Legal status of the Gulf of Aqaba', 53 *A.J.I.L.* (1959), p. 412.

Merani, P. T., and Sterling, J. L., 'Legal consideration of the Israeli–Egyptian dispute involving the right of innocent passage through the Straits of Tiran', 11 *Indian J.I.L.* (1971), p. 411.

Miravahabi, Farin, 'Claims to oil resources in the Persian Gulf: will the world economy be controlled by the Gulf in the future?', 11 *Texas International Law Journal* (1976), p. 75.

Misra, K. P., 'India and the status of Aqaba and Tiran', in Anand, R. P. (ed.), *Asian States and the Development of Universal International Law* (Delhi and London, 1972), p. 99; also in Boasson, Charles, and Nurock, Max (eds.), *The Changing International Community,* (The Hague and Paris, 1974), p. 283.

Moore, John Norton (ed.), *The Arab–Israeli Conflict*, 3 vols. (sponsored by the American Association of International Law, New Jersey, 1974).

Mouton, M. W., 'The continental shelf', 85 *Hague Recueil* (1954–I), p. 420.

Murti, B. S. N., 'The legal status of the Gulf of Aqaba', 7 *Indian J.I.L.* (1967), p. 201.

Nawaz, M. K., 'The limits of the coastal jurisdiction: continental shelf, fisheries and economic zone', 14 *Indian J.I.L.* (1974), p. 261.

Nelson, L. D. M., 'The patrimonial sea', *I.C.L.Q.* (1973), p. 668.

Nutting, Anthony, 'Middle East—Britain's role: don't take sides', *Sunday Times* 28 May 1967, p. 10.

O'Connell, D. P., 1 *International Law* (London, 1970).

— 'The juridicial nature of the territorial sea', 45 *B.Y.I.L.* (1971), p. 303.

— *The Influence of Law on Sea Power* (Manchester University Press, 1975).

Oda, Shigeru, 'Boundary of the continental shelf', II, 12 *Japanese Annual of International Law* (1967–68), p. 264.

— 'International law of the resources of the sea', 127 *Hague Recueil* (1969–II), p. 355.

— 'New developments in the United Nations Sea Bed Committee', 3 *J. Mar. L. and Comm.* (1971–72), p. 107.

— 'Towards a new regime for ocean development', 1 *Ocean Development* (1973–74), p. 291.

— *The International Law of Ocean Development, Basic Documents*, 2 vols. (Leyden, 1972 and 1975 respectively).

Onorato, William T., 'Apportionment of an international common petroleum deposit', 17 *I.C.L.Q.* (1968), p. 85.

SELECTED BIBLIOGRAPHY

— 'Apportionment of an international common petroleum deposit' (dissertation submitted for Ph.D. degree, University of Cambridge, 1971).
Oppenheim, L., I *International Law* (1st edn., 1905); 4th edn., ed. Arnold McNair (1928) and 8th edn., ed. Sir H. Lauterpacht (1955).
Organisation of Petroleum Exporting Countries (OPEC), *Selected Documents of the International Petroleum Industry, 1968* (Vienna, 1969).
Oxman, Bernard H., 'The preparation of Article 1 of the Convention on the Continental Shelf', 3 *J. Mar. L and Comm.* (1971–72), 3 parts, pp. 245, 445 and 683.
— *The Third United Nations Conference on the Law of the Sea: The 1970 New York Sessions,* 71 *A.J.I.L.* (1977), p. 247.
Padwa, D. J., 'Submarine boundaries', 9 *I.C.L.Q.* (1960), p. 628.
Parry, Clive (ed.), 2b *British Digest of International Law* (London, 1967).
Phillips, J. C., 'The exclusive economic zone as a concept in international law', 26 *I.C.L.Q.* (1977), p. 585.
Phylactopoulos, A., 'Territorial waters and sea-bed rights of islands in international law' (dissertation submitted for the Diploma in International Law, University of Cambridge, 1973).
Pontocorro, Giulio, 'Reflections on the economics of the common heritage of mankind: the organization of deep-sea mining industry and the expected benefits from resources exploitation', 2 *Ocean Development* (1974), p. 203.
Queneudec, Jean-Pierre, 'France', in Churchill, R., Simmonds, K. R., and Welch, Jane (eds.), *New Directions in the Law of the Sea,* vol. III (London and New York, 1973), p. 257.
Ramazani, Rouhallah K., 'The settlement of the Bahrain dispute', 12 *Indian J.I.L.,* (1972), p. 1.
— *The Persian Gulf: Iran's Role* (Virginia, 1972).
Rao, K., 'The legal regime of the sea bed and the ocean floor', 9 *Indian J.I.L.* (1969), p. 1.
Reilingh, O. G. de Vries, 'Warships in territorial waters: their right of innocent passage', II *Netherlands Y.I.L.* (1971), p. 29.
Reyner, Anthony S., 'The Strait of Tiran and the sovereignty of the sea', XXI *Middle East Journal* (1967), p. 403.
Robbins, Robert R., 'The legal status of Aden Colony and the Aden Protectorate', 33 *A.J.I.L.* (1939), p. 700.
Rothpfeffer, Tomas, 'Equity in the North Sea Continental Shelf cases', 42 *Nordisk Tidsskrift for International Ret.* (1972), p. 81.
Rovine, Arthur W., *Digest of United States Practice in International Law, 1973* (Washington, D.C., 1974) and *1974* (Washington, D.C., 1975).
Sadik, M. T., and Snavely, W. P., *Bahrain, Qatar and the United Arab Emirates: Colonial Past, Present Problems, and Future Prospects* (London and Toronto, 1972).
Salans, Carl F., 'Gulf of Aqaba and Strait of Tiran—troubled waters', 94 *U.S. Naval Institute Proceedings,* December 1968, p. 54.
Saudi Arabia, Government of, 'Memorandum registering the Saudi Arabia Government's legal and historical rights in the Straits of Tiran and the Gulf of Aqaba' (U.N. Doc. A/3575, 15 April 1957).
Shalowitz, Aaron L., *Shore and Sea Boundaries,* 2 vols. (Washington, D.C.,

1962 and 1964).
— 'Straits of Tiran and the law', *Washington Post*, 4 June 1967.
Schermers, H. G., 'The suitability of reservations to multilateral treaties', VI *Netherlands I.L.R.* (1959), p. 350.
Schram, Gunner G., 'Economic significance in terms of sea-bed mineral resources of the various limits proposed for national jurisdiction', 2 *Ocean Management* (1974), p. 249.
Selak, Charles B., 'A consideration of the legal status of the Gulf of Aqaba', 52 *A.J.I.L.* (1958), p. 660.
Shaym, Manjula, 'International straits and ocean law', 15 *Indian J.I.L.* (1975), p. 17.
Showcross, Lord, 'The law of the continental shelf, with special reference to the North Sea', in *Discourses to the Twentieth International Geographical Congress* (London, 1964); also in *The World Land Use Survey*, Occasional Paper No. 5 (London, 1964), p. 35.
Shukairy, Ahmad, *Territorial and Historical Waters in International Law*, Palestine Monograph No. 24 (Beirut).
Shukri, Mohammed Aziz, *The Problem of Islands in the Arabian Gulf and International Law* (in Arabic, 1972).
Sinclair, I. M., *The Vienna Convention on the Law of Treaties* (Manchester, 1973).
Slonim, Solomon, 'The right of innocent passage and the 1958 Geneva conference', 5 *Columbia Journal of Transnational Law* (1966), p. 96.
Sohn, Louis, *The United Nations and the Oceans: Current Issues in the Law of the Sea, 23 Report, Commission to Study the Organization of Peace* (New York, 1973).
Sorenson, Max, *Law of the Sea*, 520 *Int. Conc.* (1958), p. 193.
Stocking, George W., *Middle East Oil* (London, 1971).
Strohl, Mitchell P., *The International Law of Bays* (The Hague, 1963).
Swarztrauber, Sayre A., *The Three-mile Limit of Territorial Sea* (Maryland, 1972).
Sztucki, Jerzy (ed.), *Symposium on the International Regime of the Sea Bed* (Rome, 1970).
Tandon, Yashpal, 'UNEF, the Secretary General, and international diplomacy in the third Arab–Israeli war', 22 *Int. Organization* (1958), p. 529.
Tooms, J. S., 'Metal deposits in the Red Sea', *Underwater Science and Technology Journal*, March 1970, p. 28.
— 'Review of knowledge of metalliferous brines and related deposits', *Institute of Mining and Metallurgy*, Section B, Bulletin 79 (1970), p. 116.
Toriguian, Shavarsh, *Legal Aspects of Oil Concessions in the Middle East* (Beirut, 1972).
Trevelyn, Humphrey, *The Middle East in Revolution* (Boston, Mass., 1970).
Twiss, Sir T., *The Law of Nations: Rights and Duties in Time of Peace* (2nd edn., 1884).
United Nations, First Conference on the Law of the Sea, Geneva, 1958, *Official Records*, 1958, 7 vols.
— Second Conference on the Law of the Sea, Geneva, 1960, *Official Records*, 1960.

SELECTED BIBLIOGRAPHY

— Third Conference on the Law of the Sea, Caracas, Geneva, New York 1973, vols. I–IV (1975), vol. V (1976) and vol. VI (1977).
United States, Department of State, the Geographer, *Sovereignty of the Sea*, Geographic Bulletin No. 3, revised October 1969.
— *Continental Shelf Boundary: Italy–Yugoslavia, Limits in the Seas*, No. 9, 20 February 1970.
— *Continental Shelf Boundary: Bahrain–Saudi Arabia, Limits in the Seas*, No. 12, 20 March 1970.
— *Continental Shelf Boundary: Abu Dhabi–Qatar, Limits in the Seas*, No. 18, 29 May 1970.
— *Straight Baselines: Saudi Arabia, Limits in the Seas*, No. 20 8 June 1970.
— *Straight Baselines: United Arab Republic, Limits in the Seas*, No. 22, 22 June 1970.
— *Continental Shelf Boundary: Iran–Saudi Arabia, Limits in the Seas*, No. 24, 6 July 1970.
— *Continental Shelf Boundary: Iran–Qatar, Limits in the Seas*, No. 25, 9 July 1970.
— 'World straits affected by a twelve-mile territorial sea' (map, 510376 2–71).
— *Theoretical Area Allocations of Sea Bed to Coastal States, Based on certain U.N. Sea Bed Committee Proposals, Limits in the Seas*, No. 46, 12 August 1972.
— *Straight Baselines: Syria, Limits in the Seas*, No. 53, 10 October 1973.
— *Continental Shelf Boundary: Bahrain–Iran, Limits in the Seas*, No. 58, 13 September 1974.
— *Straight Baselines: Oman (Hypothetical), Limits in the Seas*, No. 61, 4 June 1975.
— *Continental Shelf Boundary: Iran–United Arab Emirates (Dubai), Limits in the Seas*, No. 63, 30 September 1975.
— *National Claims to Maritime Jurisdictions, Limits in the Seas*, No. 36 (3rd revision), 23 December 1975.
— *Continental Shelf Boundary: Iran–Oman, Limits in the Seas*, No. 67, 1 January 1976.
Utton, Albert E., 'A survey of national laws on the control of pollution from oil and gas operations on the continental shelf', 9 *Columbia Journal of Transnational Law*, No. 2, fall 1970, p. 331.
Verzijl, J. H. W., 'The United Nations Conference on the Law of the Sea, Geneva, 1958', VI *Netherlands I.L.R.* (1959), pp. 1–43 and 115–40.
— *International Law in Historical Perspective*, vols. III (Leyden, 1970), IV (1971) and VI (1973).
Waldichuk, M., 'International approach to marine pollution problem', 1 *Ocean Management* (1973), p. 211.
Warbrick, Colin, 'The regulation of navigation', in Churchill, R., Simmonds, K. R., Welch, Jane (eds.), *New Directions in the Law of the Sea*, vol. III (London and New York, 1973), p. 137.
Whitemann, M. M., 'Conference on the law of the sea; convention on the continental shelf', 52 *A.J.I.L.* (1958), p. 629.
— 4 *Digest of International Law* (Washington, D.C., April 1965).

SELECTED BIBLIOGRAPHY

Wilson, Sir A. T., *The Persian Gulf* (1928, reprinted 1954).
Wolf, Atwood C., 'The U.N. Declaration of Principles Governing the Deep Sea Bed', in Rodley, N., and Ronning, C. (eds.), *International Law in the Western Hemisphere* (The Hague, 1974).
Wright, Quincy, 'Legal aspects of the Middle East situation', 33 *Law and Contemporary Problems* (1968), p. 1.
— 'The Middle East crisis', in Shapiro, Isaac (ed.), *The Middle East: Prospects for Peace*, Background Papers and Proceedings of the Thirteenth Hammarskjold Forum (New York, 1969).
Yaari, D., 'Why Sharm el-Sheikh is necessary', *New Middle East*, March–April 1972, p. 26.
Yaroslavtsev, V., 'The world ocean and international law', 21 *International Affairs* (Moscow, 1975), p. 61.
Young, R., 'Saudi Arabian offshore legislation', 43 *A.J.I.L.* (1949), p. 530.
— 'Legal status of submarine areas beneath the high seas', 45 *A.J.I.L.* (1951), p. 225.
Young, R., 'Lord Asquith and the continental shelf', 46 *A.J.I.L.* (1952), p. 512.
— 'Legal problems of offshore concessions', in Young, T. Cuyler (ed.), *Middle East Focus: the Persian Gulf,* Proceedings of the Twentieth Annual Near East Conference and the Princeton University Conference (October 1968), p. 87.
— 'Equitable solution for offshore boundaries: the 1968 Saudi Arabia–Iran Agreement', 64 *A.J.I.L.* (1970), p. 152.
— 'The Persian Gulf', in Churchill, R., Simmonds, K. R., and Welch, Jane (eds.), *New Directions in the Law of the Sea*, vol. III (London and New York, 1973) p. 231.
Zacklin, Ralph, 'Latin America and the development of the law of the sea', 4 *Annals of International Studies* (Geneva, 1973), p. 31.
— *The Changing Law of the Sea—Western Hemisphere Perspective* (Leyden, 1974).

INDEX

Abu Dhabi, 195; –Dubai boundary agreement, 99, 198; –Qatar boundary agreement, 95–9, 198
Abu Dhabi Marine Areas Ltd, 98
Abu Musa island, 66, 103, 122–4, 125, 127–8, 199, 208–11, 254–5n
Acts of State doctrine, 126
Aden, Gulf of, 233n
Aden, Perim and Kuria Muria Act, 20
Agip-Minerarie (SIRIP), 35
Aircraft, flight over territorial waters, 50f
Al-Arabiyah island, 91f, 94, 198
Al-Ashat island, 97
Al-Bunduq oilfield, 98
Al-Fayyarin island, 105
Al-Ghanam island, 105
Al Uquair convention, 107, 109
American Independent Oil Co., 109
Ammoun, Judge, 91
Anglo-Turkish agreement, 109
Aqaba, Gulf of, 4f, 45; closed sea status, 140f, 144–5, 149f; description, 133–5; exceptional case, 152, 172–3, 176f; history, 164; international status, 141, 145, 155, 169, 176; Israeli shipping in, 167–71, 229n; juridical status, 144–9, 172; legal status, 143f, 176–7, 189; passage through, 132, 139–42, 143, 151, 152–62, 177; political issues, 132; shipping practice in, 162–6; territorial waters, 145, 147, 149, 152–62, 166, 176; United Nations Emergency Force role, 139, 169f
Aqaba port, 135, 154, 164f
Arab-Israeli conflict, 15, 132, 135–6, 138–9, 140
Arab league, 6, 44f, 46–7, 228–9n; Educational, Cultural and Scientific Organisation, 23
Arabian Gulf, 83, 85; boundary problems, 83–131; coastlines, 224n; continental shelf, 37, 38–40, 57, 61, 63, 191, 225n; enclosed sea proposals, 64–5; fishing, 220n; living resources, 29; oil tanker traffic, 21, 217n; pearl fishing, 40–2; pollution control, 23, 75; territorial waters, 214n
Arabian Oil Co. of Japan, 110
Artificial islands and structures, 55, 64
Asian–African Legal Consultative Committee, 49
Atlantis II, RV, 178

Bab el-Mandeb Straits, 49f, 52, 66
Bahrain, 7, 48, 195; continental shelf, 31, 62; exclusive economic zone, 58, 232n; –Iran boundary agreement, 100, 102–3, 199; –Qatar boundary, 121; –Saudi Arabia boundary agreement, 86–91, 198
Baxter, R. R., 143, 160, 163
Bays, 9–10, 47, 144, 189; as closed seas, 150; free passage in, 175; inland waters, 29, 147–8; multi-State, 145–9; special situations, 148–9, 153, 172–3, 176
Belgium, 117, 174–5
Bell, Sir Gawain, 124f
Ben-Gurion, David, 138, 169
Blissenbach, E., 179f
Blum, Y., 159f
Bouchez, Leo J., 175
Boundaries delimitation, 63, 83, 89f, 100, 117, 131, 189–90; offshore in Arabian Gulf, 83–131, 189–90
Brine deposits, xx, 58, 63, 178–9, 181; economic potential, 179–80; exploration licences, 185f, 188; mineral content, 179; Saudi claim to, 183–4, 188
Brown, E. H., 110
Brüel, E., 163
Bubiyan island, 118–20
Buttes Gas & Oil Co., 123, 125ff, 210n

Canadian Arctic Waters Pollution Act, 219n
Caspian Sea, 26, 219n, 224n
Chain, RV, 178

INDEX

Charteris, A. H., 161
Chetumal Bay, 172, 173–4, 175
Cobalt, sea-bed production, 72
Codification of international law, 158
Committee of Arab Experts, 44, 46, 227n, 228n
Common heritage of mankind, 68, 69–70, 77, 238n
Contiguous zone, 20–1, 47, 52–3
Continental Oil of Dubai, 99
Continental shelf, conservation, 39; definition, 31, 39–40, 221n, 225n; delimitation, 32–8, 57, 63–4, 222n; delimitation of national boundaries, 4, 84, 92, 93ff, 97, 100, 103, 105, 130–1, 200; exclusive economic zone, 60–3; legal history, 29–31; oil concessions, 222n; sovereignty over, 33, 222–3n
Continental Shelf, Geneva Convention, 4, 30–1, 33, 37, 39, 56, 62, 84, 88, 130, 180, 184, 190
Coral Sea, tanker, 15
Corfu Channel case, 14, 17, 45, 52, 143ff, 151ff, 155, 157f, 160, 163, 167

Dayyinah island, 97
Dean, A. H., 37, 157–8
Deep-sea mining, *see* Sea bed, economic exploitation
Denmark, 115
Denning, Lord, 126
Discovery, RV, 178
Djibouti, 12, 14
Dohat al-Salwa, 121
Dubai, 195; –Abu Dhabi boundary agreement, 99, 103
Dulles, John F., 171

Egypt, 71, 195; bays, 9; contiguous zone, 21; continental shelf, 31, 33, 222–3n; –Democratic Yemen agreement, 15; exclusive economic zone, 58; –Israeli blockade, 15, 164, 166; –Israeli conflict, 132, 135, 167–70; oil pollution prevention, 22, 24, 75; territorial sea, 5, 8ff, 49, 51f
Eilat, 132, 135, 138, 140, 154, 164–5, 256n
Eisenhower, Dwight D., 169f
El-Ghoneimy, M. T., 109

Empire Roche, SS, 138
Enclosed seas, 64–7, 75f, 235–6n
Equidistance principle, 84, 88ff, 94, 97f, 100, 103, 105, 115, 117
Equitable or just principle, 83, 89f, 100, 117, 131
Exclusive economic zone, 27, 47, 53–63, 74ff, 78–9, 183, 191, 232–3n

Failaka island, 112, 118
Farsi island, 91f, 94, 198
Fasht Bu Saafa oil deposit, 86, 88, 91
Fateh oilfield, 99
Federal Republic of Germany, 107, 113, 117
Fish resources, xx, 6f, 28
Fishing zones, 26–9, 54, 56, 60, 200, 232n
Fonseca, Gulf of, 140, 149–50, 172, 176
Francois, M., 152f, 172f
Functional zones, 20, 200

Gap island, 105
Geographically disadvantaged States, 59
Gidel, G., 146
Great Quoin island, 105
Gross, Leo, 158
Group of Seventy-seven, 70, 76
Gulf Area Oil Companies Mutual Aid Organisation, 23

Halul island, 97
Harvard Territorial Waters Convention, 147–8
Hawar island, 121, 229n
Hay, R., 97, 121
Hengam island, 105
Higgins, Rosalyn, 171
Historic bays, 10, 47, 140, 144, 149f, 228n
Historic rights, 41, 47, 139, 220n, 228n
Hormoz island, 105
Hormuz, Straits of, 45, 49f, 65–6, 105, 127, 216n
Hyde, C. C., 147, 160

INDEX

Informal Composite Negotiating Text (ICNT), 11, 43, 44; on contiguous zone, 20; continental shelf, 61, 63f; enclosed seas, 67; exclusive economic zone, 55, 60; innocent passage, 230n; International Sea Bed Authority, 71, 73; median line, 215n; pollution control, 239n; scientific research, 76; sea-bed area, 69; straits, 143; transit passage, 162, 230n; uninhabited rocks, 223n

Innocent passage, 10–11, 14, 17, 44–6, 49, 50, 153ff, 158, 160, 162, 230n; definition, 166–7, 270n

Inter-American Natural Resources Conservation Conference, 39

Inter-governmental Maritime Consultative Organisation, 75

Inter-governmental Oceanographic Commission, 77

International Court of Justice, on boundaries, 89–91, 98, 117

International Hydrographic Bureau, 77

International Law Commission, Gulf of Aqaba issue, 152–4, 172, 176; on multinational bays, 148

International waterways, 163

Iran, 17, 51, 196; Abu Musa dispute, 122–3, 130, 208–11; continental shelf, 31, 35–7, 62, 64, 223n; enclosed sea proposals, 64–5; exclusive economic zone, 59; fishing zone limits, 27–8, 59; marine pollution control, 76; Neutral Zone offshore boundary, 110; on International Sea Bed Authority, 71; Petroleum Act, 26; scientific research regulation, 77; territorial sea, 8, 10, 15, 49; Tumbs islands dispute, 128–30; –Bahrain boundary, 100, 102–3, 199; –Iraq–Kuwait boundary, 111–18; –Oman boundary, 105f, 199; –Qatar boundary, 100f, 198; –Saudi Arabia boundary, 91–5; –Saudi Arabia Continental Shelf Agreement, 37; –Sharjah memorandum of understanding, 125, 127–8; –United Arab Emirates boundary, 103f, 199

Iran-Italian Petroleum Co., 112

Iran-Pan American Oil Co., 111f

Iraq contiguous zone, 21; continental shelf, 31, 34–5, 62, 84, 223–4n; enclosed sea proposals, 65–6; exclusive economic zone, 56, 58–9, 228n; freedom of passage, 45–6, 51; legislation, 196; marine pollution control, 25–6, 76; on International Sea Bed Authority, 70; scientific research regulation, 77–8; territorial sea, 5, 8, 10, 115–17; –Iran–Kuwait boundaries, 111–18

Islands, 8–9, 14, 17–20, 36ff, 64; in boundary delimitation, 84, 86, 88, 90, 92, 97, 100, 103, 105, 111, 115, 120, 131, 224n, 245n

Israel occupation of Umm Rashrash, 132f, 135–6; passage through Gulf of Aqaba, 167–71; shipping statistics, 165; withdrawal from occupied territory, 167–70, 177; –Arab conflict, 15, 132, 135, 138–9

Jabrin island, 103
Jazirat al-Muharrag islet, 100, 103
Jedda Declaration, 23
Jessup, Judge P., 148
Jordan exclusive economic zone, 56; legislation, 196; on oil pollution, 22; sea outlet, 213n; territorial sea, 7, 49

Kamaran islands, 14, 17, 18–19
Kennedy, R. H., 12, 172
Khafji oilfield, 108
Kharg island, 94f, 111f
Khor Abdullah, 119
Kubar island, 109, 118
Kuria Muria islands, 17f, 217n
Kuwait contiguous zone, 21; continental shelf, 31, 62; exclusive economic zone, 60; fishing industry, 220–1n; freedom of passage, 45–6, 51; islands, 109–10; legislation, 196; marine pollution control, 22f, 26; on International Sea Bed Authority, 70; territorial sea, 6, 8, 10, 49, 114f; –Iran–Iraq boundary, 111–18; –Iraq islands dispute, 118–20; –Saudi Arabia boundary, 107–9, 110–12
Kuwait Oil Co., 118
Kuwait Shell Group, 111ff
Kuwait Spanish Petroleum Co., 118

Land-locked States, 55, 59–60
Larak island, 105

INDEX

Lauterpacht, E., 38–9
Lauterpacht, H., 38, 161
Law of the sea, OAU Declaration, 46
Law of the sea, First Conference, 53
Law of the sea, Third Conference, xix, 3, 27, 43–4, 78, 149, 183, 188f; contiguous zone concept, 53; marine pollution control, 73–6; Middle Eastern participation, 48, 78, 228n; sea-bed mining, 72; territorial sea limits, 49; transit passage, 161–2
Lebanon continental shelf, 62–3; exclusive economic zone, 60; freedom of passage, 45, 52; legislation, 196; oil pollution control, 22, 24; territorial sea, 7
Libya continental shelf, 31, 34, 64; exclusive economic zone, 58; Gulf of Surt, 9, 215n; legislation, 196; marine pollution control, 22, 75; on innocent passage, 52; on International Sea Bed Authority, 71; semi-enclosed sea, 66; territorial sea, 6, 213n
Lima island, 105
Lorimer, J. G., 41, 97, 109, 118
Love, Kenneth, 171
Lubainah al-Kabirah, 86, 88
Lubainah al-Sagirah, 86, 88
Luce, Sir William, 125

Manganese nodules, 72f
Marjan-Fereydoon oil reservoir, 94f
Mauritania, 46, 228n
May, Justice, 126
Mediterranean Sea continental shelf, 34; enclosed sea status, 64–5; pollution contol 22, 24, 75; Pollution Protection Convention, 24, 219n
Meteor, RV, 178
Meteorology network proposal, 23, 192
Middle East, xix, xxii
Middle Eastern States continental shelf doctrine, 62; environmental conservation, 23, 191–2; law of the sea attitudes, 78–9, 188–92, 212n; regional co-operation, 23, 191–2; sea-bed exploitation, 56ff, 61
Musandam island, 105

Nakhilu island, 100, 103
National Iranian Oil Co., 35, 111, 123, 210

Netherlands, 115, 174–5
Neutral Zone, 107f, 110–11
North Sea Continental Shelf cases, 31, 56, 63, 89–91, 98, 107, 113, 117, 131, 159, 185, 187, 190

Occidental Petroleum Corporation, 123–6
Oceanographer, survey vessel, 179, 182
O'Connell, D. P., 163
Oil, common deposits of, 91, 95, 105, 107, 131; concessions, 84, 111–13, 222n; resources, xx; tankers, 49, 50, 230n; *see* Pollution
Oman continental shelf, 31, 33, 84; exclusive economic zone, 56, 58; fishing industry, 27–8, 219–20n; freedom of passage, 45–6, 49, 52; Kuria Muria islands, 18; legislation, 197; marine pollution control, 25; territorial sea, 6, 8, 10, 15, 17, 49; –Iran boundary, 105f, 199; –Ras Alkhaimah boundary, 105; –Sharjah boundary, 105
Oman, Gulf of, 75, 233n
Oppenheim, L., 146–7, 159–60

Pardo, Arvid, 67
Patrimonial sea, 54, 232n
Pearl fisheries, 29, 40–2, 226n
Perim island, 14f, 17–18, 19–20
Pollution, marine, control of, 21–6, 73–6, 218n; Pollution by Dumping of Wastes Convention, 23, 74; Pollution from Ships Convention, 23, 74f, 218n; Pollution of Sea by Oil Convention, 22, 218n
Preussag, 185ff

Qaru island, 107, 109–10, 111, 118
Qatar continental shelf, 31; fishing zone, 28, 202–3, 219n; freedom of passage, 45; legislation, 197; territorial sea, 7; –Abu Dhabi boundary, 95–9, 198; –Bahrain boundary, 121; –Iran boundary, 100f, 198; –Saudi Arabia boundary, 121
Qeshm island, 105, 128

INDEX

Ras al-Khaimah, 105, 128–30, 195
Red Sea, xxi, 58, 63f, 75, 143, 180f, 183f, 187–8, 189–90; *see* Brine deposits

Safaniya oilfield, 108
Sanafir island, 133, 136, 137ff
Saudi Arabia contiguous zone, 21; continental shelf, 31; exclusive economic zone, 58; islands, 95; legislation, 197; oil pollution control, 22; Red Sea bed resources, 180, 183–7, 199; territorial sea, 5, 8, 10; –Bahrain boundary, 86–91, 198; –Iran boundary, 91–5; –Kuwait boundary, 107–9, 110–12; –Qatar boundary, 121; –Sudan Red Sea Commission, 186f
Scheldt estuary, 173ff
Scientific research regulation, 76–8
Sea bed, 44, 47, 69; Declaration, 68, 70f; economic exploitation, 71–3; pollution control, 74; proposed Economic Planning Commission, 73; proposed International Regime and Authority, 67–73, 77, 79, 188, 191; *see* Brine deposits
Selak, Charles B., 136
Shara'iwah island, 97
Sharjah, Abu Musa dispute, 122–3; continental shelf, 201; legislation, 195; territorial sea, 7f, 10f, 214n; Umm al-Qaiwain dispute, 123–7; –Dubai boundary, 103; –Iran memorandum of understanding, 125, 127–8, 208–11; –Oman boundary, 105
Shatt al-Arab, 5–6, 113
Sir Bani Yas island, 103
Sirri island, 103, 123
Somalia, 46, 228n
Soviet Union, 66
Straits, 11, 48, 78, 143, 227n; international navigation, 45–6, 50–2, 65–6, 142, 154, 158, 160–1, 162–4, 189, 231n; transit passage, 161–2, 230n
Strohl, M. P., 148, 172–3
Sudan contiguous zone, 21; continental shelf, 31, 33; exclusive economic zone, 58; legislation, 197; scientific research regulation, 77; territorial sea, 6, 8, 10f; –Saudi Arabia Red Sea Commission, 186f

Sudanese Minerals Ltd, 185f
Syria contiguous zone, 21; continental shelf, 31, 33; legislation, 198; territorial sea, 6, 8, 10f

Tana lagoon, 172, 174f
Technology, transfer of, 77
Territorial sea extent, 5–10, 48–9, 200; only access to port, 152–62, 172–3, 175; overflight of, 50; right of passage, 49, 141–2, 145f, 163, 166, 189, 229n
Territorial Sea, Geneva Convention, 4, 7–8, 10, 14, 21, 48, 51, 53, 144, 148; Arab States non-adherence, 156, 159; Art. 16(4), 140, 142ff, 145, 151, 153, 154–61, 162, 177; innocent passage, 11, 49, 140, 155, 166; reservations, 156f
Third World countries, 53, 191f
Tiran island, 133, 136f, 138–9
Tiran Straits, 4, 45, 51f, 132, 133–5; innocent passage, 140ff, 151, 154, 177; legal status, 143, 155, 160, 176f, 189; navigation control, 136–9, 140–1; right of passage, 143, 151, 154f, 157–61, 162, 166, 167–71; United Nations Emergency Force role, 168ff, 171
Transit passage, 17, 50, 161–2, 230n
Trieste, Gulf of, 150
Trucial States continental shelf, 31, 33; Mediation, 124f, 201
Truman Proclamation, 30, 32, 184
Tumbs islands, 66, 103, 127, 128–30, 251n, 254–5n

Umm al-Maradim island, 107, 109–11, 118
Umm al-Qaiwain, 123–7, 196
Umm Qasr, 118
Umm Rashrash, 132f, 135–6, 140; *see* Eilat
United Arab Emirates continental shelf, 31; exclusive economic zone, 58; freedom of passage, 45, 52; legislation, 195; territorial sea, 7, 49; –Iran boundary, 103f, 199; –Sharjah, 7, 8, 11, 128
United Kingdom intervention, Sharjah–Umm al-Qaiwain, 124; withdrawal from Arabian Gulf,

292

18–19, 129, 216n; –Norway agreement, 107
United Nations 'consensus' on Aden, 17f; Israeli-Arab conflict, 138, 167–71; Sea Bed Declaration, 68, 70f
Unity of a deposit, 91, 95, 98, 105, 107

Valdivia, RV, 179
Verzijl, J. H. W., 148, 159, 175f

Warbah island, 118–20
Warships in territorial waters, 11, 46, 49ff, 52, 146, 151, 166, 230n

Yemen Arab Republic contiguous zone, 21; continental shelf, 31, 33, 207; exclusive economic zone, 58; freedom of passage, 49; legislation, 198; on closed seas, 66; territorial sea, 6, 8, 10f, 14, 205–6, 213n
Yemen Democratic Republic, 17; contiguous zone, 21; continental shelf, 31, 34; exclusive economic zone, 29, 56, 58; legislation, 198; territorial sea, 6, 8, 10f, 45–6, 52
Young, R., 38
Yugoslavia, 67

Zubarah, 121